Base Politics

Base Politics

Democratic Change and the U.S. Military Overseas

Alexander Cooley

Cornell University Press
Ithaca and London

Copyright © 2008 by Cornell University

First published 2008 by Cornell University Press

Printed in the United States of America

Library of Congress Cataloging-in-Publication Data

Cooley, Alexander, 1972-
  Base politics : democratic change and the U.S. military overseas / Alexander Cooley.
    p. cm.
  Includes bibliographical references and index.
  ISBN 978-0-8014-4605-4 (cloth : alk. paper)
  1. Military bases, American—Political aspects—Foreign countries. 2. United States—Armed Forces—Foreign countries.   I. Title.
  UA26.A2C67 2008
  355.7—dc22
                        2007042635

Cornell University Press strives to use environmentally responsible suppliers and materials to the fullest extent possible in the publishing of its books. Such materials include vegetable-based, low-VOC inks and acid-free papers that are recycled, totally chlorine-free, or partly composed of nonwood fibers. For further information, visit our website at www.cornellpress.cornell.edu.

Cloth printing   10 9 8 7 6 5 4 3 2 1

For Nicole Jacoby

Contents

Figures and Tables

Figures

Tables

Preface

Originally a scholar of post-Soviet politics, I was amazed when the United States established military bases on former Soviet territory in Central Asia to support its 2001 campaign in Afghanistan. As the security partnership between the United States and Uzbekistan and Kyrgyzstan strengthened over the next few years, I suspected that the internal consequences of the presence of U.S. bases were far more important than Western officials and the media acknowledged or cared about. Whether intended or not, the U.S. military presence in these countries functioned as a U.S. endorsement of host governments and their actions. Hence, as political challenges to these regimes mounted in 2005, the U.S. military found itself in the crosshairs of the region's internal democratizing shifts and backlashes. Now, in late 2007, the United States has been evicted from Uzbekistan, and its position in Kyrgyzstan looks increasingly precarious.

The "base politics" of Central Asia are just the latest recurrence of a set of political dynamics that have surrounded U.S. bases in other eras and regions. Although U.S. policymakers and scholars have consistently overlooked the internal political dimension for host countries, U.S. overseas bases and their governing arrangements repeatedly have been implicated in those countries' democratic struggles, authoritarian propaganda, populist election campaigns, and political infighting and factionalism. These internal political developments have also had tangible operational consequences, as several base hosts have challenged and evicted U.S. forces from their territory, often for reasons that had little to do with the conduct or policy of the United States. Given the hundreds of U.S. military installations scattered across more than a hundred overseas countries and territories, the dearth of comparative political analysis on the issue is puzzling.

As I pursued this topic, I was not fully prepared for the scale of the project to which I was committing myself. From 2003 to 2006, I conducted field research in ten base hosts, across Asia, Europe, and the postcommunist states; this research now comprises the main case studies of this book. Each trip yielded fascinating insights and fresh understandings of these political dynamics. I made it a point to interview as many actors as possible with different interests and stakes in the basing issue. U.S. political and military officials, host-country defense officials, local politicians, antibase activists, journalists, academics, security analysts, contractors, business representatives, and base workers all contributed to my research findings and the development of these arguments. I learned as much about these countries' rich political histories and institutions as I did about the basing issue.

In short, I found that the U.S. basing presence means different things to different actors and that these views, even for the same actor, vary considerably over time. For some a basing agreement with the United States is a guarantee of security and alliance, whereas for others it may be a political endorsement of the ruling regime or a lucrative economic opportunity. Some politicians regard an American base as a symbol of violated national sovereignty, U.S. imperialism, and political struggle, whereas others aren't particularly bothered by its presence or regard it as a routine matter for technocrats to manage.

From an academic perspective, the study of base politics is not easily slotted into either of the established political science subfields of international relations or comparative politics. Bases are the products of international security agreements, but as discrete communities they also interface politically, economically, and socially with their hosts. Moreover, many base-related issues traverse additional disciplines such as international law, international negotiation, institutional economics, sociology, and media studies. I suspect that the boundaries of our modern social sciences, as well as the persistent walls that separate specialists of different regions, are the reasons we don't have more comparative studies on the subject.

Yet I am now convinced, even if we allow for historical nuance and regional specificity, that many of these political patterns can be analytically identified and even predicted. This book attempts to make some sense of "base politics" and provides a theory that explains some of its major trends across different countries and eras.

• • •

The funds required to complete this research have been considerable, and I deeply appreciate various organizations for their support and commitment to the project. A grant from the Carnegie Corporation of New York to Columbia University's Institute for War and Peace Studies allowed me, along with my colleague Kimberly Marten (with Page Fortna and Tanisha Fazal as fellow grantees), to conduct field research in Okinawa and the Japanese main islands (May–June 2003), South Korea (June 2004), and Kyrgyzstan (January 2005).

I am also grateful to the German Marshall Fund of the United States (GMF), which not only supported me as a research fellow during my academic leave (2004–5) but also awarded me a Transatlantic Fellowship that supported my residence at the GMF Transatlantic Center in Brussels in 2005 and provided a world-class network of resources and contacts. These greatly facilitated my trips to Spain (April 2005), Portugal and the Azores (May 2005), and Romania (July 2005). In particular I thank Ron Asmus, Bill Drozdiak (now President of the American Council on Germany), John Glenn, and Corinna Hörst. A travel grant from Barnard College, as part of my Special Assistant Professor Leave, supported these trips as well as my visits to Greece (October 2004), Turkey (November 2004), and Italy (April 2006). I also thank the Smith Richardson Foundation for awarding me a Junior Faculty International Security and Foreign Policy grant for 2007 that allowed me to update and finish the book in a timely fashion. Finally, publication of this book was made possible in part by Columbia University's Harriman Institute, and I am grateful for the institute's enduring support.

This research would have been inconceivable without the extensive network of contacts provided by generous colleagues. Fortunately, I had at least one such pivotal person to help me navigate the research terrain on each of my trips; I am indebted to Kim Byungki (Korea), Ambassador Angel Viñas (Spain), Takako Hikotani (Japan), Sami Kohen (Turkey), Miguel Monjardino (Portugal and the Azores), Leopoldo Nuti (Italy) and George Vlad Niculescu (Romania) for all of their organizational efforts and generous commitment to the project. I also thank representatives in the U.S. military from the U.S. European Command (EUCOM) and Pacific

Command (PACOM) for facilitating my interviews and base visits, as well as various U.S. embassy and defense officials for taking the time to organize meetings and conferences on the topic.

The project greatly benefited from the suggestions and comments I gathered when I presented earlier versions at Northwestern University, MIT's Security Studies Program, Brown University's Watson Institute, Columbia University's Harriman Institute and Weatherhead East Asian Institute, the University of Pennsylvania's Brown Center, Princeton University's Near East Studies Department, the German Marshall Fund's Transatlantic Center in Brussels and office in Washington, D.C., the National Defense Academy of Japan, the Korea University Graduate School of International Studies, the Korean National Defense University, City University of London's Public Policy Program, the University of London's School of Oriental and African Studies, the University of Toronto's Munk Centre, the City Council of Vila de Porto (Santa María, Azores), and the annual policy conferences of the Program on New Approaches to Russian Security (PONARS) at the Center for Strategic and International Studies.

The book was critically shaped and vastly improved by the insightful comments of two anonymous reviewers for Cornell University Press. I also owe a great intellectual debt to my colleague Kimberly Marten, who not only conducted joint interviews with me in Japan, Korea, and Kyrgyzstan, but contributed to the formulation of these arguments, read and commented on an entire earlier draft of the manuscript, and supported the project at its every stage. She and the rest of my remarkable colleagues at Barnard and Columbia provide a wonderful research community and support network. Jonathan Hopkin (London School of Economics) conducted interviews with me in Spain and greatly contributed to my thinking about the case.

I am also fortunate that several distinguished experts, whose detailed understanding of these individual country cases greatly surpasses mine, generously read and commented on earlier draft chapters, although they are in no way responsible for the book's remaining errors and shortcomings. I thank Fiona Adamson, Charles Armstrong, Henri Barkey, Ambassador Adrian Basora, Nur Bilge Criss, Renato De Castro, Richard Eldridge, George Gavrilis, Olimpio Guidi, Rajan Menon, Paul Midford, Miguel Monjardino, Katharine Moon, Leopoldo Nuti, Luis Nuno Rodrigues, Radu Tudor, Ambassador Angel Viñas, and Andrew Yeo for their expert feedback. Rawi Abdelal, Mark Blyth, Robert Jervis, Dan Nexon, and Jack Snyder offered insightful comments on earlier drafts of the theoretical and concluding chapters. For their helpful comments and input on the broader project, I also thank Deborah Avant, Gordon Bardos, Amy Belasco, Richard Betts, Alessandro Brogi, Bruce Cumings, Dan Deudney, Simon Duke, John Dyer, Page Fortna, Erik Gartzke, Robert Harkavy, Amy Holmes, Scott Horton, Ian Hurd, Patrick Jackson, Peter Katzenstein, Bradey Kiesling, Mark Kramer, James Kurth, David Lake, Stephen Larrabee, Robert Legvold, Catherine Lutz, Paul MacDonald, Guido Maranzana, Andy Markovitz, Katherin McInnis, Martha Merrill, Miguel Moniz, Carla Monteleone, Alex Motyl, Michael Mousseau, Barry Posen, Charles Powell, Dick Samuels, Ed Schatz, Hendrik Spruyt, Robin Varghese, Celeste Wallander, and Thomas Wood. Stephanie Boyum, Adelle Tilebalieva, and Laura Stoiffel provided excellent research assistance. Finally, I once again extend my appreciation to Roger Haydon, my editor. His refreshing candor, expert guidance, and intellectual challenges over many months have vastly improved every part of this work. I am privileged to have worked on another book with him and the outstanding production team at Cornell University Press.

For their continued unwavering support and remarkable generosity of spirit I thank my parents, John Cooley and Vania Katelani Cooley, as well as my relatives and friends at home and abroad who have endured more than their fair share of my babble about U.S. base minutiae. First among them is my wife, Nicole. The book is dedicated to her with my love and gratitude for her inspiration, support, and, above all, enduring good humor.

ALEXANDER COOLEY

Base Politics

CHAPTER 1

Political Change and the Overseas American Military Presence

In March 2004, just days after his surprising election victory, Spain's president-elect José Luis Rodríguez Zapatero ordered the withdrawal of Spanish troops from Iraq. Zapatero's dramatic decision fulfilled an election campaign pledge but also created acrimony between Spain and the United States; the previous administration of José María Aznar had offered nearly unqualified support for Operation Iraqi Freedom (OIF). Less noticed at the time was that during Spain's withdrawal, the United States continued to fly daily sorties and logistical missions in support of OIF from the Morón airbase and Rota naval station on Spanish territory. Yet the Spanish media and major political parties ignored the matter, even though public opinion polls showed that a solid majority of the Spanish public opposed granting the United States this base access.[1] U.S. defense and policy planners had expected the new administration to withdraw its blanket authorization for the use of the bases and were surprised when no such request materialized.[2] After all, they reasoned, why would a regime that had withdrawn from a military campaign in response to domestic political pressures not also oppose the use of its territory to support the same unpopular war?

1. Instituto de Cuestiones Internacionales y Política Exterior (INCIPE) 2003, 219.
2. Author's interviews with U.S. foreign policy and defense officials, Madrid, April 2005.

Just sixteen months later, the government of Uzbekistan formally notified the United States that it was terminating U.S. access to the Karshi-Khanabad (K2) base in the south of the country. Since the fall of 2001, the U.S. military had used K2 as a major staging facility to support reconnaissance, combat, and humanitarian missions in neighboring Afghanistan. The eviction notice was the culmination of tensions that had been growing between the countries after the Uzbek government cracked down harshly on antigovernment demonstrators in the eastern city of Andijon in May 2005.[3] Throughout June, the U.S. State Department and Congress had grown increasingly critical of the Uzbek government's actions and human rights records, even while U.S. defense officials continued to support their Uzbek counterparts.

Despite their different geographical settings and political systems, these base-related episodes in Spain and Uzbekistan share important features. First, the processes of politicization and depoliticization of the U.S. military basing presence within each of these host countries varied considerably over time. Although the American use of bases on Spanish territory was depoliticized as an issue in 2004, eighteen years earlier another Socialist (PSOE) government headed by President Felipe González had aggressively denounced U.S. air strikes against Libya and prohibited the use of Spanish bases for the campaign. Why did a PSOE government curtail base access for one American military action unsanctioned by the United Nations against Libya in 1986 but not another against Iraq in 2004? Similarly, why did an Uzbek government that had so vigorously courted a U.S. military presence in September 2001 suddenly reverse its decision four years later?

The second common feature of these cases is that neither the broader security relations between the United States and the host country nor domestic public opinion determined the dynamics of these political shifts. In the case of Spain, a NATO ally, the Zapatero government allowed the use of bases for OIF even as bilateral security relations between the two countries were plummeting after the Spanish pullout. At the same time, anti-Americanism in Spain was high, and public opinion on basing rights was firmly against the government's continued permissive stance. In the case of Uzbekistan, the security climate in Afghanistan had hardly changed in 2005 in a manner that would compel the Uzbek government to recalculate the external security benefits it derived from the presence

3. See Cooley 2005a.

of U.S. forces at K2. Moreover, local residents near K2 favored retaining the base because of its positive economic impact in an otherwise impoverished part of the country—although for the authoritarian Uzbek regime public opinion was scarcely important anyway. Neither security factors nor changes in public opinion can explain the depoliticization of the basing issue in Spain and its subsequent politicization in Uzbekistan. How, then, should we understand these and other cases of the changing politics of U.S. overseas bases?

This book develops a theory of base politics to explain when and why bilateral military basing agreements become accepted, politicized, or challenged by host countries. Rulers and political elites in base hosts use the benefits and political opportunities provided by basing agreements to promote their domestic political self-interest. Changes in a host country's domestic political institutions—from authoritarian rule to democratic transition or from democratic transition to democratic consolidation—independently affect the types of benefits that elites can derive from the base issue and, in turn, their propensity to contest the bilateral basing contract. Certain political environments, especially periods of volatile democratic transition, afford considerable political benefits to elites who contest basing agreements. Conversely, the consolidation of a base host's democratic institutions tends to lead to the depoliticization of the issue, regardless of prevailing public opinion or anti-U.S. sentiment. The exact causal mechanisms and political pathways through which the base issue is politicized or depoliticized vary and are the theoretical focus of this book. Accordingly, this work is certainly not the first comparative study of U.S. military bases abroad, but it is the first to focus on the changing domestic politics of bases and base access within hosts across different regions, rather than on the operational or security dimensions.[4]

Further, this book identifies and clarifies the variety of political issues that become associated with or activated by the presence of overseas bases. Granting base access for a U.S. military campaign against a third party, such as the 2003 military campaign against Iraq, is an enduring issue that relates to a host state's sovereignty, but other base-related issues also can claim the national political spotlight. Domestic politicians or nongovernmental organizations (NGOs) may campaign to prohibit the stationing of nuclear weapons or other types of weapons or may protest

4. Some comparative studies also contain helpful political analysis. See esp. Sandars 2000; Duke and Krieger 1993; McDonald and Bendahmane 1990; Duke 1989.

a base's adverse environmental impact. U.S. troops involved in accidents with local populations increase media and public scrutiny of the special legal status granted to U.S. forces in the host country. And host countries may demand increased economic payments as a quid pro quo for accepting the American military presence. Such issues have periodically dominated U.S. bilateral relations with major and minor base hosts, yet we lack a systematic framework for assessing when and why these issues become politically paramount. In this book I offer some answers to these questions.

The Enduring Significance of U.S. Bases

At first glance, the topic of base politics itself may seem anachronistic, for the term "overseas bases" conjures images of superpowers during the cold war maneuvering across the third world to secure geopolitical access and advantage.[5] But securing overseas basing access remains a critical aspect of current U.S. defense policy and the global war on terrorism, especially as U.S. planners reconfigure the force structure and basing posture to cope with more regionally based threats.[6] Moreover, for host countries, base issues can still dominate bilateral relations with the United States—a fact that is not always shared or sufficiently appreciated by U.S. officials—and the manner in which base-related issues are managed (or mismanaged) can symbolize the broader relationship between the base host and the United States. Finally, studying the politics of bases reveals some unexpected aspects of how U.S. allies and military clients engage with American unipolarism or the "American Empire." Most important, this account of base politics reveals an emerging, if unexpected, tension inherent in the current U.S. strategy of promoting democracy abroad while maintaining an extensive global basing presence—the pursuit of one may actually undermine the viability of the other in any given base host.

5. The defining work on cold war base functions and access is Harkavy 1989.
6. For example, according to the 2002 National Security Strategy, "to contend with uncertainty and to meet the many security challenges we face, the United States will require bases and stations within and beyond Western Europe and Northeast Asia, as well as temporary access arrangements for the long-distance deployment of U.S. forces." National Security Council (NSC) 2002, 29.

Projecting American Power

U.S. overseas bases and access rights are the linchpin of American global power and its military supremacy of the global commons.[7] Overseas bases in countries such as Spain and Uzbekistan act as "force multipliers" and enable U.S. planners to rapidly project power both within and across regions.[8] Securing overseas bases and access agreements with a number of countries was critical for the recent U.S.-led military campaigns in Afghanistan and Iraq.[9] For example, the K2 base in Uzbekistan was staging facility for the OIF mission, whereas facilities in Spain were used for both the Afghanistan and Iraq campaigns. Even when not used for combat purposes, bases are significant when they guarantee U.S. access to neighboring assets, territories, or resources that are of critical importance.[10]

Beyond their military roles and strategic functions, bases also provide service and repair facilities, storage, training facilities, and logistical staging posts. Bases can also be used to conduct surveillance, coordinate tasks, collect intelligence, and facilitate command, control, and communications (C3).[11] As it turns out, overseas bases such as K2 have been used to transport enemy combatants and terror suspects as part of the CIA's program of extraordinary rendition and may even have been used as sites to detain and interrogate some suspects.[12]

The sheer number of U.S. overseas bases is staggering (see table 1.1). According to the Department of Defense's 2006 *Base Structure Report*, the United States officially maintains 766 military installations overseas and another 77 in noncontinental U.S. territories. Fifteen of these facilities were estimated to be worth more than $1.6 billion each, whereas an additional 19 were valued at between $862 million and $1.6 billion.[13] Of course, such official figures do not include the numerous secret installations and jointly operated bases and/or tacit governance arrangements that are scattered

7. See Posen 2003.
8. Desch 1992.
9. See Harkavy 2005, 31–33.
10. Desch 1989. Desch argues that bases should be placed in countries or regions with extrinsic value, that is, countries lacking in value but in which a presence is necessary to guard regions that do have intrinsic value.
11. For a comprehensive list of functions and discussion, see Harkavy 1989.
12. See Grey 2006, esp. 170–89, for a discussion of Uzbekistan. Also see European Parliament 2007; Priest 2005, A1.
13. U.S. Department of Defense (DoD) 2006, 22. Estimated values are based on the official plant replacement value (PRV) of each installation.

TABLE 1.1
Location, size, and value of U.S. military installations, 2006

Location	Service	No. of large installations	No. of medium installations	No. of small installations	No. of other installations	Total locations
United States	All	98	90	2,338	362	2,888
U.S. territories	All	3	2	63	9	77
Overseas	Army	1	8	351	11	371
	Navy	5	3	84	2	94
	Air Force	8	5	246	15	274
	Marine Corp	1	3	17	6	27
All overseas		15	19	698	34	766

Source: U.S. Department of Defense, *Base Structure Report, Fiscal Year 2006 Baseline* (Washington, DC, 2006), 22.

Notes: Large installation, Total plant replacement value (PRV) ≥ $1.61B; medium installation, $862M to < $1.61B; small installation, < $862M; and other installation, PRV = 0 (primarily land records).

overseas.[14] Not surprisingly, some commentators refer to this vast overseas network of bases and troop deployments as the U.S. Empire and compare it to the peripheral holdings of previous imperial powers.[15]

The structure of this global basing network is also changing. The Pentagon's current Global Defense Posture Review (GDPR) marks the first fundamental transformation of U.S. basing posture since World War II as U.S. defense planners adjust to new strategic imperatives such as the global war on terror.[16] The GDPR will reduce U.S. forces in several major cold war base hosts—especially Germany, Korea, and Japan—and will establish a global network of smaller, more flexible facilities. These new-style bases or "lily pads" will be located in several regions where the United States has not traditionally maintained a presence, including Africa, Central Asia, and the Black Sea. As a result, the United States seems set to abandon its traditional role as an "offshore balancer" and, using its new

14. See Johnson 2004, 151–85.
15. See the contrasting perspectives offered by Kaplan 2005; Johnson 2004.
16. See Campbell and Ward 2003.

basing posture, to more directly engage regional threats such as terrorists and insurgents.[17] One explicitly political goal of the GDPR is to reduce the footprint and local friction caused by a large U.S. military presence and establish smaller facilities of a less permanent nature that will be less politically controversial and socially intrusive within host countries.

Bases as Diplomatic Symbols

Overseas bases, however, are not merely installations that serve a military purpose. For host governments and citizens, U.S. bases are also concrete institutions and embodiments of U.S. power, identity, and diplomacy. The physical presence of overseas U.S. troops and installations—from the large garrison towns in Germany that look like imported American counties to the small but restricted sites in Central Asia—serves as a daily reminder of the scope of U.S. global influence and signifies that the host country has sacrificed some of its domestic sovereignty.[18] Negotiations over bases and their governing agreements can become the most pressing bilateral issue that host countries face with the United States, as they were in Spain in the mid-1980s and Uzbekistan from 2001 to 2005, and displace all other political and security concerns.[19] Moreover, host countries often view the basing relationship as a symbol of the broader state of U.S.-host relations. Hence, Korean antibase activists campaign for a more "equal relationship" between U.S. forces and Korean sovereignty, whereas Romanian politicians proudly refer to the new U.S. bases on the Black Sea as symbols of the country's new status as a strong partner in the U.S.-led Western security system. Politically, bases are the most immediate issue through which a host country's politicians and its public experience, debate, and even contest U.S. global power.

Often, basing agreements may even signal political and social commitments that U.S. officials did not necessarily intend to make. For example, America's western European allies strongly opposed the U.S.-Spain 1953 Madrid Pact and argued that the deal bestowed international legitimacy on the autocrat General Francisco Franco when he was otherwise ostracized from the international community. Similarly, although the basing agreement with Uzbekistan focused on fighting common terrorist elements in

17. On offshore balancing, see Layne 2006; Mearsheimer 2001.
18. On the comparative political significance of spatial planning in bases, see Gillem 2004. On the social and political impact of different overseas camp towns, see Baker 2004.
19. See McDonald and Bendahmane 1990.

the Central Asian region, other states and publics across Central Asia saw the deal as a U.S. endorsement of the Uzbek regime's repressive policies and undemocratic tendencies. Historically, U.S. officials have found it difficult to limit basing agreements from being perceived as broader political endorsements of host-country regimes and their domestic political and social practices.[20]

Rethinking Debates about American Empire

A comparative study of the domestic politics of the base issue also challenges many of the conventional assumptions that we hold about the overseas impact of American hegemony and U.S. relations with global security partners and clients. Most prevailing studies of U.S. overseas bases or American Empire—whether supportive or critical—assume that the U.S. military is fairly unconstrained in its capacity to establish bases and project power from these various overseas installations.[21]

Yet, as events in Uzbekistan suggest, the considerable differential in military power between the United States and its overseas base hosts does not always guarantee enduring American access and influence. The U.S. military presence abroad, even in relatively weak countries, is more frequently politicized and contested by host states than is commonly assumed. Both supportive and critical accounts of American Empire usually ignore how otherwise weak base hosts often nudge, manipulate, and even resist the American presence, often for their own independent political purposes.[22] As in other empires of the past, "pericentric developments" within a base host's territory frequently constrain the preferences of U.S. policymakers.[23] U.S. planners certainly try to influence base-related

20. See Cooley 2005a.
21. See esp. Johnson 2000, 2004, 2007; Bacevich 2002. Also see Ferguson 2002, 2004; but also see Motyl 2006. On the importance of institutional constraints on American hierarchy, see Ikenberry 2001. On the distinct structural properties and analytical distinctions among hegemony, empire, and different hierarchical orders, see Nexon and Wright 2007; Ikenberry 2004.
22. For an important exception, see Lundestad 1986 for the author's "empire by invitation" thesis.
23. The term "pericentric" is taken from Michael Doyle's theoretical overview of historical empires and refers to theories that view peripheral political developments as the key determinants of the timing and form of imperial rule. Such pericentric theories can be contrasted to metrocentric theories, which focus on imperatives and factors in the metropole as key variables. See Doyle 1986. The most influential pericentric and revisionist account of the British Empire can be found in Robinson 1968.

developments, but the historical record suggests that often they do not adequately apprehend or cannot exert influence over these internal political processes.[24] The Uzbek eviction was one of the latest examples of this host-driven contestation of U.S. power, but it is certainly no exception.

On the other hand, a focus on base politics suggests that the transatlantic rift generated by the 2003 Iraq War may not be as acute as it is commonly portrayed, at least not in this important area of security cooperation.[25] When examined through the prism of securing base access, transatlantic cooperation has remained significantly high, even during the Iraq campaign. The Spanish policy of opposing the war while at the same time granting base access to the United States may seem paradoxical, but other European countries such as Greece and Germany did so as well. In fact, in 2002 German chancellor Gerhardt Schroeder used an antiwar plank to win reelection and then proceeded to grant base access to the United States for the very same campaign. As in Spain, basing issues in these other European countries have evolved from issues of high politics—that is, topics openly debated by political parties, the media, and elites—to routine and even bureaucratic issues not subject to public scrutiny or political debate. European governments, even those that have been openly critical of U.S. foreign and security policy, no longer question the purpose or role of U.S. facilities on their territory, even when they are used for politically unpopular purposes such as the Iraq War or CIA rendition flights.

Thus, focusing on base issues paints a picture of the overseas reception of American hegemony dramatically different from our conventional understanding. The political attitudes toward U.S. bases among those living in a host country often diverge from the prevailing state of bilateral security relations. Elites in otherwise weak states may be the best situated, as a result of their domestic political volatility, to challenge the United States on base rights, whereas stronger allies, usually consolidated democracies, are the most constrained in their capacity to contest base issues, even as they question the actual content of U.S. security policy. Accordingly, the politics of basing relations offers important new insights into how the United States, especially in this unipolar era, establishes, redefines, and renegotiates its relations with allies and military clients.

---

24. On why relations of international hierarchy do not usually promote institutional change within political peripheries, see Cooley 2005d.
25. For representative examples, see Daalder 2003; Asmus 2003. For an academic perspective, see Andrews 2005.

The Argument

Political Survival and Two-Level Politics

To better understand the interplay between domestic political imperatives and these bilateral security contracts, we must go beyond traditional security-based theories and apply a number of seemingly disparate concepts in political science—including studies of democratic transition and consolidation, hierarchical relations among patrons and clients, and new institutional theories of contracting—to the basing issue.

This book assumes that rulers of base-host countries value and pursue, above all else, their own domestic political survival.[26] Rulers certainly value other things, such as following their political ideologies, improving domestic conditions, and securing the national interest, but rulers wield power in both the domestic and foreign policy arenas in order to maximize their own political benefit and maintain their office.[27] Base contracts provide a variety of benefits, resources, and opportunities to elites in host countries for these ends.

Host states enter into basing agreements by voluntarily signing a contract or by having such an arrangement imposed on them by a stronger power in the aftermath of war or a military occupation. Whether initially established by contract or by imposition, all basing agreements are, to some extent, a hierarchical security contract in which a base host legally cedes part of its sovereignty when it accepts a foreign military presence on its territory.[28] Of course, not all agreements are hierarchical to the same degree. Contracts can vary from arrangements of almost pure hierarchy, in which the sending country occupies or imposes all of the terms and conditions on the base host, to one of modified hierarchy, in which the host country retains some sovereignty and exercises decision-making authority over the use of the bases.[29] Nevertheless, rulers of host countries are involved

---

26. On the imperatives of political survivorship, see Bueno de Mesquita et al. 2003.

27. On why and how rulers violate their sovereignty for domestic political gain, see Krasner 1999.

28. Thus, David Lake's study (2007) of hierarchy in international politics appropriately uses foreign troop deployments as an indicator of the degree of hierarchy that characterizes a bilateral relationship. On security contracts and hierarchy, also see Lake 1999; Weber 2000. Chapter 2 of this book explores how the exact provisions and terms of basing agreements vary.

29. On the continuum of hierarchical security relations, see Lake 1996, 1999. On the ability of states to design bilateral security contracts to parse the various property rights associated with sovereignty, see Cooley 2000–2001.

in two sets of hierarchical political relationships, or nested hierarchies, in that they manage relations with the sending state while simultaneously providing public goods and selective incentives to their domestic political clients and supporters, who are also known as the "selectorate."[30]

These dual imperatives interact in a two-level game in which rulers use base-related issues and resources for their domestic political purposes but can also invoke domestic constraints in their negotiations with the sender.[31] For example, when in December 2001 the United States established the Ganci airbase in Kyrgyzstan, it awarded multi-million-dollar refueling contracts to a firm controlled by Kyrgyz president Askar Akayev's immediate family. The deal provided a significant revenue stream that the regime used to dispense patronage to domestic political allies and consolidate its rule.[32] However, after Akayev was ousted in 2005, the new Kyrgyz government insisted that the United States significantly increase its base-related lease payments to compensate the Kyrgyz people for supporting the corruption and antidemocratic practices of the Akayev regime. This continuous interaction of domestic and international factors is a hallmark of basing politics, with its nested nature, and makes two-level games as important for hierarchical settings as they are for anarchical ones.

Specifically, the contractual politics of any prevailing basing agreement are usually shaped by two such interactions: the host regime's dependence on the contract for its political survival and the credibility of the base host's political institutions. The host regime's political dependence on the contract determines the degree of hierarchy or balance of terms within the basing contract, whereas the host country's political institutions determine the agreement's legitimacy, credibility, and susceptibility to renegotiation.

Base Benefits and Regime Dependence

Basing agreements provide a range of benefits and resources to host regimes. Of these, the most obvious benefit to the host nation is security. The presence of foreign troops can deter aggressors and permits a host to spend less on its national security than it otherwise would. In his study

---

30. On the importance of the selectorate and the imperatives of political survivorship, see Bueno de Mesquita et al. 2003.
31. See Evans, Jacobson, and Putnam 1993; Putnam 1988. For an application to U.S. base negotiations in Denmark and Greenland, see Archer 2003.
32. Cloud 2005.

of hierarchy in international politics, David Lake finds that base hosts and subordinate states in security arrangements tend to spend less on their security than do states with no such foreign troop deployments.[33] In turn, spending less on security allows regimes to spend more on goods that will enhance their political survival. For example, the bilateral security guarantees and military bases offered by the United States to East Asia in the postwar periods allowed Japan and Korea to minimize security spending and instead pursue state-led neomercantilist policies under the U.S. security umbrella.[34] Moreover, a foreign military presence can offer internal security and a guarantee that the host regime will survive an internal threat. In the 1950s, regimes in Japan and Italy signed basing agreements that actually allowed for U.S. military intervention in their internal affairs.

Security need not be the only, or even the main, base-related benefit for a host country's regime. Economic aid and assistance packages can be granted in exchange for securing basing rights. For example, during the 1970s then president Ferdinand Marcos of the Philippines extracted billions of dollars in economic and military assistance from the United States, as well as loan guarantees from international financial institutions, in exchange for granting U.S. basing rights. These flows allowed Marcos to pay off his political clients and consolidate his domestic political base (see chap. 3). Beyond direct quid pro quo and private benefits, bases also can make critical contributions to a host country's economy by providing jobs and supporting local small businesses.

Basing agreements can also provide intangible benefits such as prestige, legitimacy, and association with the United States and the West. Such a connection may be invaluable to host-country elites who seek international legitimacy and support for their regime. Both the U.S.-Spain 1953 Madrid Pact and the 2001 base deal with Uzbekistan, for instance, offered these authoritarian hosts U.S. recognition and security cooperation at a time when their authoritarian tendencies were being questioned by members of the international community. Similarly, U.S. bases in Italy in the 1950s were always referred to as NATO bases by the Christian Democrats and were portrayed as symbols of Italy's newly attained membership in the Western security community and its association with Western democratic states.[35] In certain political environments, moreover, domestic elites

33. Lake 2007.
34. Kurth 1989.
35. See Cremasco 1988. On NATO as a democratic community, see Risse-Kappan 1996.

demand greater benefits and renegotiation of existing basing contracts in order to appear strong on issues of national importance. Because basing agreements and their negotiations are inherently tied to issues of national defense and domestic sovereignty, they offer important political opportunities to political elites, especially during an election campaign.

The nature of goods and benefits sought by base hosts varies and depends on the base host's security situation, economic size, and domestic institutional arrangements. Base hosts that face an immediate security threat, such as South Korea or West Germany during the cold war, value security above other benefits. Base hosts with a small economy are more likely to benefit significantly from the economic flows that accompany a basing agreement than are hosts with a larger or more advanced economy. And although authoritarian and patrimonial democratic regimes benefit from the private goods and economic incentives provided by a basing contract, rulers of consolidated democracies in which the selectorate is much broader require more visible public goods from a basing deal.[36]

Regardless of the exact type of benefit a basing agreement bestows on a ruler, it is generally true that the more a regime depends on the basing contract for its political survival, the more likely the terms of the basing agreement are unbalanced or otherwise favor the sending country. In the most extreme cases of external military occupation, when U.S. forces initially established or critically supported a ruling regime such as that of postwar Japan, Germany, Korea, Italy, or the Philippines, the accompanying base deals were extremely unbalanced and tilted toward the U.S. side.

Contractual Credibility of Political Institutions

A base's political fate depends not only on the regime in power but also on the credibility of the political institutions within the host country. The political institutions of autocracies, consolidated democracies, and democratizing states vary in their propensity to honor international contracts, including security agreements. In general, consolidated democracies offer the most credible contracting environment, whereas states that are democratizing or experiencing other sorts of political transition are the most uncertain, especially when a contract was concluded before the democratic transition. Three specific mechanisms—procedural legitimacy, institutional competition, and party system consolidation—account for

---

36. I thank Robert Jervis for underlining this point.

these varying patterns of politicization and depoliticization. Given that authoritarian governments typically lack independent domestic institutions, their decisions to honor an existing basing contract are usually a function of the ruler's domestic political interests and survival strategy, not of intervening institutions.

Authoritarian Regimes: Lack of Independent Institutions

Because authoritarian regimes lack independent institutions such as a parliament, opposition parties, or an independent judiciary, decisions to politicize or contest basing issues are determined by the political calculations of the host ruler. As a result, the credibility of authoritarian rulers and their propensity to honor security contracts are mixed.

According to the popular "strongman" view of international agreements, authoritarian regimes make stable contracting partners because they can negotiate deals without public accountability and consent.[37] Decision making tends to be centralized, allowing autocrats to rapidly conclude international agreements such as security contracts without having to consult a legislature or political party. Moreover, through their control of the media and political institutions, autocrats can publicize aspects of the agreement that may be of political benefit while they conceal or mischaracterize those provisions that might be political damaging. For example, most contemporary accounts in the Spanish media of the 1953 Madrid Pact portrayed the basing accords as steadfastly guarding Spanish sovereignty, even though the secret technical agreements of the accords granted the United States virtually unhindered access to bases throughout the country.[38] As long as contracts provide some set of political benefits or private goods, authoritarian rulers adhere to their contractual commitments.

The lack of independent domestic institutions, however, leaves authoritarian rulers relatively free to arbitrarily demand revisions and adjustments to agreements according to their own political whims and interests. For example, Uzbek president Karimov faced minimal domestic constraints when he unilaterally terminated his country's basing contract with the United States. Furthermore, security contracts signed with nondemocracies are valid only as long as the ruling regime or coalition maintains power and may not survive the fall of a nondemocratic regime. For example, when Colonel Muammar Gaddafi led a revolutionary coup in

---

37. For an overview, see Martin 2000.
38. On the coverage of the 1953 agreements in the Spanish press, see Viñas 2003a, 2003b.

Libya to depose King Idris, he insisted on the withdrawal of the U.S. Air Force from Wheelus base on the grounds that the U.S. and British military presence had propped up the previous monarchy.[39] Similarly, the coming to power of the Derg in Ethiopia in the mid-1970s and of Ayatollah Khomeini in Iran in 1979 invalidated the agreements that had been signed with previous authoritarian clients guaranteeing the United States access to key communications installations in those countries.[40] Absent independent political institutions, the personalization of a security contract in an autocracy and the private benefits it provides make it likely that the contract will be challenged in the event of a regime change.

Consolidated Democracies: High Contractual Credibility

Consolidated democracies offer the most credible domestic institutions for negotiating and abiding by basing agreements and other security contracts. This credibility is achieved through three causal mechanisms and political pathways: procedural legitimacy, institutional stability and delegation, and a consolidated party system.

First, contracts signed with mature democracies are procedurally legitimate. In Charles Lipson's formulation, mature democracies make for "reliable partners" because to preserve their credibility they are obliged to adhere to contractual commitments made by their democratic predecessors.[41] A legislature's ratification of a security contract or treaty institutionalizes the host government's commitment and inhibits the arbitrary reneging that characterizes nondemocracies.[42] A contract concluded with a previous democratic regime, even one with different policy preferences, usually cannot be unilaterally invalidated or have its legitimacy challenged on procedural grounds.

Second, consolidated democracies are characterized by jurisdictional stability in policymaking and implementation. Policy matters are delegated to specialized bureaucracies and agencies for implementation. These organs assume jurisdiction and routinize the management and com-

---

39. For background on Wheelus, see the globalsecurity Web site: http://www.global security.org/wmd/facility/wheelus.htm (accessed May 2007).
40. In the Ethiopian case, the United States had signed a twenty-five-year arms-for-base deal with Emperor Haile Selassie to use the Kagnew communications station in present-day Eritrea. In Iran, during the rule of Shah Pahlavi, the United States maintained two important listening posts north of Tehran that allowed it to monitor intercontinental ballistic missile tests. See Bamford 1983, 256–59; Bamford 2002, 160–162.
41. Lipson 2003.
42. Martin 2000.

pliance with contractual commitments, treaties, and international accords. Over time, bureaucracies and implementing agencies tend to become entrenched in the policymaking process and act as "veto players" in that issue area. The higher the number of veto players within the political system, the lower the likelihood that policy agendas can be altered or revised.[43]

Third, the political party systems of consolidated democracies tend to moderate political stances on controversial foreign policy and sovereignty issues. Political competition among well-institutionalized parties tends to temper ideologically based policy positions on foreign policy matters in order to compete for and attract more moderate or median voters.[44] For example, during the 1970s the Italian Communist Party (PCI) adopted a pro-NATO and pro-U.S. bases platform in order to take the issue off the political agenda, appeal to moderate voters, and focus its campaign on domestic policy.[45] Further, once in power, parties that were once ideological must govern pragmatically, maintain winning coalitions, and cooperate with other parties on foreign policy and security affairs.[46] That cooperation includes honoring security agreements and other contracts that were concluded by democratic predecessors, even if they are policy positions to which the party's platform is ideologically opposed. In consolidated democracies, only fringe parties are likely to draw attention to base issues or any other international contractual commitment, and usually as a mobilization strategy directed at attracting ideological voters, an act that mainstream parties often point to as an indicator of a radical platform.[47]

Overall, in consolidated democracies these three institutional features "lock in" basing commitments and make the implementation of these contracts routine policy matters that are managed by technocrats, not political elites.

Democratizing Regimes: Low Contractual Credibility

The least credible contractual institutions are found in states undergoing a democratic transition from authoritarian rule, especially if the contract

43. Tsebelis 2002, 2. For an application of this argument to the similar sovereignty-related issue of decolonization and territorial disengagement, see Spruyt 2005.
44. The classic argument about policy convergence around the median voter is made in Downs 1957.
45. See chap. 6.
46. Cooley and Hopkin 2006, 11.
47. For example, in Spain only the leftist Izquierda Unida regularly brings up the issue of U.S. bases. In Greece, the newly formed National Front has discussed the Souda Bay naval base in reference to possible CIA detentions there.

in question was signed before the transition.[48] Basing agreements under-taken in such democratizing countries lack procedural legitimacy, whereas the hosts are characterized by institutional competition and party-system fragmentation.

First, existing contracts in democratizing states lack procedural legiti-macy. Contracts that were signed by a previous authoritarian govern-ment or that were imposed by an external power during an occupation lack validity, especially when they have not been democratically ratified since. As a result, the legitimacy of base contracts is an attractive issue for rulers and political elites during election campaigns. Jack Snyder and Edward Mansfield point out how democratizing polities are particularly prone to elite-induced populism, nationalism, and aggressive mobiliza-tion strategies for use as electoral issues.[49] The topic of basing agreements and infringement of national sovereignty is an ideal issue for this type of election campaigning and populist mobilization. Democratizing elites may demand adjustments to or renegotiations of what have become ille-gitimate basing accords, or they may present their opposition to the U.S. bases as a symbol of their commitment to breaking from the authoritarian past. In post-authoritarian Spain, Turkey, Greece, the Philippines, Thai-land, Okinawa, Japan, and Korea, major candidates running for national or regional office publicly questioned the validity of prevailing U.S. basing contracts. In their campaigns they argued that the deals had been signed by previous autocrats or that the United States had unfairly imposed them during a time of occupation.

Jurisdictional uncertainty within democratizing states may further ex-acerbate political debates about contractual validity. Unlike consolidated democracies, where policy implementation is bureaucratized and clearly delineated, new domestic political institutions such as legislatures, consti-tutions, political parties, independent courts, and local governments vie to assert jurisdiction over foreign policy matters, including security contract-ing, in order to define and probe the extent of their institutional authority.[50] Thus legislatures are more likely to demand that external contracts be sub-jected to ratification, new political parties are likely to address foreign-policy issues in their emergent platforms, and courts may insist on reviewing the

48. On democratic transitions, see Anderson 1999; Huntington 1993; O'Donnell and Schmitter 1986.
49. See Mansfield and Snyder 2005; Snyder 2000.
50. On the dynamics of institutional competition and democratic consolidation, see Diamond and Gunther 2001; Linz and Stepan 1996; Gunther, Diamandouros, and Pule 1995.

legality of external treaties and agreements. Local governments, especially ones that have recently acquired decentralized powers, may challenge the authority of central governments over base-related matters. Further, new social actors such as citizens' groups and the media may use the base issue and related security matters to enter the political process.

Finally, the competitive and fragmented party system in a democratizing host may further undermine the validity of existing contracts by rewarding ideological mobilization and the politicization of foreign policy and security issues. Nascent party systems—where political parties are underdeveloped and concentrate on mobilizing core activists and constituencies with ideological appeals—may further encourage politicians and their parties to adopt uncompromising, antibase stances and platforms.[51] As a result, rulers and politicians in democratizing states with multiple parties can campaign on the base issue without worrying about capturing the median voter. These domestic institutional mechanisms are summarized in table 1.2.

Outcomes of Base Politics

A base-host regime's political dependence on a security contract and a political institution's contractual credibility broadly determine how and when basing agreements become politicized, challenged, or accepted by a host country. Figure 1.1 presents a typology of these various dependence/credibility configurations and depicts four different political environments or outcomes of the basing relationship. The arrows represent typical shifts in the politics of the issue following a regime change, democratic transition, or some other major institutional transformation in the domestic politics of a base host. In general, democratic transitions within base hosts often lead them to politicize and contest security contracts, whereas democratic consolidation leads base hosts to accept or depoliticize them. We could describe these four political environments as acceptance, politicization, indifference, and contestation. The key point here is that a host regime's political stance toward the basing contract is determined by broader institutional changes within the base host and the regime's dependence on the contract, not by purely external factors such as the state of bilateral relations or the prevailing security environment.

51. On the consolidation party systems, see Sartori 1976. For a further expansion of this logic and application to the base issue in democracies, see Cooley and Hopkin 2006.

TABLE 1.2
Effects of a host country's political institutions on contractual credibility

Domestic institutional characteristic	Authoritarian regime	Democratizing regime	Consolidated democracy
Procedural legitimacy of base contract	Legitimate as long as ruler remains in power	LOW: Contracts signed with previous nondemocratic government, not ratified	HIGH: Contracts signed by democratic regime and ratified by legislature
Jurisdictional stability	None; no independent political institutions	LOW: Uncertain; domestic institutions compete for jurisdiction and policy-making authority; policy instability	HIGH: Bureaucratization, delegation, and routinized management; multiple veto points lead to policy stability
Nature of the party system	None; one-party rule	Fragmented and competitive; need to mobilize ideological base, appeal to nationalism to secure position in electoral market	Stable and institutionalized; need to appeal to median voter; mobilization around competence, not ideology
Overall credibility of commitment to base contract	Mixed; political interests and survival strategies will determine commitment	LOW: Contracts subject to politicization, contestation, renegotiation, and possible abrogation	HIGH: Contracts signed with a democratic government; need to preserve credibility of commitment

The northeast quadrant of figure 1.1 characterizes credible hosts that have signed basing agreements highly dependent on the sending country. The terms of these arrangements favor the sender but nevertheless are accepted, even begrudgingly, by host polities as legitimate contracts. This cell includes the newly democratic post–World War II regimes of Germany and Italy, with their initial U.S. basing arrangements, as well the democratic regimes in Greece and Turkey during the 1950s, with their original bilateral facilities agreements signed before their authoritarian turn when they became U.S. security clients. The cell also includes mainland Japan after its democratic consolidation in the 1960s, following the fierce political battle waged over the 1960 Mutual Security Treaty.

The northwest quadrant depicts political settings in which host regimes are highly dependent on the sender, but their domestic institutions lack

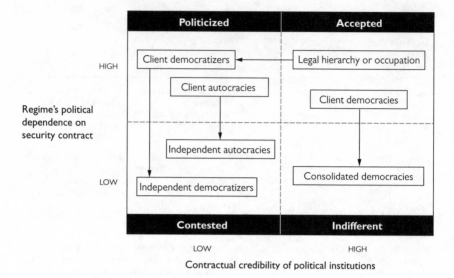

Figure 1.1. Configurations of base politics within base hosts

contractual credibility. Base hosts in this cell are likely to politicize prevailing basing agreements and challenge certain contractual terms. However, their dependence on the contract also prevents these hosts from contesting the actual necessity of the presence of U.S. forces or unilaterally abrogating the agreement. Hosts in this cell usually had initial basing agreements imposed on them during a military occupation but during their subsequent independence almost immediately questioned the validity of these original deals. This cell includes the Philippines and Japan in their push for the renegotiation of base accords in the 1950s, and the island prefecture of Okinawa post-1972, where local politicians and social movements challenged the unrestricted base rights and legal status that the U.S. military had enjoyed during its twenty-year administration (1952–72). Economically dependent authoritarian regimes, such as the Akayev regime in Kyrgyzstan, that of Syngman Rhee in Korea, or of Ferdinand Marcos in the Philippines, would also fall into this category.

In the southeast quadrant are hosts whose regimes are not politically dependent on the sender and that maintain credible contracting institutions. Security contracts with these states tend to be relatively depoliticized as political elites in these countries remain indifferent to the bases and treat the issue as a part of a broader bundle of bilateral security relations and commitments. This political outcome characterizes the basing arrangements that the United States currently enjoys with nearly all of its democratic allies in Europe, Australia, and mainland Japan.[52] Basing issues in this cell are part of a broader set of routine bilateral security cooperation and access agreements and are generally removed from everyday party politics and debate.[53] The extreme example within this cell is Great Britain, which has institutionalized basing cooperation with the United States since World War II without actually ever signing a formal military facilities agreement.[54] This statement does not imply that certain groups or politicians do not question base issues in these countries. Rather, antibase movements or protest campaigns in these base hosts lack a formal political vehicle or channel to address the concerns. For example, during the 1970s and 1980s, antinuclear campaigns and NGOs in Germany and Britain mobilized against the stationing of nuclear weapons on German and British soil, but governing political parties, even those of a more left-wing orientation, were severely constrained in their ability to meet these demands.[55] Similarly, when in February 2007 many of the left-wing elements of Prime Minister Romano Prodi's coalition protested the planned expansion of the U.S. base in Vicenza, Prodi opposed his own coalition supporters and committed to the agreement signed by his right-wing predecessor and ratified by the Italian parliament.

Finally, the southwest quadrant represents host states whose regimes are not dependent on the United States and whose domestic institutions lack contractual credibility. Not only are these states likely to contest the terms of prevailing basing contracts, but they are also the most likely, of all base hosts, to unilaterally abrogate the contract and evict the U.S. military.

Two types of states fill this cell. The first type, nondependent autocracies such as Uzbekistan in 2005, will expel a foreign military presence when the basing agreement does more to threaten than enhance their regime's political survival. The second type comprises nondependent

---

52. Despite their different modes of base acquisition, Germany and Britain have both proven remarkably reliable base hosts, and with the exception of some antinuclear campaigns in the 1970s and 1980s, the base issues have remained relatively depoliticized by the main political parties in these countries.

53. For a critical account of this political indifference in the Australian case, see Ball 1980.

54. See Duke 1987.

55. For instance, in 1979 Chancellor Helmut Schmidt, in a controversial move, bucked the base of his Social Democratic Party by agreeing to station medium-range nuclear weapons (Euromissiles) on German territory. On the evolution of the nuclear issue and U.S. relations with western Europe, see Lundestad 2003, 201–25; Joffe 1987.

democratizers—states transitioning from authoritarian rule but no longer requiring the sending country's patronage or support. In such states, the external costs for contesting a bilateral security contract are low, whereas the internal political gains may be high. Indeed, within a democratizing climate, questioning the legitimacy and validity of previous contracts on procedural grounds may become an optimal competitive political strategy and effective campaign issue. In base hosts such as democratizing Greece, Spain, Panama, Turkey, and Thailand in the 1970s and 1980s, new left-leaning parties and populist elites took a more assertive and confrontational stance toward the bases than their political predecessors had. In all of these negotiations, host countries claimed that prevailing basing agreements were procedurally invalid because they had been signed with previous nondemocratic regimes and the current voting populace would not support their extension. In Turkey (1974–78), Spain (1988), Thailand (1975–76), and the Philippines (1991), democratizing governments actually suspended the basing agreement or expelled the U.S. military.

In addition, within nondependent democratizing base hosts, new social actors, particularly civic groups and the media, can further politicize and contest the base issue. Over the last two decades, NGOs have become increasingly important actors in world politics, using new information technologies to create transnational advocacy networks.[56] In relatively late democratizers such as Korea, the explosion of civil society has generated hundreds of NGOs that work on base-related issues such as the impact of the U.S. military presence on the environment, crimes perpetrated by U.S. personnel, and the plight of sexual workers in basing areas.[57] Media outlets in democratizing states also play a critical role because they are segmented by political affiliation and retain strong ties to political parties.[58] Reporters

---

56. On transnational networks of human rights activists, see Keck and Sikkink 1998. On NGOs as important new normative actors in international politics, see Price 2003. On NGOs and global anti-base activism, see Lutz 2008.

57. For a discussion of these groups in Korea, see Moon 2003. From the 1990s onward, Korean NGOs have used the United States Forces Korea (USFK) presence as a vehicle for increasing their voice and influence in Korean political affairs. To argue that the basing issue offers political opportunities for NGOs, however, does not impute their normative motivations or invalidate their concerns about these issues. On the need to decouple the ideas of NGOs from the strategies that they employ, see Sell and Prakash 2004.

58. Hallin and Mancini 2004. In their study of such polarized systems, including the southern European states, the authors further observe that "journalism is not as strongly differentiated from political activism and the autonomy of journalism is often limited" (74). On how the media promotes nationalism in democratizing states, see Snyder 2000; Snyder and Ballentine 1996.

and outlets that hold strong views about the basing presence actively seek out news stories to promote this agenda.[59] Just as democratizing politicians explicitly link the presence of the bases to support of a previous nondemocratic regime, democratizing media outlets can point to the bases issue as a symbol of previous state censorship and media secrecy.

Hypotheses on Base Politics, Security Contracts, and Domestic Institutional Change

This examination of the imperatives of base-host elites, their political dependence, and their contractual credibility yields the following general hypotheses on the relationship between domestic institutional change and political attitudes toward honoring basing agreements and security contracts:

Hypothesis 1: Authoritarian hosts will use bilateral basing agreements to extract private goods to further regime survival.

Corollary 1a: Authoritarian regimes will honor basing agreements as long as the benefits that they derive from base-related private goods exceed their political costs.

Corollary 1b: Authoritarian regimes will contest basing agreements when the political costs of honoring the contract exceed the benefits that they derive from base-related private goods.

Hypothesis 2: If prevailing agreements were signed before a democratic transition, the new democratizing regimes and elites will politicize or contest bilateral contracts.

Corollary 2a: Democratizing elites and regimes dependent on the basing power (i.e., the sending nation) for political support will politicize contracts and demand renegotiations but will stop short of abrogating or terminating the contract.

Corollary 2b: Democratizing elites and regimes that do not depend on the basing power for political support are the most likely to abrogate or terminate the contract.

59. On the dynamics of democratization and the media, see Milton 2001. Milton observes that "the news media are a tool to help identify political problems and develop solutions to them. In the initial phases of the transition to democracy the news media have the crucial role of explaining what is politically and economically plausible and realistic" (497).

Hypothesis 3: Regimes and elites in consolidated democracies will honor prevailing bilateral contracts that were signed with a democratic government, regardless of their policy differences with the basing power.

Corollary 3a: Consolidated democracies will honor prevailing contracts, regardless of public opinion toward basing issues, social mobilization, or changes in the international security environment.

Alternative Explanations and Perspectives

These hypotheses and the theory of two-level base politics advanced in this book can be usefully contrasted with a number of alternative explanations laid out in the international relations literature and suggested in other discussion of U.S. overseas bases.

The first and most important competing set of explanations explains internal base politics as a function of systemic pressures and the security imperatives faced by the base host and sending country. According to a standard realist theory, debates over base issues should be subsumed by security concerns and are determined by a host country's alliance orientation and its perceptions of external threat.[60] Issues pertaining to the bases should be managed within the broader security relationship of the host and sending countries. From the structural realist perspective, the greater the common threat faced by sending and host countries, the more likely the bases would be accepted as installations necessary for mutual security. A liberal systemic argument (either neoliberal or constructivist) would view base politics as a function of the international or multilateral institutions that govern these countries' security ties.[61] Thus, bases specifically earmarked for multilateral functions (e.g., NATO bases) and common alliance activities may be less contentious than bases used only by the United States to unilaterally project power.[62]

A second alternative explanation focuses on the size of the base and the number of overseas troops as the critical factors in determining domestic political reactions to a foreign basing presence. From this perspective a large base or heavy foreign troop presence is more likely to evoke domestic resentment and mobilize political opposition, whereas a smaller base

---

60. The classic neorealist statement about balancing behavior is made in Waltz 1979. On alliance formation as a response to threat, see Walt 1987. For an updated account of "offensive realism," see Mearsheimer 2001.
61. On security communities, see Adler and Barnett 2002; Risse-Kapan 1996.
62. On the consequences of bilateral versus multilateral security contracting in East Asia and Europe, see Katzenstein 2005; Hemmer and Katzenstein 2002.

or reduced troop presence is correlated with acceptance or indifference to the basing presence.[63] In fact, the assumption that a lighter basing footprint may diminish the base's political impact is a key assumption in the U.S. Pentagon's current Global Defense Posture Initiative.[64] By reducing the size of large cold war–era bases and replacing them with a network of smaller, more flexible installations and access arrangements, U.S. policymakers hope to avoid entanglement in the host country's domestic politics. This assumption is critically challenged in chapter 7, which traces the sudden politicization and contestation of the relatively small U.S. basing presence in Uzbekistan and Kyrgyzstan.

A third set of alternative explanations focuses not on a base's size but on its functions and use. From this perspective, U.S. use of a foreign military base to wage an unpopular military campaign, such as the Iraq War, would generate domestic political reactions to and mobilization against the terms of a basing agreement. Alternatively, a set of base-related accidents, incidents, or possible criminal acts involving U.S. personnel, especially if the victims are host-country nationals, would trigger a political backlash against the base and its underlying agreements.

Finally, a fourth rival set of explanations focuses on the social characteristics of a base-hosting country, such as public opinion regarding the United States and the host's political culture, as the determining factors in its prevailing political stance toward the U.S. military presence. Recent scholarship suggests that anti-Americanism is itself a complex phenomena that draws on the various domestic cultural sources, ideologies, and historical narratives of a particular society or political community.[65] But we could hypothesize that the higher the intensity and popularity of anti-American sentiments, the more likely a U.S. basing presence would be politicized or contested by domestic elites. Conversely, lower levels of anti-Americanism should correlate with less political mobilization against the bases. Similarly, a political culture perspective would expect societies with widespread norms against militarism to also exhibit the most political activism against a continuing foreign military presence.[66]

---

63. Although his work doesn't directly address the basing issue, Robert Pape, in his study of the political logic of suicide bombers, observes that al-Qaeda's suicide terrorists mostly come from countries that host a heavy presence of U.S. combat troops. See Pape 2005a. I thank Jack Snyder for suggesting this analogy.

64. See Cooley 2005a; Campbell and Ward 2003.

65. On the diversity of anti-Americanism and its different drivers, see Katzenstein and Keohane 2006.

66. On the importance of antimilitarist norms in shaping security policy in Japan and Germany, see Berger 1998; Katzenstein 1996.

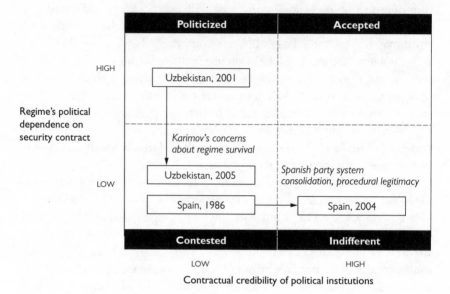

Figure 1.2. Changes in base politics, Spain and Uzbekistan

In sum, this book's theory of base politics as a function of domestic institutional change and consolidation can be usefully contrasted with the predictions of theories that examine systemic sources of security relations, the size of bases, the functions of bases, and the prevailing political culture within a host.

Understanding Base Politics: Spain and Uzbekistan Reprised

Returning to the examples of base politics described at the outset of the chapter, we find that the shifting positions of Spain and Uzbekistan reflect underlying institutional changes in their respective domestic political environments, not reactions to the international security environment or domestic public opinion (see figure 1.2). The use of Spanish bases by the U.S. military for its 1986 Libya campaign was considered illegitimate by the PSOE because the governing agreements had been established during the Franco era and had not been subject to democratic ratification.[67]

---

67. Moreover, at the time, the PSOE was mobilizing support for a referendum on NATO membership and did not want to appear weak on the basing issue.

After publicly receiving credit for "successfully" solving the base issue by renegotiating the Franco-era agreement and then securing its ratification democratically in 1988, the PSOE abandoned its aggressive stance on the basing issue and removed it from the policy agenda. Revisiting the issue in 2004 held no political gain for PSOE leaders. As the Spanish party system was consolidated across four successive PSOE governments, the leaders had come to portray their party as moderate, competent, and responsible on foreign affairs and security issues. In 2004 President Zapatero may have disagreed with the American military campaign in Iraq and withdrawn Spanish forces from that theater, but he honored the base access granted Operation Iraqi Freedom, viewing it as a credible and legitimate contract signed with a previous democratic government. Only Izquierda Unida, a leftist political party with the support of about 5 percent of the electorate, criticized the PSOE government on the base issue.

Similarly, in 2001 the government of Uzbekistan was eager to offer its cooperation and airbase facilities to the United States in order to jointly fight terrorists and Islamic extremists in Central Asia and be associated with the U.S.-led coalition. This security agreement with the United States helped President Islam Karimov eliminate political opponents, equip his security services with modern hardware, and publicly justify his tough internal policies. In May 2005, after Andijon, the Uzbek government regarded a continued American presence as a potential security threat to its regime, especially in light of the recent series of U.S.-backed revolutions in other post-Soviet states. By contrast it viewed Russia and China as alternate security partners that would be unconcerned with Uzbek democratization and would support the Karimov regime's hard-line tactics. The regime, with its authoritarian character, faced few domestic constraints after evicting the United States, even if the action displeased elements of the local population who had benefited economically from the presence of the K2 base. Domestic politics and the imperatives of political survivorship altered Karimov's calculations regarding the purpose and political utility of the U.S. base.

One of my main findings is that as domestic political institutions change within host countries, so too do political attitudes toward security contracts. Importantly, democratic rule in a base host does not necessarily guarantee that its basing relationship with the United States will remain stable. Although consolidated democracies accept basing agreements and honor contracts, just as Spain did in 2004, democratizing states are more likely to aggressively challenge the validity of these contracts, especially if they were signed before the transition.

These arguments have critical policy implications. They reveal important but as yet unacknowledged negative interactions between the foreign policy objective of promoting democracy abroad and the strategic objective of maintaining a global network of military bases. Maintaining permanent bases in democratizing hosts such as Afghanistan and Iraq may become politically impossible for the United States when these regimes no longer depend on the United States for their political support. Further, pressing for democratization within base-host countries that lack consolidated institutions and in which anti-Americanism is already high may actually trigger a populist antibase backlash and jeopardize the future legal status of the U.S. military presence. These are important and perhaps disconcerting lessons for U.S. planners to consider as they attempt to promote democratic change abroad while they simultaneously negotiate basing rights with these same polities.

CHAPTER 2

Overseas Military Basing Agreements

Issues and Methodology

Before we can assess the evolution of U.S. base contracts in particular cases, we need to identify the issues that the contracts cover. In this chapter I provide a framework for understanding the dimensions of basing agreements and for tracking how these provisions change across time and case, as well as a methodological justification for my selection of case studies. International legal scholars have examined some of these governance issues, and much of their work offers useful analytical insights.[1] Here I focus on the features of basing agreements that have been most frequently politicized and place them in a theoretical context that is more familiar to political analysts and social scientists. Although I refer to the American overseas military presence, these analytical categories just as easily could be applied to the study of other countries' basing arrangements.

Base contracts typically cover three broad categories of issues. First, they detail the precise installations, troop levels, and assets that a sending power can deploy in a host country. Second, base agreements govern issues of sovereignty, especially questions involving the legal status of bases, the consultation procedures for their use, and the criminal jurisdiction procedures that govern foreign troops stationed in the host country. Third, basing agreements may be linked to various economic and political

1. See especially Woodliffe 1992; Lazareff 1971.

demands made by the host country or to bargains struck in exchange for granting basing rights. Across all three of these dimensions, contractual arrangements vary considerably: some are hierarchical, or tilted exclusively toward favoring the sending power, whereas others are relatively more balanced in their provisions. So although a foreign military presence indicates some degree of hierarchy between a sending and host state, some basing agreements are considerably more imbalanced than others. In the next section, after a brief overview of the different forms of basing contracts, I overview these areas of governance and discuss the controversies that have historically arisen. In the final section of this chapter, I explain my case selection criteria and the methodology of the subsequent empirical chapters.

The Various Dimensions of Basing Contracts

Acquisition of Base Rights

Great powers have established their basing networks through a number of means, including conquest, alliance politics, colonization, and commercial transaction.[2] The United States mostly established its basing network after World War II, an era when the international norm of colonialism was considerably weakened.[3] As a result, and with a few notable exceptions, U.S. planners had to use mechanisms other than outright territorial conquest and military occupation to secure their basing needs.[4] The bulk of the basing network was acquired in the late 1940s and the 1950s through one of two modes: postwar occupation or bilateral contracting. In some cases, such as those of Japan and Korea in Asia, or West Germany in Europe, the U.S. basing presence remains a direct legacy of postwar occupation regimes. In other cases, such as that of Spain in the 1950s or more contemporary agreements with Kyrgyzstan and Uzbekistan, bases were established through a mutual contract, with facilities leased in exchange for

2. See Harkavy 2005; Stambuk 1963a, 474–76.
3. On norms and decolonization, see Jackson 1993.
4. For an overview, see Sandars 2000. Sandars refers to this extensive bundle of leasing agreements and basing contracts as a "leasehold empire" and differentiates these arrangements from the acquisition of overseas territory for military purposes that characterized previous imperial powers. His neocolonial exceptions are Philippines, Panama, and Guantánamo Bay (104–45). One could also consider U.S. Commonwealth possessions that host major U.S. military installations, such as Puerto Rico and the Mariana Islands, and unincorporated territories, such as Guam, as part of this category.

aid payments or some other quid pro quo. As the cases show, these modes of acquisition are not mutually exclusive; some bases originally acquired by occupation (Philippines and Japan) were later renegotiated at the initiative of the host country to secure more favorable terms.

Forms of Basing Contracts

In almost every instance of peacetime use of an overseas military base, some type of accord that codifies mutual consent governs the presence of the foreign force. These agreements can take an astonishing range of contractual forms and include formal bilateral or multilateral treaties, executive agreements, exchange of diplomatic notes, or military-to-military protocols.[5] The duration of these leases varies, with some agreements lasting ninety-nine years (Philippines, 1947) or even indefinitely (Japan, 1951), whereas others specify a length of just a few years. Governing agreements may be part of an overall bilateral comprehensive security package or defense and economic cooperation agreement (DECA), as was the case with Greece, Turkey, and Spain during the 1970s and 1980s, that also provides for transfers of military assistance and economic aid. The U.S.-UK arrangement is perhaps a unique case in that the vast network of airbases and other facilities used by the United States for decades has been governed by a series of informal rules and procedures, not an explicit agreement or defense treaty.[6] In the Australian case, the main agreement that has governed U.S. installations and joint facilities on Australian territory, most of them used for intelligence gathering and surveillance, is the UK-USA agreement of 1947–48 on signals intelligence (SIGINT) cooperation and exchange, not the actual Australia, New Zealand, United States (ANZUS) Security Treaty.[7]

Agreements on basing can also vary in the scope of issues that they cover. In some cases basing agreements only govern the specific terms and duration of the overseas military presence. Others may be part of a bilateral security or defense cooperation agreement between the countries that, even when signed with NATO countries, may include other important bilateral elements.[8] In other cases agreements may emphasize the

5. For an overview, see Woodliffe 1992, 29–47.
6. See Duke 1987. Duke also points to the accountability issues created by the lack of a formal contract.
7. See Ball 1980, 2001; Richelson and Ball 1985.
8. See Murphy 1991.

multilateral security purpose, as opposed to the bilateral legal framework, in order to give the agreement broader domestic legitimacy as an international accord. For instance, the text of the 1980 Defense and Economic Cooperation Agreement (DECA) between the United States and Turkey repeatedly emphasized the NATO purposes of the U.S. basing presence, whereas the 1983 DECA signed with Greece under Prime Minister Papandreou, who two years earlier had campaigned against Greek involvement in NATO, made absolutely no mention of the Western security organization.[9] The case studies I present show how the form as well as the substance of various basing agreements have been shaped consistently by prevailing domestic conditions within base hosts.

In still other cases basing accords may comprise part of a much broader set of bilateral accords and provisions that bundle together nonsecurity issues and agreements. For example, in the Spanish case the 1970 agreement granted the United States base rights in Spain, but the agreement also included provisions for cultural, educational, and scientific exchanges between the two countries because Spanish negotiators hoped to present the agreement to its public as a broader framework for cooperation and Western integration.[10] Similarly, the 1995 Agreement on Cooperation and Defense between Portugal and the United States specified a number of technical and scientific areas of cooperation that the United States agreed to pursue with the regional island government of the Azores.

Transparency of Agreements and Political Considerations
A base host's domestic political considerations often dictate the forms and transparency of governing contracts. Basing agreements with authoritarian states tend to be secretive and conducted at the executive level. For example, the technical arrangements and legal details of the 1953 Madrid Pact were kept classified, at the insistence of Spanish dictator Francisco Franco, to avoid publicizing the clauses that detailed how U.S. forces could infringe upon Spanish sovereignty.[11] Basing accords that are carried over from an authoritarian regime and that lack transparency and legislative approval tend to become prime political targets in the immediate democratization period.

9. On these contrasting DECAs, see Stearns 1992, 20–21.
10. "Agreement on Friendship and Co-operation between the United States of America and the Kingdom of Spain," signed August 6, 1970, in *Treaties and Other International Acts Series (TIAS)* (Washington, DC: Department of State), 6924, 6977 (defense chapter).
11. See Viñas 1981.

In most democratic base hosts, by contrast, the substance of base accords tends to be more transparent (with some notable exceptions) and may be subject to legislative consultation or ratification. In democratizing hosts, parliamentary ratification of agreements has often been a politically volatile and even tumultuous affair, as was the case of the 1960 Mutual Security Treaty in the Japanese Diet. In some cases legislative institutions have even rejected base accords previously agreed to by the executive. In the now famous 1991 Philippine Senate vote, the new base treaty extension that had been signed by President Aquino failed to win the necessary two-thirds majority for approval, thereby effectively terminating the U.S. military presence. However, not all basing agreements reached with democracies have been made public or transparent, especially during the 1950s. For example, in Italy the Christian Democratic government's concern that left-wing parties might raise politically damaging objections over certain provisions prompted it to insist that all base-related technical agreements take the form of an executive exchange of notes, not a treaty subject to parliamentary vote (see chap. 6).

The Status of Forces Agreement

A detailed set of rules, protocols, and promises—known as a status of forces agreement (SOFA)—governs the actual stationing of foreign troops. SOFAs are signed with every base host, although many remain classified; the agreements define the rights and duties of U.S. military personnel and their dependents while stationed overseas. As of 2000, the United States maintained 105 SOFAs with 101 countries, a significant increase from the 65 agreements it had signed as of 1959.[12] Typically, SOFAs cover legal issues such as the freedom of movement of U.S. troops, taxation, criminal jurisdiction, import and export rights and duties, drivers' licenses, registration fees, entitlements, and any other areas in which the presence of U.S. forces must be reconciled with the laws of a host country.[13] Accordingly, SOFAs can vary considerably in their scope and terms. Some of the more hierarchical ones may guarantee near or actual extra-territoriality for U.S. forces, much like international diplomatic immunity. Others may have more restrictive clauses that regulate U.S. military members in accordance with host-nation law.

12. Eichelman 2000, 23; Stambuk 1963b, 483. Both sources offer good overviews of the evolution of SOFAs.
13. On the range of issues covered by SOFAs, see Erickson 1994.

For U.S. forces stationed in NATO countries, the multilateral NATO SOFA, signed in 1951, governs relations among treaty members stationed on each other's territory.[14] The agreement has its origins in the post–World War II reconstruction of Europe. When U.S. soldiers remained in Europe as an occupying force and then as a standing military presence, European countries were no longer willing to give U.S. forces full immunity from their legal codes, as they had done during wartime. After Britain in 1948 threatened to withdraw the concessions it had made to U.S. forces in 1942 for wartime procedures, U.S. officials agreed to form a NATO Working Group that in 1951 drafted the NATO SOFA. The accord struck a compromise between the United States' wish for continuing full legal immunity for its personnel and host countries' attempts to bring these foreign deployments under domestic law.[15] Still in effect today, the multilateral agreement details a number of innovative governance procedures, cooperative norms, and principles, such as the concept of concurrent jurisdiction, and many have since evolved according to case law and practice. Unlike other bilateral SOFAs, the NATO SOFA is reciprocal and governs the status of NATO troops stationed or training in the United States or other member countries. In contrast, SOFAs with East Asian base hosts have been amended or periodically renegotiated on a bilateral basis, which has often led to competition and ratcheting effects among base hosts.[16] For example, Philippine officials in the 1950s deeply resented that Japan, a recently vanquished belligerent, received a more favorable arrangement in line with NATO SOFA criminal jurisdiction.[17] Over time, there has been convergence toward aspects of the NATO SOFA as a favorable model for base hosts.

Issue 1: Basing Agreements and Facilities

The first set of issues governed by basing agreements is the range of facilities ceded by the host state to a sending state. Facilities comprise installations, assets, and troop levels, and all three can be subject to political scrutiny and debate within the base host.

14. On the NATO SOFA's origins and evolution, see Delbrück 1993.
15. See Baxter 1958, 73–74.
16. On multilateral versus bilateral U.S. security regimes and organizational forms in Europe and East Asia and their political consequences, see Katzenstein 2005; Hemmer and Katzenstein 2002.
17. See Berry 1989, 63–65.

Installations and Territory

Identifying and classifying the range of overseas military installations is tricky. A military installation can be as small as an isolated meteorological station or as prominent as a large airbase. Indeed, until its reversion to Japanese rule in 1972, the entire Japanese island province of Okinawa (Ryukyu Islands) was itself exclusively administered by the U.S. Department of Defense. In a comprehensive study of great power access to foreign military facilities, Robert Harkavy distinguishes ten types of installations that correspond to different security functions: airfields, naval ports, army bases, missile sites, space-related sites, communications and control facilities, intelligence and command, environmental monitoring stations, research and testing sites, and logistical hubs.[18] Not all installations carry the formal designation "military base." For lesser sites, small teams of foreign troops may staff a particular installation or work in cooperation with the host country as embedded advisers. Under the Department of Defense's global base posture review, many new installations are to be known as cooperative security locations, meaning that they are not formal bases but sites, some with pre-positioned equipment, that can be rapidly accessed by the U.S. military when needed (see chap. 7).

From a political perspective, the location of U.S. installations can be especially important. Military installations located near major cities or population centers are more likely to be politically contentious than those in more remote sites. Across different base hosts, installations located in or near capital cities have been pointed to as visible reminders of a host nation's diminished sovereignty. Observers of Turkey in the 1950s recall how large U.S. military convoys that routinely drove through Ankara served as daily reminders to the Turkish press and public of their country's subordinate role in the security relationship.[19] The U.S. airbases in Torrejón, Spain, and in Hellenikon, Greece, were located just outside these countries' capital cities, and both countries in the 1980s insisted that these bases be closed and remaining U.S. forces be moved to more remote locations. Perhaps the best example of how a single base can become a political lightening rod is Camp Yongsan, a massive 690-acre installation

18. Harkavy 1989, 17. James Blaker (1990) identifies six types of functions and installations in his account of the organizational structure of the U.S. global basing network.
19. Author's interview with the editor of a major Turkish daily newspaper, Ankara, November 2004. Not surprisingly, the United States withdrew its heavy presence from Ankara in the 1960s.

located in the center of modern Seoul and which for decades has hosted the headquarters of the United Nations command, the Combined Forces Command, the United States Forces Korea, and the U.S. Eighth Army in Korea.[20] However, geographically remote base locations can generate their own type of politics. In chapter 5 I focus on the evolution of base politics on the island hosts of the Azores and Okinawa and examine how the basing issue on these islands has become embedded in broader questions of center-periphery relations and domestic political development.[21]

Agreements may also specify property rights should the base be closed or relocated, as well as the condition in which an installation should be returned. One particularly sensitive issue for antibase activists and local administrators on Okinawa is Article IV of the governing SOFA agreement of the 1960 U.S.-Japan Mutual Security Treaty, which states, "the United States is not obliged, when it returns facilities and areas to Japan . . . to restore the facilities and areas to the condition in which they were at the time they became available to the United States armed forces, or to compensate Japan in lieu of such restoration."[22] Article IV has been invoked by the United States when faced with local claims and compensation requests for environmental damage allegedly inflicted by the bases.[23] As a result, the government of Japan's Defense Facilities Administration Agency in Tokyo has established a number of programs and mechanisms to compensate base-hosting communities.

Assets

Basing agreements can also specify or prohibit the actual military assets that are deployed on installations. Accords may set limits on the number and type of weapon systems, aircraft, ships, radar, or surveillance equipment

20. The installation was initially built on the site of the former Japanese Imperial Head-quarters on the outskirts of Seoul in the 1950s, but as a result of the city's expansion, Camp Yongsan now lies in the very heart of the capital. On its political significance, see Cooley 2005b; Kim 2002–3. For a historical background and local maps, see the globalsecurity assessment, http://www.globalsecurity.org/military/facility/yongsan.htm (accessed May 2007).
21. On base negotiations of a triangular nature involving Greenland, see Dragsdahl 2005; Archer 2003.
22. "Agreement under Article VI of the Treaty of Mutual Cooperation and Security between Japan and the United States of America, Regarding Facilities and Areas and the Status of United States Armed Forces in Japan," signed January 19, 1960, TIAS 4510, Article IV.
23. Various authors' interviews with Okinawan local administrators, U.S. military officials, and DFAA representatives, Okinawa and Tokyo, May–June 2003.

that the sending country can operate. Certain weapons associated with offensive capability may be particularly politically sensitive to a base host and its public. For example, in the 1960s the stationing of B-52 bombers for the U.S. campaign in Vietnam was especially controversial in Okinawa and mainland Japan.

Without a doubt, the most politically controversial of military assets has been the presence, status, and transit of nuclear weapons on a base host's territory. During the cold war an extensive global chain of nuclear installations and bases spanned hundreds of sites in dozens of overseas host countries.[24] Official U.S. nuclear policy has been to "neither confirm nor deny" the presence and location of its nuclear weapons.[25] Not surprisingly, this intentional ambiguity has clashed with demands by several base hosts that the United States not introduce nuclear weapons onto its bases. In 1958 France insisted that nuclear weapons be removed from its territory.[26] After Japan's adoption of its three nonnuclear principles in the late 1960s, Tokyo demanded that all nuclear deployments be subject to its prior approval; the denuclearization of Okinawa was the major contentious issue of the 1969 U.S.-Japan reversion talks (see chap. 6). The 1986 Constitution of the Philippines banned the deployment of nuclear weapons, whereas Panama, Iceland, and Spain formally requested that the United States not station nuclear weapons on their territory.[27]

Even trickier than the permanent stationing of nuclear weapons has been the issue of nuclear transit rights through or above a host state. One of the few countries to which the United States has conceded on this issue is Denmark. After a U.S. B-52 bomber carrying four 1.1-megaton bombs crashed near the Thule base in Greenland in 1962, the United States agreed to prohibit U.S. aircraft carrying nuclear arms from overflying Greenland.[28] The transit issue has proven particularly thorny for U.S. naval vessels carrying nuclear weapons. For example, when in 1987 the New Zealand parliament passed a law banning the transit of vessels carrying nuclear weapons, the United States responded by suspending its security commitments to New Zealand under the 1951 ANZUS treaty.[29]

---

24. For a detailed inventory, see Arkin and Fieldhouse 1985, 214–49.
25. For a fascinating chronology of the policy, see Kristensen 2006.
26. On the nuclear question and U.S. bases in France, see Facon 1993.
27. Sandars 2000, 306.
28. Archer 2003, 133–35.
29. For details of the relevant political and legal issues, see Pugh 1989.

Personnel

Agreements on facilities usually detail the number and types of military personnel that the sending country can deploy. Agreements usually establish ceilings for permanently stationed troops as well for civilians and dependents. As David Lake argues, the number of foreign troops in any given country is a relatively good reflection of the degree of hierarchy between the sending and host countries.[30] Beyond mere numbers of troops, the service associated with a particular base may also have special political connotations. For example, the presence of the Third Marine Expeditionary Force on Okinawa—the only forward-deployed marine division—has been particularly associated with Okinawa's heavy "base burden." Ground forces and the army may also be associated with a previous "occupying force" and, in the Japanese case, were removed from the main islands in the later 1950s for political reasons (see chap. 6).

A related, and more recent personnel issue concerns the role of private contractors who operate and maintain military bases. Since the early 1990s, many base functions and operations, as well as new base construction, have been tendered to private firms—most notably Kellogg, Brown and Root, a subsidiary of Halliburton—and jobs that were once performed on base by U.S. military personnel are now carried out by contractors.[31] Practically speaking, the reliance on contractors for base-related functions and maintenance has freed U.S. troops to pursue other tasks. However, the widespread use of contractors also has created accountability problems because SOFAs do not usually cover the legal status and actions of contractors and their employees.[32] For example, highly publicized base-related scandals have implicated U.S. private contractors in human trafficking in the Balkans and overbilling for meals in Kuwait.[33] And although the Department of Defense may distinguish between civilian contractors and military personnel, the vast majority of politicians and citizens in

30. Lake 2007. Official overseas deployments for any given country since 1953 can be tracked using DoD data. For an analysis and the complete data set, see Kane 2004.
31. On the origins of the private sector's involvement in the construction and maintenance of bases, see Johnson 2004, 131–49.
32. On the broader problem of accountability in the private military industry, see Avant 2005; Singer 2003.
33. On the Balkans human-trafficking scandal and the relationship between contractors and DoD, see Mendelson 2005, esp. 39–50.

base-hosting countries do not.[34] Accordingly, poor behavior or illegal actions by contractors taint local perceptions of the U.S. military. Politically, increasing the number of contractors on a base may carry political benefit, for both the sending and host states, of lowering the official number of foreign troops stationed at that base.[35]

Political motives may also inform decisions to restrict troop movements within the host country. One remarkable case involved the Icelandic government's insistence during the 1950s and 1960s that U.S. soldiers stationed at Keflavik, near the capital Reykjavík, be confined to the base areas out of fear that U.S. personnel would fraternize with Icelandic women and disrupt local social relations.[36] U.S. base commanders who would rather not deal with the political consequences and media scrutiny of an incident or accident involving a U.S. service member may also restrict off-base movements.[37]

Issue 2: Matters of Sovereignty

Questions of sovereignty are a second set of issues covered by basing agreements. The presence of a foreign military force on the territory of another sovereign country goes against the most fundamental analytic principles of Westphalian sovereignty and nonintrusion in the domestic affairs of a host country. In the field of international relations, however, few scholars of sovereignty have examined foreign military bases and the types of institutions and procedures that regulate their presence. For example, in his otherwise comprehensive study Stephen Krasner does not include foreign military bases in his account of the ways in which powerful state actors have regularly violated the institution of sovereignty in the international system.[38]

---

34. In my interviews, especially in the new base-hosting countries in Central Asia and the Black Sea, the legal distinction between civilians, troops, and contractors was meaningless to local observers.
35. Avant makes this argument about how an increase in the number of contractors lowers troop numbers in reference to Iraq. See Avant 2005, 2006.
36. Ingimundarson 2004. The author also argues that at the same time the Icelandic government secretly requested that the U.S. military not station black servicemen in Iceland.
37. In Kyrgyzstan, the U.S. base commander imposed restrictions on off-base movements after a 2002 accident in which a U.S. officer in a military vehicle ran into two pedestrians. Author's interviews with U.S. military officials in Bishkek, Kyrgyzstan, January 2005.
38. Krasner 1999.

Nevertheless, questions of sovereignty are central to the practical and political governance of overseas bases. These sovereign issues range from the symbolic, such as the appropriate flag to be displayed over a facility, to the severe, as in the oversight and consultation procedures to be followed before use of the base for military missions. Here I examine three major issues: the sovereign status of bases, the host country's right to restrict the use of the base, and the criminal jurisdiction procedures that govern the legal status of U.S. troops accused of crimes while in the host country.

Sovereign Status

The precise sovereign status of bases is itself fraught with political undertones and significance. A base can be exclusively a sovereign U.S. territory, exclusively a host-country territory, or a "joint-use" facility; in Europe, many bases are designated as NATO bases. These distinctions are often adopted for domestic political purposes. For example, bases in Italy, despite the heavy U.S. troop presence, have always been referred to as Italian or NATO bases, and their operations have always been presented to the Italian public as essential to the multilateral organization's mission.[39] Similarly, critical commentators on the "joint facilities" in Australia have argued that the label belies the de facto control that U.S. officials have exerted over these installations' operations and staffing.[40] Most U.S. bases in Japan, on the other hand, have been designated as exclusively American facilities, in part because the Japanese government, for political reasons, has wanted to distinguish between U.S. forces and the constitutionally restricted activities of the Japanese Self-Defense Forces.

Aspects of the sovereign status of bases have also been subject to renegotiation and change, especially in the Philippines, Portugal, Spain, Greece, and Turkey. These host states all demanded that a host-nation commander formally be placed in charge of a base's operations and that the host nation assume responsibility for an installation's security and policing. On occasion, states themselves have erred in their understanding of the sovereign status of these facilities and, in the process, have suffered politically embarrassing consequences. For example, when U.S. authorities in 1985 diverted a jet carrying wanted hijackers from Egypt and forced it to land on an installation in Sigonella, Sicily, they mistakenly assumed that the

39. See Cremasco 1988.
40. See Ball 1980, 149–57. Duke 1987 makes a similar argument about facilities in Great Britain.

base was American when it was in fact Italian.[41] In the end, the legal mistake was critical as U.S. Special Forces, not their Italian counterparts, had to back down from a confrontation on the base's tarmac and reluctantly accept Italian jurisdiction over the downed plane and its passengers.

On occasion, bases have also yielded unusual or unique sovereign forms or modes of governance. The government of Japan was granted "residual sovereignty" over Okinawa in 1952, even though the U.S. military governed the island from 1952 to 1972 without constraint. However, the legal status implied Japan's eventual claim over the island and became the main basis for the 1969 reversion agreement. In other cases, the sovereignty of a base territory has been transferred from one state to another. For example, in 1940 the British government transferred sovereign basing rights in the Caribbean and Newfoundland to the United States in exchange for fifty destroyers.[42] Similarly, in 1965 the British government demanded that it retain control of the Chagos islands in the Indian Ocean, previously administered by Mauritius, in exchange for granting Mauritius its independence. Just one year later, the British leased to the U.S. military the island of Diego Garcia in the renamed British Indian Ocean Territory for fifty years.[43] In other cases the sending country may exert exclusive sovereignty over a base territory, without any legal right or promise to return the installation. For example, the ninety-nine square miles in Cyprus that host the British bases of Dhekelia and Akrotiri are constitutionally sovereign British territories, not leased military installations.[44]

Use Rights

The use rights of a military facility define the extent to which the host country can restrict or veto base-related activities and operations.[45] Such restrictions can take different institutional forms. Constitutionally, a host country may have provisions that require the domestic legislature to approve the use of foreign military bases for missions that are not sanctioned by mutual security institutions or international law. This proviso was why the Turkish parliament in March 2003 was required to vote to grant the United States access to its territory for the Operation Iraqi

41. This was part of the *Achille Lauro* episode. For details see chapter 6.
42. Sandars 2000, 42–47.
43. See Woodliffe 1992, 89–90. A controversial aspect of the agreement was the forcible displacement of 2,000 inhabitants (Ilois) of Diego Garcia and their relocation to Mauritius.
44. Woodliffe 1992, 72–76.
45. On use rights and sovereignty, see Cooley 2000–2001.

Freedom campaign (see chap. 4). In general, the United States has retained unrestricted use rights only in the most exceptional and hierarchical of cases. For example, it retained unrestricted use rights during its formal administration of Okinawa and in the Philippines as a result of the 1947 Military Bases Agreement.

In most cases, base use for military purposes is subject to some sort of "prior consultation" requirement by which the U.S. military must inform or secure the consent of the host country. One major concession made by the United States to Japan in the 1960 Mutual Security Treaty was the agreement that the U.S. military would consult with the government of Japan on any mission that did not directly involve the defense of Japan or U.S. installations on Japanese territory. In Europe, the United States' use of its bases for "out-of-area" missions not sanctioned by NATO, particularly in the Middle East, was one of the most politically inflammatory base issues during the cold war.[46] For example, during the 1973 Arab-Israeli War, the governments of nearly all western European allies refused the United States permission to use military bases on their territory to support Israel.[47] Portugal allowed the use of the Azores bases during the conflict and subsequently faced a costly oil embargo by Arab states, prompting the Portuguese government in 1975 to declare that the bases could no longer be used for U.S. missions in the Middle East. Similarly, all of the Mediterranean base hosts denied the use of their bases and airspace to the United States for its 1986 air strike on Libya.[48] The use-rights question has surfaced once again in the post–cold war era in the context of the Global Defense Posture Review. In negotiating new accords for the global network of smaller facilities, U.S. negotiators have been demanding "strategic flexibility" from hosts or the right to use the bases for any regional mission without previous consultation.

SOFA Criminal Jurisdiction Procedures

The final sovereignty issue is also frequently the most contentious and politically sensitive of SOFA provisions—the criminal jurisdiction procedures that govern U.S. military personnel. As a legal institutional form,

46. For a broad overview of U.S. and western European out-of-area disagreements, including base-access issues, see Lundestad 2003.
47. For discussions of both of these cases and out-of-area operations in the southern European states, see Grimmett 1986.
48. See Grimmett 1986.

SOFAs must reconcile U.S. military law with the criminal code of the host state.

Specifying jurisdiction over criminal law violations committed by both U.S. troops and host-country nationals working on the base has often been the hardest of base-related negotiations to successfully conclude. Host countries are reluctant to cede their right to detain, try, and punish U.S. personnel accused of a crime, whereas the U.S. military is eager to ensure that its troops are not subjected to alien rules or criminal procedures. Moreover, the issue of jurisdiction, especially after a high-profile accident or crime, can be politically explosive. For example, the acquittal by a U.S. military court in November 2002 of two American service personnel who accidentally ran over two Korean girls while driving an armored car generated fierce resentment among the Korean public. After the verdict Korean politicians and citizens' groups staged massive demonstrations and complained that the criminal jurisdiction procedures of the SOFA were fundamentally unfair.[49]

As with other base-related issues, criminal jurisdiction procedures can vary considerably across base hosts. Commentators who view a SOFA as providing legal immunity for U.S. troops are mistaken in the strictly legal sense, although some SOFAs have been so favorable to the United States that, practically speaking, they have guaranteed near extraterritoriality to U.S. troops—akin to the custom of diplomatic immunity. In these cases, such as the 2001 U.S. SOFA with Kyrgyzstan, the U.S. tends to exercise "exclusive" jurisdiction over its personnel and their actions, meaning that host countries must formally file an extradition warrant to obtain custody over a U.S. serviceperson. On the other hand, as in the cases of Thailand and Yemen in the 1990s, U.S. visiting forces did not operate under a SOFA and were therefore subject to criminal prosecution by these countries' legal systems.[50] In most cases, however, including that of the NATO SOFA, criminal jurisdiction is allocated according to both exclusive and shared jurisdiction. In the NATO formulation, the sending country exercises exclusive jurisdiction over its personnel for all crimes that are punishable by the laws of the sending state but not the laws of the receiving state. Conversely, the receiving state exercises exclusive jurisdiction over the sending country's forces, civilian components, and dependents for crimes punishable by the laws of the receiving state but not the sending state.[51]

49. On the 2002 Korean case, see Cooley 2005b.
50. Egan 2006, 305–6.
51. NATO SOFA, Article VII, para. 2, as reprinted in Duke and Krieger 1993, 370–87.

Central to the NATO SOFA and other recent bilateral agreements with allies such as Japan and Korea is the principle of concurrent jurisdiction, which applies to all cases that do not fall under exclusive jurisdiction categories. Under concurrent jurisdiction, primary authority over a member of a foreign military is awarded based on a number of predefined categories, procedures, and norms.[52] Under Article VII the sending country retains the primary right of jurisdiction over offenses "arising out of an act or omission done in the performance of official duty" and offenses committed against the property and security of the sending state or its troops, civilians, and dependents.[53] Off-duty offenses committed against host nationals or the domestic country's criminal code fall within the primary jurisdiction of the host state. Technically, if neither side exercises its primary right, the other party has the option of exercising its secondary right over the same case. The procedures by which distinctions are made between "on duty" and "off duty" are not specified in the NATO SOFA and have been subject to intense scrutiny, debate, and negotiation.[54] As in the U.S. legal system, the NATO SOFA prevents "double jeopardy," so once jurisdiction has been exercised and a defendant acquitted or convicted, he or she cannot be tried again by the other country.[55]

Norms and informal understandings also play an important part in implementing criminal jurisdiction procedures. Foremost among these is the NATO SOFA's "waiver" norm, which states that "the State having the primary right shall give sympathetic request from the other authorities of the other State for a waiver of its right in cases where that other State considers such a waiver to be of particular importance."[56] However, it has been U.S. policy from the inception of the NATO SOFA to secure jurisdiction over all criminal offenses and accidents committed by its troops, even when the primary right of jurisdiction clearly lies with the host state.[57] Furthermore, under the terms of a 1959 supplementary agreement to the NATO SOFA, host countries agree to waive jurisdiction in all but the "most serious cases," and the agreement stipulates that a host country that does not assert its jurisdiction over the foreign-based forces within twenty-one days automatically waives its jurisdictional right.[58]

---

52. For a helpful analysis, see Woodliffe 1992, 169–81; Rouse 1957.
53. NATO SOFA, Article VII, para. 3.
54. On the tricky issue of how contracting states determine on-duty status, see Woodliffe 1992, 178–80; Stambuk 1963a, 84–96.
55. NATO SOFA, Article VII, para. 8.
56. NATO SOFA, Article VII, para. 3.
57. Woodliffe 1992, 181.
58. For a clarifying discussion with specific reference to Germany, see Davis 1988.

TABLE 2.1
Worldwide waivers of host-country primary authority in cases of concurrent jurisdiction

Year (Dec. 1–Nov. 30)	1997	1998	1999	2000	2001	2002	2003	2004	2005
No. of concurrent jurisdiction cases with host-country primary authority	3,196	3,402	3,704	2,996	3,268	4,028	4,268	3,218	3,156
Host-country waivers of primary jurisdiction	2,752	2,972	3,144	2,740	3,078	3,731	3,706	2,844	2,963
Waiver rate (%)	86.1	87.4	84.9	91.5	94.2	92.6	86.8	88.4	93.9

Sources: Compiled from data provided in Judge Advocate General of the Army, *Annual Reports on Military Justice* (Washington, DC, 1997–2000) and U.S. Court of Appeals for the Armed Forces, *Annual Report of the Code Committee on Military Justice* (Washington, DC, 2001–2006).

Accordingly, the waiver by the host state of its primary jurisdiction has developed into a strong norm, albeit one that is influenced by U.S. relational power, as host states ordinarily waive their right to assert jurisdiction over all but a handful of the most serious crimes.[59] In 1958 there was a 57 percent waiver rate of primary jurisdiction among NATO countries, but by 1988 the United States secured host-country waivers in 96.5 percent of all criminal cases throughout the NATO area.[60] From 1954 to 1958, the beginning of recorded statistics on these rates, the worldwide waiver rate of primary authority in all host countries with concurrent jurisdiction was 69 percent.[61] By the 1990s and 2000s, these rates had risen to a range of 85–94 percent (see table 2.1).

The criminal jurisdiction waiver rate is also a useful indicator of the level of politicization within the host country surrounding the presence of U.S. forces. Waiver rates vary and can be heavily influenced by the host's domestic political climate. Given the waiver norm for most offenses, significant fluctuations in waiver rates (assuming that the types of crimes and incidents involved are constant) are usually indicative of increased political pressure on a host government to assert its jurisdiction and sovereignty in basing matters. For example, host-country waiver rights declined significantly in Spain (mid-1980s) and in Korea (since the mid-1990s)

59. On the origins and legal consequences of jurisdiction waivers, see Rouse 1957.
60. The 1988 figure is from Woodliffe 1992, 184. For the 1958 data, see Stambuk 1963a, 115. Typically, the vast majority of these local jurisdiction cases are traffic offenses.
61. Stambuk 1963a, 115. The total number of cases was 59,689.

during times of intense politicization and scrutiny of the basing issue more broadly. Unfortunately, researchers cannot always obtain consistent data on criminal jurisdiction waivers because of political sensitivities over the issue.

In sum, criminal jurisdiction procedures and their implementation vary considerably across agreements. In broad terms, a more hierarchical SOFA often provides for exclusive jurisdiction, whereas a less hierarchical agreement, such as the NATO SOFA, provides for concurrent jurisdiction. These procedures can also change within cases over time. For example, in the Korean case, U.S. troops initially were granted immunity from local prosecution by the 1953 Mutual Defense Treaty; U.S. officials first agreed to a SOFA with concurrent jurisdiction in 1966, which was later revised in 1991 and 2001.[62]

Issue 3: Bargains and Basing Agreements

Beyond issues relating to installations and sovereignty, base agreements vary in the types of bargains and concessions offered by the sending country to the receiving country in exchange for securing basing rights. Such bargains can take the form of both economic and political concessions.

Economic Bargains: Quid Pro Quo

Determining the exact terms of a compensation package to a base host can be difficult because although some assistance levels and transfers are specified in agreements, others are kept de-linked, often for political purposes. At different times, U.S. negotiators have offered base hosts economic assistance, military hardware, technology transfers, export credits, and debt write-offs as quid pro quo.

During the cold war the most common types of assistance offered for base rights were economic aid under the Economic Support Fund (ESF) and military aid under the Foreign Military Financing (FMF) program and Military Assistance Programs (MAP). The United States awarded FMF for the purchase of U.S. military equipment and training at concessionary interest rates on long repayment schedules. MAP was a grant program, established in 1954 (successor to the Mutual Defense Assistance Program),

62. See Egan 2006, 314–15; Jung and Hwang 2003.

that financed arms and military hardware to anticommunist countries to promote collective security. It evolved into a principle instrument for securing political agreements, including basing rights, until the Carter administration ordered its phaseout in 1981.[63] Although MAP and FMF were not granted solely to those countries hosting major bases, countries hosting major U.S. installations received much larger arms transfers and program funds than did countries not hosting major U.S. facilities.[64]

The United States has always refused to refer to base-rights payments as rent, insisting instead that military and economic payments are designated to support military allies and meet common security objectives.[65] In reality, however, the governments of Spain, Greece, Turkey, and the Philippines routinely referred to these payments as rent, and during the 1970s and 1980s they demanded increasing economic and military assistance for hosting U.S. troops and facilities.[66] These rental sums reached their peak in the mid-1980s as various base hosts invoked financial agreements with other countries as new aid-level baselines.[67] Between 1974 and 1987, the cost to the United States of securing base rights increased from $200 million to $2 billion per year, whereas the total cost of operating U.S. overseas bases grew from $1 billion in 1974 to $4.6 billion in 1986.[68] One of the more contentious periods in base negotiations arose in the late 1980s when the U.S. Congress reduced funding levels that had been agreed to by U.S. negotiators, in the process severely straining relations with base-hosting countries and damaging U.S. credibility to guarantee payment of its base-rights obligations.

Base hosts have also demanded specific military equipment or technologies in exchange for rights. In the 1950s, the United states completely overhauled and modernized the air defense systems of Spain, which it then transferred back to Spanish control shortly after. In the 1980s, the U.S. pledged to support the development of Turkey's arms industry as part of the Defense and Cooperation Agreement, whereas in dealing with Greece negotiators agreed to provide NASA surveillance equipment. More recently, the Kyrgyz and Uzbek governments asked the United States to provide electronic surveillance equipment to their security

63. For a critical overview of the politics of FMF, see Shaw 1983.
64. See the painstaking analysis done in Harkavy 1989, 340–56.
65. On the "rent" issue, see Clarke and O'Connor 1993.
66. See Clarke and O'Connor 1993.
67. Cooley and Spruyt 2003.
68. *Financial Times* 1988.

services as part of their informal Operation Enduring Freedom basing-rights package.[69]

Perhaps the most remarkable case of economic bargaining for basing access can be found on the Japanese island prefecture of Okinawa and the triangular relationship among the United States military, the government of Japan, and the citizens and authorities on Okinawa. As a tacit quid pro quo for hosting 75 percent of all exclusive-use U.S. military facilities in Japan, the island receives an array of rental payments, burden payments, and public works and construction funds from the government of Japan. As I explore in chapter 4, these economic incentives provided by the mainland have been sufficient to ensure that a tacit majority of Okinawan citizens supports the U.S. military presence, despite the island's bloody World War II history, its pervasive culture of antimilitarism, and the vocal protests of local antibase NGOs.[70]

The political converse of quid pro quo is host-nation support, payments made by base hosts to the United States to defer the operating costs of U.S. facilities on their territory. Such support arrangements first arose in Germany (since 1961) and Japan (1977) as a result of U.S. pressures on host governments to contribute to base operating expenses after an unfavorable dollar exchange rate had dramatically increased base costs. In Germany Chancellor Konrad Adenauer objected to the political appearance of paying for the stationing of U.S. forces on German territory and so instead reached agreements in the 1960s to purchase U.S. military equipment and increase payments to the NATO infrastructure budget.[71] In Japan, too, burden sharing was initially resisted in the late 1970s but soon after institutionalized itself within the Japanese political system as established domestic interest groups, such as base unions and construction firms, lobbied for its expansion.[72] Not coincidently, the countries with the largest number of U.S. troops—Germany, Japan, Korea, and Italy—have tended to provide the highest percentage of base cost sharing.[73] By 1998, Japan was paying 76 percent ($4.0 billion) of U.S. overseas stationing costs, whereas Italy contributed 60 percent ($1.1 billion), Korea 41 percent ($751 million),

69. Personal correspondence with a U.S. military official involved in U.S.-Kyrgyz base negotiations.
70. See Cooley and Marten 2006.
71. See Sandars 2000, 211–13. For time-series budget data and details of the U.S.–West German offset negotiations of 1966 and 1967, see Treverton 1978.
72. See Calder 2006; Yoda 2006.
73. Members of the Gulf Cooperation Council that have hosted U.S. forces have also contributed a high percentage of base operation costs.

TABLE 2.2
Selected host-nation support for U.S. stationing costs

Country	1998 US$ Mil (Offset %)	2000 US$ Mil (Offset %)	2002 US$ Mil (Offset %)
Japan	4,013 (76)	5,003 (79)	4,411 (75)
Germany	957.0 (22)	1,211 (21)	1,564 (33)
Korea	751.3 (41)	796.3 (42)	842.8 (40)
Italy	1,113 (60)	364.2 (37)	366 (41)
United Kingdom	127.5 (n/a)	132.9 (17)	238.5 (27)
Kuwait	176.0 (n/a)	245.0 (47)	253.0 (58)
Spain	101.9 (45)	115.3 (50)	127.3 (58)
Turkey	23.8 (26)	4.7 (3)	116.9 (54)
Greece	19.0 (42)	19.5 (29)	17.7 (32)

Sources: U.S. Department of Defense (DoD), *2004 Statistical Compendium on Allied Contributions to the Common Defense* (Washington, DC, 2004); DoD, *Report on Allied Contributions to the Common Defense, June 2002* (Washington, DC, 2002); and DoD, *Responsibility Sharing Report, March 2000* (Washington, DC, 2000b).
Notes: The amounts are given in US$ million. The percentages indicate the amount offset by the host country. The amounts include direct and indirect costs paid by the host nation.

and Germany 22 percent ($957 million) (see table 2.2). Interestingly, that same year Spain, Greece, and Turkey—countries that had demanded large compensation packages for basing rights in the 1970s and 1980s—all paid a substantial offset: Spain, 45 percent; Greece, 42 percent; and Turkey, 26 percent.[74]

Political Bargains: Security and Policy Links

Base-related concessions can also take the form of political or security demands. The mere presence of U.S. troops has not always been accompanied by a security guarantee for the receiving country, even if a host state requests one. For example, Spanish negotiators during the Franco period repeatedly tried to extract a security guarantee from the United States, something U.S. negotiators refused to offer, given the Franco regime's international isolation and exclusion from NATO. The U.S.-Japan 1951 Security Treaty was heavily criticized in Japan in part because it offered

74. U.S. Department of Defense 2000a, III-30.

no explicit U.S. guarantee of Japan's security, a provision that was added to the revised 1960 Mutual Security Treaty.

Base hosts have also linked basing-rights negotiations to specific U.S. foreign policy stances on matters unrelated to the use of the bases. In 1954 the Italian government demanded that the United States officially support Italy's claim on the divided city of Trieste in exchange for accepting a military facilities agreement. In the 1960s, the Portuguese government of António Salazar tabled the renewal of the Azores basing agreement and demanded that the United States stop both covert and public support of anticolonial movements in Portugal's African colonies of Angola and Mozambique.[75] In these and other cases, American officials agreed to make political concessions in order to obtain or maintain base-access arrangements.

Summary: Installations, Sovereignty, and Bargains

Basing agreements can take a variety of legal and institutional forms. In this chapter I have identified three different types of issues covered by basing accords: facilities (installations, assets, and troops), sovereignty (status, use rights, and criminal jurisdiction), and bargains (economic and political). Not all of these issues necessarily will be politicized in all base hosts. For example, criminal jurisdiction, especially after the adoption of the NATO SOFA, has tended to be a far more politically controversial issue in the East Asian hosts than in the southern European ones. But understanding the various dimensions of basing issues is critical for charting their relative politicization across different time periods and cases, as well as for judging the relative balance or hierarchy of their provisions. As I outlined in chapter 1, changes in the domestic political institutions of a base host, particularly the processes of democratic transition and democratic consolidation, should be associated with the degree of politicization of these various base-related issues.

Case Selection and Methodology

In the next four chapters I track the evolution of basing agreements across the issues of facilities, sovereignty, and bargains in eight overseas hosts;

---

75. See Cooley 2005a; chap. 5 of this volume.

four cases are drawn from southern Europe (Azores/Portugal, Italy, Spain, and Turkey) and four from East Asia (mainland Japan, Okinawa, Korea, and the Philippines). In each chapter, in a perhaps somewhat unorthodox fashion, I compare and contrast base politics in one European and one Asian case. By executing these cross-regional comparisons, I move away from region-specific accounts or purely historical narratives and explore theoretically comparable institutional characteristics within the political systems of these different base hosts.[76]

In chapter 3 I examine how authoritarian rulers in Spain and the Philippines used the base issue to further their domestic political survival, how these basing agreements became contested during subsequent democratic transitions, and then how they were depoliticized after democratic consolidation. In chapter 4 on South Korea and Turkey, I examine how U.S. bases were initially established with a clear common security purpose but subsequently became enmeshed in the political turbulence of bouts of authoritarian rule and democratic transitions. In chapter 5 I compare and contrast how democratic transition and consolidation within the island territories of Okinawa and the Azores became enmeshed within the triangular bargaining relationship among the U.S. military, regional governments, and mainland national governments and how these internal changes created different forms of compensation politics in each case. In chapter 6 I explore how the early institutionalization of one-party democratic systems in mainland Japan and Italy steadily depoliticized the basing issue and led oppositional parties to gradually moderate their stances on the bases for electoral purposes.

The cases should not be considered comprehensive accounts of the political history of the bases in these hosts, nor can they substitute for the more definitive histories of U.S. overseas forces or political histories written by experts on these countries. Rather, the cases are meant to track the important changes in basing contracts and are designed to show how rulers of these base hosts, especially during democratic transition and consolidation, strategically politicized and contested the base issue in response to domestic political pressures and institutional changes. Many of the episodes discussed in the cases—Japan's contentious ratification of the 1960 Mutual Security Treaty, the aftermath of the 1962 accident involving a nuclear bomber near Palomares in Spain, the massacre of student

---

76. For other studies that compare the domestic determinants of security policies in Europe and Asia, see Katzenstein 2005; Samuels 2003.

demonstrators in 1980 at Kwangju in Korea, and the Turkish parliament's vote against authorizing a U.S. military presence for the 2003 campaign against Iraq—are political episodes that have acquired their own special significance in the historiography of the U.S. military presence in these countries. I argue that most are readily explainable by the theoretical framework of base politics advanced in chapter 1.

Case Selection Logic

My choice of cases from these two distinct regions and their integrated discussion are critical aspects of this book's methodology and contribution to comparative political study. Three main reasons justify this exact case selection.

First, the East Asian and southern European base hosts were recipients of some of the heaviest and most significant overseas U.S. deployments in the postwar era (see table 2.3). Overall, these 8 countries or territories represented 7 out of the 12 largest overseas deployments in 1960 and 7 out of the largest 10 in 1980. The most notable overseas peacetime deployments not included in the study are those in Germany, Britain, France, and Panama.

The German case, in particular, is a significant omission from this study. The massive size of U.S. forces in Germany (over 200,000 during the cold war) and their significant penetration of entire regions and towns make this case the most complex and difficult to comprehensively examine.[77] The British case also is a noteworthy omission, although it too is relatively unique in that so many of the agreements that govern the stationing of U.S. troops are informal.[78] Nevertheless, the broad predictions of the argument could be applied to both cases: in particular, how phases of political party competition determined the politicization of the bases and how these hosts maintained their long-term commitment to the United States despite policy differences. France's expulsion of U.S. forces in 1966 under Charles de Gaulle's Fifth Republic and the refusal of the Panamanian government to renew U.S. basing rights during the 1990s could also fruitfully be explained by using this study's theoretical perspectives. Despite these omissions, the southern European and East Asian regions still host

---

77. For a cold war political history, see Nelson 1987.
78. See Duke 1987.

TABLE 2.3
U.S. troop deployments for selected major overseas hosts

U.S. troops in case study host countries	1951	1960	1970	1980	1990	2000
East Asia						
Japan	172,861	83,462	82,264	46,004	46,593	40,159
South Korea	326,863	55,864	52,197	46,004	41,344	36,565
Philippines	12,755	11,334	23,440	13,387	13,863	79
Southern Europe						
Italy	6,518	10,339	9,645	11,903	14,204	11,190
Spain	35	11,232	8,744	8,974	6,986	2,007
Turkey	745	7,454	6,681	5,269	4,382	2,006
Portugal	958	2,238	1,588	1,367	1669	1,005
Most significant excluded cases						
Germany	176,084	232,256	202,935	244,320	227,586	69,203
France	22,876	40,059	68	77	85	67
United Kingdom	26,313	31,992	21,168	24,312	25,111	11,207
Iceland	1,784	3,897	3,157	2,868	3,196	1,636
Canada	10,072	14,312	2,643	691	560	688
Thailand	68	338	39,212	95	213	526
Panama	12,384	7,807	11,297	9,146	11,042	20
Morocco	6,953	8,031	1755	40	50	17
Total worldwide	805,425	551,879	885.051	425,872	446,605	209,083

Source: U.S. Troop Deployment Data Set, compiled by Tim Kane, Heritage Foundation. Data available at http://www.dior.whs.mil/mmid/military/history/309hist.htm.

at least two-thirds of the countries with the heaviest U.S. overseas military deployments since World War II.

Second, broadening the scope of the empirical analysis to multiple cases drawn from both Europe and Asia allows us to control for the peculiarities of any one region. Other studies of the politics of U.S. bases tend to be single-country cases or to focus exclusively on the politics of basing agreements in a specific region. Accordingly, some tend to attribute political developments surrounding the U.S. bases to a host country's particular historical experiences and legacies (e.g., Franco's egotistical rule) or to a distinct political culture (e.g., Okinawa's pacifist culture). Further, each of these regions has been embedded in a contrasting institutional logic of security. Whereas the southern European countries, with the exception of Spain until 1986, were NATO members and often stressed the multilateral purpose of military facilities, the East Asian countries reached bilateral security agreements and basing arrangements with the United States.[79] Certainly the presence of NATO served as an important institutional and ideational source of transatlantic security ties, however this study shows that internal institutional factors and domestic political change remained more important in determining the political evolution of the base issue.

Most significantly, both the southern European and East Asian cases demonstrate considerable variation in terms of the timing and sequencing of their internal democratic transitions and consolidation—the independent factors critical to this book's account of when and why base issues become politicized. In southern Europe, both Portugal and Spain maintained authoritarian regimes until the mid-1970s, whereas Turkey entered the cold war as a democracy and then experienced three separate military coups (1960, 1970, 1980) and subsequent redemocratization. Italy differed internally in that it hosted the largest Communist Party in western Europe; its political party system, however, was institutionalized early on, by the election of 1948, and would last for the duration of the cold war. In East Asia, too, democratization trends varied across cases and time. Japan's one-party, Liberal Democratic Party (LDP)–led "democratic hegemony" was institutionalized in the late 1950s, whereas Korea only experienced real democratic transition in the 1990s. The Philippines began as a democracy but was interrupted by the rule of Ferdinand Marcos in the late 1960s until its democratic revolution in 1986. Finally, the U.S. military formally governed Okinawa (unlike the Japanese mainland) until its reversion in 1972, when the island experienced a tumultuous period of simultaneous democratization and integration into the institutions of the Japanese state.

One noteworthy difference between this study and other accounts of the politics of U.S. bases in Japan is the deliberate separation of the politics of the basing issue on the Japanese mainland from that of Okinawa. This distinction may strike some readers as unnecessary or confusing, but it is dictated by the approach I've outlined. Different political logics and

79. See Katzenstein 2005.

institutional changes have driven the base issue on the Japanese mainland and on Okinawa at different times. Whereas the issue of U.S. bases reached the peak of contestation on the Japanese mainland in 1960 and has since dissipated with the consolidation and bureaucratization of the Japanese political system, the issue remains highly charged on the island prefecture precisely because the basing question remains embedded in island-mainland disputes about Okinawa's marginal status as prefecture and its unequal economic development. Moreover, many Okinawans believe that the Japanese mainland government colludes with the U.S. military to foist the greater part of the heavy U.S. military presence in Japan on the small island prefecture. Disaggregating the politics of the U.S. basing presence in Okinawa from that in the rest of Japan—and comparing each to a European case with similar institutional characteristics (Azores and Italy)—is critical for understanding the precise sources and timing of politicization in each setting.

Having laid out a theory of base politics, the various dimensions of basing agreements, and the logic of the cases, I now turn to the case comparisons. I begin with an account of the political evolution of U.S. bases in Spain and the Philippines, two of the most individually studied, yet rarely compared, U.S. base hosts.

CHAPTER 3

The Philippines and Spain

In the Shadow of the Dictator

The evolution of the U.S. basing presence in Spain and the Philippines offers strong support for the theory of base politics advanced in chapter 1. In both countries, patterns of contesting or depoliticizing the issue of U.S. bases were heavily influenced by periods of democratic transition or consolidation in the base hosts. In both countries, the bases' association with the regimes of high-profile authoritarian figures would eventually undermine their contractual legitimacy. To this day, a segment of public opinion in both countries attributes the political longevity of Francisco Franco and Ferdinand Marcos to the U.S. military presence and American political support for their authoritarian rule. In the Philippines, President Marcos declared martial law and used the military and economic assistance from basing agreements to dispense patronage to his political clients and maintain his control over the Philippine armed forces. The Franco regime also gained economically from hosting U.S. bases, but more importantly the U.S. presence bestowed international legitimacy on Franco—a more valuable benefit at a time when his regime remained internationally isolated. Although American officials did not favor or publicly condone the human rights abuses or excesses of either of these dictators, they subordinated their calls for political liberalization in these countries to the operational needs of securing and extending U.S. basing arrangements.

The accommodation that the United States showed to these authoritarian rulers undermined the credibility of the basing contracts and made the

U.S. military presence the target of a significant political backlash when these countries democratized. Populist politicians, new civic groups, left-leaning political parties, and the newly independent media pointed to the U.S. military presence as a symbol of previous undemocratic practices and human rights abuses as well as a violator of the host country's sovereignty. As a result, both countries challenged and renegotiated existing basing agreements with the United States, in the process dramatically reducing the U.S. military presence against the expressed wishes of U.S. defense officials. The exact domestic institutional pressures that undermined the basing contracts differed across the cases. In Spain, the reelected Socialist Party in 1986 used an artfully worded NATO referendum as leverage to conclude a new basing agreement that mandated the withdrawal of the United States from its airbases near Madrid and Zaragoza. In the Philippines, the post-Marcos political climate was characterized by intense nationalism and anti-Americanism as new political elites and institutions sought to define their institutional authority under the interim presidency of former political dissident Corazón Aquino. In September 1991, in perhaps the most dramatic instance of domestic base politics, the Philippine Senate voted against an agreement that would have extended the U.S. military presence for another ten years. A year later, the U.S. military left the Philippines.

In this chapter I compare and contrast the evolution of base politics in Spain and the Philippines across three distinct periods. In the first section I explore how military bases were established in each country and trace their evolution through the end of the Franco and Marcos regimes. I show how these authoritarian rulers depended on these basing agreements for political legitimacy and economic assistance. In the next section I examine how democratization pressures politicized the basing issue, delegitimized existing base contracts, and led to fundamental changes in the status of the U.S. military presence. In the final section I examine how the basing presence in Spain then became depoliticized as the Spanish democratic system consolidated; I also analyze political reaction to the 2000 reintroduction of U.S. troops into the Philippines on a "visiting basis."

Contracts with Dictators: Establishing the U.S. Military Presence

Spain: The 1953 Madrid Pact

The U.S. military presence in Spain was established by the Madrid Pact of 1953, now considered a landmark event both for Spain's defense relations with the West and for the internal consolidation of Franco's rule.[1] Before the pact, the Spanish dictator remained isolated by western European countries because of his regime's cooperation with fascist forces and its spotty human rights record. Excluded from Western institutions such as NATO and excommunicated from the United Nations in 1946, Spain under Franco's regime entered the 1950s impoverished and a European pariah, without access to the Marshall Plan or any external source of reconstruction funds.[2]

U.S. president Harry Truman openly disliked Franco, but the election of Dwight Eisenhower in 1950 ushered in a more conciliatory American stance toward his regime. The Korean War and the loss of U.S. base access in Morocco underscored to U.S. defense planners the need to establish a military foothold on the Iberian peninsula and to integrate the anticommunist Spanish military regime into the Western security sphere.[3] After two years of transatlantic shuttling and negotiations, the landmark accords, signed on September 26, 1953, allowed U.S. armed forces to be stationed throughout Spain in exchange for an economic assistance package and military hardware. The public agreement was composed of three official pacts: a defense agreement, mutual defense assistance, and an economic aid agreement.[4] The defense agreement also included several secret technical annexes, classified at the request of the Spanish government, that governed operational issues, sensitive installations, nuclear questions, and the legal status of U.S. forces in Spain.[5] Among the dozen or so installations specified in the agreement, the four most important (and enduring) were an airbase at Torrejón (just outside the capital Madrid), a naval station at Rota (near Cádiz), and airbases and training facilities in Morón (near Seville) and Zaragoza (see fig. 3.1). In addition, the agreement allowed for the construction of a pipeline network linking these facilities, air defense warning installations, and seismic and nuclear-testing monitoring stations that were listed as weather stations.[6]

---

1. For overviews, see Liedke 1999; Dabrowski 1996; Seidel 1993; Viñas 1981; Whitaker 1962, esp. 44–62.
2. Seidel 1993.
3. See Jarque Iñiguez 1988.
4. "Use of Military Facilities in Spain," signed September 26, 1953, *TIAS* 2850; text also published in the *Los Angeles Times,* September 27, 1953.
5. See Viñas 1981.
6. For a near-comprehensive list of the facilities (exempting redacted nuclear sites), see Nash 1957, 43. A Spanish base negotiator confirmed the dual purpose of the weather station, author's interview with 1988 Spanish negotiator, Madrid, April 2005.

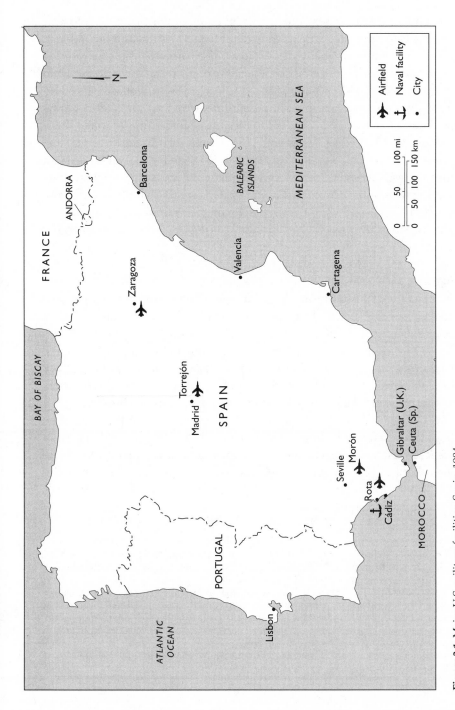

Figure 3.1. Major U.S. military facilities, Spain, 1984.
Source: Congressional Research Service

Compared with other agreements, even others of the early cold war era, the U.S.-Spanish pact was considerably hierarchical and favorable to the United States on many dimensions. The United States was granted "virtually complete jurisdiction over its forces in Spain" and retained the right to "house, provide security, discipline and welfare, store and maintain provisions, supplies and equipment, and maintain and operate facilities as necessary."[7] In regard to status of forces and criminal jurisdiction, the United States retained exclusive jurisdiction over all the activities of its personnel in Spain.[8] In exchange for granting the right to use these facilities, Spain received $226 million in aid, of which $141 million was in the form of end-item assistance and $85 million in defense support aid. Over the next ten years, Spain received about $1.1 billion in aid and an additional $300 million in export-import credits for hosting the bases.

Impact of the Accords

Although a major political victory for Franco himself, the Madrid Pact and subsequent agreements did not completely satisfy Franco's main domestic allies, the Spanish military and the Catholic Church. Some conservative officers still harbored anti-U.S. resentment from the 1898 Spanish-American War, whereas others resented the poor quality of the military hardware provided by the United States.[9] A few Spanish defense planners also expressed concern that by allowing construction of important U.S. facilities, many of which stationed nuclear weapons, near major Spanish population centers, the regime had made those cities potential targets in an East-West nuclear exchange. The Spanish church, too, had deep misgivings about the potential for non-Catholic American chaplains to proselytize and the likely adverse impact of thousands of young American troops on traditional Spanish social values.[10]

---

7. National Security Council, "Progress Report on United States Policy Toward Spain," NSC 72/6, February 15, 1954, *Declassified Document Reference System* (henceforth *DDRS*).

8. The Nash (1957, 157–58) report emphasized that the original status of forces agreement favored the United States: "More Americans in Spain will bring to the fore the question of criminal jurisdiction. At present the arrangements are favorable to us and have amounted in practice to exclusive jurisdiction. A sizable increase of cases may cause the Spaniards to request reconsideration of these arrangements."

9. Author's interview with former high-ranking Spanish diplomatic official to the United States, Madrid, April 2005.

10. Nash 1957, 156, 157.

Nevertheless, all of Franco's internal allies accepted that the 1953 agreement brought a measure of international legitimacy and connection to the West that the regime had desperately sought. The state-controlled media emphasized that the pact was a vindication of Franco's unilateralism and distinct type of foreign policy making.[11] In turn, this newly acquired legitimacy brought other successful international memberships. The Madrid Pact was decisive in allowing the Vatican to conclude a concordat with Spain (although for political reasons U.S. officials allowed the Spanish government to sign it before the basing agreements). Most importantly, acceptance by the United States also paved the way for Spain's readmission to the United Nations in 1955. But despite the Madrid Pact and Spain's normalization within the international community, western European countries continued to marginalize the Spanish dictator until his death. No European head of state or prime minister ever visited Franco in an official capacity, and European NATO members made it clear that they would veto any attempt to admit Spain into NATO as long as Franco was alive.[12] For this reason, historians view the Madrid Pact as a critical turning point in the consolidation of the regime: it was an agreement that served Franco's own political survival more than it did Spain's European integration or even Spanish security. As a prominent biographer of Franco observed, "the Caudillo had bargained away neutrality and sovereignty without distinguishing between the good of Spain and the good of Franco."[13]

Subsequent Negotiations and Modifications

The 1953 Pact was amended or updated on four further occasions during Franco's rule—in 1958, 1963, 1968, and 1970—with a fifth, the 1976 agreement, finalized just after his death.[14] Over the course of these subsequent negotiations, some parts of the agreement were revised, but the basic formula of 1953 was always preserved: Spain authorized the use of these military facilities and in exchange received economic and military assistance without an explicit mutual security guarantee.[15] Attaining the latter was always a priority for Spanish negotiators, who viewed a mutual security pact as the ultimate recognition of Spain's place as a valued American ally.

11. On reactions to the pact, see Dabrowski 1996, 118–39.
12. I am indebted to Dr. Pere Vilanova Vias of the University of Barcelona for bringing this point about European recognition to my attention.
13. Preston 1993, 624.
14. The 1976 accord remains one of the most analyzed. See Druckman 1986.
15. For overviews of these subsequent negotiations and agreements, see Viñas 2003b.

However, despite much convoluted language, Spanish negotiators failed to extract concrete security commitments or support for NATO membership.[16] Spanish negotiators secured some limited concessions in the area of use rights in the 1968 and 1970 agreements, including the right to decide the permissibility of flights to "areas of special tensions" on a case-by-case basis and a pledge from the United States to consult with Spain before changing the operational use of the bases.[17]

The remarkable 1970 Agreement of Friendship and Cooperation best embodied Spain's need to present the base agreements to its public as a form of broader cooperation and Western integration.[18] The agreement covered all facets of U.S.-Spanish relations, including promoting educational, cultural, and scientific exchanges and agricultural cooperation. In the absence of an official security treaty, Spanish negotiators wanted to deemphasize that they were providing military facilities without a military return. Once again, American negotiators tried to distance themselves from condoning the regime while retaining Spanish cooperation for base operations. Practically, such distinctions proved difficult to maintain in the eyes of the Spanish public.

The Accident at Palomares

No single incident is more representative of the Franco regime's self-interest and strict control over the media on base-related issues than is the accident at Palomares, the United States' first widely publicized nuclear weapons accident near a populated area.[19] On January 16, 1966, an Amer-

16. For instance, the 1965 joint declaration of U.S.-Spanish relations states that "threat to either country, and to the joint facilities that each provides for the common defense, would be a matter of common concern to both and each country would take such action within the framework of its constitutional processes." *TIAS* 5437, as quoted in Dabrowski 1996, 171.

17. The latter was invoked when the Spanish side refused to authorize U.S. use of the bases in 1973 in support of Israel.

18. "Agreement of Friendship and Cooperation between the United States of America and the Kingdom of Spain," signed August 6, 1970, *TIAS* 6924 and 6977. U.S. negotiators believed that offering such nonmilitary areas for quid pro quo would satisfy Spanish desires for more multilateral links, including U.S. support for Spanish-European Community negotiations. A strategy paper of the National Security Council (NSC) on the 1970 negotiations reasoned, "it is evident that the intangible quid pro quo which we can offer the Spanish outweighs the tangible. The items of primary importance in the negotiations, therefore, are those which will build Spanish goodwill toward our continued presence. . . . To the extent that these give the Spanish a sense of partnership with the Western Alliance and with the U.S., we hope that they will weigh heavily in Spanish attitudes toward retention of our military facilities." NSC Undersecretary Committee, "Spanish Base Negotiations—Quid Pro Quo," March 4, 1970, *DDRS*.

19. For detailed accounts of the incident, see Maydew 1997; Szulc 1967.

ican B-52 bomber collided with a KC-135 tanker based in Morón while attempting to refuel above the southeastern coast of Spain. The tanker exploded immediately, whereas the B-52 bomber, which was carrying four B28 atomic bombs, broke up into pieces. Three of the bombs fell in or near the vicinity of the village of Palomares, and the fourth fell into the sea about five miles offshore. As they crashed, two of the Palomares bombs detonated and left massive craters, scattering contaminated debris, including about seven pounds of plutonium, across 552 acres surrounding the village. Approximately 1,700 U.S. troops and Spanish civil guards worked to decontaminate the area, while U.S. ships and divers searched for eighty days before finally retrieving the submerged bomb on April 7.

At first, the U.S. military and the Spanish government withheld details about the accident. The U.S. side did not report the nuclear dimension; the Spanish media too ignored the atomic devices and downplayed the danger to local communities.[20] A U.S. embassy cable reporting on the Spanish media's reaction to the accident observed that "Spanish dailies continued to give [the] story heavy play, with emphasis on 'return to normalcy' and in rural region[s], continued search activities, compensation for financial losses, and lack of serious health hazards. Most reports refer vaguely to 'missing devices' or 'remnants of planes' without mention of nuclear nature."[21]

As the international media started to piece together more information and report on local contamination checks, however, the true extent of the nuclear issue started to surface. In a move calculated to make the regime appear tough, the Franco public relations machine began to criticize the U.S. transit of nuclear weapons in Spain. In response, the United States stepped up its own public relations effort and announced on January 25 that it would stop flying nuclear weapons over Spain. Four days later, however, the Spanish government announced that it would ban all flights carrying nuclear bombs above Spanish territory. Then, after a few days, the regime staged a vocal protest at the U.S. embassy in Madrid and gave heavy media coverage to the demonstrators.[22] The United States, not

20. On the evolving media coverage of the incident, see Stiles 2006.
21. Embassy of Madrid Telegram to Department of State, "Local Press," January 26, 1966, *DDRS*.
22. Stiles 2006, 59. As the author also observes of Franco's survival imperative and the aftermath of the Palomares accident, "although General Franco was a dictator, it would have been politically risky to appear overly supportive of the United States, especially because some officials in his own office did not approve of his military treaties with the United States."

having recovered the stray bomb by the beginning of March, released a "fact report" that sought to alleviate rumors of potential harm caused by device. But the grandest piece of propaganda was offered on March 8 when U.S. ambassador Angier Biddle Duke and Spanish information minister Manuel Fraga staged a public swim for the Spanish and American media at a beach near Palomares.[23] The resulting AP photo, published on front pages of Spanish newspapers and the *New York Times,* is now regarded as one of the most recognized images of U.S.-Spanish relations. Overall, the evolution of the Palomares incident shows how domestic political calculations constantly informed the Spanish dictator's reaction to the accident and his media policy. As a result, Palomares has acquired a particularly symbolic significance in the post-Franco media and among Spanish political commentators.[24]

The Philippines: From Independence to Marcos

Unlike the U.S. military presence in Spain, which the United States established by courting the Franco regime, a number of major U.S. installations in the Philippines were a direct legacy of World War II. The American presence in the Philippines dates back to 1898, when the United States acquired the islands during the Spanish-American War and subsequently governed them as a colony with "unincorporated" status. A 1934 accord to allow independence in ten years was interrupted by the Japanese occupation in 1941. After expelling Japanese forces from the islands, the United States granted the Philippines independence on July 4, 1946, on the condition that the U.S. Joint Chiefs of Staff acquire forty army and navy facilities, including the Subic Bay naval station and Clark Air Base.[25] The independence treaty—the 1946 Treaty of General Relations—explicitly excluded U.S. base facilities from the sovereignty transfer.

The 1947 Military Bases Agreement
The precise status and terms of the bases were codified in the Military Bases Agreement (MBA) of 1947. Commentators have referred to the agreement as "neo-imperial" with good reason. In it the United States secured

23. For more on the propaganda surrounding the episode, see Szulc 1967, 219–28. Until 2005, Fraga, at eighty-three, was still active in Spanish politics as the recently reelected governor of Galicia.
24. This significance has been confirmed by the author's interviews with Spanish media editorial writers and foreign affairs columnists, Madrid, April 2005.
25. Berry 1989, 17–19.

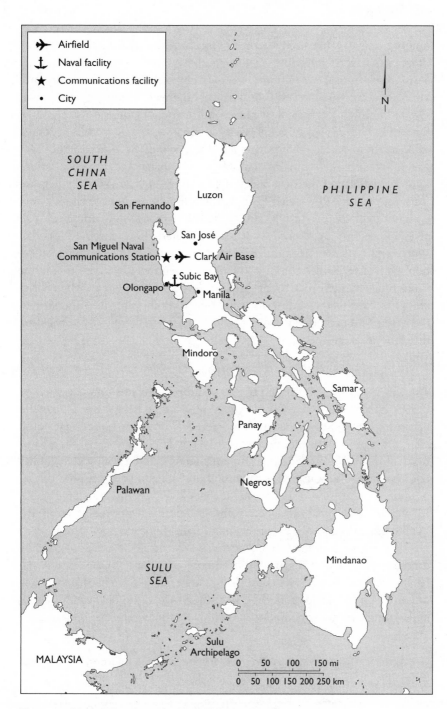

Figure 3.2. Major U.S. military facilities, Philippines, 1979.
Source: National Defense University

ninety-nine-year, rent-free leases to Subic and Clark along with fourteen other sites in the Philippines (see fig. 3.2). An additional seven sites were earmarked for use "by military necessity" in exchange for the future provision of some military aid.[26] In terms of sovereignty, the agreement was also extremely hierarchical. It placed no restrictions on the use rights of the bases and explicitly acknowledged that the bases were designated exclusively to project U.S. power into the Pacific. The United States was granted the power to govern, maintain, and construct on the installations without consulting the host and to freely move equipment and weapons from one facility to another.[27] The United States retained exclusive sovereignty over the bases, which included the city of Olongapo, and over all Filipinos employed on the bases. The United States assumed jurisdiction over all crimes committed by Americans and Filipinos on the installations as well as crimes committed by U.S. personnel anywhere else in the Philippines while "on duty" or during a "state of emergency." All facilities and personnel were exempt from any type of Philippine taxation. Finally, the agreement prohibited either government from unilaterally abrogating its terms and conditions.

Democratization and Nationalism, 1948–1966
The MBA was signed, ratified by the Philippine Senate, and accepted by the Philippine Supreme Court, yet almost immediately the agreement became the target of intense political scrutiny and new nationalist political campaigns that questioned its legitimacy. This politicking was a function of the MBA's one-sided nature but also reflected the intense volatility of postwar Philippine democratization and its competitive, elite-driven politics. A succession of Philippine leaders leveraged this unstable political climate in order to extract economic and political concessions from the United States to consolidate and expand their domestic power base.

The security guarantees conspicuously absent in the 1947 treaty were granted in the early 1950s. In 1951, under the presidency of the vocal populist Elpidio Quirino, the two countries signed a mutual defense treaty laying down the principles of collective security between the parties (Article II) and stating that an armed attack on either party "would be dangerous to

26. "Agreement between the Republic of the Philippines and the United States of America concerning Military Bases," signed at Manila, March 14, 1947, Article I, *TIAS* 1775.
27. *TIAS* 1775, "Description of Rights," Article III.

its peace and safety."[28] In 1953, a military assistance treaty provided modest amounts of military aid and training, and in 1954 the Philippines signed the South East Asia Collective Defense Treaty. These agreements ignored issues specific to the bases and their governance.

When the flamboyant and openly pro-American Ramon Magsaysay was elected in 1954 with the full support of the United States, U.S. officials assumed that they would quickly implement new needed base policies. Given the bases' proximity to conflict zones in Southeast Asia, the Pentagon sought a new agreement to expand and modernize Clark and Subic in order to accommodate more traffic, troops, and training facilities.[29]

Yet it was the Philippine president who skillfully used his pro-U.S. reputation both to entrench himself politically and, in turn, to use these domestic pressures as leverage on basing matters. Philippine landowners and industrialists, who were already being undercut by extensive black market trading on the bases, opposed the proposed expansion, as did the media and nationalists who were concerned that the United States would unlawfully secure rights to unexplored mineral wealth and pry open protected Philippine markets.[30] Unable to appease these constituents through government transfers because U.S. aid had been severely cut by Eisenhower after Magsaysay's election, Magsaysay postponed talks in 1955 to placate these protests.[31] The leak of the Brownell memorandum—a document drafted by U.S. lawyer Herbert Brownell arguing that the United States already possessed the legal right to appropriate new lands—inflamed Philippine public opinion and roused the Philippine Senate. When talks reopened in 1956, Magsaysay demanded that a whole new range of issues related to Philippine sovereignty—including taxation, customs, and criminal

28. "Mutual Defense Treaty between the Republic of the Philippines and the United States of America," signed at Washington, D.C., August 30, 1951, Article IV, *TIAS* 2529. In 1954, Secretary of State John Foster Dulles extended the scope of the 1951 agreement by stating that "any military attack on the Philippines could not but be an attack on the military forces of the United States." Sandars 2000, 110.
29. With the United States anticipating military operations in China and Vietnam, the bases were considered a linchpin for supporting the Asian campaigns. In addition, under a decision taken by Eisenhower in 1953, one-third to one-half of U.S. nuclear weapons were to be dispersed to foreign bases, including the Philippines, to decrease the stockpile's vulnerability to Soviet attack.
30. Cullather 1994, 136–41. On the base-related shadow economy and its organization, see Madison 1996, 158–66.
31. For the U.S. perspective on the rise of nationalism and the bases question in the 1950s, see the National Security documents compiled in Cullather 1992; Taylor 1964.

jurisdiction—be revised in the new agreement, a move that caught the United States off guard. With negotiations again halted by the turmoil of the 1957 Philippine election campaign, the U.S. military operated on the basis of informal agreements and arrangements, through which Magsaysay "could help the United States and augment his patronage base without incurring the political risks of open collaboration."[32] Far from being a passive pawn of the United States, Magsaysay skillfully used the base issue to his internal political advantage before dying in a plane crash in March 1957, still not having signed the agreement that Washington wanted.[33]

The Bohlen-Serrano Agreement

Washington lamented the loss of Magsaysay. Although he had failed to deliver in a number of areas, U.S. officials feared that the tide of nationalism now engulfing Philippine politics, coupled with the "indecisive and corrupt" new Garcia administration, could severely destabilize the security relationship and sabotage the base negotiations.[34] Accordingly, U.S. officials decided to grant the concessions necessary to reach an accord. Talks recommenced in 1958 and were concluded in October 1959 with an agreement reached by Philippine foreign minister Felixberto Serrano and U.S. ambassador Charles Bohlen. The Bohlen-Serrano Agreement of 1959 was the first major amendment to the 1947 MBA, and it revised several provisions of the original hierarchical contract.[35] In the area of facilities, the United States agreed to cede 117,982 hectares of territory and return exclusive jurisdiction over the town of Olongapo and the port of Manila to Philippine authorities.[36] In addition, the lease period of ninety-nine years was replaced by a new period of twenty-five years, although the new period only formally went into effect at a separate signing of the provision in September 1966. The United States paid a number of fees and prom-

32. Cullather 1994, 150, 151.
33. As Cullather 1994 summarizes, "Magsaysay attempted to establish himself as a broker between his American and Philippine clients, but after the first thousand days, he found himself caught between increasing demands of indigenous interests and the shrinking largesse of the United States. Realizing that his political fortunes lay with his Filipino supporters, he sided with them in disputes that became numerous and intractable . . . he did not shrink from holding U.S. objectives—like the bases treaty—hostage to the political and economic demands of his Philippine allies" (121).
34. See Cullather 1992, 163–85.
35. Amendment of the 1959 agreement was formalized as the "Agreement between the United States of America and the Republic of the Philippines concerning Military Bases, Amendment of August 10, 1965."
36. Taylor 1964, 238–39.

ised to arrange for International Monetary Fund (IMF) and export-import loans. The U.S. side also made some concessions on issues of sovereignty. The agreement established a joint Mutual Defense Board to consider grievances and placed a Philippine liaison officer on site at every facility. The United States agreed to consult with the Philippine government before using the bases for purposes other than mutual defense, including the stationing of any intermediate or intercontinental ballistic missiles.

One area in which no progress was made in 1959 was the contentious issue of criminal jurisdiction. By the late 1950s, Philippine newspapers were publishing a steady stream of stories about U.S. base guards shooting Filipinos who had strayed onto base territory as well as reports of abuses of Philippine base workers in Olongapo.[37] The issue had become so politicized that, from 1957 to 1964, the Philippine government practically stopped granting waivers of jurisdiction to the United States for its limited category of offenses, after having granted waivers in 79 percent of cases in 1954 (see table 3.1). The jurisdiction issue was repeatedly brought up by Manila, and in February 1965 new talks were held that focused exclusively on the SOFA issue. In August 1965, an agreement was reached that brought the U.S.-Philippine SOFA in line with the NATO and Japan accords, implementing a system of concurrent jurisdiction.[38] The United States ceased to exercise jurisdiction over the criminal actions of Filipinos on the bases, although it was awarded primary jurisdiction over the actions of all U.S. servicemen on the islands subject to the certification of their "on-duty" status.[39] In addition, the sides established a joint Criminal Jurisdictional Implementation Committee, and both sides agreed to give "sympathetic consideration" to waive jurisdiction in those cases of a "particular national interest."

Marcos and the Politics of Authoritarian Survival, 1966–1979

The election of Senator Ferdinand Marcos to the presidency in 1965 marked a new chapter in Philippine politics and in bilateral basing relations. Much like Magsaysay before him, Marcos initially was vocally pro-American, but he also used this affiliation to insulate himself from U.S. pressure. In 1969,

37. For details, see Meadows 1965, 305–18. Julian Madison estimates that more than thirty Filipinos were killed while on or near the base from 1948 to 1965. None of the cases were tried in Philippine court. See Madison 1996, 152–74.
38. On the evolution and details of the U.S.-Philippine SOFA, see Porrata-Doria 1992.
39. Berry 1989, 142–43.

TABLE 3.1
Waivers of criminal jurisdiction in the Philippines, 1954–64

Year	1954	1955	1956	1957	1958	1959	1960	1961	1962	1963	1964
New cases	156	99	47	49	182	82	72	60	85	67	132
Waived	123	41	22	1	1	1	1	2	0	2	0
Percentage waived (%)	79	47	41	2	1	1	2	3	0	3	0

Source: U.S. Department of Defense figures, as cited in Berry 1989, 127–28.

Marcos called for another round of base negotiations and soon after was reelected despite widespread allegations of intimidation and vote fraud. In 1971–72, prohibited by the constitution from running for a third term, Marcos played up a number of internal and external threats to the country's stability, and in September 1972 he declared martial law. Afterward the Philippine president routinely clamped down on political opponents, jailed dissidents, and muzzled the press, while supporting and growing the military, his key domestic constituency and ally. Throughout the 1970s and early 1980s, political dissidents and left-wing activists adopted the term "the U.S.-Marcos dictatorship," a phrase that became accepted even among Philippine conservatives.[40] During this time, Marcos and his political cronies ran the economy into a standstill, while they mismanaged and embezzled hundreds of millions of dollars in aid and overseas development loans.[41]

From early on, Marcos showed great skill in playing two-level basing politics. During the terms of five U.S. presidents, Marcos understood that Washington's first priority in bilateral relations would always be to maintain basing access. Starting with his 1969 reelection campaign, during which he wanted to shed his pro-American image in the face of growing nationalism, Marcos called for a general review of the U.S.-Philippine relationship and another renegotiation of the basing agreement.[42] From that point, Marcos would maintain a tough, pro-Philippine sovereignty domestically, but he did so while maintaining unwavering U.S. support

40. Kessler 1986, 42.
41. By the time Marcos left office, the country's external debt was greater than $25 billion, with debt service about 35 percent of the government's budget. On the relationship among international lenders, the United States, and the Marcos regime, see Broad 1990.
42. Berry 1988, 131–39. Marcos's decision in 1965 to send some troops to Vietnam ingratiated him with the Johnson administration and netted him a number of IFI loans.

that he leveraged for base-related payments.[43] In turn, these substantial quid pro quo payments allowed him to provide patronage for his military supporters and political base.

In 1971, Marcos and his foreign minister Carlos Romulo formally requested that a new agreement be negotiated to replace the 1947 MBA. His main reason was that the bases were now being used by the United States solely to support "American experiments in Asia."[44] Over the next three years, a technical committee revisited a number of issues, including consolidating and reducing the size of the facilities, shifting command and control jurisdiction, revising criminal jurisdiction provisions, and encouraging Philippine military self-reliance.[45] These negotiations were protracted and difficult, and the United States complained that Marcos deliberately used the media to emphasize base-related accidents in order to incite public opinion and strengthen his negotiating hand.[46]

With the two sides finally narrowing the gap on most issues by 1976, the greatest outstanding Philippine demand was its request for a substantial increase in compensation payments.[47] In 1976, Henry Kissinger and Romulo had reached a tentative agreement for an unprecedented $1 billion payment over five years, but Marcos himself rejected the figure the following day and the talks collapsed.[48] Negotiations recommenced in fall 1977, and an agreement on basic guidelines for a new treaty, which included granting full Philippine sovereignty over the facilities and holding future renewal talks every five years, was issued in 1978 after Vice President Walter Mondale's visit to Manila.[49] In October 1978, after talks had stalled again, U.S. senator Daniel Inouye, chairman of the Senate Appropriations Subcommittee on Foreign Operations, visited the Philippines to negotiate with Marcos a level of compensation that would be deemed acceptable by the U.S. Senate. Inouye stressed that any compensation package in the realm of $1 billion would not be ratified, and he underscored the importance of rapidly concluding an agreement so as to make the appropriations deadline for the FY 1980 budget.[50] Convinced by the senator's

43. Richard Kennedy, "Fiscal Year 1976 Aid Review," National Security Memorandum for Brent Scowcroft, December 10, 1974, 31, *DDRS*.
44. Berry 1989, 147.
45. On the 1970s negotiations, see Berry 1989; Paez 1985, 27–105.
46. See Newsom 1990.
47. On the negotiations, see Berry 1989, 190–228.
48. See Bonner 1988, 210–12.
49. See Castro 1985, 139.
50. Sandars 2000, 113–14.

arguments, Marcos ordered negotiations to restart, and an agreement was concluded on December 26, 1978, with the formal MBA document signed on January 7, 1979.

The 1979 agreement revised the 1947 MBA on almost every issue. Technically, the 1979 accords formally amended the 1947 agreement.[51] The agreement stipulated that the leasing period be renegotiated every five years until the ultimate 1991 expiration date. In terms of sovereignty, the agreement emphasized that all the territory hosting U.S. installations was exclusively Philippine, and a Philippine base commander was appointed to head each basing facility. For the first time ever, Philippines armed forces were made exclusively responsible for the perimeter security of the facilities. Significant territorial modifications were also agreed upon. At Clark Air Base, the United States formally ceded 92 percent or 119,000 acres out of the original 130,000, leaving it with about 10,550 acres. Annex II reduced U.S. territory in Subic Bay to 14,400 acres, about 40 percent of the previously held 62,000 acres (land and water area).[52] The other facilities were either transferred to Philippine jurisdiction or were consolidated and appended to the governing structures of Clark and Subic.[53]

In terms of compensation, the 1979 agreement represented a huge leap over previous levels. The final package of $500 million over five years was a substantial increase from the $45 million annual payment agreed to in 1966. The annual sum of $100 million was less than the $1 billion that had been rejected by Marcos two years before, but it established that the compensation packages from that point onward would be of significant proportions.

Reagan and Marcos: Declining Support and Endgame
The election of Ronald Reagan, who Marcos had first met as governor of California, calmed bilateral relations considerably. Despite protests from Philippine political exiles (many of them living in the United States) and more liberal members of the U.S. Congress, the Reagan administration

51. "Arrangements Regarding Delineation of United States Facilities at Clark Air Base and Subic Naval Base; Powers and Responsibilities of the Philippine Base Commanders and Related Powers of the United States Facility Commanders and the Tabones Complex," signed January 7, 1979, *TIAS* 9224.
52. *TIAS* 9224, Article I, Annex I and II.
53. The U.S. facilities at Wallace Air Station, the Crow Valley Weapons range, and the John Hay Air Station were transferred to Clark, while the Zambales Amphibious Training Area and the San Miguel Naval Communications Station became extensions of Subic. See Berry 1989, 230–32.

placed strategic concerns above all other issues. It quickly dropped any pretense of criticizing Marcos's human rights policy and strongly backed the Philippine president and his anticommunist credentials.[54] Marcos was invited to Washington for a state visit in 1982, his first since 1966, where the two sides agreed to begin the next round of base renegotiations in April 1983. The 1983 talks were successfully concluded in less than two months and were the antithesis of the contentious 1970s negotiations.[55] The two sides maintained the bases-for-aid formula and kept the substance of almost all of the other clauses unchanged. The United States willingly raised the amount of compensation, with the sides agreeing to a new five-year package for $900 million, an 80 percent increase of the 1979 accord.

Soon after the agreement was signed, political events started to unravel in the Philippines. In August 1983, opposition figurehead Benigno Aquino was assassinated, unleashing a wave of discontent and anti-Marcos mobilization. In 1984 Marcos went into seclusion to recover from illness, while political dissidents, opposition forces, and antibase activists started to rally around Aquino's widow, Corazón Aquino, as the new opposition figurehead. Among its demands, the opposition called for removal of the U.S. bases and the drafting of a new constitution. The U.S. State Department and U.S. Congress criticized Marcos and nudged him toward reforms, but the Philippine president returned to political visibility in 1985 fully anticipating that the U.S. president and the Pentagon would remain his staunch allies. In a move designed to shore up his political base, Marcos called a sudden presidential election for February 7, 1986. He clearly did not expect the ensuing tidal wave of support for Aquino. At the same time, opinion within the U.S. State Department over the last year had shifted decisively against the Philippines president, and the elections attracted intense American media coverage.[56] After Marcos fraudulently claimed victory, popular demonstrations erupted in Manila and continued for eighteen days. On February 25, in the final symbolic act linking Marcos to the U.S. military, U.S. helicopters airlifted the Philippine autocrat from the presidential palace to Clark airfield, where he was flown out of the country. Immediately after the dictator's ouster, Richard Kessler, reflecting on U.S.-Philippine relations, observed that

54. See Bonner 1988, 295–341.
55. "Defense Memorandum of Agreement," signed June 1, 1983, *TIAS* 10699.
56. I thank Mark Kramer for his comments on this point.

in assessing American policy throughout the Marcos period . . . one is struck by how much better Marcos understood the Americans than the Americans understood Marcos. He found that all five American presidents he dealt with from 1965 to 1985 were unwilling to jeopardize the U.S.-Marcos relationship, even when basic American values such as respect for human life and freedom of speech were at stake. Marcos, an astute observer of the American scene, came to understand that, under any administration, the overriding concern of U.S. policy would be the protection of the U.S. military bases in the Philippines.[57]

Democratization and the Renegotiation of the Base Agreements

The Franco and Marcos eras cast a shadow over U.S.-host base negotiations in the subsequent democratization period and eroded the credibility of these original security contracts. Negotiating teams for both base hosts came to the table determined to scale back the presence of U.S. military personnel, correct imbalances in previous agreements, and place the new security relationship on a more equal footing. Ultimately, new democratic pressures reduced the U.S. military footprint, although these played out in different ways. In Spain, an orderly transition of elite pacts gave way to a more contested party system that catapulted the socialist PSOE and its anti-NATO platform to power. In the Philippines, a constitutional revision and jurisdictional competition between the legislature and the executive characterized the tumultuous post-Marcos political environment, generating a veto point for a proposed base extension.

Democratization in Spain

From Managed Pact to Party Competition
Spain, with its democratic transition, has been invoked as a model of a smooth "pacted" transition, where elites form temporary pacts over contentious issues and agree to establish working democratic institutions in the interests of promoting the transition.[58] The unity government of the Democratic Center Union (UCD) admitted the Communists (PCE) back into the political system and looked to set aside politically divisive and

57. Kessler 1986, 43.
58. See Hopkin 2004; Colomer 1991.

ideological issues. With both the UCD and the PCE concerned about the rising political fortunes of the Socialists (PSOE), the two parties reached a tacit agreement on foreign policy that depoliticized the basing issue. Leaders of the PCE agreed not to oppose the presence of U.S. bases as long as the UCD made no sudden push for Spanish membership in NATO.[59] The NATO issue was rapidly developing into the major foreign policy topic in Spanish politics and was generating considerable political traction for the PSOE.

The foreign policy pact effectively ended during the UCD's second term. In 1981 the prime minister (also known as president of the Spanish government) Adolfo Suárez resigned and precipitated a failed coup by junior military officers. After the coup attempt, the newly appointed head of government Leopoldo Calvo-Sotelo launched an aggressive public campaign in 1982 to promote NATO membership, shattering the party consensus to remain silent on the issue. Sotelo's aggressive drive was both a calculated attempt to irreversibly subordinate the Spanish military to civilian rule and a move designed to placate more conservative factions within the UCD.

In July 1982, just two weeks after Spain was offered NATO membership, the Calvo-Sotelo government also concluded a bilateral bases pact with the United States. The talks were more contentious in tone than those preceding the 1976 agreement, in part because Calvo-Sotelo did not want to appear too soft on the issue in the run-up to the national election. The 1982 Agreement on Friendship, Defense, and Cooperation extended the long-standing "bases-for-aid" formula, with some concessions to the Spanish side.[60] Spain was offered the standard NATO status of forces agreement and a veto over out-of-area operations. The treaty also established a joint council to review base-related issues semiannually. Despite the negotiations' more contentious tone, the Spanish government did not secure a reduction in U.S. forces. Indeed, U.S. negotiators later expressed surprise that their Spanish counterparts had not insisted on lowering the troop ceiling.[61] Calvo-Sotelo later justified this relatively pliant stance by reasoning that the UCD had no future as a party and that he wanted to use his remaining time in office to cement Spain's integration into the Western security community, regardless of the electoral consequences.[62]

---

59. See Cooley and Hopkin 2006; Mesa 1992, 157.
60. "Agreement on Friendship, Defense and Cooperation between the United States of America and the Kingdom of Spain," signed July 2, 1982, *TIAS* 10589.
61. See the comments made by U.S. negotiator Donald Planty in Planty 1990.
62. See Calvo-Sotelo 1990.

Election of the PSOE and the NATO Referendum

Putting NATO membership back on the table played straight into the hands of the PSOE, which was led by the charismatic Felipe González. On the verge of a historic triumph, the PSOE adopted an anti-NATO party platform in 1981 and entered the 1982 presidential campaign with security issues front and center. Polling indicated a Spanish public deeply suspicious of NATO and highly critical of the United States' commitment to a democratic Spain.[63] González vowed to hold a referendum on NATO membership, and on the subject of the bases the PSOE candidate talked of the need to bring "greater balance" to the accord, although he did not make any speeches during the campaign that threatened outright expulsion.

After a decisive victory in October 1982, González froze Spain's integration into NATO's military command structure and delayed ratification of the bilateral bases accord signed by the Sotelo government. On February 24, 1983, González signed a protocol that decoupled the NATO and basing issue, ensuring that in the event of withdrawal from NATO the basing agreement would still be valid.[64] The rank-and-file PSOE membership were not pleased with the protocol, especially because many of them did not distinguish between the issues of NATO membership and the U.S. bases. The PCE denounced the protocol and called for the removal of all American bases from Spanish territory.

During his first term in office González also felt increasing pressure from local politicians on the bases issue. After Spain's first municipal elections in 1979, PSOE mayors controlled three of the four major base-hosting cities (with the exception of conservative Seville) and vigorously complained to the national party about issues such as their inability to collect local road taxes from the bases, SOFA procedures, and lack of compensation from Madrid.[65] During the early 1980s, local politicians joined forces with antibase activists to stage regular demonstrations in front of the base compounds in Rota, Zaragoza, and Madrid, chanting the slogan "No NATO! Bases must go!" The most dramatic of these was a 100,000-person demonstration in March 1984 protesting the PSOE's seemingly hesitant stance on these security matters. Tensions also mounted within

63. Many elements of the Spanish left had long equated the American military presence with support for Franco. This image was confirmed by Defense secretary Alexander Haig's imprudent remarks in 1981 that the attempted military coup in Spain was an "internal matter" in Spanish politics. On the PSOE's foreign policy positions in 1982, see Mujal-Leon 1983.

64. Duke 1989, 258–59.

65. See Dabrowski 1996, 228–30.

the PSOE as the leadership tried to deflect local calls for legislative action on these base-related issues.[66]

With his first term running out and opinion polls showing continued public hostility to NATO membership, González finally set a date for the NATO referendum, which he now supported and regarded as vital for the country's impending EU accession. The framing of the referendum itself was a remarkably crafty exercise in agenda setting. Rather than present a simple question on whether Spain should remain a member of NATO, González worded the query so that voters were asked whether Spain should continue its membership in the organization subject to three conditions:

1. The participation of Spain in the Atlantic Alliance will not include its incorporation into the integrated military structure.

2. The prohibition on the installation, storing, or introduction of nuclear arms on Spanish territory will be continued.

3. The progressive reduction of the military presence of the United States in Spain will be proceeded with.[67]

With antibase sentiments running high, González effectively conflated the NATO and U.S. basing issues in two of three of the referendum's conditions, after having previously decoupled the issues in his 1983 protocol. Some wavering PSOE members viewed the vote as an opportunity to express their support for a U.S. troop withdrawal, and these provisions put them at greater ease with González's turnaround on NATO. In effect, González made the vote more about the competence and credibility of the PSOE rather than about the actual NATO issue. Despite polls showing a probable "no" vote just days before, the referendum passed with 52.5 percent voting yes and 39.9 percent voting no, while 7.7 percent abstained or cast a blank ballot. Notably, seven out ten PSOE members voted yes, defying the party's platform on the issue, while the same percentage of conservatives abstained and nationalists and Communists voted no.[68] This geographical and party distribution of the vote coincided almost

66. Roldán 1998, 145–47.
67. The exact wording was: "Do you consider it advisable for Spain to remain in the Atlantic Alliance according to the terms set forth by the Government of the nation?" Holman 1996, 106.
68. For the exact numbers and analysis, see Boix and Alt 1991.

identically with the results of national elections, held three months later, which gave the PSOE its second term with a comfortable majority.

The Contentious 1986–1988 Negotiation and Eviction from Torrejón
Having secured a referendum victory and reelection, the PSOE now turned its attention to negotiations for a new basing agreement, one that it insisted should break decisively with those of the Franco era that lacked democratic credibility. This base negotiation would be the first one conducted by the Socialists, and President González had already announced that he would abandon previous aid-based formulas. Armed with the base-related provisions in the approved NATO referendum, PSOE negotiators could also credibly proclaim a public mandate and use it to demand a significant reduction in the 12,500 U.S. troops. Controversial air strikes by the United States on Libya in April 1986 further fueled antibase public sentiment, especially when it was revealed that the United States had relocated Spanish-based bombers to Great Britain for the Libyan mission right after González had refused to authorize the use of Spanish bases and airspace for the campaign.[69]

Spanish negotiators were adamant on two points when starting negotiations in late 1986: the United States would have to abandon the airbase at Torrejón near the Spanish capital, and Spain would not seek monetary compensation.[70] For Spain, the latter was particularly important because it signaled that no amount of military or economic aid could reverse its decision about Torrejón, and that the basing question had to be separated from all other areas of bilateral relations.[71]

The negotiations over the next two years were tense, protracted, and contentious, with each side publicly criticizing the other's positions and tactics. Throughout the talks, Spanish negotiators insisted that only a new agreement that brought "balance" to the relationship could be accepted by the Spanish public and would rid the basing agreement of its Franco-era legacies.[72] Besides, the results of the NATO referendum committed Spanish negotiators to securing a significant drawdown in U.S. presence. From the end of 1986 throughout 1987, Spain rejected several U.S. proposals

69. See Grimmett 1986, 18–19.
70. Author's interview with high-ranking Spanish base negotiator of the 1988 agreements, Madrid, April 2005.
71. For the Spanish perspective on these negotiations, see Viñas 2003a, 471–510; 2003b, 19–22.
72. Author's interview with high-ranking Spanish base negotiator of the 1988 agreements, Madrid, April 2005. Several U.S. newspapers covering the negotiations also reported on the Franco-era baggage being used as a tactic by the Spanish side.

and stated that removal of the entire fighter squadron from Torrejón was nonnegotiable.[73]

In November 1987, the Spanish negotiators formally notified their U.S. counterparts that the agreement that expired in May 1988 would not be renewed, which threatened the U.S. forces with the prospect of imminent expulsion. The Americans responded that the domestic political concerns of the Spanish team were threatening the stability of the alliance, and both Secretary of Defense Caspar Weinberger and Secretary of State George Schultz visited Madrid in the hope of changing the Spanish position.[74] The deadlock was only broken in June 1988 when the Italian government announced that it would accept all of the Torrejón-based F-16s on Italian territory. For its part, the Spanish government gave the United States three years to complete the Torrejón relocation and dropped its calls for the right to inspect ships in Rota for nuclear weapons, agreeing to a variant of the U.S. "neither-confirm-nor-deny" policy. The final treaty, signed in December 1988, was to continue for eight years; it reduced U.S. troops in Spain by 40 percent, closed the airbases at Torrejón and Zaragoza, and provided no military or economic compensation to Spain. Despite some public concern with the nuclear issue, the new treaty was easily confirmed by the Spanish parliament on a vote of 270 to 10 and earned praise from the mainstream media and editorial boards as a "promise kept" by the González government.[75]

Contrasting the 1988 PSOE-negotiated accord with the 1953 Madrid Pact, Spanish historian Angel Viñas writes: "In the history of the bilateral relationship this agreement is the exact counterpoint of what the Franco regime had consented to in 1953. The enshrined imbalances, dependence, and trends toward a lack of proper supervision of U.S. activities in Spain were transformed into a well-balanced compact of duties, rights and responsibilities strictly respecting the full sovereignty of both parties."[76] The PSOE, which had come to power on an anti-NATO platform and a vow to get tough on the basing issue, had delivered a new agreement and U.S. troop reduction. With the new accord signed and democratically ratified, the issue lost its political significance among Spain's mainstream political parties. The U.S. bases in Spain would again be used for controversial military campaigns, but the issue itself would never attract the

73. See Burns 1987; *New York Times* 1987a.
74. See *New York Times* 1987b.
75. See, e.g., *El País* 1988a, 1988b.
76. Viñas 2003b, 21.

same amount of domestic political attention and party competition as it had in the 1980s.

Democratization in the Philippines: Confronting the Marcos Legacy

The post-Marcos era was characterized by intense nationalism, jurisdictional uncertainty, and failed coup attempts by segments of the military uncertain of their standing in the new democratic Philippine state.[77] In her first major policy initiative in 1986, interim president Aquino appointed a forty-eight-member committee of diverse political leanings, including several antibase activists, to draft a new constitution and submit it directly for a national referendum. The document contained two particular clauses that directly addressed base issues: Article II (8) prohibited the stationing of nuclear weapons on Philippine territory, and Article XXVIII prohibited the United States from extending the Military Bases Agreement beyond 1991 without the explicit "concurrence" (ratification) of the Philippine Senate and, if requested by the Philippine Congress, an additional popular referendum. The same article worried the United States because the document interpreted the 1991 deadline as a final termination date, as opposed to a date after which either side could serve notice regarding the bases' future. In April 1987 the referendum on the new constitution passed overwhelmingly, with 80 percent of voters affirming it. The document created a new institutional context for base negotiations and ratifications.[78]

The intense nationalism generated by the new democratizing climate had also flared up during the 1988 MBA review. Initially, U.S. negotiators had entered the 1988 talks with limited goals, hoping to offer some aid increases over the next two years until new negotiations regarding the bases' future began at the end of 1989. Instead, U.S. negotiators were barraged by public and media frenzy about the bases and faced intense criticism in the Philippine Senate. President Aquino remained publicly silent throughout the tense seven-month negotiation period, even as Foreign Secretary Raúl Manglapus declared that the Americans should "move out" if they were unwilling to pay the new $1.2 billion per year price tag demanded by the Philippine side.[79] The review agreement was finalized

---

77. On post-Marcos democratization and consolidation in the Philippines, see Thompson 1996.
78. On the importance of the new constitution with regard to the bases issue, see Berry 1989, 286–87.
79. Stromseth 1989.

in October 1988, with the Americans agreeing to a substantially increased quid pro quo of $962 million for the agreement's remaining two years in addition to accepting the new constitution's prohibition on the stationing of nuclear weapons. The negotiations also showed how the changing institutional context of democratization had generated audience costs for Philippine negotiators and shifted bargaining power to the new government in Manila.[80]

The final negotiations of 1990–91 were enmeshed in a complex set of domestic and international factors. In September 1990 the Philippines Base Panel (PBP), appointed by President Aquino, began its negotiations with the U.S. team, led by Richard Armitage, by serving formal notice that U.S. forces must be withdrawn by 1991, the date authorized in the new constitution.[81] The Philippine side was aware of the 1988 Spanish-U.S. negotiation and troop reduction, and it began the talks with the main aim of securing a treaty of withdrawal, as opposed to renewal, that would put the bilateral relationship on a more "equal" footing.[82] The Philippine panel favored removing U.S. military personnel from all installations except Subic Bay naval station, for which a five- to seven-year additional nonrenewable extension would be granted. The U.S. side agreed in principle to withdraw from Clark but stuck firm to a ten- to twelve-year extension for Subic, with a guarantee for visitation rights for U.S. vessels afterward. The sides were also considerably apart on compensation issues and the perennially tricky criminal jurisdiction provisions of a future SOFA.[83]

In the later part of 1991 the U.S. negotiators managed to take advantage of emerging cracks within the Philippine government among the president, the PBP, the business community, and various pro-American conservatives who were concerned that the PBP was adopting a too-aggressive negotiating posture. Then, in June 1991, Mount Pinatubo erupted unexpectedly. The eruption covered Clark Air Base in ash, prompting the evacuation of all U.S. personnel and virtually ending the United States' tenure at the facility. The volcanic disaster and ensuing governmental disarray

80. As Stromseth observed, "a more open Philippine polity has both complicated the negotiations and diminished U.S. bargaining leverage" (1989, 185–86).
81. Both Richard Armitage and Alfredo Bengzon, chief base negotiator for the Philippines, have published their accounts of the talks. Bengzon's is particularly helpful for the insights it provides into the domestic political institutions and actors on the Philippines side. See Bengzon 1997.
82. For a helpful collection of the key communications in the talks, see Castro-Guevara 1997.
83. Bengzon 1997.

prompted a near capitulation of the PBP to U.S. terms. In August 1991 President Aquino signed the new Treaty of Friendship, Cooperation and Security. The proposed lease for Subic would run for ten years, and compensation was set at just $200 million a year.

The deal seemed to be a victory for the United States, but it immediately set up a showdown between a skeptical Senate and President Aquino. Throughout the negotiations, many senators had openly stated that the new deal needed to fundamentally break with the past either by increasing levels of compensation or by setting a firm U.S. withdrawal deadline. With neither of these conditions fulfilled and a two-thirds vote required for ratification, passage was going to be difficult. On September 16, 1991, the very day that the old Military Bases Agreement expired, the Philippine Senate defeated the bill by a vote of 12 to 11, well short of the 18 votes needed.[84] The United States had not counted on the institutional veto provided by the Senate or perhaps believed that it could be overridden. Indeed, in the days after the dramatic Senate vote, Aquino considered holding a popular referendum on the issue or revoking its 1990 withdrawal notice, but the constitutionality of either course of action was challenged by the media and the Justice Department.[85] President Aquino backed off from the constitutional confrontation, and the United States was given until the end of 1992 to accomplish a full withdrawal from all of its facilities in the Philippines. On November 24, 1992, the American flag was lowered from Subic, and U.S. military forces completed their withdrawal.

Democratic Consolidation and Depoliticization

The Rapid Decline of the Basing Issue in Spain

President González's political skill in resolving foreign policy matters, especially his ability to help Spain secure admission to the EU in 1986 and to renegotiate the bases treaty, was again rewarded by the electorate. In 1989, González and the PSOE won their third successive general election. After seven years in power, the Spanish president had led his party away from its original anti-Western and antimarket campaign platform and turned it into a promarket party that touted its own competence and experience in foreign policy issues. The Spanish party system itself was

84. The vote required a two-thirds majority. On the Senate vote and debate, see Legislative Publications Staff of the Senate of the Philippines 1991.
85. For details, see Bengzon 1997, 270–94.

institutionalizing into a stable two-party system at the national level, with well-entrenched and well-financed party organizations.[86] Only the fringe party Izquierda Unida, formed from the old Communist Party, now maintained a publicly antibases party platform. With the new 1988 agreement, the U.S. basing presence now had the democratic sanctioning and procedural legitimacy that it previously lacked.

Democratic consolidation further demobilized the basing issue from the political agenda, even as the bases continued to be used for high-profile military missions.[87] This change was dramatically illustrated by González's attitude toward Operation Desert Storm in 1991. During the initial crisis, the Spanish government moved quickly to offer its full political support to U.S.-led efforts and then gave unrestricted use of the bases for the military campaign. The Gulf War offered the PSOE an opportunity to consolidate Spain's new status as a member of various Western organizations.[88] Demonstrations against the war took place off the bases, but they were not nearly as big as previous anti-NATO rallies, nor did they receive the same amount of national media attention.[89] Despite some attempts by the Partido Popular (PP) and Izquierda Unida (IU) to clarify the government's position on the terms of base use for military campaigns, the issue did not gain much political traction.[90] The IU, with well under 10 percent in the polls, was too marginal, whereas the PP could hardly make a convincing argument because the Socialists had just "corrected" the lopsided and illegitimate base deals of the Franco era.

On the criminal jurisdiction issue, too, Spanish authorities significantly increased their number of waivers of criminal jurisdiction (see table 3.2). From 1989 to 2005, U.S. officials secured jurisdiction in 98.4 percent of criminal cases involving U.S. bases in Spain, with Spain denying just 18 out of 1,066 requests for jurisdiction over a period of sixteen years. These numbers represented a significant increase from those of May 1983 through May 1989, under the more politicized 1982 agreement, when Spanish authorities asserted jurisdiction in 80 out of 1,096 cases.

---

86. Van Biezen 2003, chap. 4; Gunther, Sani, and Shabad 1988.
87. Some may argue that it was the change in the international system in the late 1980s and the decline of communism that explain the depoliticization of the base issue. Yet such an explanation is indeterminate. Left-wing parties may just as easily claim that absent the Soviet threat, Spain has no compelling security interests in hosting the bases and should therefore expedite their removal.
88. Powell 2001, 467–68.
89. See Roldán 1988, 148–50.
90. *El País* 1991.

TABLE 3.2
Criminal jurisdiction in Spain under the 1982 and 1989 agreements

Criminal jurisdiction agreement	Duration	Total no. of criminal jurisdiction cases	No. retained by Spain	Total exercised by U.S. or dismissed	U.S. exercise rate (%)
1982 agreement	May 1983 to May 1989 (6 years)	1294	80	1214	94
1989 agreement	May 1989 to April 2005[a] (16 years)	1096	18	1078	98.4

Source: Office of the Staff Judge Advocate, Office of Defense Cooperation, Madrid, Spain.
[a] End of reporting period; agreement is still in effect.

For the rest of the 1990s, political party competition focused on issues relating to the economy, decentralization and regionalism, and political corruption. The election of the PP's José Aznar as prime minister in 1996, breaking four consecutive terms of PSOE government, did not change the political demobilization of the bases issue. In fact, Aznar was eager to promote Atlantic ties and initiated Spain's full integration into NATO's military structure. In addition, Aznar established a NATO subregional command on Spanish territory and strongly backed the U.S. bombing of Iraq in 1998. The PSOE, in internal turmoil after the departure of González, did not contest any of these actions or in any way revisit the bases issue.

The broad PP-PSOE consensus on foreign policy matters came to a close after Aznar's reelection in 2000. He later showed unqualified support for the post-9/11 U.S.-led global war on terror and took pains to link his own hard-line anti-ETA position to that effort. Moreover, Aznar's misgivings about the benefits of European cooperation for increased security seemed justified when France refused to back Spain's claim to sovereignty during the Spanish-Moroccan skirmish over uninhabited Perejil Island in summer 2002. Aznar emerged from the episode with an understanding that Spanish security interests would be better promoted if Spain became an unwavering ally of the United States on the global stage.[91] In 2002, he signed an extension of the U.S. basing agreement that allowed the United States to construct more airplane hangars and a runway extension in

91. Author's interviews with Spanish senators from the Partido Popular, Madrid, April 2005.

Rota and granted a U.S. criminal intelligence team the right to conduct terrorism-related investigations on Spanish soil.[92] Despite some media attention and criticism of the intelligence team provision, the 2002 accord passed Parliament and was supported by both main parties.[93]

The greatest split between the PP and PSOE came over the issue of supporting U.S.-led military action against Iraq. Aznar's strong backing of OIF, including his high-profile appearance with Bush and Blair at an eleventh-hour summit in the Azores, was opposed by 85–90 percent of the Spanish public. Despite Aznar's stance on Iraq, the public broadly trusted his competence and credibility, and most opinion polls showed his PP successor Mariano Rajoy comfortably ahead of his inexperienced PSOE challenger, José Luis Rodríguez Zapatero, just days before the March 2004 elections. On March 11, however, the largest single terrorist attack on Spanish soil—a series of coordinated train bombs—killed two hundred commuters in Madrid. Aznar was convinced that it was the work of ETA and called newspaper editors to assure them of the accuracy of his sources. However, the investigation revealed that the bombings were the work of an al-Qaeda cell, not Basque separatists, at which point Aznar's credibility took a significant hit whereas Zapatero's anti-Iraq stance seemed justified. In a stunning election result, Zapatero defeated Rajoy and shortly after announced that he would fulfill his campaign pledge and withdraw Spanish troops from the Iraqi theater.

After Zapatero's announcement, U.S.-Spanish relations markedly deteriorated, although at no point did the Zapatero government entertain the possibility of withdrawing the blanket permission given to the United States to use Rota and Morón in support of OIF.[94] U.S. airplanes continued to fly dozens of daily sorties from the bases. Unlike the mid-1980s, when González denounced the U.S. campaign against Libya and prevented the United States from using bases on Spanish soil as points from which to attack Libya, in 2004 PSOE officials decoupled the issue of Spanish troops in Iraq with authorization of base access for the Iraq campaign. When asked about the two issues, officials from the new PSOE government explained that the troop withdrawal honored the democratic wishes of the Spanish public, while maintaining a security commitment to an ally.[95] Even though

---

92. I am grateful to Charles Powell of the Real Instituto Elcano for informing me about the intelligence team provision.
93. *FBIS* 2002.
94. Author's interviews with Spanish and American defense officials, Madrid, April 2005.
95. Personal communication with high-ranking Spanish PSOE official, October 2005.

most opinion polls suggested that the Spanish public overwhelmingly opposed the use of bases for OIF-related missions—polling before the war found that only 20 percent favored the use of the bases, whereas 74 percent opposed their use for OIF[96]—only Izquierda Unida among political parties paid any attention to the issue, and the media seemed to take little interest in the matter. The basing issue, in the midst of significant bilateral strains and political campaigning, was still demobilized and politically stable. Similarly, revelations that the CIA in 2004 and 2005 had used airports in the Canary Islands to transfer prisoners to secret interrogation sites precipitated an internal investigation by the Spanish government that found the government and appropriate ministries had "acted in conformity with the law."[97] The European Parliament would later challenge this finding after its own investigation into host-country complicity with the CIA.[98] However, the CIA scandal underscored how, despite their use for a number of controversial military campaigns, the U.S. bases in Spain are no longer a matter for high politics and debate among the major parties. Base access agreements with the United States are now regarded as institutionalized democratic commitments, whether their use is supported by the Spanish public or not, and are now a stable feature of the bilateral relationship.

U.S. Troops Reenter the Philippines under the Visiting Forces Agreement

U.S. forces departed their permanent base at Subic Bay in November 1992, but U.S. troops reentered the Philippines in 2000, albeit in a visiting or rotational capacity to participate in joint military exercises in Balikatan on the southern island of Mindanao. This renewed security cooperation was driven by Philippine fears of a growing Chinese regional threat; by growing Islamic and communist insurgencies in the south of the country; and by the Armed Forces of the Philippines (AFP)'s need to modernize and update itself through U.S. military transfers and training.[99] In 1999 the Philippine Senate ratified the Visiting Forces Agreement (VFA), originally signed in 1998, to govern the renewed "temporary" presence of U.S. troops in the Philippines. As in Spain, the procedural legitimacy of the new governing arrangement has helped to depoliticize the renewed U.S. military

96. Del Campo and Camacho 2003, 108–9.
97. BBC News 2005.
98. European Parliament 2007, 19.
99. An analytically helpful overview of the political economy of the AFP and its needs is offered in De Castro 2005.

presence, although elements of the new agreement have been subjected to some political scrutiny and debate.

In the wake of the 9/11 attacks, this renewed cooperation has expanded and intensified. Philippine president Gloria Macapagal-Arroyo immediately offered overflight rights and the use of Subic Bay and Clark to international coalition partners for the Afghanistan campaign. In summer 2002, 1,200 U.S. troops conducted joint exercises with host-country troops during a six-month high-profile exercise on Mindanao known as Balikatan 02-1. The exercises, coupled with $19 million in military aid in 2002 to the AFP, were designed to improve the capacity of the Philippine army to fight Islamist separatists linked with al-Qaeda, most notably the Islamist Abu Sayyaf group. And in November 2002 the two countries signed a five-year Military Logistic Support Arrangement (MLSA) that provided a formal framework for bilateral logistical cooperation, transfers, and interoperability.[100]

In February 2003 the two governments announced that nearly 2,000 troops, including 400 U.S. Special Forces and 1,000 U.S. Marines, would join Philippine troops in a combined forces operation against Abu Sayyaf on the island of Sulu.[101] The exercise would have coincided with Operation Iraqi Freedom, with the U.S. Pentagon keen to emphasize the alleged links between Abu Sayyaf and the Iraqi government. However, news of the impending operation generated a media storm in the Philippines, so on February 28, 2003, officials of both nations announced the cancellation of the operation.[102] Remarkably, Pentagon officials admitted that the Philippine government had asked them to reclassify the operation as an "exercise," to avoid domestic criticism on constitutional grounds.[103] But ever since, U.S. forces have maintained a presence in Mindanao under the VFA, although much of their exact role and purpose remains secret and underreported, while the AFP has received a steady stream of military and technical assistance from the U.S. side.[104]

The "temporary" reintroduction of U.S. forces under the VFA initially generated some opposition among a disjointed coalition of media commentators, left-leaning NGOs, right-wing nationalists, and anti-Macapagal critics, especially because of the standing constitutional prohibition on the

100. De Castro 2005, 491.
101. BBC News 2003. On the Abu Sayyaf–Iraq link, see Hookway 2003.
102. See De Castro 2006, 114–16.
103. *Houston Chronicle* 2003.
104. For overviews, see De Castro 2005, 2006.

stationing foreign troops and military bases.[105] Yet, with a few exceptions, including the February 2003 aborted exercise, the increased frequency and scale of this bilateral military cooperation was widely supported by the Philippine public as part of the overall campaign to defeat insurgents in the south. Only a handful of protestors turned up at public demonstrations against the U.S. deployment, and according to one report in early 2002, 84 percent of respondents to a survey favored U.S. military assistance and involvement in the southern campaign.[106]

The Smith Incident and Custody Dispute

The domestic politics of the VFA as opposed to those of the previous MBA and SOFA are highlighted by the aftermath of a high-profile sexual assault case involving U.S. military personnel. In November 2005 at Subic Bay, Corporal Lance Smith, a twenty-one-year old marine, raped a twenty-two-year old Filipina. In December 2006 a local Philippine court convicted Smith and sentenced him to forty years in prison; three other off-duty marines were acquitted of being accessories to the crime. Immediately following his conviction and sentencing, U.S. authorities demanded that Smith be handed over and held in U.S. custody for the duration of his appeal, as stipulated by the VFA criminal jurisdiction guidelines. In their attempts to regain custody, U.S. officials threatened to cancel future bilateral military exercises and cut off military aid if Smith was not handed over.[107] The Philippine Executive, Foreign Affairs office, and Department of Justice all backed the U.S. position, as did the AFP, whereas elements of the media and NGOs denounced the action as heavy-handed and not respecting the equality and sovereignty of the host state.[108] In February 2007 the Philippine Supreme Court dismissed a petition, brought by the rape victim's layers, to void the VFA's one-year limit for judicial proceedings against accused U.S. personnel.

The aftermath of the Smith case also testifies to the relative lack of political concern for and the legitimate status of the VFA and U.S. forces in the Philippines, especially when compared with the turbulent politics of the immediate post-Marcos era. Unlike the earlier MBA, the VFA has contractual legitimacy, despite its unpopular criminal jurisdiction procedures regarding custody. For example, in response to criticism of the custody

105. De Castro 2003, 982–85.
106. Hookway 2002.
107. Conde 2006.
108. Shanker 2006.

transfer, interior secretary Ronaldo Puno insisted that the legal terms of the VFA had to be honored and noted that "we cannot treat our international agreements conditionally."[109] Moreover, a comfortable majority of Philippine senators, including members of the opposition, refused to publicly call for renegotiation of the VFA.[110] And despite a steady diet of media articles and editorials on the VFA in spring 2007, the issue played a minimal role in the national legislative elections in May 2007.[111] As in the case of post-1988 Spain, the U.S. military presence in the Philippines under the VFA has been institutionalized as a democratically ratified commitment. Regardless of occasional publicized incidents or controversial exercises involving U.S. forces, the U.S. troop presence is not politically contested at the level that the U.S. basing presence had been during the democratization era.

Conclusion: Dictatorship and Subsequent Contractual Legitimacy

In Spain and the Philippines the politics of the U.S. basing presence has varied broadly, according to institutional developments and political incentives within these host countries (see fig. 3.3).

During different political eras, dictators and democrats have used various aspects of the U.S. basing presence to further their domestic political interests. The initial basing agreements signed with Spain and the Philippines were hierarchical and reflected the high degree of host-regime dependence on these contracts. In Spain, the Madrid Pact offered a lifeline of international recognition and legitimacy to the Franco regime, allowing it to slowly integrate into the international community over the next twenty years. In the Philippines, the benefits of hosting bases were more material. The 1947 Military Bases Agreement, along with the accompanying trade accord, stemmed from the weak position in which the government found itself after World War II and its need to maintain close relations with the United States. Rising nationalism in the democratizing

---

109. Philippine Information Agency 2007.

110. Tan 2007. The story also notes that in his support of the transfer of custody, opposition Senator Alfredo S. Kim commented, "every state has the duty to carry out in good faith its obligations arising from treaties and other sources of international law, and it may not invoke provisions in its Constitution or its laws as an excuse for failure to perform this duty." I also thank Andrew Yeo for his observations on the issue.

111. I thank Prof. Renato De Castro of the University of LaSalle for his insights on this point.

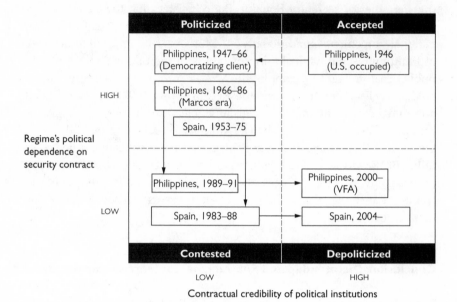

Figure 3.3. Evolution of base politics, Spain and Philippines

climate of the 1950s allowed domestic leaders to challenge the credibility of the agreement for domestic political purposes, culminating in the 1959 Bohlen-Serrano revised accord. The authoritarian Ferdinand Marcos perfected the two-level game of base politics and strategically used base renegotiations to secure large aid payments, which he then used to consolidate his political power and his network of cronies.

After both dictators fell, the credibility of the contracts that governed the U.S. military presence was questioned and undermined. For populist politicians and media commentators, the faces of Franco and Marcos were inextricably entwined with the U.S. basing presence, thereby rendering these previous agreements undemocratic and invalid. In both cases, this contractual uncertainty combined with the dynamics of democratization to inflict an operational price on the U.S. military. In Spain, after the initial pacted transition, the PSOE campaigned on an anti-NATO platform to gain power. After including a provision for base reductions in the 1986 NATO referendum, PSOE negotiators successfully used the referendum and its public support to fundamentally overhaul the Franco-era agreement. In the process they broke with the traditional bases-for-cash formula and effectively evicted U.S. forces from Torrejón and Zaragoza. However, the consolidation of the Spanish party system and the PSOE's refusal to engage with the issue after it ratified the 1988 agreement ensured that the United States could continue its basing operations, even for controversial missions such as OIF. After the Spanish political system got over the "hump" of democratization and backlash, democratic consolidation effectively locked in the credibility of the basing contract within the institutions of the Spanish political state, turning it from a contested issue of party politics into an inviolable democratic commitment and bureaucratic matter.

In the Philippines, too, democratization produced a wave of debate and domestic political competition over the U.S. basing presence and its legal status. Political dissidents, who had once accused the United States of supporting the Marcos regime to retain its basing access, now found themselves in the position of negotiating a new basing agreement. Ultimately, the Philippine Senate, which had been mandated by the new constitution to ratify all new agreements on foreign military bases, vetoed the extension. The failed vote reflected not so much popular antibase sentiment but rather the tense relationship that had developed during the post-Marcos democratic transition between the legislature and the Aquino-led executive. The reintroduction of U.S. troops in 2002 to train Philippine armed forces and the ambiguous legal status of those troops once again reopened these constitutional controversies.

The cases of Spain and the Philippines have instructive political analogs in the cases of Greece and Thailand. In Greece, the United States established a number of military bases in the 1950s in the wake of its intervention in the Greek civil war, and it forged close ties with Greek intelligence and security services.[112] In 1967, a group of junior colonels led by George Papadopoulos, possibly backed by the CIA, orchestrated a coup against the Center Union's democratic government. The new military regime preserved its close ties with the United States and even negotiated an agreement with the U.S. Navy to home-port the Sixth Fleet at the port of Elefsina, near Athens.[113] But just as in Spain and the Philippines, the collapse of the dictatorship in 1974 triggered a number of democratizing dynamics

112. The founding agreement was "Agreement between the United States of America and the Kingdom of Greece concerning Military Facilities," signed October 12, 1953, *TIAS* 2868. For domestic political reactions, see Couloumbis 1966. For a comprehensive account of the bases and bilateral defense relations in the 1950s, see Stefanidis 2002. For an English-language overview, see Laganis 1993.

113. On the evolution of the home-porting agreement, see Woodhouse 1985.

that undermined the credibility of these deals and generated a political backlash against the U.S. military presence.[114] Interim prime minister Constantine Karamanlis cancelled the 1973 home-porting agreement, immediately renegotiated the legal status of the other military facilities, and demanded a significant increase in compensation under a new DECA.[115] In 1981, the fiery populist Andreas Papandreou and the Greek Socialists (PASOK) swept into power for the first time, largely on a platform calling for the removal of U.S. bases from Greece and withdrawal from NATO.[116] And just like his Socialist counterpart in Spain, Papandreou once in office moderated his anti-American foreign policy demands and signed a new five-year bases accord in 1983.[117] When the accord expired, Greece demanded the closure of the Hellenikon airbase, near Athens, which was finally shut down in 1991. After Greece secured this new agreement and significant U.S. troop reduction, the remaining U.S. facility in Souda Bay, Crete, never again became a salient national political issue. And just as Spain did in 2003 and 2004, Greece under Socialist auspices granted the use of Souda Bay to the U.S. military for the Iraq campaign, even though the PASOK government officially opposed the military action and despite intense Greek public opposition to the war. Tellingly, the Greek Defense Ministry refused an invitation from the U.S. Pentagon to hold a joint press conference about the Souda access agreement for OIF.[118]

In the Thai case, the United States supported anticommunist military governments in the 1950s with large amounts of military and economic assistance.[119] As a U.S. client state under successive military regimes in the 1960s, Thailand was developed into a launching pad for American operations in Vietnam. U.S. forces used Thai bases to carry out 75 percent of U.S. bombing campaigns in North Vietnam as well as surveillance and reconnaissance missions.[120] Over the decade, Thailand hosted up to 50,000 U.S. troops, 750 aircraft, and an extensive network of air and naval bases, as

114. On the Greek transition, see Diamandouros 1986.
115. See *New York Times* 1975. On the post-junta DECA negotiations, see Stearns 1992, 46–49.
116. For an overview, see Larrabee 1981–82.
117. On this evolution, see Couloumbis 1993; Loulis 1984–85.
118. Personal communication from high-ranking official in the Greek Ministry of Defense, April 2006.
119. See Fineman 1997.
120. Randolph 1986, 49–81. On the alliance and military campaign in the 1960s, see also Flynn 2001.

the country became awash in U.S.-sponsored military construction projects and foreign aid.[121] In addition, Bangkok was used as the transportation hub of the "secret war" in neighboring Laos, which by 1970 had escalated into a full-fledged bombing campaign.[122] With the end of the Vietnam War and Bangkok's turn toward China and Vietnam, both countries demanded that the Thai government evict all U.S. troops. In 1975, U.S. forces began a yearlong withdrawal.

Even under these considerable international pressures, however, the dynamics of democratization played a critical role in the actual termination of the U.S. presence. In November 1975 the Thai government indicated that it was willing to accept a residual deployment of 3,000 U.S. troops for a renewable two-year stay beyond the scheduled March 1976 withdrawal deadline. However, Prime Minister Kukrit Pramoj called for national elections in April 1976, and not wanting to appear weak on issues of Thai sovereignty, Kukrit attached a set of conditions for concluding a future U.S. base deal that included applying Thai domestic law to U.S. troops. U.S. negotiators could not agree to the provision and insisted that the United States at least retain exclusive jurisdiction for all on-duty offenses.[123] In the middle of a hotly contested election campaign, the Thai government refused to budge, and the final 4,500 U.S. troops were evacuated over the next four months without a new basing accord. On the eve of the national election, Kukrit proudly defended his stance by declaring, "We had to decide: Do we want 4,000 U.S. Ambassadors in Thailand?"[124]

The cases of Spain, Philippines, and Greece (less so Thailand) share the feature that the U.S. basing presence was seldom deemed vital by these host governments as critical to their national security. Rather, bases were used by the United States to support missions and campaigns in countries and regions outside that of the host. Accordingly, critics of the base politics theory might claim that these base hosts were able to renegotiate and terminate security contracts with the United States because such actions did not incur immediate security-related costs. In the next chapter, by contrast, I examine the evolution of base politics in Turkey and South

---

121. See Randolph 1986, 82–125; Viksnins 1973.
122. In 1971, 47 percent of tactical air strikes against Laos were flown from bases in Thailand. Randolph 1986, 148.
123. Previously, U.S. troops had enjoyed extraterritoriality because the countries had not signed a formal SOFA. Flynn 2001, 308–9; Randolph 1986, 189–92.
124. Flynn 2001, 309.

Korea, two cases in which the U.S. basing presence played a more vital security and deterrence function in the defense of these hosts. However, even in these more security-intensive environments, the basing issue again became implicated in the political dynamics of domestic democratization and institutional change.

CHAPTER 4

South Korea and Turkey

From Common Defense to Political Uncertainty

U.S. forces in South Korea and Turkey, unlike those in Spain and the Philippines, were first deployed for mutual defense and to deter the aggression of a common enemy. During the 1950s, the regimes of Syngman Rhee in Korea and Adnan Menderes in Turkey strategically used the U.S. military presence and the accompanying heavy flow of aid to solidify their military alliances and to consolidate their internal political rule. After this initial period, however, with its clear, common purpose of security, the political status of the bases in these two countries diverged as domestic political change and democratization undermined the credibility of U.S. base contracts in both countries. The timing of these challenges varied as a function of Korea's punctuated late democratization and Turkey's democratizing fits and starts.

Whereas in Korea the domestic political system was characterized by authoritarian rule for several decades until it opened up rapidly and deeply in the early 1990s, in Turkey democratization occurred in bursts from the 1960s through the 1980s, as the military intervened in domestic politics on three separate occasions (1960, 1971, and 1980). In Korea, the repressive regimes of Park Chung Hee (1961–79) and Chun Doo Hwan (1980–88) depended heavily on the substantial U.S. military presence to provide security and deter North Korea, but these autocrats also viewed the U.S. military presence as critical to their domestic legitimacy and as an underlying social contract that guaranteed security to South Korean society. As a result, Republic of Korea (ROK) regimes in the 1960s and 1970s fiercely opposed unilateral attempts by the United States to draw down troops and consistently emphasized the magnitude of the existential security threat posed by the North. By contrast, during the democratizing and politically turbulent 1960s in Turkey, the U.S. basing presence rapidly became a highly charged domestic issue. Rising anti-American sentiment, the growing influence of new leftist parties and social movements, and a number of base-related incidents and sovereign infringements by the U.S. military prompted the Turkish government to renegotiate many of these basing provisions. In the 1970s, after another military coup and restoration of civilian rule, a democratizing Turkish government actually halted U.S. base operations and declared the governing base contract invalid after the United States imposed an arms embargo.

After the end of the cold war, regional and internal changes once again altered the credibility of the basing contracts and recast the political significance of the remaining U.S. bases in these countries. In Korea, the late but comprehensive democratization of Korean society engendered an intense backlash against the U.S. military presence and its governing agreements. As in Spain and the Philippines, former political dissidents and activists linked U.S. bases with support for previous nondemocratic governments and argued that many elements of the relationship, especially the status of forces agreement and its environmental and criminal jurisdiction procedures, should be revised and made more evenhanded. These campaigns acquired a strength and political potency unmatched in other cases in this book by virtue of the ability of antibase NGOs and media outlets to develop and then exploit political networks, to employ new information technologies to magnify base-related incidents, and to place basing issues on the national political agenda.

The role and purpose of the U.S. military presence in Turkey were also questioned in the 1990s, despite the significant reduction in U.S. troop levels and the closure of many cold war–era military installations. As the United States and its Western allies used airbases in Turkey to enforce a no-fly zone against Iraq, Turkish politicians, the media, and even the military questioned whether these operations undermined fundamental Turkish national interests. In March 2003 the Turkish parliament denied U.S. forces passage into Turkish territory for the U.S. military campaign against Iraq. The vote reflected persistent fears among individual parliamentarians about the destabilization of Turkish borders and the U.S. military, but it also illustrated how a volatile party system and jurisdictional competition can veto base access, even when the sitting prime minister actually intended to approve the measure.

Establishing the Common Defense, 1945–1960

Korea: Occupation, War, and Clientelism

The origins of the U.S. military presence in Korea can be traced to the latter stages of the Second World War. With U.S. planners focusing squarely on Japan, they failed to conjure a detailed blueprint for Korea's future governance. In August 1945, a U.S. military coordinating committee reached an agreement with the Soviets to divide up the Korean peninsula along the 38th parallel and accept the surrender of Japanese forces in their respective sectors. Subsequently, the U.S. Seventh Infantry Division under the command of General John Hodge was sent to the south to establish administrative headquarters.

Hodge may have been an able military strategist, but by all accounts he lacked the necessary political and administrative experience to effectively govern Korea's political institutions.[1] Rather than allow Korean political institutions and civic organizations to develop from within, Hodge viewed any leftist or communal group as a potential Soviet-sponsored movement and security threat. For example, in 1946 he used American forces to put down a protest in Taegu and declared martial law. Hodge also allowed a group of landlords and wealthy elites, most of whom had collaborated with occupying Japanese forces, to help administer the U.S. occupation.[2] Finally, in an attempt to install Korean leaders who would share "an American point of view," Hodge repatriated a small group of Korean conservatives living in exile, the most important of whom was the seventy-year-old, long-term U.S. resident Syngman Rhee.[3] Rhee assumed the first presidency of the South when it was granted its independence in August 1948.

In late 1948, the United Nations passed a resolution calling for the withdrawal of all foreign troops from the Korean peninsula, and by June 1949, 47,500 U.S. troops had departed, leaving a small contingent of about 500.[4]

1. See Matray 1995.
2. Cumings 1997, 193–94. Also see Marten 2005, 155–56.
3. Cumings 1997, 197.
4. Sandars 2000, 181.

Just one year later, North Korea invaded the South. The United States, along with a sixteen-nation coalition including Turkey, sent troops to fight a three-year bloody conflict. Tellingly, Rhee used the war to consolidate his internal powers and do away with all pretense of running a democratic state. In 1952, with his term expiring, Rhee declared martial law and overrode the constitution, granting himself the presidency and autocratic powers.[5] Shrewdly, the Korean president used the murder of four American soldiers as the pretext for this power grab by blaming the killings on communists.[6]

The move plunged Korea into political crisis, but it also embarrassed Rhee's foreign allies, who had justified their intervention in terms of fighting for a democratic Korea. Ignoring opposition politicians' requests for intervention, the United States backed Rhee after deciding that despite his unsavory political behavior, he was a known quantity among ROK elites. In practice, however, Rhee rarely followed Washington's domestic political directives and strongly opposed elements of the war's conduct, including Washington's negotiated settlement in 1953. In the words of General Mark Clark, who described U.S.-ROK relations during the Korean War, "I found myself engaged in a two-front diplomatic battle . . . with the Communists at Panmunjom and with President Syngman Rhee in Seoul . . . the biggest trouble came from Rhee."[7] In 1953 U.S. planners formulated a secret contingency plan, known as Operation Everready, to depose Rhee and replace him with one of his generals, but the South Korean ruler proved remarkably adept at maintaining the loyalty of his military and survived politically.[8]

The Clientelist State of Syngman Rhee

Rhee's ability to use the U.S. military presence for his own domestic political purposes was amply demonstrated after the armistice for the remainder of his rule. He secured a mutual defense treaty in October 1953 very much along the lines of the U.S. agreement with the Philippines.[9] Rhee was not pleased that the treaty promised "mutual consultation" in the event of an external attack rather than an ironclad defense guarantee (Article II), but

5. Ra 1992.
6. Cumings 1997, 342.
7. As quoted in Park 1975, 97.
8. I thank Charles Armstrong for bringing this point to my attention.
9. "Mutual Defense Treaty between the United States of America and the Republic of Korea," signed October 1, 1953, *TIAS* 3097.

the indefinite duration of the treaty (Article VI) gave him some degree of security.[10] Article IV of the agreement granted the U.S. military "the right to dispose land, air and sea forces in and about the territory of the Republic of Korea," a clause that amounted to granting full and unrestricted use rights. After the war, American troops were reduced to about 60,000 and scattered across hundreds of facilities throughout the country, with a major set of army installations, including the Second and Seventh Infantry Divisions, concentrated along the demilitarized zone (DMZ) just north of Seoul. These U.S. Army "tripwire" installations were established to deter a North Korean offensive and still include the massive 3.5-acre Camp Casey and Camp Red Cloud, current headquarters to the Second Infantry Division. A network of airbases was created throughout the country, including bases at Osan, Taegu, Pusan, and Kunsan, along with the Fourth Missile Command, and a number of logistics and training facilities were spread throughout the ROK territory.[11] Yongsan Army Garrison, a 690-acre facility in the capital city Seoul, served as the headquarters of United States Army Korea, the Eighth Army, the United Nations command, and the combined U.S.-Korea command (see fig. 4.1).

Emphasizing the hierarchical nature of the arrangement, the ROK agreed to keep its forces under the UN command of the United States, a command that had been established initially in 1950 for operational purposes.[12] During this time, U.S. troops enjoyed near extraterritoriality under the Daejon Agreement, a wartime arrangement, because a SOFA was not signed until 1966.[13] South Korea had become a military client of the United States, but this military dependency did not always translate into actual political leverage over Rhee's heavy-handed internal rule.

Nevertheless, massive amounts of U.S. economic assistance accompanied this security support. American military commanders actually administered these aid flows from 1951 to 1959, which amounted to nearly 100 percent of the ROK government budget.[14] Although this assistance was originally intended to help establish a market-based system in

10. Sandars 2000, 183.
11. For details and individual base histories, see http://www.globalsecurity.org/military/facility/korea.htm.
12. The bilateral Combined Forces Command was established in 1978. The CFC is now commanded by a U.S. four-star general, with a Korean general serving as deputy commander.
13. The full texts of the 1966 and 1991 SOFAs and ancillary accords can be viewed at http://www.shaps.hawaii.edu/security/us/sofa1966_1991.html (accessed May 2007).
14. Cumings 1997, 304.

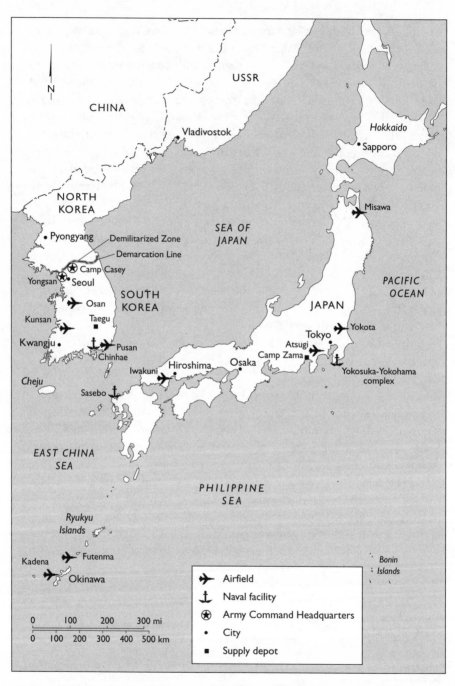

Figure 4.1. Major U.S. military facilities, South Korea and Japan, 1979.
Source: National Defense University

South Korea, Rhee used the money instead to implement a program of import-substitution industrialization in an attempt to rapidly construct a Japanese-style self-sufficient industrial base behind a protective wall.[15] Rhee's political clients and cronies also benefited from the assistance. The ROK ruler used a collection of complex exchange-rate regimes and import licenses to allow political clients to capture arbitrage from market differentials in aid goods and foreign exchange.[16] In addition, Rhee funneled supply contracts for the U.S. military to client firms, such as Samsung and Korean Airlines, that later established themselves as Korea's main industrial conglomerates. Just like Magsaysay or Marcos in the Philippines, Rhee knew exactly how to translate the U.S. military presence into economic support for his private political purposes and patronage machine. As Bruce Cumings observes, "Rhee extracted 'maximum rents from the global hegemon,' using the ROK's immense geopolitical leverage granted by the Cold War and his own inveterate skills as a tough poker player willing to cash in on the whole game, knowing the United States had no one else to rely on but him."[17] Economic dependence on the United States, nevertheless, did not diminish Rhee's leverage with his superpower patron or his two-level games and brinkmanship.[18]

Turkey: The Truman Doctrine, Regime Dependence, and the Depoliticized 1950s

The establishment of bases in Turkey and U.S. relations with the ruling Turkish Democratic Party in the 1950s exhibited important similarities to the Korean case. After its World War II–era doctrine of neutrality, Turkey found that the formation of NATO and the Soviet threat forced it to rapidly integrate into the U.S. security orbit. Throughout World War II, Moscow had pressured Ankara to establish Soviet bases in the Bosporus and Dardanelles, a request that Ankara refused for the last time in 1946.[19] American officials feared that such bases would be used to project Soviet power throughout the Eastern Mediterranean and Middle East, so they pressed to draw Turkey into the Western security sphere.[20] The Truman

15. See Cumings 1997, 304–9; Haggard 1990, 54–61.
16. Haggard 1990, 57.
17. Cumings 1997, 306.
18. Also see Haggard 1990, 60–61.
19. I thank Prof. Nur Bilge Criss of Bilkent University for clarifying this issue.
20. See Leffler 1985.

Doctrine in 1947 brought $792 million in general aid and $687 million in military aid to Turkey over the next five years.[21] Rebuffed by Washington for immediate NATO membership in 1949, Turkey impressed Washington by sending 4,500 troops to fight in the Korean War, the third largest allied contingent. On February 1952 Turkey, along with Greece, was admitted to NATO, paving the way for the United States to rapidly construct an extensive network of new facilities on Turkish territory that aimed to counter the Soviet Union.

As U.S. forces were moved throughout Turkey, the two sides signed a number of base agreements and related security contracts, most of them secret or even informal. A public agreement—the Exchange of Letters and Memos—was signed in January 1952, while the NATO Status of Forces Agreement was ratified by the Turkish parliament in 1954, with a secret military facilities agreement concluded the same year.[22] The bundle of agreements reflected the broad array of functions and assorted installations that were constructed on Turkish territory. The most important operational installations were the airbases at Incirlik, near the city of Adana close to the Syrian border, and Izmir, which in 1957 became headquarters for the NATO Sixth Allied Tactical Air Force.[23] Additional airfields were established at Diyarbakir, Yesilkoy, and Balikesir. A docking and storage naval facility at Iskenderun was constructed to accommodate and resupply the Sixth Fleet. Along the northern border and Black Sea coasts—in Marmara, Karamursel, Samsun, and Sinop—the United States constructed a network of early warning radar installations and facilities to gather intelligence and monitor Soviet missile and nuclear tests.[24] By 1961, class Jupiter intermediate-range ballistic missiles had been deployed in Çigli, near the city of Izmir (see fig. 4.2).

While these various sites were under construction, the total number of American troops, officials, and dependents in Turkey reached about 24,000.[25] American military personnel were particularly visible in large cities such as Ankara, Izmir, and Adana. With the exception of the criminal jurisdiction issue, which drew some criticism in the Turkish military, relations over the bases during the 1950s were generally positive and

---

21. Criss 1993, 341.
22. "Exchange of Letters on Mutual Security," January 7, 1952, *TIAS* 2621.
23. See Nash 1957, 173.
24. For useful individual functional descriptions, see Gunter 2005, 115–16.
25. Harris 1972, 56.

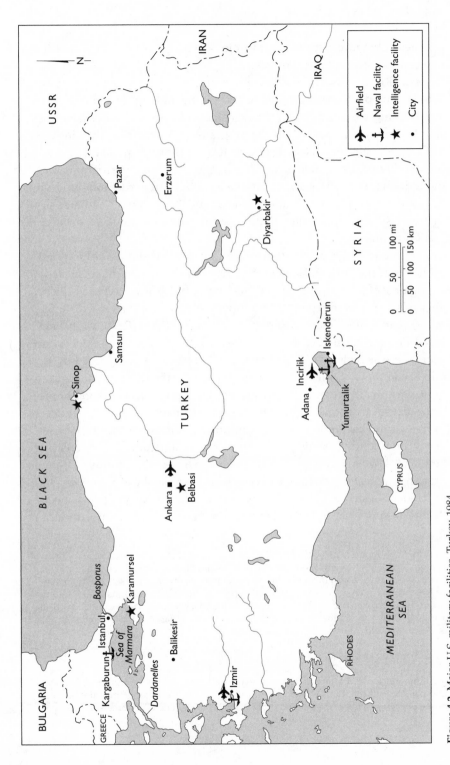

Figure 4.2. Major U.S. military facilities, Turkey, 1984.
Source: Congressional Research Service

reflected a broad consensus within the Turkish political system that the two countries shared common security goals.[26]

As in Korea, a broad set of aid agreements and exchange programs supplemented the basing agreements. Strong military-to-military links and training were conducted through the Joint American Military Mission for Aid to Turkey (JAMMAT) program (later renamed the Joint U.S. Military Mission for Aid to Turkey, or JUSMAT, program), and hundreds of Turkish officers participated in exchange and training programs with the U.S. military. American aid targeted various infrastructural improvements with security implications, including the country's rudimentary highway system. The United States also funded education and development programs.

This broad array of assistance programs served the domestic political needs of the Turkish Democratic Party (DP). The DP, which enjoyed a strong base of support among the Turkish peasantry, was elected in 1950 in Turkey's first fully independent multiparty elections, inflicting a historical first defeat on the Kemalist Republican People's Party (RPP). At its helm stood Prime Minister Adnan Menderes, who governed for a total of ten years (he was reelected in 1954 and 1957) before he was deposed by the military in 1960.[27] Over the course of the decade, the DP used its access to these various aid programs to reward domestic political clients and implement distributive policies through its vast patronage network.[28] Menderes oversaw a Turkish economy that continually teetered on the brink of solvency, and he used American aid to subsidize agriculture and construct large state-owned projects rather than implement market reforms.[29] Despite growing domestic and American criticisms over aid abuse, Menderes and DP leaders eagerly fostered the impression that their party enjoyed special American support.[30] In 1958, Menderes once again turned to his American

26. The Nash report (1957, 175) described this commonality of purpose in the following manner: "Turkey's relations with the United States have been unusually close and friendly since 1947, mainly due to the mutuality of our objectives in achieving security against the Soviet threat. Turkey relies for her security on the United States, and, realizing this, has willingly placed her real estate at our disposal for bases that serve our mutual interests. That she has not lost in the arrangement can be seen by a glance at the enormous total of our economic and military aid in the past decade."
27. Menderes himself was hanged in 1961.
28. Sunar and Sayari 1986, 173.
29. See Harris 1972, 71–76.
30. A number of devastating critiques were leveled in the American press about fraud and abuse in U.S. aid programs to Turkey and the DP's use of funds for its own political purposes. See Drake 1958. See also Manly 1959a, 1959b, 1959c, a detailed three-story critique.

patron for domestic purposes when he secured a bilateral agreement with the U.S. that promised American intervention in Turkish politics in the event that communists or other forms of "internal aggression" threatened the integrity of the regime.[31] This agreement, together with Menderes's abuse of U.S. aid flows, caused opposition political leaders, the press, the bureaucracy, and even members of the military to resent the DP's grip on power, which was actively supported by Washington in the interests of preserving its Turkish basing rights and security cooperation.[32]

On May 27, 1960, growing political turmoil came to a head as the Turkish military deposed Menderes and established the National Unity Committee. The committee guaranteed existing basing rights and security agreements, although some members of the junta expressed concerns that the basing accords had undermined Turkish sovereignty and that the country was becoming an "American colony." Throughout the 1950s, Menderes had granted basing rights in return for economic and military assistance packages that kept the country and his regime afloat.[33] However, during the next two decades, Turkey's volatile democratization ignited a more politically charged debate over the scope and legitimacy of these base rights.

Cold War Security Relations and Domestic Interactions

South Korea, 1960s–1980s: Supporting Strongmen

Over the next three decades the U.S. military presence in South Korea was linked to the undemocratic tendencies and repressive policies of a series

---

31. On the bilateral agreement, see Ahmad 1977, 297; Harris 1972, 221–23.

32. Harris 1972, 81. Harris further observed that "Menderes and his colleagues apparently expected that the U.S. government would bail them out of their economic difficulties. The DP leadership believed that Turkey's political importance to the West would induce its allies to provide extensive economic assistance even if the Turks refused to follow the course recommended by their partners. Such a calculation was by no means farfetched. While the U.S. aid mission continually pressed the Turkish government to retrench and follow a more rational economic policy, in the end the United States always came forward to provide essential assistance to keep the Turkish economy afloat. Indeed, American aid nearly doubled over its previous rate during these crucial years" (73). However, the military's preparation for the coup could be traced back to 1955 because the majority of officers favored the RPP. I thank Prof. Henri Barkey for his insights on this issue.

33. On the basing rights as the fundamental U.S.-Turkish bargain in the Menderes era, also see Pope and Pope 1998, 84–93.

of Korean strongmen. However, ROK rulers themselves also manipulated the U.S. military presence and the command structure to justify their internal actions and political crackdowns. Even in situations in which the United States did not condone the brutal actions of ROK rulers—the most dramatic being the Kwangju crackdown in 1980—the ROK regime deliberately fostered the impression that the United States fully supported its hard-line policies. In his assessment of how authoritarian military rulers managed at least some basis of support in Korean society, Victor Cha observes that "the provision of security (and economic growth) in this security-scarce environment became the Korean social contract. By providing the security good, authoritarian political regimes purchased their political legitimacy from the electorate despite acceding to power through the most illegitimate of means and draconian practices."[34] The U.S. military presence was a critical part of this internal security contract, one that Korean rulers depended on for their internal political legitimacy and survival.

Korea's Security-Dependent Autocrats: From Rhee to Chun

From 1961 to 1988, Korea was ruled by three successive strongmen with military ties, and the ROK armed forces played some role in each regime's transfer and consolidation of power. Given the combined command structure, the U.S. military was also implicated in bringing about these regime changes, although its actual capacity to control the domestic activities of the ROK military probably has been overestimated.

For a brief period in 1960, Rhee's wavering rule created an opening for political liberalization. Rhee fraudulently won a national election in March 1960, and the victory ignited student protests throughout the country. Rhee asked for, and received, permission from the U.S. commander to dispatch Korean marines to trouble spots within South Korea, and he declared martial law.[35] On April 19, the situation dramatically escalated as more than 100,000 political dissidents marched on the presidential palace. One week later, the U.S. ambassador and commanding general visited Rhee to demand his resignation, and on April 29 the leader left for exile in Hawaii. Over the next year, the opposition Democratic Party organized and administered the government, however, weak economic conditions, growing popular unrest, and a perceived leftward

34. Cha 2003, 205.
35. Cumings 1997, 344.

drift convinced the Korean military that it needed to intervene in national political affairs.

On May 16, 1961, Park Chung Hee and a small group of officers carried out a coup and asserted military control, creating a government that would last uninterrupted for another three decades. U.S. forces did not intervene in this internal crisis. Park's government, like Rhee's rule before him, was characterized by repression, constant constitutional abrogation, and the suppression of political dissidents. Park justified his rule through a civilian election in 1963, but he retained a predominantly military cabinet, and periodically dissolved the National Assembly and declared martial law. In his dealings with U.S. officials, Park repeatedly emphasized the country's tense security environment to justify his heavy-handed internal rule. For example, when U.S. president Jimmy Carter confronted Park about his spotty human rights record at a July 5, 1979, meeting, Park justified his record by stating:

> Our capital is only 25 miles from the DMZ. Right across the DMZ hundreds of thousands of soldiers are poised. We must deal with the situation whether we like it or not, otherwise we might fall into the same situation as the Vietnamese. Some time ago several members of Congress came to call on me. I told them that if dozens of Soviet divisions were deployed at Baltimore, the U.S. Government could not permit its people to enjoy the same freedoms they do now. If these Soviets dug tunnels and sent commando troops into the District of Columbia, then U.S. freedoms would be more limited. We support the human rights policy. . . . But the survival of 37 million people is at stake, and some restraint is required.[36]

Park's eighteen-year tenure dramatically ended in 1979 when the head of the Korean CIA assassinated him over his hard-line handling of domestic unrest and political dissent. On December 12 of the same year, General Chun Doo Hwan assumed power through yet another military coup with the aid of South Korean forces that, without U.S. authorization, had left their posts at the DMZ under the command of General Roh Tae Woo (who would succeed Chun in 1988).[37] Again, although U.S. forces were nominally in control, they were not in communication with the dissenters until the group had consolidated power. And although neither American

---

36. "Memorandum of Conversation," Carter-Park meeting, White House, Washington, D.C., July 5, 1979, *DDRS*.
37. Oberdorfer 2001, 116–18.

civilians nor the U.S. military was impressed with the new regime, they eventually accepted it as a fait accompli.[38]

The long-standing perception that the United States preferred South Korean strongmen to democratically elected leaders was reinforced in February 1981 when President Reagan invited Chun to the White House as the new administration's first visiting foreign head of state. The trip, coming just a few months after the explosive Kwangju incident (described later in this chapter), crystallized the notion among Korea's wavering political elite that Chun's takeover was irreversible.[39] And despite Chun agreeing to lift martial law and commute political dissident Kim Dae Jung's death sentence to life imprisonment, Korean political dissidents felt betrayed by Washington's decisive support for yet another ROK military ruler.

ROK Opposition to U.S. Troop Reductions

Victor Cha's observation about the nature of the Korean social contract and the dependence of Korean leaders on the U.S. military is critically important for understanding why South Korea's authoritarian rulers so vehemently opposed U.S. proposals for force reductions on the peninsula. The presence of U.S. forces in Korea was essential not only for deterring the North but for serving as an internal reminder that the South constantly "needed security" and hence military rule. Accordingly, reductions in U.S. troops gave the appearance of U.S. abandonment and threatened the internal sources of Korean rulers' legitimacy as well as the balance of forces with the North.[40] During the 1960s, U.S. officials had pressured Seoul to contribute to the war effort in Vietnam. Partially out of fear that the U.S. troop commitment on the peninsula might shrink, Korean officials steadily increased its contribution to Vietnam as ROK troops reached 50,000 by 1969. In exchange, United States Forces Korea (USFK) commanders and President Lyndon Johnson guaranteed that the U.S. force level would be

---

38. In a cable to Washington right after the coup, U.S. ambassador William Gleysteen wrote: "the December 12 incident is bad news from our point of view. The military of Korea who have remained remarkably united for 18 years under the firm hand of Park Chung Hee have now engaged in acts of insubordination which have not only generated animosities that may take years to work their way out but have also set a precedent for others to follow. In doing so, they totally ignored the Combined Forces Command's responsibilities, either ignoring impact on the U.S. or coolly calculating that it would not make a difference." As quoted in Oberdorfer 2001, 119.
39. Oberdorfer 2001, 137–38.
40. On the politics of abandonment, see Cha 2000; Nam 1986.

maintained and could only be changed subject to consultations with the ROK government.[41]

The pledge, however, did not extend into the Nixon administration. As part of a broader plan to reduce its forces in Asia and shift the defense bur-den further onto host countries, President Richard Nixon announced in 1970 that the United States would withdraw the Seventh Infantry Division, about 20,000 troops, from the Korean peninsula. Made without prior consultation, the announcement was greeted with shock and disbelief in the ROK government.[42] Within a week of the troop reduction announcement, the ROK National Assembly unanimously passed a resolution declaring that the United States had betrayed the loyalty that Korea had shown in Vietnam.[43] Different segments of Korean society such as the media and the military also expressed their vehement objection to the plan.[44] The psychological impact of abandonment was so politically devastating that the ROK government took out advertisements in major American newspapers and Prime Minister Chong Ilkwon threatened to withdraw troops from Vietnam and even abandon a section of the DMZ. None of these threats materialized, although the ROK government demanded $4 billion as compensation when the 20,000 men of the Seventh Infantry Division were finally pulled in March 1971 (in actuality ROK received about $1.5 billion).[45] A similar attempt by President Carter in the late 1970s to withdraw another 10,000 troops without consultation was halted by vehement Korean lobbying of the U.S. Congress and by the U.S. Defense Intelligence Agency's dramatic announcement in January 1979 that the numbers of North Korean forces were far greater than previous estimates.[46]

The Social and Economic Impact of the Bases

The bases themselves generated their own social dynamics and fair share of tensions, especially after the mid-1970s. Throughout the 1950s and 1960s, base relations with local communities tended to be cordial and economically lucrative. Still an economically impoverished country, ROK appreciated that the bases infused hard currency into the Korean economy and generated entire small towns designed to cater to U.S. troops. As in

41. Sandars 2000, 190.
42. Cha 2003, 65–69; Moon 1997, 58–67.
43. Cha 2003, 64.
44. Moon 1997, 58–67.
45. Sandars 2000, 190–91.
46. On the Carter troop reduction episode, see Oberdorfer 2001, 84–108. Carter later expressed his doubts about the accuracy and timing of the DIA estimate.

other base hosts, the black market for trading goods that were imported tax free onto U.S. bases was widespread.

Perhaps the most important of these ties, from both a social and economic perspective, was the growth and institutionalization of prostitution near the U.S. bases. Katharine Moon points out that the ROK government not only tolerated the activities of "comfort women" but also actively encouraged and regulated the practice, only clamping down after it received U.S. requests to do so in the 1970s.[47] Initially, prostitutes were brought onto the bases on weekends, but as the bases developed into permanent fixtures, clubs, bars, and brothels became common features of basing towns.[48] By some Korean organizations' estimates, over one million Korean women worked in the camp towns through the 1980s, or about one in six South Korean women between the ages of eighteen to thirty-five.[49] The sex industry also spawned countless illegitimate children and led to an extremely high rate of venereal disease among U.S. troops in Korea.[50]

Base relations markedly deteriorated throughout the country in the 1970s. The withdrawal of 20,000 troops under Nixon decimated several camp towns and local communities. Local property values plummeted, and comfort women and small business owners became unemployed or were forced to relocate to areas that retained U.S. forces. Also, racial tensions within the U.S. military peaked at the beginning of the 1970s, as black U.S. soldiers complained of open discrimination in camp towns and the informal segregation of base towns. During this time as well, USFK pressured the ROK to improve social conditions on the remaining bases, an initiative reluctantly met by ROK officials after twenty years of not addressing such issues at the highest level.[51]

Korea's spectacular economic development also generated indirect base-related tensions. As the Korean economy roared into the 1970s and 1980s, the gap in the economic power of U.S. troops versus that of average Korean citizens shrank and then disappeared altogether. Base-related businesses lost their economic appeal for Koreans, who were now part of a modern and dynamic economy. By the late 1990s Korean women had

47. Moon 1997.
48. Also see Cumings 1992.
49. Baker 2004, 156.
50. According to Moon (1997, 92–93), a medical study in 1972 revealed that more than 75 percent of U.S. troops were infected with venereal disease.
51. Moon 1997, 106–24. Moon provides a fascinating account of the political impact of the cleanup campaign.

almost entirely gotten out of the sex trade; most base-area comfort women were now foreign nationals such as Russians and Filipinas, who were brought to Korea on entertainment visas.[52]

Demographic change also generated community tensions. Originally, most U.S. facilities had been dispersed to relatively isolated areas or the edge of cities and towns.[53] Economic development brought increased urbanization, and the expanding cities enveloped many bases. As Korea's economy grew, many of the USFK bases became the more blighted socio-economic areas of these cities. The most striking, and politically controversial, example of urban growth can be seen at Camp Yongsan, the massive 690-acre facility in Seoul that has served as the headquarters of U.S. Forces Korea, the Eighth Army, and the base for the Common Forces Command. Initially located on the outskirts of Seoul, the Korean capital, on the site of former Japanese Imperial Army headquarters, Yongsan base was eventually encircled as a result of Seoul's rapid expansion, turning the camp into a massive American installation located at the heart of South Korea's capital.

Massacre at Kwangju, 1980

No single episode has generated more criticism about the role of the U.S. forces in internal Korean politics than the ROK's brutal suppression of a student-led revolt at Kwangju in May 1980. Kwangju's continued political symbolism—like that of the Palomares incident in Spain or the 1995 rape incident in Okinawa—has crystallized for many Koreans the view that the U.S. military remained utterly indifferent toward and even supportive of the authoritarian ROK and its repressive excesses. During the democratization era of the 1990s and 2000s, Kwangju became an important narrative and a powerful symbol for mobilizing antibasing activists and anti-American protests.[54]

Events at Kwangju were triggered when students and activists protested Chun's seizure of power. In May 1980, tens of thousands of student protestors took to the streets to demand elections and an end to military rule. ROK civilian and military officials raised the possibility with their American counterparts of using military force to control the demonstrations. On May 13, Chun proclaimed that the protests had been instigated by North

52. Author's interviews with U.S. public affairs and military officials, Seoul, May 2004.
53. Author's interview with U.S. political affairs official, Seoul, May 2004.
54. On the continuing symbolic importance of Kwangju, see Woo-Cumings 2005; Cumings 2005; Drennan 2005—all of which are essays in Steinberg 2005. Also see Shin 1996, 793–94.

Korea in preparation for an attack, and four days later ROK police arrested leading political dissidents, including Kim Dae Jung, and declared martial law, banning all public demonstrations. As the army occupied key domestic institutions and centers of protests, demonstrators in Kwangju flooded into the streets and sporadically clashed with Korean Special Forces and police. On May 27, Korean Special Forces and Twentieth Division troops swiftly and brutally brought an end to the insurrection, killing 170 by official estimates, a figure that was later revised to 240.[55]

Whatever the exact facts of the case, as Kimberly Marten suggests, the United States, when defending its conduct during the incident, tends to focus on legal arguments regarding operational control of the Combined Forces Command (CFC) troops, whereas when political dissidents reflect on Kwangju, they criticize the United States' political passivity.[56] U.S. officials maintain that they did not authorize a massacre, whereas some observers maintain that the acquiescence of the CFC to releasing troops was of marginal importance at best in that the Korean forces would have been released even without approval and Chun had already purged the military of democratic reformers.[57] Critics respond that the United States was at least complicit in the Kwangju crackdown. The United States may not have explicitly authorized the massacre, but it did not take steps to actively block it. ROK commanders notified the United States that they were removing elements of the Twentieth Division from CFC operational command on May 16, and Americans approved their subsequent use in Kwangju, but Americans also assumed that military troops would be preferable to the dreaded Special Forces.[58] Radio broadcasts by official ROK media during the crisis stated for propagandistic purposes that the United States had approved the use of ROK Special Forces, even though U.S. officials vehemently denied granting such permission.[59]

---

55. The official death toll was revised in 1995. Political activists claim that the actual toll exceeded a thousand.
56. See Marten 2005, 171. Marten provides a concise and analytically helpful analysis of the issues involved; see 170–77.
57. Fowler 1999, 277–80.
58. Oberdorfer 2001, 128–30.
59. Oberdorfer 2001, 129. According to a cable from U.S. ambassador Gleysteen describing his communications with ROK officials during the crackdown, "I explained that we had been very bothered by broadcasts in the Kwangju area asserting that General Wickham [U.S. commanding general] had not only authorized the shift of troops to Kwangju but had also encouraged the movement of military forces to control the city. We had told the military authorities that such crude efforts to shift the blame to us were unacceptable and if continued, would necessitate a firm U.S. denial."

Indeed, the very "structural" elements of the ROK-U.S. relationship that make Kwangju an important symbol of U.S. complicity in internal antidemocratic practices—the hierarchical nature of CFC operational control, U.S. recognition of Chun, and regular ROK-U.S. civilian and military contacts—are the same elements that allowed Chun to invoke the United States' sanctioning of his actions at Kwangju as political cover.[60] Chun used the legitimacy afforded by the U.S. troop presence and the perception that the United States controlled Korean forces to justify his repressive crackdown. Kwangju was an illustrative example, although extremely brutal, of a leader playing two-level base politics between the nested hierarchies of international security and domestic politics to secure his political survival.

Turkey: Cycles of Democratization and Military Rule

While Korea endured the rule of a succession of autocrats, the 1960–80 period in Turkey was characterized by democratic fits and starts, interrupted by three political interventions by the Turkish armed forces. Consequently, the United States' basing presence and its governing contracts themselves periodically became politicized and contested as a function of these volatile changes within the Turkish political system.

Political Liberalization and the Turbulent 1960s

In contrast to Korea's decade of entrenched authoritarianism and dependence on the United States, the 1960s in Turkey saw widespread democratization and political upheaval in which that country's relationship with the United States was denounced and contested by emerging left-wing forces. Also in the 1960s, a number of base-related incidents and scandals emphasized that Turkey did not exercise full sovereignty over the military bases, which polarized Turkish society and politicized the U.S. presence.[61]

A number of base-related incidents highlighted for Turkish politicians, the military, and the public the reality of U.S. sovereign control over base functions—a control greater than the Menderes government

---

Cable from U.S. Embassy in Seoul to U.S. Secretary of State, "May 26 Meeting with Blue House Syg Choi," May 26, 1980, *DDRS*.

60. See Cumings 2005.

61. For a more detailed account of Turkish antibasing movements in the 1960s, see Holmes 2006.

had admitted. The first such incident occurred in 1958, when the United States, without first consulting the Turkish government, used Incirlik to support a landing of U.S. Marines in Lebanon—a mission that clearly fell outside the parameters of NATO use.[62] In 1960 the U-2 incident implicated Turkey in the violation of Soviet airspace, with seemingly no previous knowledge of these reconnaissance flights by Ankara, and prompted the Soviet government to send a diplomatic note of protest against the use of Turkish territory for anti-Soviet intelligence missions. In 1962 the Cuban missile crisis again brought issues of nonconsultation and sovereignty to the public eye, as the Turkish military and public were outraged that the United States unilaterally conceded to remove the Jupiter missiles on Turkish soil as part of the agreement that removed Soviet missiles from Cuba.[63] But the most inflammatory episode occurred in 1964, when President Johnson, in a hasty attempt to prevent a possible Turkish intervention in Cyprus, wrote a heavy-handed note to Turkish president Ismet Inonu. The "Johnson letter" warned that the United States did not agree to the use of American-supplied equipment for a military campaign in Cyprus and that in the event of a Soviet response to Turkish actions, the United States would not feel bound by its NATO obligations to defend Turkey.[64] The Johnson letter reinforced the prevailing perception that the United States routinely ignored Turkish sovereignty and did not consider Turkey to be a true alliance partner.[65]

When, in December 1965, an Incirlik-based RB-47 reconnaissance aircraft crashed in the Black Sea close to Soviet territory, the U.S. Navy attempted to recover the aircraft's black box even though the Turkish

62. Author's interview with the editor of a Turkish national daily newspaper, Ankara, November 2004. See also Harris 1972, 66–68, which points out that although members of the international press were granted access to Incirlik to cover the story, the Turkish press were denied entry to the base, further underscoring the lack of balance in the bilateral partnership.

63. The precise nature of the bargain is difficult to pinpoint because President Kennedy had asked Turkey to remove the Jupiters one month before the missile crisis. Nevertheless, as Nur Bilge Criss (1993, 346–47) points out, the political issue was once again the seeming lack of consultation with the Turkish side. On the Jupiters and their removal, see Criss 1997.

64. Much has been written about the Johnson letter. A good overview of the episode and the different drafts of the letter can be found in Stearns 1992, 36–39.

65. The importance of the Johnson letter in fostering this perception was emphasized to me by a number of Turkish defense analysts and foreign policy observers. Some even speculated that Inonu strategically leaked the letter in order to justify his inaction on the Cyprus issue.

military refused it permission to do so.[66] An American destroyer on its way to the crash site was actually stopped by the Turkish navy, which then proceeded to recover the box. The incident piled parliamentary pressure on the Turkish leadership to reassert its sovereignty over base-related functions, and shortly after, Prime Minister Süleyman Demirel announced that the Turkish government would discontinue reconnaissance flights and would initiate a comprehensive review of its basing agreements.[67]

These base-related incidents were amplified by intense political polarization, growing nationalism, and anti-Americanism in domestic Turkish politics. In 1961, the reintroduction of democracy brought with it a "widening of the political spectrum" that included the growth of leftist parties and unions, nationalist and far-right parties, and Islamic groups, and an increase in urban populations and students—social segments that would become increasingly politically active.[68] The new Turkish Constitution's system of proportional representation was designed to institutionalize a multiparty system of governance that would force major parties into coalition agreements and avoid the excessive buildup of power that had characterized the DP under Menderes.[69] From 1961 to 1965, the institutional overhaul seemingly worked as the RPP ruled in coalition with different smaller parties under the leadership of Inonu. However, in 1965, the recently formed Justice Party headed by Süleyman Demirel swept into power, crushing the RPP and winning an outright majority as a result of its strong grassroots outreach and campaigning. Smaller ideologically charged parties and groups increasingly became vocal on foreign policy matters and questioned, both from the left and right, the value of Turkey's orientation to the West and relations with the United States.[70] Increased radicalization on all sides coincided with escalating political violence.

In this volatile political climate, Prime Minister Demirel was forced into increasing confrontations with parliament and pressure groups that demanded increased transparency and more favorable terms for Turkey on the basing issue. In 1966 Demirel called for a new basing agreement, and in 1967 Turkey refused the United States permission to use its territory in support of Israel. The new basing accord, known as the Defense

---

66. Criss 1993, 348.
67. Sandars 2000, 273.
68. An excellent account of Turkish democratization in the 1960s and 1970s and its foreign policy consequences is given by Adamson 2001.
69. See Ahmad 1977, 212–87.
70. Karaosmanoğlu 1988, 304–5.

and Cooperation Agreement (DCA), was signed in 1969. In his address to parliament in early 1970, Demirel announced that the DCA would replace the previous fifty-plus agreements, many informal, and would ensure that "the control of the Turkish Government over the joint defence installations and the activities from them will be full and absolute."[71] The agreement also gave the Turkish government the right to inspect all facilities and specified that it must agree to any non-NATO use of the bases.[72]

With growing terrorist activity, radicalism, and anti-Americanism, the U.S. military in the late 1960s had been transformed for many from a symbol of Turkey's integration into the West to an "imperial power." At the same time, the U.S. military presence in Turkey peaked in 1967: 26,000 personnel and dependents, of which 5,000 and an additional 1,000 civilians were living in Ankara.[73] A detailed study of social conditions of U.S. troops in Turkey in the 1960s found that U.S. personnel and dependents routinely faced hostile demonstrations, poor community relations, and legal problems.[74] Port calls by the Sixth Fleet became tense and violent affairs in 1968 and 1969, as some U.S. sailors were attacked by groups of radicalized Turkish students while on shore, prompting Turkish right-wing groups to clash with anti-American demonstrators during U.S. visits.[75] In March 12, 1971, the Turkish military, having witnessed an out-of-control political party system and ensuing political anarchy and violence, once again reasserted control over the government.

The 1970s: Cyprus and the Base Closures

The period of military rule from 1971 to 1973 has been described as one of the most repressive in Turkey's recent history. Political organizations and media outlets that were active in the 1960s were banned in the interests of restoring political order. Democratic elections were held again in 1973, but the electoral environment continued to be volatile because Turkey's party system remained fragmented.[76] Although the newly constituted RPP, now a moderate social democratic party led by Bülent Ecevit, won a plurality, the electorate overwhelmingly voted for a number of individually smaller right-leaning parties. Demirel's Justice Party refused to join an RPP-led

71. As quoted in Sandars 2000, 273.
72. Duke 1989, 76.
73. Criss 1993, 344.
74. Wolf 1969.
75. Cohen 1969.
76. Adamson 2001, 284–85.

coalition, as did the Democratic Party, so the RPP joined the Islamist National Salvation Party (NSP) led by Necmettin Erbakan, even though Ecevit and Erbakan "shared little besides a stated desire to stand-up to American hegemony in matters of both foreign and domestic policy."[77] The RPP-Islamist coalition faced a skeptical and highly politicized parliament that was ready to scrutinize its foreign policy decisions.

Just one year later, Ecevit's waning coalition was put to the test by the outbreak of a major political crisis in Cyprus. When the Greek-backed Cypriot National Guard overthrew the elected president Archbishop Makarios and replaced him with Nikos Sampson, a supporter of Greek political union with Cyprus, the political pressure on Ecevit to intervene was overwhelming. Aware of how previous Turkish leaders had bowed to U.S. pressure against intervention in 1964 (the Johnson letter) and 1967, Ecevit gave the go-ahead to the Turkish military to intervene on July 20, 1974. This initial campaign established a foothold on the island and precipitated the fall of the Greek military regime in Athens. Buoyed by a wave of nationalism and overwhelming support among the Turkish public, media, and other political parties, Ecevit ordered a second military campaign on August 13, 1974, that claimed 40 percent of the island and formed a north-south partition. In response, the U.S. Congress—urged by a powerful pro-Greek faction—imposed an arms embargo on Turkey in October 1974, deferring its implementation until February 1975 to allow for further negotiations.[78]

The Turkish response, with a Demirel-led coalition having taken over the government soon after the Cyprus campaign but still operating in a highly politically charged and nationalist environment, was quick and decisive. In a move that would have been unthinkable fifteen years earlier, the Turkish government suspended all military activity by the United States except for NATO-related Incirlik missions. In an announcement that interrupted national television programming, the government declared that the 1969 DCA and all other bilateral defense treaties regarding the bases had "lost their legal validity" and that all bases in Turkey used by the United States would be "turned over to the full control and supervision of the Turkish armed forces."[79] The action curtailed U.S. military activities throughout the country, but also halted intelligence-gathering activities at

77. Adamson 2001, 284.
78. Sandars 2000, 276.
79. Berger 1975. Also see Grimmet 1986, 50.

Belbasi, Karamursel, Diyarbakir, and Sinop.[80] When the U.S. Congress once again voted in August 1975 to keep the embargo in place, Ecevit, now the leading opposition figure, called for the closure of all U.S. military bases and the removal of American troops from Turkey.[81] A new Defense and Economic Cooperation Agreement (DECA) was negotiated in 1976, but the U.S. Congress did not approve it, and U.S. operations in Turkey remained suspended until the Carter administration negotiated a deal in October 1978. Negotiations for another DECA began, and Ecevit, once again prime minister, declared that any new accord on the use of bases would depend on the United States providing long-term economic aid to Turkey.[82]

These negotiations produced the 1980 DECA agreement just months before the Turkish military once again intervened in the face of growing political violence and terrorism gripping the country.[83] The DECA—which was fully honored by the military—emphasized repeatedly that the use of the bases would be limited to NATO purposes.[84] On issues of sovereignty, the agreement emphasized that the bases were under Turkish jurisdiction and Turkish security, and created a joint defense support commission. The economic quid pro quo was also raised as the United States committed its "best efforts" to secure $450 million per year over the agreement's five-year duration and another $350 in debt rescheduling.[85] After the volatility and low point of U.S.-Turkish relations in the 1970s, the DECA institutionalized a more stable agreement.

The 1980s: Another Coup and Rehabilitation under Özal

The Turkish military relinquished power in 1983 after thirty months of rule. In November 1982, the Turkish parliament adopted a new constitution that vested the "right to allow foreign forces to be stationed in Turkey" in the Turkish parliament, thereby finally institutionalizing authority for base-related activity in the legislative body. Just as they had in the Philippines, these new constitutional provisions on base activity established the institutional dynamic for the controversial votes on the

---

80. Duke 1989, 177.
81. Onis 1975.
82. Sandars 2000, 277.
83. "Agreement for Cooperation on Defense and Economy," signed March 29, 1980, *TIAS* 9901.
84. For analyses of the NATO dimension, see Stearns 1992, 21–23. For an insider's perspective on the 1980 negotiations, see the account by U.S. ambassador James Spain (1984).
85. Gunter 2005, 116; Sandars 2000, 280. According to Gunter, the 1980 DECA made Turkey the third largest recipient of U.S. military aid after Israel and South Korea.

use of Turkish bases for the American-led operations against Iraq in 1991 and 2003.

In the meantime, under the premiership of Turgut Özal, the basing issue remained in play but retained a much less controversial profile than it had in the previous two decades. For the rest of the 1980s, Özal's priorities remained domestic: he reformed the Turkish economy, initiating widespread privatization (including broad privatization of the media), and he managed to combine a generally pro-Western outlook with a personal faith in Islam.[86] But his domestic political fortunes were once again linked to the presence of U.S. forces when the Gulf Crisis erupted in 1990.

The Cold War Ends and Political Uncertainty Intensifies

Korean Democratization and Its Consequences

Korean democratization accelerated in the 1990s with the election of Kim Young Sam in 1992. Five years later former leading political dissident Kim Dae Jung became the first candidate from an opposition party to win as a candidate of that party, making his election the first significant break with Korea's conservative political past.[87]

Not coincidentally, Korea's democratization in the mid-1990s also brought new scrutiny of the U.S. military and the basing contracts, especially the U.S.-ROK SOFA. As with other cases of democratization of base hosts, the U.S. military presence became linked with U.S. support for previous undemocratic practices by Korea's military regimes. Opposition figures and progressive figureheads accused the United States of contributing to ROK internal repression, especially the tragedy at Kwangju. Korea's party system remained nascent and personalized, making it volatile and more responsive to such nationalist appeals and identity-based mobilization strategies.[88] President Roh Moo Hyun's emotionally charged election campaign of 2002, which called for "greater balance" in ROK-U.S. security ties, is a case in point. New civic groups and social movements also began to challenge USFK's presence. For the first time in ROK history,

86. See Pope and Pope 1998, 158–79.
87. For overviews, see Moon and Mo 2004; S. S. Kim 2003; Diamond and Shin 2000.
88. According to S. S. Kim (2003, 39), "the extreme personalization of political power has also combined with abiding regional patronage to generate breathtaking turbulence in the Korean party system, with parties constantly changing names and identities keyed to the rise and fall of individual party leaders."

students and NGOs staged antibase demonstrations and openly campaigned for the withdrawal of American troops and the revision of the SOFA. Furthermore, for many progressives, the U.S. military presence was viewed more as an obstacle to reestablishing relations with North Korea than as a security guarantor against the North. President Kim Dae Jung's new Sunshine Policy, which called for improving relations with the North, further called into question the fundamental purpose of the U.S. troop presence.[89] Certain external events also impacted these democratization trends, as U.S. actions in the wake of the 1997 East Asian financial crisis and President George W. Bush's "axis of evil" fueled elements of this new anti-Americanism.[90]

Even while ROK public attitudes toward the United States have grown significantly more critical, public opinion about the necessity of the U.S. military presence is considerably more ambiguous, despite the acute politicization of the issue.[91] In a 1997 poll of 1,400 Yonsei students in Seoul, 47.1 percent of respondents described themselves as anti-American and just 21.2 percent as pro-American, yet 31.8 percent opposed the stationing of U.S. forces in the country and 50.2 percent responded that the USFK presence was "needed." In September 2000, in the midst of the inter-Korean conciliation, a national poll of 1,000 respondents by the newspaper *Korean People* found that 70.6 percent of respondents agreed with the statement that "the USFK should continue to stay here to deter a potential North Korean invasion into South Korea." Even after the controversial events of 2002 involving the accidental deaths of two Korean girls (discussed in the following section), a January 2003 poll of 1,200 Koreans by the *Chungang Ilbo* newspaper found that only 13.8 percent favored a complete or substantial withdrawal of USFK, whereas 42.8 percent favored small-scale reductions and 41.5 percent favored maintaining the current troop levels. In fact, compared with polls in other base-hosting countries, these figures show relatively strong support for the continued USFK presence.

New Democratizing Actors and the Basing Issue
Despite the relatively strong domestic support for continued USFK presence, Korea's democratization has generated new actors who have targeted the basing issue. Helped by new information technologies and

---

89. See Levin 2004; Levin and Han 2002.
90. Kim 2002–3.
91. The following polling data are quoted in Kim 2004, 271, 278.

networking, NGOs and new media outlets have effectively politicized the issue and made it appear far more contested than broader public surveys suggest.

The rise of NGOs and social movements working on basing issues is part of a much broader recent upsurge in the importance and activities of transnational activists working on a range of social issues.[92] On this dimension, the recent democratization of Korea is a comparatively distinct case among base hosts, with the possible exception of Okinawa. Since the 1980s, South Korea has witnessed an unprecedented "activation" of civil society and the rapid growth of citizens' movements and nongovernmental organizations into some of the most significant actors in Korean domestic politics.[93] On base-related issues, Korean NGOs have campaigned to raise awareness of women's sexual labor in U.S. base districts, crimes committed by U.S. military personnel, land usage, environmental issues, and revisions of the status of forces agreement.[94] Many of the most prominent organizations are linked through the umbrella organization People's Action for Reform of the Unjust SOFA (or PAR-SOFA).

Mostly as a result of these NGO campaigns and pressure, U.S. officials in 2001 agreed to amend the SOFA's criminal jurisdiction to bring it into line with most of the concurrent jurisdiction procedures of the NATO SOFA.[95] The agreement also allowed the ROK to exercise jurisdiction in the custody phase for twelve serious crimes—including murder, kidnapping, and rape—as long as due process rights are guaranteed for U.S. personnel during pretrial confinement. However, the revised agreement did little to quell NGO criticism. For example, the Civil Network for a Peaceful Korea demanded that the 2001 SOFA be further revised, and a spokesperson for the group insisted that ICC jurisdiction should replace the SOFA's.[96] Interestingly, NGO campaigns targeting the U.S.-Korea SOFA, both before and after the 2001 revision, have occurred during a period of decreasing crimes and accidents involving U.S. personnel (see table 4.1).[97]

92. On NGOs, activism, and transnational networks, see Keck and Sikkink 1998.
93. For discussions, see S. S. Kim 2003; Lee 1993.
94. For background, see Moon 1999.
95. For legal analysis with some comparative references, see Jung and Hwang 2003. The authors conclude that the agreement grants more rights to the host country than does the NATO SOFA and that the agreement's biggest problem lies in its politicized implementation.
96. Civil Network for a Peaceful Korea 2004, 11. Author's interview with CNPK member, Seoul, May 2004.
97. Data provided by JAG office, USFK Legal Affairs, Camp Yongsan, Seoul, June 2004.

TABLE 4.1
Criminal jurisdiction and waiver rates under the U.S.-ROK SOFA

| Year[a] | SOFA incidents (no. of people) | | | | ROK exercise of jurisdiction | |
	Military	Civilians	Depen-dents	Total	Military	Rate (%)
1967	1,290	38	2	1,330	9	0.70
1968	1,282	62	9	1,353	16	1.25
1969	1,192	89	7	1,288	11	0.92
1970	1,550	46	44	1,640	14	0.90
1971	1,321	71	35	1,427	28	2.12
1972	1,495	74	17	1,586	31	2.07
1973	1,635	78	69	1,782	24	1.47
1974	1,723	76	85	1,884	32	1.86
1975	2,121	99	73	2,293	29	1.37
1976	2,145	128	92	2,365	23	1.07
1977	2,016	108	70	2,194	15	0.74
1978	2,350	101	96	2,547	19	0.81
1979	2,297	77	92	2,466	16	0.70
1980	Suspension of criminal jurisdiction due to martial law					
1981	2,218	102	103	2,423	4	0.18
1982	2,224	108	103	2,435	13	0.58
1983	1,967	148	182	2,297	7	0.36
1984	1,961	157	163	2,281	8	0.40
1985	1,702	175	157	2,034	11	0.65
1986	1,451	150	135	1,736	11	0.76
1987	1,543	164	125	1,832	5	0.32
1988	1,554	146	133	1,833	9	0.57
1989	1,387	128	126	1,641	12	0.86
1990	1,278	136	124	1,538	13	1.02
1991	1,434	124	145	1,703	16	1.11
1992	790	97	119	1,006	11	1.30
1993	677	118	96	891	20	2.95
1994	861	110	101	1,072	26	3.02
1995	847	161	102	651	43	5.08

(cont.)

TABLE 4.1—*(cont.)*

Year[a]	SOFA incidents (no. of people)				ROK exercise of jurisdiction	
	Military	Civilians	Dependents	Total	Military	Rate (%)
1996	602	109	72	783	24	3.97
1997	622	104	49	775	42	6.75
1998	563	107	46	716	23	3.21
1999	702	106	85	893	22	3.12
2000[b]	396	112	120	628	33	8.33
2001	461	129	112	702	36	7.80
2002	392	80	69	541	20	5.10
2003	360	87	88	535	96	26.67

Source: Office of the Judge Advocate, United States Forces Korea.
[a] The reporting period is December 1–November 30.
[b] Starting December 1, 1999, minor traffic accidents are not reported as criminal cases.

From 1999 to 2003, the period of the most intense politicization of the SOFA, total SOFA crimes and incidents actually declined by more than 40 percent—from 893 to 535—even though criticism of the SOFA's criminal jurisdiction procedures grew during this same period. Moreover, ROK waiver rates significantly declined from 1992 to 2002, especially under later progressive governments, dropping from a 98–99 percent waiver rate before 1993 to a 93–95 percent rate afterward.[98] That is, since the start of the democratization period in the mid-1990s, the ROK has exercised its right of jurisdiction three to four times more frequently than in the past. The actual data on criminal jurisdiction, then, suggest that whatever the merits of the claim that the U.S.-ROK SOFA is unfair, the issue has steadily become more politicized during a period in which USFK crimes and ROK jurisdiction waiver rates have actually declined.

The agenda-setting power of NGO antibase movements has been enhanced by the informational revolution that has coincided with Korea's democratization. Koreans are among the global leaders in their use of cell phones, the Internet, and e-mail, and these technologies have allowed the various groups to network easily and to quickly disseminate their information campaigns to the broader public. As a result, Korean antibase

98. Data provided by the USFK Legal Affairs office, Camp Yongsan, Seoul, June 2004.

NGOs campaign more effectively and can reach a broader audience than that reached by previous antibase movements of the 1970s and 1980s.

The democratization of Korea's media has also focused attention on the basing issue. During military rule, the ROK media was heavily controlled by the state and was prevented from reporting on security matters or the country's *chaebol,* or large conglomerates.[99] As a result, media politics has become an important issue in its own right. Both presidents Kim Dae Jung and Roh Moo Hyun complained about "conservative" press bias and made media reform a central issue of their governments.[100] Accordingly, the coverage of base-related issues and stories by new media outlets signifies a break from previous practices. U.S. officials vigorously complain about the press's bias in its coverage of basing issues, noting that newspapers focus on negative stories and intentionally distort stories and press releases.[101]

The progressive media's attention to crimes committed by USFK personnel has been particularly influential. Internet sites managed by activist groups and NGOs (such as usacrime.org.kr or koreatruth.org) post discussions and stories about the adverse affect of the USFK on Korean politics and society; they also link to other Web sites and antibase campaigns. Yonghoi Song has observed that these progressive media outlets focus overwhelmingly on anti-U.S. themes, and he observes that the "[Korean] news plays a crucial role of shaping the public perception of the [USFK] crimes because news is virtually the only window through which most people can make sense of the crimes of U.S. military personnel . . . the way the news media constructs the crimes or misdeeds of the U.S. military personnel have the significant implications for the future of the Korea-US relationship."[102] Younger generations tend to use these Web sites, blogs, and online sites as their main source of news.

As in Spain or the Philippines, democratization in South Korea has generated significant nationalism and anti-American sentiment, with accompanying attention to base-related issues. What distinguishes the seemingly more virulent Korean antibase activism is not its veracity or emotional content, but its skillful and effective use of new media and technologies to keep its message on the national political agenda.

---

99. On Korea's media reform, see H. S. Kim 2003.
100. See Manyin 2003, 8; *Economist* 2003.
101. Author's interviews with U.S. Public Affairs representatives, Seoul, June 2004.
102. Song 2004, 5.

Highway 56 and the 2002 Presidential Campaign

The significant impact of Korea's new democratizing actors on the basing issue was dramatically illustrated during the summer of 2002 and the subsequent presidential election campaign. On June 13, 2002, during a training exercise, an American armored vehicle ran over and killed two Korean schoolgirls on a narrow turn on Highway 56. Just minutes after the accident, an observer photographed the girls' mangled corpses, and within hours, activists' antibase Web sites (including usacrime.or.kr) and Internet news outlets had posted the gruesome images and e-mailed them to hundreds of thousands of personal e-mail accounts.[103]

NGOs and sympathetic political elites organized widespread protests, including a rally of 100,000 in Seoul in August. Commanders from the U.S. Eighth Army personally expressed their regrets to the girls' families, but Washington imprudently refused to issue an official apology. Soon, the ROK-U.S. SOFA and procedures for determining criminal jurisdiction were at the center of Korean criticism. Even though the training exercise designated the two American drivers as on duty and thus clearly under U.S. military jurisdiction, the Korean government and NGOs demanded that the servicemen be turned over to the Korean legal system. The slogan "Unfair SOFA" became a mobilizing cry for both NGOs and Korean politicians commenting on the events.

The new Korean media also played an important role in fueling anti-American sentiment in the aftermath of the incident. Progressive online outlets focused overwhelmingly on covering the antibase protests precipitated by the various aspects of the case and portrayed them as "legitimate public anger at the injustice inflicted by the United States."[104] Online news sites such as OhMyNews and PRESSian commanded more than 2.5 million page hits a day in 2002. But as Song observes, the sites were far more reliant on unnamed "guerilla sources" during the major phases of the incident than were the major conservative newspapers, with nonofficial Korean sources accounting for more than three times the combined use of Korean government and U.S. official sources.[105]

When in November 2002 the U.S. drivers were acquitted of all criminal charges—including negligent homicide—the issue reached a political boil in South Korea. The ruling Millennium Party expressed its disapproval

103. Author's interviews with public relations representatives of USFK, Seoul, June 2004. Also see Song 2004, 9.
104. Song 2004, 123.
105. Song 2004, 139, table 6.4.

of the verdict, as did the Ministry of Justice. Coming in the midst of a presidential campaign, just one month before polling day, the verdict was declared unfair by all major candidates, and each vowed, if elected, to challenge the terms of the SOFA. Politically, these events particularly favored the progressive candidate and former political dissident Roh Moo Hyun, who vowed not to kowtow to the United States.[106] With the support of most progressive NGOs and civil society networks, Roh won a surprising national victory in 2002. The basing issue had been transformed into a political asset in Korea's democratizing political environment.

Readjusting U.S. Forces and Democratic Consolidation
The anti-USFK protests of 2002 marked a low point in more recent U.S.-ROK relations, but will such NGO-driven mobilization and antibase activism come to define the state of the basing issue in the future? Katharine Moon has argued that the proliferation of antibase activists and confrontational NGOs within the ROK was testament to Korea's ongoing democratic consolidation.[107] According to this view, the basing issue and other matters of security policy are likely to remain monitored and politicized by NGOs now that these actors have entrenched themselves as important players in Korea's democratic political system.

I predict, however, that as long as Korea's political system continues to consolidate, the basing issue will become steadily depoliticized. Specifically, as Korea's political party system stabilizes and the governance of security issues is routinized among Korea's political parties, governmental institutions, and bureaucratic agencies, the use of U.S. bases as an issue by political elites should become a less-attractive political strategy. In other words, although NGOs may continue to push for base-related reforms, their capacity to actually sway median voters and party followers is likely to diminish. Just as the issue became depoliticized in Spain, Greece, or Japan, continuing democratic consolidation in Korea over the next two electoral cycles should cut against, not for, the politicization of USFK, regardless of the actual policies or base-related incidents that might occur in the meantime.[108]

---

106. On the 2002 campaign, see Cha 2005; Levin 2004, 21–22.
107. Moon 2003.
108. The political consequences of future Korean reunification and reconciliation remain an important unknown, however. Reunification may even have negative consequences for Korea's future democratic consolidation. I thank Kathy Moon for highlighting this point.

Impending adjustments to the basing structure of U.S. forces in Korea should also help depoliticize the issue. Among the major changes to be implemented include reducing U.S. troops to 25,000 by 2008, consolidating a number of scattered installations along the DMZ into two complexes (Camp Casey and Camp Red Cloud), repositioning some 14,000 troops from the DMZ to the south of the country, and relocating USFK headquarters and most of the Eighth Army away from Yongsan to the south by 2008. Under the new strategy, U.S. forces will not only serve their long-standing purpose of deterring North Korea but will also focus on promoting stability in the greater northeast Asia region. These changes are consistent with the Pentagon's more general readjustment of its global basing posture (see chap. 7), but commentators agree that the highly charged events of 2002 provided added impetus for the drawdown and realignment.[109]

Already there are signs that political elites who once used the basing issue for electoral gain are now reformulating their positions and playing down its political significance. For instance, President Roh himself demonstrated more moderating tendencies after his election as he visited USFK troops and asked antibase NGOs to moderate their views.[110] Roh declared that U.S. troops should remain on the peninsula to guarantee peace and stability, helped to negotiate the final details concerning U.S. force adjustments, and also bucked his own progressive base by offering unqualified support for the unpopular Iraq War.[111] In this respect, Roh's turnaround on basing issues is reminiscent of that of other national leaders, such as Felipe González or Andreas Papandreou, who successfully campaigned on antibase and renegotiation platforms but became pragmatists on the issue once they came to power.

Turkey's Territorial Integrity: Bases, Iraq, and the Kurdish Question, 1990–

Turkey's democratic consolidation under Özal in the 1980s also coincided with a marked reduction in bilateral tensions over basing matters. During the 1990s and 2000s, the issue of U.S. bases once again became politicized and implicated in Turkish domestic politics, although to a lesser degree and for different reasons than during the contentious 1960s and 1970s. The

109. Author's interviews with U.S. political and military officials, Seoul, June 2004. On the origins and possible consequences of these changes, see Cha 2004.
110. Levin 2004, 23.
111. Cha 2005, 132. Cha offers an excellent account of the reasons behind Roh's postelection moderation (132–35).

1991 Gulf War marked a new era during which the U.S. basing presence was linked to the composition of Turkey's immediate borders, its regional conflict against Kurdish militants and separatists, and its very territorial integrity. Turkish politicians once again periodically questioned the compatibility of Turkish national interests with the U.S. basing presence, especially because the country's party political system underwent fundamental changes and realignments with the decline of traditional parties and the rise of Islamic-oriented parties. The U.S. military presence was brought to the fore of bilateral relations when the 2003 Turkish parliament voted to deny U.S. troops access to Turkish territory for the Iraq campaign, which was itself the result of a mismanaged vote by the new majority Welfare Party.

The Gulf War and Özal

For Özal, the 1990 Gulf Crisis and ensuing war offered him a political opportunity to recover his dwindling popularity, which had resulted from corruption scandals, and his authority.[112] Since 1988 when he assumed the presidency, Özal had remained locked in a power struggle with parliament regarding executive authority and the separation of powers.

Özal aggressively supported the United States during the Gulf Crisis and broke with the long-standing Turkish position of regional neutrality, despite opposition from a skeptical public, opposition parties, the media, and the military itself. Moreover, the Turkish president took advantage of the international crisis to bypass normal cabinet and parliament consultations and personally negotiate deals involving the use of Turkish bases for the impending war. In response, Özal's foreign minister, defense minister, and chief of general staff all resigned over his pro-U.S. position and bypassing of normal cabinet procedures.

On January 17, 1991, just three days before U.S.-led hostilities against Iraq began, the Turkish parliament in a controversial move approved the use of Incirlik for coalition forces. Despite polling indicating that more than two-thirds of the Turkish public disapproved of Turkey's active support for the coalition, Özal's strong leadership drew praise domestically and in international circles and galvanized public support for the war effort.[113] Television images of American warplanes conducting around-the-clock sorties from Incirlik were broadcast across multiple new Turkish

---

112. According to Pope and Pope (1998, 218), Saddam Hussein's invasion of Kuwait was "a godsend for Turgut Özal, and the President rose to the occasion."
113. Pope and Pope 1998, 218–32.

outlets and constantly underscored the base's importance for the Turkish public.[114] But despite a successful military campaign, Özal had his hopes for a place at the postwar negotiating table dashed when George H. W. Bush decided not to continue the military pursuit into Baghdad, leaving the Iraqi president contained but in power.

In Whose National Interest?
The No-Fly Zone and Renewed Party Competition
The end of the Gulf War precipitated a new regional crisis and brought renewed political problems for Özal and his successor. Saddam Hussein's aggressive crackdown of the Iraqi Kurds in the north created a refugee and humanitarian crisis, as thousands of displaced Kurds came streaming over the Iraqi border into Turkey. In response, the United States, backed by Britain and France, planned to create a safe haven in northern Iraq for Kurdish refugees and proposed using Incirlik to support this new Operation Provide Comfort (OPC). OPC required some 2,000 troops and, once again for constitutional reasons, a new mission authorization by the Turkish parliament. The first OPC approval was granted in September 1991, with subsequent authorizations required every six months.[115] These renewals turned into highly politicized but staged affairs, with the opposition's criticism intensifying after Özal's sudden death in 1993. Opposition parties and the public denounced OPC for securing a safe haven and de facto state for Kurdish separatists in Iraq and Turkey. The military tolerated the mission, but intelligence that Kurds were increasingly using the safe havens as bases from which to launch incursions into Turkish territory made them uneasy.[116] The most vocal critics came from two different domestic parties, Bülent Ecevit's left-nationalist Democratic Left Party and Necmettin Erbakan's Islamist Welfare Party, who referred to OPC in the 1995 election campaign as an "infidel invasion force."[117] Erbakan vowed to terminate OPC, and his election to head a fragile coalition government in 1995 seemed to spell the end for the mission. At his victory celebration on July 25, 1995, Erbakan wished OPE a "speedy good-bye" and extended the deal for a final time in summer 1995.[118]

114. Author's interviews with Turkish and foreign media commentators, Istanbul, November 2004.
115. Author's interview with U.S. defense official, Ankara, November 2004.
116. Sandars 2000, 282. Author's interviews with Turkish military officials, Istanbul, November 2004.
117. See Barkey 2000, 115–17.
118. Barkey 2000, 116; Bruce 1996.

The end of OPC, however, redefined the U.S. mission from that of actively protecting the safe havens to patrolling the airspace, under the new name Operation Northern Watch (ONW). Once in power Erbakan backed off from much of the fiery rhetoric about expelling the United States, but he boasted that he had secured a number of concessions from the United States for transforming OPC into ONW.[119] For its part, the United States quelled its criticism of Turkey's cross-border raids and military operations and downplayed reports of human rights violations by Turkey in Kurdish areas. Under the design of UN regime-sanctions agreements, Turkish leaders also secured the transit of at least 50 percent of all Iraqi exports under the UN oil-for-food program through Turkish soil and were granted an exemption to the embargo for Turkish trade with northern Iraq. Nevertheless, the Turkish public, political elites, and media remained skeptical of OPC and ONW during the 1990s, regarding the purpose of these operations as fundamentally incompatible with Turkey's national interests and its territorial integrity.

The AKP "Revolution" and the 2003 Parliamentary Vote on Iraq

On March 2003, the Turkish parliament voted against authorizing the United States' use of Turkish territory and bases to support its impending military campaign in Iraq. The negative vote generated significant operational difficulties for the United States, which had planned on encircling the Iraqi army by establishing a northern front of about 60,000 troops. Although contingency plans had been drawn up, the decision came as a surprise to most military planners, and disgruntled political analysts accused Turkey of abandoning its superpower ally in a time of need.

Many U.S.-based analysts have interpreted the vote as a product of strong anti-American sentiment among the Turkish public, which had forced Turkish leaders to reject the U.S. request, or even an instance of Turkish "soft-balancing" against U.S. hegemonic power.[120] As we have seen, however, widespread anti-Americanism and popular disapproval of basing access also occurred in Spain and Greece, yet these governments allowed basing access for OIF. What was different about the Turkish case?

---

119. Barkey 2000, 116. As Henri Barkey observes, "although Erbakan claimed to have received concessions from the United States in June 1996, which allowed him to claim credit for the transformation of OPC into ONW and thus fulfill his election promise, this change did not significantly alter U.S. policy in Iraq."
120. On the failed vote as deliberate "soft-balancing" or "balking" against the United States and U.S. primacy, see Walt 2005, 131, 142, 143; Pape 2005b, 39.

The immediate cause of the negative March vote was neither the prevailing high level of anti-Americanism nor the uneasy security relations between the countries. Instead, the vote was the product of domestic institutional pressures and party political competition introduced by the country's new political climate. Unlike the other southern European cases, in which it was a government that directly guaranteed access to U.S. officials, in Turkey the constitution mandated that the parliament approve the use of bases for any mission not sanctioned by the United Nations or NATO.

This institutional requirement was complicated by a recent fundamental change in Turkey's political party system. Although U.S. officials, including Deputy Secretary of Defense Paul Wolfowitz, had begun negotiating a base-access agreement for a U.S.-led Iraq military campaign as early as summer or spring of 2002 with the Ecevit coalition government, the dynamics of Turkish politics were dramatically altered later that fall.[121] On November 3, 2002, the Turkish electorate had swept into office the Islamic-affiliated Justice and Development Party (AKP), led by the charismatic former mayor of Istanbul Tayyip Erdogan.[122] Because Turkey's electoral law sets a 10 percent threshold for party representation, many smaller parties that divided the popular vote were excluded, and the AKP gathered nearly two-thirds of parliamentary seats even though it actually won just over one-third (36 percent) of the popular vote. So although the Turkish political system as a whole was certainly democratic and had characteristics of democratic consolidation, its party system remained volatile and subject to rapid party turnover and extinction.[123] The military remained suspicious of the AKP's antisecular tendencies and its potential foreign policy orientation. Political uncertainty remained high, as the Erdogan himself did not immediately assume the prime ministership because he was not a parliamentarian at the time, but the AKP leader did embark on a series of high-profile foreign policy initiatives, including the disastrous Copenhagen EU summit where Turkey was not offered a start date for accession negotiations.[124]

Within this volatile political environment, the Iraq authorization vote was the AKP's first major legislative undertaking. During the run-up to

---

121. On the summer 2002 approaches, see Gunter 2005, 119; Olson 2005, 141.
122. For analysis, see Özel 2003.
123. On the distinction between democratic consolidation and democratization and its relevance to understanding the Turkish party system, see Heper 2002. On the origins of the institutional decline of Turkey's traditional parties in the 1990s, see Özbudun 2001.
124. An excellent overview of the AKP's postelection activities is given in Robins 2003.

the vote, no immediate signs of the impending electoral outcome were apparent. U.S. deputy secretary of defense Paul Wolfowitz participated in a meeting in Ankara in December 2002 that laid the groundwork for base access by offering Turkey a package of financial assistance and military modernization of Turkish facilities. On assuming power, Erdogan publicly proclaimed that he would leave all military and security-related decisions to the military. A December visit to Washington seemingly went well, and the Turkish premier gave the impression that his party would support a future campaign against Iraq.[125]

Over the next three months, however, the AKP gave mixed signals about its exact position, as many rank-and-file members expressed concerns about attacking a Middle Eastern country and underlined their recurrent fears about establishment of an independent Kurdish state. Also, the previous decade's experience with OPC and ONW was invoked in the media as analysts questioned whether U.S. and Turkish regional interests really were aligned. Turkish NGOs and social activist movements began a vigorous campaign against the impending war, as Turkish public opinion during the lead-up period ran about 85–90 percent against the war.[126] As a result, Erdogan remained publicly silent on the issue and deferred the parliamentary debate and vote until the last possible minute, with many AKP deputies adopting the public stance that war could still be averted.[127] In February Turkish domestic attention shifted to the substantial quid pro quo package that was being offered by Washington. In exchange for base access, Turkey would be offered $2 billion in grant aid and $24 billion in loan guarantees and debt write-off, on top of the upgrades to its bases, ports, and military installations.[128] The package itself led many critics to assert that the country's compliance was being bought.

Indecision led to annoyance among Turkey's political elite, media, and, most importantly, the military. Although the National Security Council had approved the military action in January, it refused to publicly back the measure after a follow-up meeting in February. The AKP's waffling seemingly confirmed to the military that the party could not be trusted on security matters, and many political analysts interpreted the military's lukewarm

---

125. Robins 2003, 561.
126. On the role of NGOs and the antiwar movement, see Altinay and Holmes 2008.
127. Author's interview with a Turkish national newspaper columnist, Ankara, November 2004.
128. A detailed account of the various components of the incentive package is given in Olson 2005, 143.

public support of the base-access agreement as an attempt to embarrass the AKP for its incompetence.[129] The Turkish land forces commander even went beyond a passive nonendorsement and, on the Wednesday before the vote, leaked in a media interview that he opposed the authorization. To make matters worse, the day before the vote President Sezer declared that a UN Security Council authorization for military action should be a prerequisite for Turkish authorization. The opposition RPP imposed a party vote against the motion, whereas the AKP did not strictly whip the vote out of fear of splitting the party. For example, Turkish-Kurdish members of the AKP from the southeast openly announced that they would not support the measure for fear of regional destabilization and the possible incursion of Turkish troops into Kurdish-controlled areas in Iraq.[130]

Even with this domestic political turmoil, however, the AKP's significant majority still led most to believe that the March 1 vote would pass comfortably, and an informal whip count of votes that morning gave the AKP a majority of 50 to 100 votes for the measure.[131] Evidently, this comfortable cushion led many AKP delegates to later switch their vote to no, assuming that it was safe to do so. As the votes were tallied, the measure seemed to have passed by a slender 264 to 251. However, the 19 abstentions meant that a majority of deputies in the Grand Assembly on the day had not supported the motion and that in fact the motion had failed by three votes; the RPP challenged the initial result and was upheld by the head of Parliament. Embarrassed and thrown into immediate political danger, Erdogan spun the vote as a "victory for democracy" while going into immediate backdoor negotiations to determine if a new follow-on vote could be secured. The chief general staff assured the United States that the vote would be brought up again, but the failure to gain Security Council approval and the domestic popularity of the rejection at home gave Erdogan no political room to do so. The parliament did vote to grant the U.S. military overflight rights, but the large contingent of U.S. forces waiting on navy ships off the Turkish coast eventually turned away to sail for the Iraqi theater through the Persian Gulf.

Tensions over U.S. policy in Iraq and Turkey's domestic political dynamics continued to inform base-related issues after 2003. The Turkish media and public grew increasingly hostile to American actions, especially after

129. Author's interviews with U.S. defense officials, Turkish defense analysts, and Turkish political commentators, Ankara and Istanbul, November 2004.
130. See Rubin 2005, 2.
131. I thank Henri Barkey for this point.

high-profile U.S. missions such as the November 2004 attack on Fallujah.
Fears that new Iraqi democracy would inevitably lead to some form of federalism and Kurdish statehood were further inflamed by the U.S. Coalition
Provisional Authority's decision to reject Ankara's offer of 10,000 Turkish
peacekeepers in spring 2005. Periodic cabinet decisions allowed Incirlik to
be used to logistically support operations in Afghanistan and in Iraq, but
in July and October 2004 the Turkish side, under considerable media scrutiny, rejected a U.S. proposal to redeploy fifty F-16 fighters from Germany
to Incirlik.[132] The proposal, part of the Pentagon's global restructuring
plan, included demands that U.S. planners have unrestricted use rights
for Incirlik missions, a requirement that Turkish negotiators, the military,
and the media underscored would violate the Turkish Constitution.[133]

Conclusions: Domestic Political Change and the Unraveling of Alliances

Despite the strong security rationale for their original establishment, over
time the U.S. military presence in both South Korea and Turkey became
implicated in domestic institutional developments, as periods of democratization eroded the credibility of the basing agreements (see fig. 4.3).
However, after the 1950s, Korean rulers remained much more politically
dependent on the U.S. basing presence than did their Turkish counterparts.

Initially, U.S. forces stationed in both countries served the mutual
defense, and U.S. aid flows tied to the security partnership in the 1950s
kept the regimes of Syngman Rhee and Adnan Menderes, and their political clients, in power. In the 1960s, base politics in the two countries varied
according to the countries' very different trajectories of political democratization and consolidation. In Korea, an initial chance to establish democratic rule after Rhee's fall was squandered, and a succession of autocratic
military rulers governed the South. Korean rulers used the presence of U.S.
forces, both operationally and symbolically, to consolidate and legitimize
their rule, often in the most brutal of circumstances such as the Kwangju
crackdown in 1980s. As with activists in other countries experiencing

132. See Sariibrahimoglu 2004, 2005.
133. In July 2005, Turkish authorities agreed that Incirlik could be used as a cargo hub for
the U.S. C-17 but insisted that no combat aircraft be stationed and that they be notified of
the contents of the shipments one month in advance.

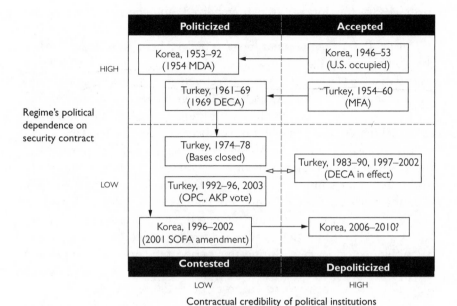

Figure 4.3. Evolution of base politics, Republic of Korea and Turkey

democratic transitions, many Korean former opposition figures and dissidents during the 1990s and 2000s linked the U.S. military presence with decades of autocratic rule and demanded the renegotiation of the basing contracts. The election of President Roh in 2002, following a high-profile accident and U.S. court martial acquittal of the U.S. servicemen involved, marked the culmination of this anti-U.S. political backlash.

In Turkey, by contrast, democratization did not follow the linear or relatively late trajectory as it did in Korea. On three separate occasions—at the beginning of the 1960s, 1970s, and 1980s—the Turkish military intervened to reestablish political order and reconfigure the Turkish political system. As a consequence, Turkey underwent democratization on several occasions, and these new civilian governments, no longer dependent on Washington for aid, enjoyed much greater room to challenge the terms of these basing contracts. The base contracts remained highly politicized during these periods, as seen by the volatile street protests and clashes of the 1960s, and were even contested and unilaterally terminated when the Ecevit government in 1974 suspended all non-NATO U.S. base activities.

In the 1980s, the Turkish system stabilized, and the prevailing basing accords were relatively depoliticized.

During the 1990s, popular perceptions in both Korea and Turkey changed regarding the purpose of U.S. forces. Critics in both base hosts argued that the U.S. military presence actively impeded their national and regional interests. In Turkey, the Gulf War generated a refugee problem and subsequent low-level conflict with Iraq's Kurds that threatened the territorial integrity and stability of southeastern Turkey. The U.S. use of Incirlik airbase to patrol the no-fly zone in support of operations OPC and ONW seemed to directly contravene Turkish national interests and constrain Turkey's military capacity to deal with the situation. In 2003, lingering concerns about the impact of the U.S. military on Turkey's borders remained, as Erdogan's inexperienced AKP lost the parliamentary vote required to authorize U.S. access to Turkish territory for the OIF campaign. Not coincidentally, during this period fundamental changes and volatility in Turkey's party system accompanied the renewed scrutiny and repoliticization of the role and purpose of U.S. forces in Turkey.

In Korea, the democratization of the 1990s generated a mushrooming of civic groups and organizations that called for changes in the U.S. basing relationship and increased ties to North Korea. The election of Kim Dae Jung and his Sunshine Policy platform led many former political dissidents and progressives to argue that the presence of U.S. forces was impeding the reconciliation of the Korean peninsula. The sense of a common security purpose, so engrained for decades during the cold war, had lost much of its resonance during Korean democratization. Despite the ongoing security dilemma with the North, Korea's governments no longer rely on the presence of U.S. forces for their internal legitimacy. And although even questioning the purpose of U.S. forces would have been illegal during much of Korea's postwar history, two progressives were swept into the presidency through political campaigns criticizing the purpose and terms of the U.S. military presence. By 2005, base politics in the ROK had evolved almost as much as Korea's political institutions themselves had.

CHAPTER 5

Okinawa and the Azores

Island Hosts and Triangular Politics

The most geographically remote, yet perhaps most analytically instructive, pair of base hosts are the island groups of Okinawa and the Azores. As with the other cases, base politics on these islands have been highly conditioned by domestic political change, especially periods of democratic transition and consolidation. However, the base politics of these islands have been mediated by an additional factor absent in the other cases—the political relation between regional island governments and their respective national governments. Okinawans and Azoreans have developed distinct political identities that often have clashed with the prevailing mainland conceptions of nation and state held in Tokyo and Lisbon. The U.S. military presence on these islands periodically has exacerbated these "internal" center-periphery tensions.

As a result, base politics in Okinawa and the Azores are best viewed as triangular political interactions involving the mainland government, the island host, and the U.S. military, as these three actors have negotiated and contested base-related issues such as sovereign authority and compensation levels. Within these two triangles, however, the configuration of political alliances has varied, with important political consequences for the legitimacy of these base contracts. In the Okinawan case, the U.S. military actually administered the island from 1952 to 1972. Most islanders regarded U.S. military rule as colonial, and even after reversion and Okinawa's democratization, Okinawan reformists have regarded the heavy U.S. basing presence as illegitimate and a nondemocratically sanctioned legacy of earlier military administrations. For reformists and other advocates of Okinawan identity, the Japanese central government continues to ignore the political wishes of the island and actively colludes with the U.S. military to place an unfair military burden upon the prefecture island. By contrast, Azoreans have traditionally retained strong ties with the United States through significant migration from the islands to North America. During the mid-1970s U.S. officials, concerned about guaranteeing base rights on the islands, reportedly colluded with Azorean nationalists to ferment an independence movement in the event that the Communists secured their rule in Lisbon. The separatist wave was diffused with Portugal's democratic consolidation and new devolution of power to the island's regional government. To this day, U.S. basing agreements in the Azores remain more widely accepted as legitimate than in Okinawa.

Understanding Triangular Politics: Islands, National Governments, and Bases

Geography and Island Identities

The development of a distinct political identity on an island territory usually depends on the island's geographical remoteness, economic dependency, and political autonomy.[1] What is immediately striking about the locations of Okinawa and the Azores is just how far they are from their respective mainlands (see figs. 5.1 and 5.2).

Okinawa is the largest island of the Ryukyu chain and lies in the East China Sea, about a thousand miles to the south of the Japanese main islands, placing it closer to Taiwan than to Tokyo. The Azores Archipelago is located on the volcanic mid-Atlantic ridge, about a thousand miles to the west of continental Portugal. The nine islands have a landmass of around 910 square miles (slightly less than Rhode Island), and the most politically important are São Miguel, the largest island and host to the Azorean capital Ponta Delgada, and Terceira, host of the Lajes airbase. This geographical positioning has made both island groupings strategically important,

---

1. For an informed overview of island politics, see Baldacchino 2004.

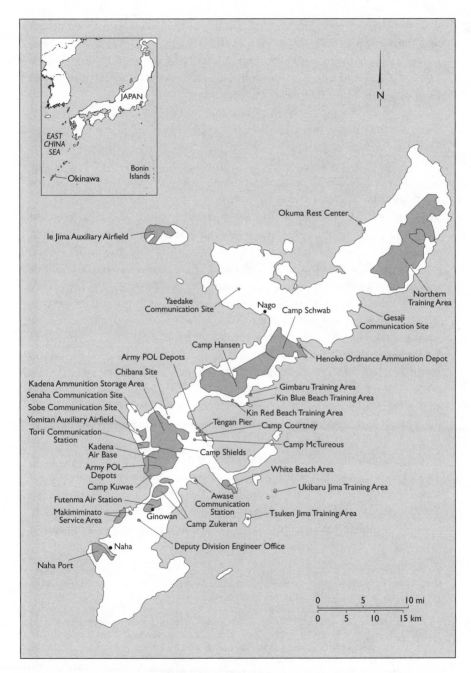

Figure 5.1. Major U.S. military facilities, Okinawa, 2000.
Source: National Defense University/DoD

with the U.S. military referring to Okinawa as the "keystone of the Pacific" and the Azores as the "crossroads of the Atlantic." But this very remoteness has also contributed to the development of indigenous political identities and fostered a sense among these islanders that they have not been fully integrated into their respective states.

Ever since the Japanese Imperial Army annexed the island in 1879, Okinawa has rested awkwardly on the periphery of Japan.[2] Although Okinawa is legally part of a unified Japanese state, its integration has always been incomplete, as the central government in Tokyo at key historical moments has treated the prefecture differently from the Japanese main islands.[3] Okinawa was the setting for one of the bloodiest battles of World War II in which Tokyo sacrificed the island and its citizens to take a stand against U.S. forces sweeping across the Pacific. More than 100,000 Japanese and Okinawan troops were killed in the battle, along with over 12,000 Americans, and another 100,000 Okinawan civilians (about one-third of the island's population) perished.[4] Just a few years later in 1952, Tokyo ceded administrative control of the island to the U.S. military under Article III of the peace treaty that secured independence for the main islands. Okinawa reverted to Japanese rule in 1972, but with a vast network of U.S. military installations still intact. In 2000 the island continued to host 75 percent of all U.S. exclusive-use military installations on Japanese territory, encompassing 50,000 troops and civilians scattered across thirty-eight separate facilities.[5] Its role as host to U.S. military bases has placed a unique burden on the island and has contributed to its awkward political relations with Tokyo.[6]

By contrast, the Azoreans view themselves as an Atlantic people with social ties to North and South America as well as to the Portuguese mainland. Portuguese explorers first claimed the deserted islands in the fifteenth century, and Lisbon has exercised sovereignty for most of the time since. From the late nineteenth to the late twentieth centuries, emigration

2. Some have viewed the incorporation of the Ryukyu Islands into the imperial Japanese state, along with the northern islands of Hokkaido, as examples of "internal colonialism" within Japan. See Siddle 1998.
3. Hook and Siddle 2003; Johnson 1999. Masaaki Gabe (2003) aptly uses the metaphor of an inverted triangle in describing Okinawa's historical relations with the United States and Japan.
4. On the internal political dimensions of the battle, see Ota 1999.
5. In 2000, this total consisted of 24,858 military personnel, 1,448 civilians, and 23,196 dependents. Okinawa Military Base Affairs Office 2000, 6.
6. See esp. Yoshida 2001; Hook and Siddle 2003; Johnson 1999.

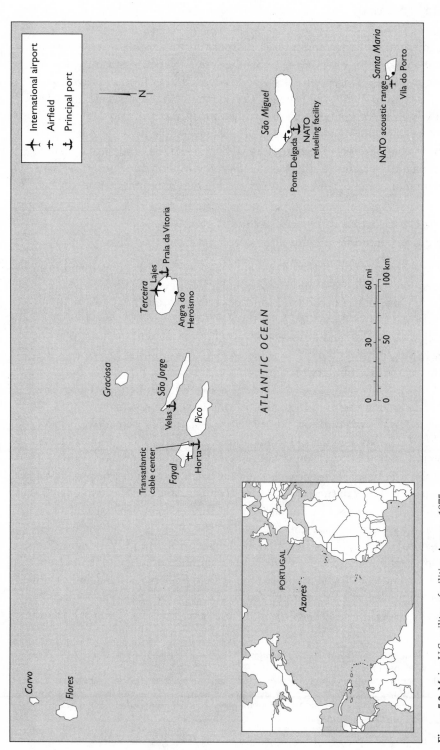

Figure 5.2. Major U.S. military facilities, Azores, 1975.
Source: University of Texas

to the United States and a large diaspora have cemented these transatlantic links: more than three times the number of Azoreans now live in communities in Massachusetts, Rhode Island, and California as live on the mid-Atlantic islands themselves.[7] Consequently, Azoreans have traditionally been more politically conservative, pro-American, and Atlanticist in their political outlook than are Portuguese mainlanders. Islanders view themselves as the very center of transatlantic relations and have remained suspicious of Lisbon's attempts to integrate them into the Portuguese state or, in more recent years, the European Union as a peripheral territory.[8]

The U.S. Military and Triangular Politics: Democratization and Compensation

The presence of the U.S. military in both cases has exacerbated and even been the root cause of these tense center-periphery relations, yielding a triangular politics involving island governments, national governments, and the U.S. military. However, the exact political alliances, democratization dynamics, and base-related bargains struck within these triangles have varied across the cases, as has the legitimacy of the agreements that govern the U.S. military presence.

In the Okinawan case, mass democratization first entailed opposing and mobilizing against U.S. military rule to secure reversion. Since 1972 Japan has absorbed the island prefecture as a judicially co-equal member, even as Okinawa continued to host the vast majority of U.S. military forces on Japanese territory. Indeed, since reversion the necessity and legitimacy of the U.S. basing presence has been the main issue of debate among the island's political parties. Okinawa's reformists have drawn attention to the destructive effects of the military bases, emphasized Okinawa's relatively unfair base burden, and complained that the island is not adequately represented at base-related negotiations between Tokyo and Washington. Yet conservative politicians, usually aligned with the dominant Liberal Democratic Party (LDP), have stressed the need to preserve national unity with mainland Japan and have pointed to the economic benefits—especially public works projects—that hosting the U.S. bases brings to the island

7. The definitive work on Azorean emigration and transnational ties is Moniz 2004. Also see Williams 2005.
8. Under the European Union, the Azores have been designated a "peripheral region." The label upsets the sensibilities of many islanders but ensures additional funds for structural development. I thank Miguel Monjardino for his helpful communications on this point.

prefecture. Although reformists regard the basing presence as an illegitimate remnant of Okinawa's colonial past, conservatives view the bases as an integral part of Japan's commitment to the mutual defense treaty with the United States (see chap. 6).

Modern Azorean state formation and democratization were shaped by the double "shocks" of 1974–75: the 1974 coup by junior officers in Lisbon that brought down the long-standing authoritarian government and the accompanying collapse of Portugal's overseas empire. Deeply suspicious of the leftward orientation of Lisbon's Revolution of the Carnations, the Azoreans generated a separatist movement (FLA) in response to growing Communist influence on the mainland. Concerned with preserving its key mid-Atlantic military outpost, the United States backed and funded the Azorean separatists. At a critical moment in Azorean and Portuguese democratization in the mid-1970s, the United States was ready to ally with the islands against the Portuguese mainland in order to preserve its basing rights, although this proved unnecessary as the Portuguese political system underwent democratic consolidation and introduced a new constitution that guaranteed political autonomy to the Atlantic islands.

Also, these distinct triangular political patterns have yielded contrasting outcomes on the quid pro quo issue. In Okinawa, the radicalization of a number of social groups opposed to the bases and the local reformist government's uneasy relationship with Tokyo periodically have politicized and contested the legitimacy of the U.S. military presence. For example, in 1995 Okinawan governor Masahide Ota refused to extend the private land leases on which U.S. military installations were located in the wake of a highly publicized rape of a local girl by three U.S. military personnel. But this very militancy and opposition to the bases have driven Tokyo to develop and institutionalize a comprehensive system of fiscal transfers, public works funds, and targeted payments to key island actors. Managed by a permanent and well-funded state bureaucracy, the Defense Facilities Administration Agency in Tokyo, these sizable transfers have established a political economy of base-related compensation that ultimately assures that a slight political majority in Okinawa continues to support the U.S. presence, albeit tacitly.[9]

By contrast, the Azoreans' generally pro-American attitudes and Atlantic political orientation have institutionalized what many islanders consider a policy of neglect and even exploitation by Lisbon on the basing issue. The

9. See Cooley and Marten 2006.

transnational ties that Azoreans share with migrants in the United States have made base-related negotiations less like bargains and, in the words of a former president of the regional government of the Azores, more like dealing "with relatives."[10] However, as supportive hosts for U.S. military installations, Azoreans believe that they have not been compensated adequately for their accommodating attitude and that the central government in Lisbon favors its mainland interests over island needs when it negotiates with the United States. In 1995 this "political neglect" was crystallized when the Portuguese government signed a new defense cooperation agreement with the United States that curtailed the annual payment that the United States had been making to the Azorean regional government and instead secured military hardware for the mainland armed forces as the deal's main quid pro quo. Ironically, the relatively more pro-American and compliant Azoreans have received far fewer material benefits for hosting U.S. military installations than have their Okinawan counterparts, who have regularly contested the terms of the U.S. presence.

Democratization, State Formation, and Okinawa's Special Bases Burden

The U.S. Occupation and Administration of Okinawa, 1952–1972

After the Battle of Okinawa, the U.S. military consolidated its presence on the island and developed it into a hub for East Asian activity. Despite strong reservations expressed by the U.S. State Department and Tokyo, Article III of the 1951 San Francisco Peace Treaty effectively turned Okinawa into a possession of the U.S. military.[11] State Department officials believed that separating Okinawa from the main islands would create significant future legal and political difficulties for the United States, but these concerns were overridden by the Department of Defense, which viewed the island as strategically invaluable. In exchange for granting sovereignty to the Japanese mainland, Tokyo agreed to cede administration of the island to the U.S. military under the legal concept of residual sovereignty. Under this formula, the islands would remain Japanese possessions but would be

10. As quoted in Monje 1992, 9.
11. The most comprehensive account is provided in Eldridge 2001.

administered by the United States with no guarantees for reversion until the "security situation in East Asia" allowed it. Thus, for Okinawans, the very origins of the U.S. military presence on the island were made possible by Tokyo's acquiescence to alien rule.

From 1952 the U.S. military administered Okinawa through a set of parallel U.S. and local institutions designed to serve the military's operational needs.[12] At the top of the administrative hierarchy was the U.S. Civilian Administration of the Ryukyu Islands (USCAR), a field agency headed by a high commissioner from the armed services appointed by the U.S. secretary of defense. Parallel to USCAR was the indigenous Government of the Ryukyu Islands (GRI), composed of an executive, a local parliament, and a local court system. The GRI governor was directly appointed by USCAR and would not be popularly elected until 1968. In practice, USCAR retained the power to veto and override all GRI executive decisions, legislation, and judicial orders, "subject to requirements of military security."[13]

U.S. defense planners considered Okinawa vital for a number of regional objectives, including defense of the Taiwan straits and the Republic of Korea, and later, support for the Vietnam War. Starting in 1951, the U.S. military constructed a vast network of airbases, naval stations, and storage and training facilities that by 1953 covered more than 14 percent of the main island.[14] A different set of legal codes and decision-making procedures also governed the U.S. military presence in Okinawa from that on the Japanese main islands. Throughout the period of U.S. administration, the United States enjoyed unrestricted use-rights for its activities on Okinawa, whereas on the main islands, after the 1960 Mutual Security Treaty, U.S. operations were subject to prior consultations with the Japanese government. Furthermore, the status of forces agreement signed with the

12. The most comprehensive English-language account of the U.S administration of Okinawa is given in Yoshida 2001.

13. "Directive for United States Civil Administration of the Ryukyu Islands," October 4, 1950, as quoted in Yoshida 2001, 43.

14. Yoshida 2001, 60. I thank Robert Eldridge for pointing out to me that today the proportion is even higher at 19 percent. Among the more important of these are Kadena airbase, which today remains the largest overseas U.S. airbase, and the U.S. Marine Corps Air Station Futenma, part of a network of facilities hosting 15,000 marines on the island, the only forward-deployed marine division. Other key facilities include the expansive northern training area, Naha Port, and Camps Hansen and Schwab in the center of the island. For details, see http://www.globalsecurity.org/military/facility/okinawa.htm (accessed May 2007).

main islands did not apply to U.S. military activities on Okinawa, and the U.S. military exercised exclusive jurisdiction and extraterritoriality over all crimes committed by U.S. personnel on the islands.

1950s: U.S. Rule and Land Confiscation

U.S. military officials initially clung to stereotypes that the Okinawans were docile by nature and would indefinitely acquiesce to military rule.[15] Some islanders supported, or at least tolerated, U.S. rule and appreciated the large investments and improvements to the island's infrastructure. However, recent studies based on Okinawan sources suggest that opposition on the island was considerably more intense than has been commonly described in American and even mainland Japanese accounts.[16]

The most contentious aspect of U.S. rule in the 1950s was the U.S. military's requisition of Okinawan land, most of it from farmers who earned their livelihoods in agriculture, in order to construct a network of military, communications, and storage facilities. Some of this land was secured by contractual agreement with local authorities, often in exchange for promises of economic development and local employment opportunities, but in other instances local inhabitants were evicted at gunpoint, often after violent struggles.[17] By early 1953, 41 percent of Okinawan farmland had been appropriated (about 14 percent of the island's total landmass) as part of the U.S. Army's $200 million base construction program.[18]

Matters were made politically worse in 1956 when the United States announced that it would compensate Okinawan landowners for the land requisitions by paying them one low lump sum rather than an annual rent that Okinawan negotiators had demanded. The declaration unleashed mass protests throughout the island, and on June 20, 1956, 160,000 demonstrators staged fifty-six separate simultaneous protests against American land requisition policies.[19] In response, U.S. authorities threatened to disband GRI officials who had provoked the demonstrations and to revoke funding from institutions such as the Ryukyu University that had served as sites for the mobilization.[20] In the interests of maintaining

15. Views on the American side are explored in Sarantakes 2000, esp. 40–78.
16. See Aldous 2003a, 485; Yoshida 2001.
17. See Yoshida 2001, 58–75.
18. Yoshida 2001, 63.
19. Aldous 2003a, 492; Sarantakes 2000, 93. This is a conservative estimate. Yoshida (2001, 72) estimates the number at between 200,000 and 300,000.
20. Yoshida 2001, 72.

political order, however, they stopped short of such actions. In 1957, U.S. authorities yielded to the growing domestic opposition to the land policy and decided to provide annual rental payments to all private owners. By 1962, 50,000 Okinawan landowners had been dispossessed, accounting for 52,000 of the 76,000 acres claimed by U.S. authorities.[21]

1960s: The Growing Movement for Reversion

During the 1960s a number of indigenous political parties and movements brought reversion to the political forefront. In 1962 the Okinawan legislature unanimously passed a resolution that accused the United States of practicing colonial rule against prevailing United Nations ordinances.[22] The single most influential pro-reversion movement was the Okinawan Teachers Association, founded by future governor Yara Chobyo, which had campaigned for the adoption of Japanese educational standards and principles in Okinawa since 1952, equating the struggle for Okinawan education with the struggle for reversion.[23] By the mid-1960s, all Okinawan political parties favored reversion to the mainland, although they differed in their stance regarding the future status of U.S. military bases and broadly reflected the positions held by their counterparts on the mainland. For example, the Okinawan Liberal Democratic Party, generally more pro–United States than the other parties, favored a reversion agreement that allowed for the retention of U.S. bases, whereas the Socialist and Communist parties demanded immediate reversion with complete withdrawal of the bases.[24]

A number of U.S. policies and political missteps further fueled the growth of reversion forces in the 1960s. The high commissioner frequently intervened in local legislative affairs, controversially asserted USCAR's jurisdiction over civil cases originally heard within the GRI court system, and even ousted the outspoken mayor of Naha, Kamejiro Senaga, after his local election.[25] Suspicious of pro-reversion forces and their links to alleged Communist sympathizers, the General Executive also imposed travel bans on prominent pro-reversion leaders and their publications, making Okinawans and Americans alike question the U.S. commitment

---

21. 1962 USCAR pamphlet, cited in Higa 1963, 419.
22. Sarantakes 2000, 61–62.
23. Aldous 2003a, 502.
24. See Higa 1963, 1967.
25. Yoshida 2001, 81–82; Sarantakes 2000, 112–14; Higa 1967, 162–63.

to upholding the islanders' human rights.[26] Meanwhile, cutbacks in aid by the U.S. Congress in the early 1960s undermined the economic argument for U.S. rule, whereas base workers and teachers unions demanded better pay and more favorable labor practices. The extraterritorial criminal jurisdiction afforded U.S. personnel also became a high-profile issue, as crimes and accidents involving U.S. personnel were heavily criticized in the Okinawan press and became powerful symbols for reversion activists. The use of the Okinawan installations to support the unpopular Vietnam War further galvanized public opinion against the bases. The introduction of B-52 bombers in Kadena in 1965, a move that most Okinawans viewed as an aggressive military measure that served no defensive purpose, and port calls by U.S. nuclear-powered submarines were particularly unpopular.[27]

By the late 1960s the reversion movement was peaking in intensity. In 1968 85 percent of the public surveyed by the national newspaper *Asahi Shimbun* in both Okinawa and on the Japanese mainland supported immediate reversion.[28] This swelling of public opinion in favor of reversion provided Japanese prime minister Sato Eisaku with his principal source of bargaining leverage or "audience costs" as he prepared for the November 1969 reversion summit with U.S. president Richard Nixon (see chap. 6).

Reversion, Democratization, and the Political Economy of Base Acceptance

Reversion Politics and the Contentious Basing Issue

Against a backdrop of intensifying public opinion in favor of reversion on both the mainland and in Okinawa, Prime Minister Sato staked his domestic political future on securing a reversion agreement at a November 1969 summit with President Nixon. The deal, successfully concluded amid a flurry of back-channel negotiations, mandated Okinawa's reversion to the Japanese by the end of 1972. In exchange, although it was publicly denied at the time, Japan agreed to impose voluntary quotas on its textile exports to the United States, a concession that Nixon considered vital for maintaining his political support in U.S. southern textile-producing states (see chap. 6).[29] To the disappointment of many reformists on Okinawa, the deal

---

26. Aldous 2003a.
27. Yoshida 2001, 145–48.
28. *Japan Quarterly* 1968, 42.
29. For a insider's full account of the 1969 negotiations and agreement, see Wakaizumi 2002.

allowed U.S. bases to remain on the island subject to the general terms of the 1960 Mutual Security Treaty between Japan and the United States, including the requirement of prior consultation for their use. The United States agreed to remove nuclear weapons from the island but insisted that Sato sign a secret memo agreeing to give favorable consideration to U.S. requests for their reintroduction in an emergency.

The 1969 reversion agreement and the beginning of Okinawa's democratization seemed to further fuel, not mollify, those constituents holding antibase sentiments. Chief among these critics was the former Teachers' Union head and leading reformist Yara Chobyo, who one year earlier had become the island's first popularly elected chief executive. Yara had defeated the Tokyo- and U.S.-backed LDP candidate Nishime Junji on a confrontational platform that opposed the presence of U.S. bases on Okinawa after reversion. Yara publicly decried the reversion deal and insisted that the U.S. military, regardless of its public statements to the contrary, would retain nuclear weapons on the island if it were allowed to stay.

The three years between the signing of the agreement and actual reversion were among the most politically volatile on the island. Okinawans staged multiple demonstrations, many of them violent, to protest the terms of reversion and aspects of the U.S. military presence, especially criminal jurisdictional procedures. For example, in December 1970, in the wake of a U.S. military court's acquittal of a U.S. officer of manslaughter, about seven hundred Okinawans rioted for over six hours, breaking into Kadena airbase and burning seventy-three cars owned by U.S. personnel in the process.[30] With the backing of local newspapers and antibase groups, Yara politically exploited the heightened uncertainty surrounding the bases' future; the Okinawan governor even boycotted the official reversion ceremony on June 1972.

Yara's strong antibase stance and visible leadership paid political dividends: he achieved an easy election victory in June 1972 in the prefecture's first post-reversion gubernatorial elections. Along with Yara, Okinawan voters elected a prefecture assembly composed of a majority of reformist parties (including Socialists and Communists) that opposed the bases and promoted Okinawan identity. Yara's tenure, along with his 1976 reformist

30. On the so-called Koza riots, see Aldous 2003b, esp. 157–60. Aldous observes of the timing of the riots that "while the outburst of anti-Americanism was unsurprising after so many years of foreign occupation, it was puzzling that it came after Prime Minister Sato's diplomatic success of 1969 when President Nixon had agreed to work towards reversion of Okinawa to Japan during 1972" (148). He explains the riots as a response to the political uncertainty over future citizenship rights generated by the reversion agreement.

successor Taira Koichi, was characterized by a number of base-related confrontations with Tokyo and the U.S. military over issues such as the reduction of Okinawan employees on the bases, the appropriate jurisdiction for base-related accidents and crimes, as well as the controversial stationing of the unpopular Japanese Self-Defense Forces on the islands.[31] At the same time, the Okinawan economy, which had been dollarized during U.S. rule, was hit hard by reversion; adoption of the yen led to severe price increases, and economic activity slumped. With the 1973 oil shocks exacerbating economic conditions and with unemployment on the island more than three times the national average, economic issues dominated the 1978 gubernatorial campaign that returned the conservative LDP to power.

State Building and the Political Economy of Base Acquiescence
The election of LDP Nishime Junji in 1978 on a pro–economic development platform marked a turning point in Okinawa's previously contentious "base politics" and began the institutionalization of a comprehensive system of economic payments designed to promote the acquiescence of the Okinawan public to the presence of U.S. forces. Nishime's campaign had been highly critical of the ideological character of previous reformist governors, arguing that the antibase policies of his predecessors had severely damaged the Okinawan economy.

Sensing an important opportunity to institutionalize a smoother set of relations with the new prefecture, Tokyo opened up its coffers almost immediately—in 1979 it increased funding by 21.4 percent over the previous year[32]—to fund large public projects on the island, including the construction of a Nakagusuku harbor, a new highway across the island, and a number of educational and recreational facilities.[33] In cooperation with the Okinawa Development Council, an agency created to aid the island's development, Nishime also formulated a more ambitious developmental plan for the next decade. With the backing of the central government, the LDP governor established an International Exchange Division and the Okinawa International Foundation, meant to turn Okinawa into a hub of international trade, exchange, and conventions in the Southeast Asian area. Nishime also aggressively courted industrial investment from the mainland and promoted domestic and international tourism.[34]

31. Egami 1994, 834–35.
32. Eldridge 2004, 26.
33. Eldridge 2004, 24–26; Egami 1994, 836.
34. Egami 1994, 836–37.

In addition to these public goods, Tokyo during the Nishime administration targeted politically key local interest groups through the use of selective economic incentives. After reversion in 1972, Tokyo increased the rent it paid to the more than 30,000 private U.S. base landowners by 600 percent, ensuring that they received rents in excess of prevailing market value. By 1982, all but 153 of the remaining 25,300 private landowners had voluntarily signed lease extensions.[35] Construction companies and their subcontractors colluded with the prefecture and Tokyo to apportion and undertake hundreds of these new public works and development projects. In 1978, Tokyo introduced "sympathy payments" as part of its new program of host national support for Okinawan base workers in order to stabilize and increase the number of locals employed on the bases.[36] As a result, even though the U.S. bases' direct contribution to the local economy steadily declined after reversion, Nishime and Tokyo introduced a variety of economic incentives to ensure local acceptance of the bases. This quid pro quo has since become institutionalized and remains a hallmark of Okinawa's relations with the Japanese mainland.[37]

As a result of these public works and selected incentives, much of the antibase sentiment that characterized the Yara-led reversion campaign and subsequent administration was politically neutralized. Nishime handily won reelection in 1982 and again in 1986, despite severe criticism from reformist opposition parties that he was too acquiescent on the basing issue. Reformist mayors in base-hosting districts also lost several elections, thereby improving base relations with local community leaders.[38] Antibase activists and reformist political parties continued to organize demonstrations throughout the 1980s, but the basing issue lost much of its appeal for most Okinawans as economic issues trumped antibase activism. Acknowledging the mixed feelings toward the bases held by the Okinawan public, Nishime himself commented about antibase protests in the 1980s: "What Okinawans say [in protesting the military bases] and what

35. Eldridge 2004, 67.
36. From a peak at reversion of 18,118 Okinawan base workers, the total number fell to 7,177 in 1979. Host-nation support stemmed this decline and stabilized the number at about 8,000 (8,349 in the year 1996). Hook and Siddle 2003, 4.
37. In 1970 the direct contribution of the bases to the Okinawan economy was 25.6 percent, whereas in 1996 it had declined to just 5.7 percent. Hook and Siddle 2003, 4–5. However, Tokyo's array of compensation and burden payments has continued to increase. For a full account of Okinawa's "compensation politics," see Cooley and Marten 2006.
38. *Los Angeles Times* 1981.

they want are two different things."[39] Nevertheless, this institutionalized pattern of base payments would be severely tested by local political developments in the 1990s.

Okinawa's New Crisis: The 1995 Rape and the Renewed Contestation of the Bases

After a period of relative calm, the basing issue once again exploded with an intensity that few would have previously predicted. On September 5, 1995, three U.S. servicemen in the town of Kin abducted and then raped a twelve-year-old Okinawan schoolgirl.[40] Initially, U.S. authorities did not hand over the perpetrators to Japanese custody, thereby drawing attention to the SOFA's criminal jurisdiction procedures. Within a few weeks, the incident had sparked a renewed crisis in local-U.S. relations and drawn considerable global media coverage. On October 21, an antibase mobilization effort produced a demonstration of 85,000 strong, the largest in more than twenty-five years, and the Okinawa basing issue was raised to the highest priority of U.S.-Japanese relations since the reversion agreement.[41] Over the next three years the legitimacy and legality of the U.S. bases were once again contested by a reformist Okinawan government supported by the local media and a powerful and networked community of antibase NGOs.

Local-Central Tensions over the Base Leases

Okinawa's governor Ota Masahide seized on the rape and its aftermath to launch an all-out political attack against the U.S. basing presence. The reformist Ota, previously a historian at the Ryukyu University, had been elected governor in 1990 in the midst of the Gulf Crisis and in the wake of some base-related accidents, ending three terms of LDP rule during which economic issues were given greater attention by the prefecture than were basing issues. Ota proved to be popular and was comfortably reelected in 1994.

Ota immediately used the 1995 rape to challenge Tokyo's jurisdictional authority over base-related matters by contesting the legal validity of the basing presence and invoking Okinawan identity to justify his efforts.

39. Abrams 1981.
40. See Johnson 1999, 116–19.
41. Millard 1999, 96–97.

Just weeks after the rape, Ota announced that he would refuse to sign the extensions to the private land leases on which U.S. military installations were situated. He also vowed to challenge the constitutionality of the lease renewals by arguing that they challenged Article 29 of the Japanese Constitution, which states that "the right to own or to hold property is inviolable."[42] Despite favorable publicity on Okinawa, Ota's legal challenge found little sympathy in the courts. With the leases about to expire in March 1996, the Naha branch of the Fukuoka court issued a speedy verdict mandating that Ota sign the leases. Then, in August 1996, the Japanese Supreme Court upheld the lower court's decision. Ruling that the special law requiring land lease renewals was constitutional, the court declared that Ota's actions "harmed the public interest." Out of legal options, Ota finally agreed to a compromise offered by Tokyo. In September 1996, the Okinawan governor met with Japanese prime minister Hashimoto, who pledged to work with all sides to reduce the basing presence and relocate facilities to less intrusive areas on the island. Hashimoto also announced the allocation of an additional ¥5 billion package to assist in the prefecture's development. Ota agreed to the deal, and the immediate crisis seemed to be diffused.

In addition to increased compensation payments and public works money, the aftermath of the rape crisis yielded a number of new institutions designed to ease Okinawa's "special burden" and improve U.S. military relations with local communities. In November 1995, Tokyo and Washington formed the Special Action Committee on Okinawa (SACO), which was charged with recommending measures to reduce and consolidate U.S. military facilities on the island. SACO delivered its recommendations in December 1996, but many of its proposals, such as relocation of the U.S. Marine air station at Futenma, involved controversial new construction or generated considerable opposition among antibase activists and community leaders.[43] U.S. forces themselves instituted new measures to curb drinking among personnel while off base and introduced a number of new community outreach programs.[44] Finally, in a remarkable act, the

---

42. As quoted in Mulgan 2000, 163. I draw on her analysis of the relevant legal issues.
43. For the full list of SACO measures, see http://www.globalsecurity.org/military/facility/okinawa.htm (accessed May 2007). On the Futenma relocation, see Gabe 2000; Eldridge 2000. On the difficulties and local barriers to implementing the SACO recommendations, see Cooley and Marten 2006.
44. Author's interviews with U.S. military and State Department consulate officials, Okinawa, May 2003.

Japanese Ministry of Foreign Affairs created an ambassadorship to Okinawa. A high-ranking official from Tokyo's Ministry of Foreign Affairs filled the post, whose main purpose was to facilitate dialogue and smooth relations between local administrators on Okinawa and the United States military, as well as educate rotating U.S. military officers on the cultural and historical sensitivities of the basing issue on the island.[45]

The Role of the Media and the Networked Antibase Movement
The Okinawan media and NGOs were Ota's strongest political backers and, with the help of global networks, played a key role in politicizing the 1995 crisis and challenging the legality of elements of the base contracts. Each of the island's two main local newspapers—the *Ryuku Shimpo* and the *Okinawa Times*—has a readership of about 200,000, and together they account for about 90 percent of the island's newspaper circulation. Since USCAR rule, both newspapers have remained strongly antibase in their news reportage and editorial stances, focusing their base coverage on "negative" stories such as social tensions, crimes by U.S. personnel, and military accidents.[46]

The *Shimpo* first reported the rape story on September 8, three days after the incident, in a small article with a follow-up the next day. However, the *Times* ran an extensive front-page story that included commentaries by police on the difficulty of securing custody of those charged and complaints about the SOFA's criminal jurisdiction procedures. The *Times*'s extended coverage sparked a subsequent competition among the local papers as both proceeded to cover the various elements of the story, including the SOFA question, on their front pages.[47] According to one content analysis of the Okinawan press, over the next two months the *Okinawa Times* ran 348 stories related to the rape and SOFA issues, only ten of which actually dealt with the facts of the crime. A total of 76 percent of all the stories run on the issue focused on local anger and "demands for change" regarding the status of the bases.[48]

45. Author's interview with MOFA official stationed in Okinawa, Naha, May 2003.
46. Author's interview with editorial board member of a major Okinawan newspaper, Naha, May 2003.
47. Okamura 1998, 9–12.
48. Hollstein 2000, 195, 196. Mark Clifford Hollstein interprets Okinawan newspaper coverage of the story as consistent with their promotion of a narrative of "unwanted military occupation" in regard to the bases.

The mainland Japanese media offered minimal coverage of the story for the first week and only started giving more attention to the issue after the *Washington Post* and *New York Times* ran stories about the incident and the basing issue on September 20. With the issue now deemed newsworthy, the mainland *Asahi Shimbun* ran nearly four hundred reports and features on base-related issues during October and November, elevating the U.S. basing issue to national awareness for first time since reversion.[49] The involvement of the U.S. and international media was the crucial factor in turning the story into a priority for the Japanese national media.

The 1995 incident also galvanized a number of NGOs working on base-related issues. Externally, NGOs and peace activists such as the Okinawan Women Act against Military Violence took their agendas to various international forums, including the United Nations International Women's Forum in Beijing and the U.S. Congress, and forged international networks with other antibase NGOs in Korea and the Philippines.[50] Internally, NGOs from various parts of the country that had been working on a number of base-related issues—such as crimes by U.S. personnel, environmental pollution, and women's issues—joined together to form a network. According to Caroline Spencer, the contentious events of the mid-1990s turned a disparate set of groups working on base-related single issues into a new and vocal antibase social movement with extensive international ties.[51] In turn, these groups supported Ota's contestation of the base leases and actively opposed the SACO recommendation to relocate the Futenma station to a new offshore heliport in the north of the country.[52]

Economic Backlash: The 1996 Referendum and Ota's 1998 Election Defeat
By fall 1996, Ota's refusal to sign the land leases coupled with the island's dramatic social mobilization and extensive media coverage created the impression that a strong majority of Okinawan citizens agreed that the U.S. bases should be withdrawn from the island. However, subsequent elections, particularly the 1996 regional referendum and the 1998 prefecture gubernatorial election, would demonstrate that the level of support for the strict antibase position and the revocation of existing basing accords

49. From the data compiled by Okamura 1998, 14.
50. Author's interview with an Okinawan prefecture assembly member and NGO activist, Naha, May 2003. Also see Spencer 2003, 134–36; Francis 1999.
51. Spencer 2003.
52. Gabe 2000; Eldridge 2000.

was not as strong as first appeared, despite widespread outrage at the 1995 rape. Tokyo's well-institutionalized system of public and selective compensation payments would politically override Ota and his followers' appeals to antimilitarism and Okinawan identity.[53]

The results of a 1996 referendum called by the Okinawan governor were the first indication that significant segments of the Okinawan population did not support Ota's open contestation of the bases. The referendum, an unusual practice in Japanese politics, was called for September 8, 1996, and was designed to directly challenge the central government's authority and legitimacy on the basing issue. The referendum language itself was left deliberately broad so as to attract maximum support. It asked that the voter agree or disagree with the two-part question: "[How do you feel about] reviewing the Japan–United States Status of Forces Agreement and reducing the American bases in our prefecture?"[54] Although 89 percent of those who voted agreed with the proposition, 40 percent of those eligible did not turn out to vote, despite a highly publicized campaign by the prefecture government to ensure a big voter turnout. Therefore just 53 percent of eligible voters agreed with the general ballot proposition. According to Robert Eldridge, this result was "remarkable" and most likely is explained by the fact that many more probase factions simply refused to vote, something the conservative LDP had lobbied for.[55] Eldridge observes that important social and political groups such as local LDP members, private landowners, local businessmen, a breakaway base workers group, and members of the self-defense forces all opposed the motion and lobbied against turnout. As a result, the referendum was hardly the strong, popular antibase mandate that the prefectural government and antibase groups had hoped for.

Then remarkably, on November 15, 1998, Ota himself was narrowly defeated in Okinawa's gubernatorial election by LDP candidate Inamine Keichi. Inamine, who was heavily backed by the central government and LDP political machinery, had campaigned on the platform of securing large amounts of development aid from Tokyo in exchange for maintaining U.S. installations under the SACO process. Like Nishime, who twenty years before had also ousted a reformist on an economic platform, Inamine accused Ota of placing his antibase ideology above the economic needs of the island. He was backed by many younger voters, who remained unhappy

53. For details, see Cooley and Marten 2006; Mulgan 2000.
54. Eldridge 1997, 879. This paragraph draws on Eldridge's helpful analysis.
55. Eldridge 1997.

with the country's high unemployment rate.[56] Despite his once significant popularity, visibility, and strong support among NGOs, activists, and the local media, Ota was defeated just three years after having contested the U.S. basing presence in the aftermath of the Kin town rape. Not surprisingly, in the comprehensive decentralization bill passed in 1999 by the mainland Diet, base-related issues and legal matters were exempted from this new devolution and enhanced local autonomy.[57] In 2002, Inamine secured a comfortable reelection on a similar economic platform and a track record of conciliatory relations with the center. Politically, Tokyo's well-institutionalized system of public goods and selective economic incentives had trumped the mobilization of the antibase reformists and their local allies.[58]

Once More: The 2004 Helicopter Crash, Realignment, and Nakaima's Election
Over the course of the next two terms, Inamine was caught between the political pressure from Tokyo to better accommodate the U.S. military and calls by the local media, mayors, and civic groups to reduce the negative impact of the bases. Notably, important parts of the SACO process continued to stall, especially on the intractable issue of moving Futenma.

On August 13, 2004, the incident that many U.S. and Japanese officials feared materialized when a U.S. Marine Corps helicopter, based in Futenma, crashed onto the grounds of the nearby Okinawa International University. U.S. military officials sealed off the crash scene and denied local police access, citing as justification a standing provision in the Agreed Minutes of the SOFA.[59] A subsequent investigation revealed that the crash had been caused by human error and poor maintenance of the helicopter's rotor. The crash and its aftermath generated a swell of public criticism among Okinawan local politicians, civic groups, and the media concerning the "occupation"-like behavior of U.S. forces on the island. On September 12, 2004, in the largest antibase protest since 1995, over 30,000 demonstrators gathered in Ginowan to demand Futenma's closure. The crash also seemed to expedite the conclusion of an agreement between the U.S. and

---

56. Eldridge 2004, 50–51.
57. Mulgan 2000, 162–63.
58. Underscoring the slight probase shift in Okinawan public opinion, a 2001 poll conducted by the Japanese cabinet office in Tokyo found that by a narrow plurality of 45.7 percent to 44.4 percent, Okinawans believed that the U.S. bases are "necessary" or "unavoidable" for Japanese security as opposed to "unnecessary" or "dangerous." See Cooley and Marten 2006.
59. For an account of the incident, see Johnson 2007, 195–98.

Japanese governments for a fundamental base realignment in Japan. In May 2006, after months of intensive negotiations, Tokyo announced plans for a dramatic realignment of U.S. forces in Japan (see chap. 6), including a plan to relocate 8,000 marines from Okinawa to Guam by 2014. The plan also renewed calls for the relocation of Futenma from its central location in Ginowan to a new northern facility at Camp Schwab near Nago, this time with the planned construction of two new runways in a V pattern that would also extend offshore from Cape Henoko.

Announcement of the realignment and future reductions did not satisfy Okinawa's vocal antibase constituency. With Governor Inamine retiring after two terms, the 2006 gubernatorial election would be critical to local acceptance and implementation of the new bilateral accord on realignment. Just as in 1998, antibase fervor seemed to initially favor the campaign of the Socialist candidate, former peace tour guide and Upper House member Itokazu Keiko, who ran principally on opposing U.S. bases and the proposed Futenma relocation plan. The local business community and the Abe government in Tokyo backed the LDP candidate Nakaima Hirokazu, a former head of the Okinawa Chamber of Commerce, whose campaign emphasized the need for economic revitalization on the island and a more conciliatory stance toward Tokyo on the Futenma move and basing issues.[60] As in 1998, the LDP candidate narrowly defeated the antibase one (this time by 36,000 votes or about 5 percent), once again underscoring the considerable hidden vote within the island's electorate that was driven by economic concerns rather than purely antibase political appeals.[61]

Just a few days after Nakaima's election, the Japanese government announced it would provide extra grants to Okinawa for the relocation of Futenma, including raising Tokyo's contribution to new public works projects to 95 percent from the usual 33–50 percent.[62] Then in February 2007, defense ministry officials withdrew the proportion of the new funds earmarked for Nago after its newly elected mayor called for a revision of the relocation plan.[63] In April 2007, as other local officials fell into line behind the realignment plan, the Lower House passed the final Law on Special Measures for U.S. Forces, which described its purpose as "to provide for special measures to enhance convenience in the daily life in communities adjacent to

60. Johnson 2006a.
61. Johnson 2006b.
62. *Japan Economic Newswire* 2006.
63. *Economist* 2007.

defense facilities and to facilitate USFJ realignment."[64] The act, which is valid until 2017, includes an array of new categories of subsidies and payoffs, conditionally sequenced into four separate stages, with benchmarks designed to monitor local communities' compliance with the realignment process.[65]

The results of the 1996 referendum and the 1998 and 2004 gubernatorial elections underscore the institutionalization of compensation payments and the political/economic ties that bind Okinawa with the central government in Tokyo. Governor Ota used the 1995 rape as an opening to criticize the bases and challenge the central government's authority to make base-related decisions on behalf of the island prefecture.[66] Ota's campaign, like Itokazu's eight years later, was backed by a vocal network of activists, local politicians, and media supporters, and it played on a recurring theme in Okinawan politics that Tokyo and Washington collude against the island. However, Tokyo has countered these local challenges to its jurisdictional authority by targeting compensation and burden payments to key segments of the Okinawan population. These selective incentives have ensured that a slight majority acquiesce, albeit tacitly, to the U.S. basing presence and its governing U.S.-Japanese security agreements. Tokyo has institutionalized this comprehensive system of material incentives because, for a large segment of the Okinawan public, the U.S. military presence lacks contractual legitimacy as a result of its historical links to occupation and military administration. This particular triangular relationship and its compensation politics operate in stark contrast to the case of the Azores, whose more accepting attitude toward the U.S. basing presence produces fewer material benefits from the central government.

The Azores: Mid-Atlantic State Formation and the Politics of Neglect

The Early Years: Establishing the Bases and the Authoritarian Rule of Salazar

As in Okinawa, the U.S. military presence in the Azores has its origins in World War II, although the United States originally gained access through

---

64. *Sankei Shimbun* 2007a.
65. *Sankei Shimbun* 2007b.
66. On Ota's view of political devolution, the bases, and his tenure as governor, see Ota 2003.

Portugal's agreement as opposed to actual combat. Dr. António de Oliveira Salazar, who since 1932 had headed a conservative authoritarian regime in Portugal, remained neutral during the first years of World War II. As Allied concerns for protecting Atlantic shipping lanes from German submarines mounted, Churchill and Roosevelt considered taking over the islands to establish a mid-Atlantic staging post. Sensing in 1943 that the war was turning decisively in favor of the Allies, Salazar agreed to invite the British to use the Terceira airbase and invoked the centuries-old Portuguese-British alliance.[67] In November 1944, after some pressure, Salazar granted the United States permission to construct and operate an additional airfield on the island of Santa Maria with unrestricted use rights.[68] The agreement was renewed in 1946 and then again in 1947 and 1948; the latter agreement granted the United States use of Lajes and Santa Maria airfields until the end of 1952. For the United States, the Azores airfields became a vital air bridge between North America and Europe/Africa, with its strategic value on a par with that of Iceland and Greenland.[69] In 1949, NATO granted Portugal membership despite its authoritarian regime, primarily because the facilities in the Azores were considered critical for the new alliance.[70]

NATO membership was not exactly embraced by Lisbon. Despite Portugal's traditional Atlanticism, Salazar personally and openly disliked the United States, mainly because of U.S. support for decolonization and national liberation movements. At the time, Portugal maintained an extensive empire scattered throughout Africa and parts of Asia, as well as its Atlantic island possessions, and Salazar regarded the overseas territories as an integral part of the Portuguese state. Preserving Portuguese sovereignty and territorial integrity was also critical for the Portuguese military, whose support Salazar depended on.[71]

From the first negotiations over the base in 1944, Salazar used the Azores as a bargaining chip to secure American support for Portuguese colonial policy. In exchange for these initial access agreements, U.S. officials promised to return East Timor to Portuguese rule after Japanese occupation. Kenneth Maxwell observes that "the concession was the first significant

67. The definitive English-language account of the behind-the-scenes maneuvering by the Allies to secure base access can be found in Herz 2004.
68. Calvet de Magalhães 1993, 276. The text of the agreement can be found in Vintras 1974, 178–80.
69. National Security Council, "Base Rights in Greenland, Iceland and the Azores," Washington, DC, November 25, 1947, in *DDRS*.
70. Monje 1992, 7.
71. See Spruyt 2005, 176–203.

breach in the United States' anticolonial position—subsequently the starting point for many of the problems which were to bedevil U.S. policy toward Portugal and Portuguese Africa thereafter."[72] Salazar cared little for the actual liberal political missions associated with NATO or U.S. foreign policy and continued to regard Portuguese membership in the Western security system as a way to preserve the integrity of Lisbon's colonial holdings. Although NATO refused to guarantee the territorial integrity of Portuguese Africa, the United States assured Salazar, in a secret addendum to the 1951 bilateral accord, that if needed it would consent to a transfer of NATO military equipment "from metropolitan Portuguese territory to any Portuguese colonial territory."[73]

On the Azores themselves, the U.S. military and the islanders generally enjoyed friendly relations over the next two decades. The islands' economy, underdeveloped even in comparison to the relatively poor Portuguese mainland, was given a considerable boost by the U.S. military presence, even though Lisbon did not demand substantial economic quid pro quo.[74] In 1957, U.S. installations employed 1,372 Portuguese nationals, and Lajes was described in an American base review as "a cooperative enterprise," with the U.S. presence contributing annually about $20 million to the economy.[75] The Portuguese authorities also signed a separate SOFA to cover the Azores, which effectively gave U.S. authorities exclusive criminal jurisdiction, but no serious incidents materialized to arouse local complaints.[76] Most important, the extensive transnational ties between the Azorean communities on the islands and in North America ensured that "the presence of American personnel on the islands never posed any problems with the local population. Americans were not only easily accepted but very much welcomed, giving employment and prosperity to the islanders."[77]

Showdown: Kennedy, the Azores Bases, and African Colonialism

In the early 1960s the bases in the Azores became embroiled in the tension between Salazar's need to preserve the integrity of the Portuguese empire

72. Maxwell 1997, 49.
73. The secret exchange of notes is quoted and discussed in Antunes 1999, 151.
74. See the analysis in Crollen 1973, 90–97.
75. Employment numbers are from Nash 1957, 133.
76. The Azorean SOFA is still in effect, whereas the NATO SOFA applies to U.S. military personnel on the Portuguese mainland. See Nash 1957, 137. Briefing by the U.S. Legal Affairs Department, Lajes airbase, May 2005.
77. Calvet de Magalhães 1993, 280.

and U.S. policy on African decolonization. After the Kennedy administration took office, it began to openly support and fund national liberation movements in Angola and Mozambique as part of its new Africa policy. In March 1961 the United States voted in the UN Security Council to condemn Portuguese military actions in Angola and supported a resolution calling for an independent investigation into the conflict.[78] Salazar was livid, in part because he considered the U.S. vote an affront to the long-term territorial integrity of the Portuguese state, but also because he was facing internal unrest among the military and the vote put him in a precarious position with his most loyal military supporters.[79]

In response, Salazar confronted the Azores issue head on. He mobilized thousands of protestors outside the U.S. embassy in Lisbon who demanded that the United States stay out of Portuguese affairs and get out of the Azores. He also formally refused an American request to build a radar and seismographic installation on the island of Madeira and threatened to expel the United States from the Azores altogether.[80] Portuguese negotiators called off talks on extending the basing agreement that was due to expire in 1962, and Salazar's attitude toward the United States was described as verging on "psychopathic."[81] The Portuguese side threatened to evict the United States if it organized or participated in any type of international embargo or sanctions against Lisbon.[82] The U.S. Pentagon, viewing the loss of the Azores as unacceptable, also pressured the administration to drop its new Africa policy toward Portugal. These pressures had their intended effect; by summer 1962 the State Department stopped criticizing Portuguese actions in Africa, and the U.S. delegation at the UN opposed all resolutions that criticized Portuguese colonialism and threatened sanctions.[83]

---

78. An excellent account of the episode can be found in Rodrigues 2004.
79. In fact, in April 1961 Salazar quashed a coup attempt by his minister of defense.
80. Rodrigues 2004, 7, 8.
81. A CIA memo in early 1962 described Salazar and the basing issue in the following terms: "United States negotiations with Portugal for renewal of base rights in the Azores are going to be made extremely difficult by the bitterness of doctor Salazar towards the United States. Source was amazed at the depth of his dislike for the government of the United States. Source had assumed that various anti-American statements made by him were political expedients but Source is now convinced the dislike is almost psychopathic. From this attitude, Source concluded that Salazar will demand extreme political concessions." Central Agency Intelligence, "Portugal: Azores Base Negotiations," February 2, 1962, in *DDRS*.
82. Central Intelligence Agency, "Significance of Portuguese and Spanish Colonial Problems for the U.S.," July 11, 1963, 2, in *DDRS*.
83. On the divisions and debates on the American side that led to this policy moderation, see Schlesinger 1965, 562–63.

Shrewdly, Salazar kept the legal status of the Azores bases in abeyance for the rest of the 1960s so as to maintain his leverage over the decolonization issue, and the bases operated informally. Like Marcos and Franco, Salazar used the basing issue to extract a political concession from the United States that was critical for his domestic political survival.

When the Nixon administration, with its more realistic orientation, assumed office, the dynamics of the issue changed somewhat. Washington dropped all mention of decolonization, and the U.S. Navy even started to take advantage of Portuguese port facilities in Angola and Mozambique.[84] After the outbreak of the Yom Kippur War in October 1973, Portugal, in a controversial move, granted unconditional transit rights at Lajes to the United States for its resupply of Israel, a role that turned out to be militarily decisive.[85] The Caetano regime, which had replaced Salazar in 1968, paid a heavy price for granting these use rights. Arab oil producers boycotted Portugal even after the embargo on other Western nations was lifted, causing the Portuguese economy to slide into crisis. Just six months later Marcelo Caetano was overthrown in a revolutionary coup that would mark the beginning of the mainland's tumultuous democratization.

Lisbon's Communist Takeover and Democratization

As Okinawa was undergoing its post-reversion turmoil, the mid-1970s in continental Portugal and the Azores was characterized by a very different set of democratizing dynamics and triangular politics.

The Revolution of Carnations and Azorean Reaction
In April 1974 a group of junior military officers, some with left-wing ties, seized power in Lisbon as part of the Armed Forces Movement (MFA), ending decades of conservative authoritarian rule.[86] The coup was broadly supported by the mainland public, but it ushered in a year of considerable

---

84. Maxwell 1997, 47.
85. The exact bargaining over the use of Lajes is still a matter of some dispute. According to then U.S. Secretary of State Henry Kissinger, Portugal initially refused the request and had demanded, as quid pro quo, military equipment for its African colonial wars. Kissinger (1982, 520) writes that he refused the Portuguese demand and drafted a "Presidential letter of unusual abruptness" to Caetano that threatened to abandon Portugal should it not grant access rights. Kenneth Maxwell (1997, 55) claims that in exchange for granting access, Portuguese officials were secretly offered a supply of "red-eye" ground-to-air missiles in support of their African wars.
86. I rely on Maxwell's (1997) account of the Portuguese Revolution.

turmoil in Portugal's internal and external affairs. Some officers of the so-called Revolution of the Carnations maintained ties to the Portuguese Communist Party (PCP) and soon after replaced the pro-Western General António de Spinola with General Francisco da Costa Gomes. In March 1975, the radical prime minister Vasco Gonçalves nationalized the country's major industries and banks and introduced a program of land reform, as the MFA jockeyed for power with the provisional government and the country's political parties.[87] By the turbulent "hot summer" of 1975, Communists had almost complete control over the country's cabinet, and political uncertainty regarding Portugal's political future had reached its peak.

The revolution also had a profound impact on Portugal's relations with the world.[88] The collapse of the Caetano regime initiated broad decolonization as timetables were finalized for the withdrawal of Portuguese troops in Africa and East Timor. Portugal's NATO allies cut military ties to the country and were concerned that Lisbon's new statement of "neutrality" might even put Portugal in the Soviet camp.[89] In the United States, President Gerald Ford and Secretary of State Henry Kissinger hinted that Portugal could be expelled from NATO, and American officials funneled money into covert support for mainland anti-Communist parties and institutions such as the Catholic Church.[90]

The Rise of the FLA in the Azores

Events in Lisbon had a profound impact on the Azores. The conservative islanders feared Communist rule, a fact made abundantly clear in the April 1975 elections in which the Communists received less than 2 percent of the vote, compared to 60 percent for the conservative Popular Democratic Party and 25 percent for the Socialists.[91]

Moreover, the revolution prompted a growth in the clandestine political activity of the Azorean Liberation Front (FLA), a movement dedicated to attaining independence for the Azores. The FLA was led by the U.S.-based migrant José de Almeida and maintained strong transnational ties with fund-raisers in the United States.[92] The movement organized

---

87. Maxwell 1997, 112–13.
88. For an overview, see Maxwell 1991; Bermeo 1988.
89. See Cook 1975.
90. Binder 1975.
91. On the mainland, the Portuguese Socialist Party had won with 37.9 percent of the vote, whereas the Popular Democrats (PPD) received 26.4 and the Communists 12.5 percent.
92. Moniz 2004, 61.

anti-Communist demonstrations, including a 30,000-person anti-left protest on the island of São Miguel in June 1975, and even instigated a small bombing campaign.[93] During the June 1975 demonstration, protestors seized the local radio station and forced the Lisbon-appointed governor to resign. A few days later, another FLA-organized mob seized the Portuguese minister of education, who had flown out to inaugurate the new Azorean University. FLA activists openly declared that if the mainland were to remain Communist, the Azores would declare independence.[94] In 1976 one poll suggested that 63 percent of Azoreans favored some sort of separation from the Portuguese state (autonomy or independence), and 70 percent of those believed it should come in the form of independence (45 percent of all Azoreans polled).[95]

In its mobilization efforts the FLA pitted the Portuguese mainland against the United States. FLA propaganda and leaflets warned that Communist rule would prohibit Azoreans from seeing their migrant relatives living in the United States and Canada. The FLA also drew attention to the Lajes base, claiming that Lisbon kept the revenues paid by the U.S. military and gave the islanders little in return for local capital investment, education, and infrastructural improvements.[96] FLA leaders and Popular Democratic Party representatives demanded that Lisbon include Azorean representatives in any future negotiations over the base's status.[97] Also, many Azoreans actually got their news from the U.S. Armed Forces radio broadcasts located on Terceira Island, which presented the revolutionary regime in Lisbon in a less than positive light.[98]

Plenty of circumstantial evidence supports allegations that the United States covertly supported the FLA, and it seems unthinkable that Washington had not finalized a plan to secure continued use of the Azores bases in the event of sustained Communist rule in Lisbon. Promoting Azorean independence was the logical course of action. As Scott Monje points out, Kissinger's publicly expressed view in 1975 that the loss of Portugal would be "inconsequential" may have been rooted in the belief that the loss of the base could be averted simply through recognizing and defending Azorean independence.[99]

93. Gallagher 1983, 219.
94. *Time* 1975.
95. *New York Times* poll, as cited in Moniz 2004, 63.
96. Sobel 1976, 110; *Washington Post* 1975.
97. Wheeler 1975.
98. Szulc 1975, 13.
99. Monje 1992, 8. Moniz (2004, 69) also suggests that although supporting independence was the most favored political stance, Kissinger considered annexing the islands.

Miguel Moniz suggests that most of the organization and mobilization of the FLA occurred within the southeastern New England Azorean communities, whose businessmen provided much of the movement's funding.[100] The CIA worked with the Catholic Church and the transnational Azorean migrant communities to establish a Catholic university on the islands.[101] During the tense summer of 1975, the FLA met with U.S. State Department officials to discuss Azorean independence and the preservation of base access.[102] Philip Agee, a former CIA agent involved in Portuguese affairs, stated in November 1975 that "the separatist movement in the Azores, already gaining momentum among U.S. residents of Azorean origin, may be promoted by the CIA as a last resort for preserving U.S. bases there."[103] Former West German chancellor Helmut Schmidt provides a final piece of strong circumstantial evidence. Schmidt recounts in his memoirs that Gerald Ford asked him in May 1975, at a NATO meeting in Brussels, "How would the Europeans react if the Azores seceded from Portugal and declared their independence?"[104] Whereas in the Okinawan case, the U.S. military worked with the government of Japan to develop institutions and economic incentives to diffuse Okinawan antibase sentiment, in the Azorean case the United States covertly backed island separatists against the mainland government to ensure that base access would be guaranteed in the event that Portuguese democratization ushered in a Communist government.

Decentralization and Constitutional Reforms

In the end, political events on the mainland and significant institutional changes diffused the FLA's campaign for independence and reassured

---

100. Moniz 2004, 69. Moniz further observes that "the Azores' important geo-strategic position had ramifications for the construction of Azorean transnational identity as the US government participated in supporting and fomenting conceptions Açorianidade among local migrant communities. The fallout of the policies worked to support and further promote conceptions of transnational Azorean identity and the link between the migrant communities living abroad and those in the islands themselves. Activities in the area were not limited to the migrant communities alone, as CIA operatives were also present on the islands working to stir up nationalist sentiments among the Azoreans there" (70).
101. Moniz 2004, 70; Szulc 1975, 11.
102. Harvey 1978, 75.
103. Dratch 1975. Dratch provides a helpful overview of the military significance of the facilities, particularly their antisubmarine activities, and their functions in 1975.
104. Schmidt (1989, 168) replied that "the East European propaganda machines would present it as American interference. Western Europe, however, would accept a separation of the Azores if the situation in Lisbon becomes untenable. But today that is not the case. Therefore at present a declaration of independence on the part of the Azores would not be justified in the eyes of Western Europe."

worried U.S. military planners. MFA rule brought considerable disarray, and its actions engendered a backlash among Portugal's democratic parties, which united behind the rapidly rising Socialist Party. In June 1976, Socialist candidate Mário Soares triumphed in the national election and became the first democratically elected prime minister of Portugal in over fifty years. In a prudent move, Soares invited several islanders into his cabinet and offered them posts in the Foreign Ministry.[105]

In April 1976, a new democratic constitution was passed that delegated new powers to the Azores and Madeira and created a new regional parliament with complete fiscal autonomy.[106] In June, in the first regional elections since passage of the constitution, the conservative Popular Democrats won with 60 percent of the vote, and the thirty-six-year-old João Mota Amaral became the region's first president. By the end of 1976, the Portuguese political crisis and immediate separatist threat had passed, and the United States and most Azoreans seemed comfortable with the direction of the Socialist government. In 1978, Lisbon granted the Azores the right to send a separate representative to U.S.-Portugal talks concerning the Lajes base.[107]

Although the autonomy afforded the islands by the 1976 Constitution (reaffirmed in 1989) took the momentum out of the FLA's campaign, a few later episodes emphasized lingering center-periphery tensions. The most serious of these occurred in April 1978 at the height of a dispute over the exact contours of regional autonomy, when the Portuguese deputy prime minister António de Almeida Santos was attacked by a separatist crowd during an island visit, as the Azorean police once again passively stood by.[108] In 1986 the Portuguese military strongly objected to a decision by the regional government to display the Azorean flag alongside the Portuguese one at official ceremonies, an episode that became known as the "war of the two flags."[109] And despite decentralization, the islands remained relatively poor, and some Azoreans complained that they received inadequate compensation from the mainland for their "contributions to the nation," which ranged from their agricultural production to hosting the U.S. base.[110]

---

105. Gallagher 1979, 356.
106. A good English-language overview of the 1976 Constitution as it pertains to the Azores can be found in Amaral 1992, 18–22.
107. Gallagher 1979, 357–58.
108. Gallagher 1979, 357.
109. Graham 1990, 31.
110. For a critical appraisal, see Leite 1992. These complaints are almost always in the context of Azorean–mainland Portugal relations, not Azorean-American relations.

The Reformalization of the Basing Agreement

Negotiations over the terms of the 1983 agreement reflected both the dynamics of democratization on the Portuguese mainland and the increased involvement of the islands' regional government as an independent actor in the triangular relationship. Kenneth Maxwell observes that the Azores "had felt [under authoritarian government] that its own needs were slighted—a feeling that could not be expressed under the authoritarian regime, but which, after the autonomy granted by the Constitution of 1976, could be forcefully articulated even in the course of bilateral negotiations with the United States."[111] On the Portuguese mainland, pressures mounted before the negotiations, with politicians and the media calling for greater Portuguese decision-making in the use of the bases and increased compensation in line with that offered to other strategically important U.S. allies such as Spain, Greece, and Turkey. The 1983 agreement and the supplemental 1984 technical agreements formally updated (although they did not replace) the 1951 agreement and authorized the continuing use of the islands' airstrips, military installations, and communications facilities.[112] Article II acknowledged Portugal's "full sovereignty" over the facilities, set ceilings on troop levels, and designated that a Portuguese commander head Lajes. In terms of use rights, the agreement required that the United States get approval from Lisbon for any non-NATO mission involving the bases. Compensation packages were significantly increased, reaching $148 million in 1984 and $208 million in 1985. Of this mix of economic and security assistance, the United States agreed to pay $40 million a year directly to the regional Azorean government.[113]

Although the Azores continued to receive its annual $40 million, tensions between Washington and Lisbon rose when U.S. congressional cutbacks in military aid greatly reduced the actual 1985–87 aid payments from the commitment levels.[114] Adopting the hard bargaining position of his southern European counterparts, Prime Minister Aníbal Cavaco Silva threatened a formal renegotiation of the agreement if the United States

---

111. Maxwell 1991, 3.
112. "Technical Agreement in Implementation of the Defense Agreement between the United States of America and Portugal of 6 September 1951," signed May 18, 1984, *TIAS* 2368.
113. Author's interviews with Azorean officials and U.S. officials in the Azores and mainland Portugal, May 2005.
114. Sandars 2000, 68.

did not fulfill its aid commitments. Intervention by U.S. defense secretary Frank Carlucci, who had been ambassador to Portugal in the aftermath of the 1974–75 revolution, diffused the situation somewhat when an agreement was reached in 1988 that provided for about $200 million in aid per year (compared to the $147 million for 1987 and $117 million for 1988).[115] But in 1990 Silva once again asked for a renegotiation that was finally concluded in 1995.

Throughout the 1980s, then, the position of the Azoreans and that of the mainland Portuguese government regarding the status and politics of the base differed. Overall, the Azoreans had few issues with the bases' actual operations and received an important budget supplement for hosting the facility. On the Portuguese mainland, however, democratization pressures, including competitive party politics and a critical media, drove rulers and negotiators to adopt many of the same bargaining tactics of Portugal's southern European NATO counterparts. Still, anti-NATO and antibase sentiment among the Portuguese public, even under Socialist rule, never reached the same level as in Spain or Greece.[116] This low level can be attributed not only to Portugal's more Atlanticist tradition but also to the fact that the U.S. military presence was more of a local, as opposed to a national, issue enmeshed within the broader Azores-Lisbon relationship.

Azorean Abandonment: Lisbon's New 1995 Base Deal

By 1995 the Azoreans found that their importance to both the U.S. military and the Portuguese mainland had diminished. The antisubmarine warfare activities previously conducted in the Atlantic had been terminated, and the U.S. Air Force's use of Lajes field remained the only U.S. military activity on the islands. Despite the prominent role of Lajes in the Gulf War, when it supported over 12,000 aircraft missions, and its use for minor missions in the early 1990s, the United States by the mid-1990s made clear to the Portuguese government that it would no longer fund base rights quid pro quo at previous cold war levels.[117] For

115. Duke 1989, 247.
116. For example, a 1985 poll found that 64 percent of Portuguese favored NATO, whereas 16 percent were against it. In Spain, by comparison—although two years earlier—just 17 percent were in favor of the alliance. See Vasconcelos 1988, 103.
117. Author's interviews with U.S. political and Department of Defense officials, U.S embassy, Lisbon, May 2005.

the Azorean regional government, however, base-related payments from the United States had become a staple of the islands' budget and development strategy.[118] Ultimately, the Ministry of Foreign Affairs in Lisbon, not the Azorean regional government, concluded the new basing accord in 1995.

The Azorean regional government and press were not satisfied with the deal. Consistent with U.S. efforts to end direct payments for "base rights" in the post–cold war era, the 1995 agreement terminated the previous levels of economic and security assistance and instead offered a one-time allocation of $173 million in military hardware to the Portuguese military and a series of bilateral cooperation initiatives.[119] Like the United States' 1970 agreement with Spain, this agreement, with its various initiatives, set out a number of measures that had little to do with either the military base or security issues. Some of the more unusual clauses of the supplemental 1995 agreement included commitments to suppress and "quarantine the Japanese beetle," "cooperate in the fields of health and medical science," and "host visits to the United States of experts and students of the Autonomous Region [Azores]."[120]

For members of the Azorean delegation and the regional government, these cooperative initiatives offered a poor substitute for the cash payments they had previously collected. Although by 1995 the islands were receiving some structural funds from the European Union, the overwhelming perception among Azoreans remained that authorities in Lisbon had undersold base rights for $173 million worth of excess defense articles that served the interests of the Portuguese military and not those of the islands' administration or inhabitants.[121] Nevertheless, the economic impact of Lajes on the islands' economy remains considerable, even if the direct quid pro quo has been terminated. For example, in 2004, the base directly employed 1,010 Portuguese civilians for a net economic value of $93 million, $47 million of which equaled the value of the base's

118. Author's interview with Azorean regional government representative, Terceira, May 2005.
119. "1995 Agreement on Cooperation and Defense between the United States and Portugal," signed June 1, 1995, Kavass ref. no. (KAV) 4969.
120. "Supplemental Minutes to the 1995 Agreement on Cooperation and Defense between the United States and Portugal," signed March 28, 1995. The minutes are unpublished but were provided to me by the Office of Defense Cooperation of the U.S. embassy in Lisbon.
121. Author's interviews with Portuguese defense experts and Azorean negotiating team representative, Terceira, Azores, May 2005.

local construction, services, and materials procurement contracts.[122] Since the 1995 agreement, the European Union has replaced the United States as the alternate external sponsor of the islands' developmental needs. The EU considers the islands one of its "most remote regions" and from 2000 to 2006 funneled €854 million in aid to the autonomous region under the PRODESA program.[123] In fact, in purely economic terms, EU structural development funds have more than covered the loss of U.S. base-related payments. However, this change in external patron does not seem to have altered the prevailing perception on the islands that they are marginalized by Lisbon.

The new narrative of "neglect" embodied by the 1995 agreement now serves as the main prism through which Azoreans view the basing question and their relations with Lisbon. As a result, after every major military campaign in which the U.S. military uses Lajes, the Portuguese and Azorean media are eager to ascertain the operational significance of the airbase.[124] But this sense of marginalization was further reinforced by an organizational change made by the U.S. military in 2002 when U.S. planners removed Lajes from the U.S. Atlantic Command and placed it under the jurisdiction of European Command (EUCOM). The move made sense for U.S. administrative needs but upset many Azoreans, who saw the reshuffle as a final indication of diminished strategic importance.[125] From being the first line of defense of the United States during the cold war, the Lajes base was relegated to the extreme periphery of European Command, in addition to its designated status as a "remote region" within the EU.

As host to an eleventh hour pre–Iraq War summit in March 2003, the islands found themselves briefly back in the international spotlight, but it is now widely acknowledged that Lajes and the mid-Atlantic islands no longer hold the same significance for the United States as they once did. At 2004 and 2005 bilateral commission meetings, representatives of the Azorean regional government launched strong complaints that the

122. "Lajes Field FY04 Economic Impact Analysis," unpublished briefing provided by the Office of Public Affairs, Lajes Field.
123. For details of EU initiatives and PRODESA, see http://ec.europa.eu/comm/ regional_policy/country/prordn/details (accessed May 2007).
124. I am thankful to Miguel Monjardino for his observations on this topic. For a Portuguese-language account, see Monjardino 2000.
125. Author's interviews with U.S. military and foreign affairs officials in Lisbon and the Azores, Portugal, May 2005.

various nonmonetary benefits offered by the 1995 agreement had not turned out to be significant, but neither Lisbon nor Washington seemed to care enough to renegotiate the 1995 accord.[126] Nevertheless, the Azorean regional government and local groups continue to be amicable and supportive hosts to the U.S. military. One remarkable indicator of just how uncontested the U.S. military presence remains in the Azores can be seen in the criminal jurisdiction issue on the islands: since 1995, the Portuguese government has only once failed to waive its primary right of criminal jurisdiction for crimes committed by U.S. personnel on the islands.[127]

Conclusions: Base Politics in Island Hosts

The island base hosts of Okinawa and the Azores show how political attitudes toward the U.S. military base presence can be implicated in broader relations between these island hosts and their mainlands. The contrasting manner in which the U.S. military presence has been implicated in the democratization of the two island groups has yielded strikingly different forms of triangular politics and perceptions about the credibility of the agreements that govern the U.S. presence. In the Okinawan case, U.S. administration of the island eventually prompted a reversion movement that regarded the United States as an occupying power and viewed Tokyo as complicit in denying Okinawans their sovereignty and full integration with the Japanese state. In the Azorean case, the islands and the basing issue initially served the interests of the Salazar regime and his quest to preserve Portuguese territorial integrity during an international era of decolonization. But strong ties between the United States and the Atlantic islands, aided by significant transatlantic migration, fostered a sense of Atlantic identity that would later encourage secession from the mainland during the Portugal's turbulent democratic revolution.

As a result of these varying triangular relations, the two island hosts and their central governments institutionalized contrasting politcal econ-

---

126. Office of Defense Cooperation, "Minutes and Analytical Observations of the 18th Meeting of the Bilateral Commission," unpublished memorandum, U.S. embassy, Lisbon, May 2005.

127. This information is according to the JAG office, Lajes airbase. Author interview, May 2005. The single exception was an alleged child molestation case in 2000, for which U.S. authorities did not vigorously pursue a waiver.

omies in relation to the U.S. basing presence. To politically neutralize Okinawan antibase activism and contestation, the Japanese government has provided an extensive array of public goods and targeted incentives to the island prefecture and key social segments. At three key junctures in Okinawan history after reversion—1978, 1998, and 2006—local political candidates who emphasized national unity and base-related economic benefits triumphed over antibase incumbents and candidates who questioned the U.S. basing presence and the legitimacy of its underlying agreements. By contrast, the relatively supportive Azoreans since 1995 have received much diminished "burden payments" and now feel as if their political and economic interests are neglected by Lisbon.

Although the Okinawan and Azorean examples illustrate a special case of base politics, the triangular interactions that characterize them hold important lessons for other countries and contexts hosting U.S. bases. Other examples of similar island politics and triangular bargaining relations include U.S.-Denmark negotiations over bases in Greenland, U.S.-Italy negotiations over facilities in Sardinia (especially La Maddalena naval repair station), and U.S.-Greek relations over the naval base at Souda Bay on Crete, which after 1991 has been the sole remaining U.S. military installation on Greek territory.[128] However, the broader point that emerges from this comparison is that when bases are located in remote areas of a host country with some degree of democratic devolution, local authorities and administrators are likely to assert their regional interests and implicate base-related issues in their negotiations with their central government. These lessons are especially important for understanding the politics that might inform future U.S. bases in Kurdish-controlled Iraq, where the contracting terms over a permanent U.S. military presence may complicate inter-ethnic federal arrangements between the Kurds and Iraq's central government. It also suggests that political decentralization in countries that already host remote bases has the potential to transform base-related political interactions from a bilateral issue to some form of triangular relationship in which the central government's preferences may not necessarily mirror those of the actual base-hosting locality.

Having examined Okinawa's triangular politics as a variation on patterns of domestic political change and base politics, I next consider the evolution of the base issue from the perspective of the Japanese main

128. On the United States-Denmark-Greenland triangle, see Dragsdahl 2005; Archer 2003. On Sardinia, see chapter 6.

islands. The evolution of base politics in Japan has followed a different institutional logic from that on Okinawa, as the U.S. bases in Japan are now considered part of a legitimate bilateral security contract. Along with Italy, Japan demonstrates how a one-party political system in a democratic client state can effectively depoliticize the basing issue, even in the presence of a radical or Communist political party that explicitly opposes the United States–host country security alliance.

CHAPTER 6

Japan and Italy

The Politics of Clientelism and One-Party Democratic Rule

The United States defeated and then occupied both Japan and Italy during the latter stages of World War II. Since the 1950s, Japan and Italy have hosted an extensive network of military bases and facilities used by U.S. armed forces and, with some instructive exceptions, have done so without contesting the terms of the U.S. basing presence. Accordingly, these cases offer the opportunity to examine the evolution of base politics in two "client" states whose internal and external affairs have been heavily influenced by the United States. In this chapter I assess whether these countries' dependence on the U.S.-led security system constitutes an exception to my argument that changes in the domestic institutions of base hosts are of paramount importance for the politicization and depoliticization of the U.S. basing presence.

Elites in both Italy and Japan were remarkably adept at playing two-level base politics, even though they were, in terms of their relative power capabilities, in structurally weaker positions when negotiating with their superpower patron. The imperatives of democratization and democratic consolidation not only drove the base issue in these countries, but Japanese and Italian policymakers blatantly used the U.S. alliance as an instrument of domestic politics. The Liberal Democratic Party (LDP) in Japan and the Christian Democrats (DC) in Italy ruled their political systems for most of the cold war era, and these parties used base-related issues to challenge the security credentials of their left-wing political opponents. At the same time, in their negotiations with the United States, LDP and DC officials strategically invoked the internal threat posed by these opposition parties to extract concessions on security matters. Japan and Italy may have been client states, but they did not passively implement American directives on base-related and security matters.

Although security alliance with the United States set broadly similar structural parameters on the basing issue in Japan and Italy, there were also politically consequential differences in the legitimacy and forms of their initial basing contracts. Japan was defeated and then occupied by a heavy U.S. military presence for six years, whereas Italy joined the Allies as a "co-belligerent" after its liberation in 1943. As a result, the United States imposed its enduring military presence and governing arrangements to a greater extent in Japan than in Italy, a fact that fostered widespread resentment in Japan against the procedural legitimacy of these initial deals. In Italy, the initial basing agreements of the 1950s were vigorously debated and criticized by the left, but they were then accepted as democratic commitments and remained unmodified until after the cold war. Furthermore, Japan was brought under the U.S. security umbrella through exclusively bilateral agreements, having to accept facilities legally designated as U.S. bases, whereas U.S. military installations and troops in Italy were designated as Italian facilities used for NATO purposes, a legal distinction that gave Italian rulers Western multilateral legitimacy and political cover.[1]

One-party democratic rule in both countries forced left-wing opposition parties to eventually moderate their position on the basing issue. But differences in the timing of the consolidation of these party political systems also explain the greater volatility of the issue in Japan in the 1950s and early 1960s. The LDP was not formed until 1955, and, in Japan's volatile and democratizing climate, it had to immediately manage intense factionalism and strong left-wing opposition to the revised 1960 Mutual Security Treaty, whose ratification proved to be one of the most contested episodes in postwar Japanese democratic politics. However, following the ratification, the LDP's systemic primacy drove a number of smaller opposition parties to moderate their positions on the basing and security issues

---

1. As Peter Katzenstein points out, the organizational forms of these security systems varied, with the United States dealing with Japan bilaterally, whereas it sought to integrate Italy within the multilateral institutions of NATO and western Europe. See Katzenstein 2005; Hemmer and Katzenstein 2002.

in exchange for their inclusion in LDP-led coalitions. Italy's political party system, by contrast, was definitively established by the landmark election of 1948 and divided into pro- and anti-Western political parties. Over the following decades, Italy's left-wing parties dramatically moderated their initial antibase position in their attempts to appeal to the median voter and to defeat, or in the case of the Socialists, to join, the DC governing coalition.

Japan: LDP Hegemony and the Rise and Decline of the Basing Issue

From Occupation to the Legalization of the Basing Presence

The postwar U.S. occupation of Japan went through a substantial evolution.[2] In an attempt to subdue and neuter the once militaristic nation, the United States imposed a new pacifist constitution on Japan, whose Article IX explicitly prohibited rearmament.[3] By 1948, however, the rise of the Communist threat in the Soviet Union and in China forced American officials to reconsider Japan's potential role in regional security. Under the "reverse course," the United States abandoned many of its attempts to reform institutions of the Japanese state and resurrected an old guard of political elites and technocrats to focus on economic development and building the security relationship. The onset of the Korean War brought outright panic in American circles and prompted U.S. officials to intensely pressure their Japanese counterparts to accept remilitarization and an increased role in regional security.[4]

On the Japanese side, Prime Minister Yoshida Shigeru was caught between seemingly irreconcilable international and domestic pressures. The United States and conservatives strongly favored a peace treaty that would grant independence and autonomy to Japan over its military affairs, whereas most Japanese, including the various left-oriented parties, advocated independence with Japan's pacifist constitution remaining unchanged. Even though he knew Japan was in a severely weak position, Yoshida skillfully played two-level base politics and manipulated these conflicting pressures. He offered the Americans long-term basing rights in

---

2. See esp. Takemae 2003; Dower 1999.
3. On the evolution of Article IX and the subsequent domestic struggles over the antimilitarist norms it established, see Berger 1998; Katzenstein 1996.
4. Takemae 2003, 501–2; Samuels 2003, 205–7.

Japan as quid pro quo for Japanese independence and insisted on keeping Article IX intact. When pushed by John Dulles and other negotiators to go further and agree to remilitarization, Yoshida played up his constrained domestic position and even secretly contacted Socialist Party leaders to organize demonstrations against rearmament in order to impress upon American negotiators the political volatility of tampering with Article IX.[5] Yoshida also managed to extract the Japanese claim of "residual sovereignty" over the Ryukyu Islands in Article III of the San Francisco Peace Treaty, despite adamant demands by the U.S. military to permanently sever Okinawa from the main islands.[6] By managing his nested hierarchies and invoking the constraints of each, Yoshida carved out a new policy position and bargaining equilibrium from the seemingly irreconcilable demands of both left-wing and conservative factions and pressures.[7] The resulting Yoshida Doctrine—enshrined in the San Francisco Peace Treaty of 1951—allowed Japan to free ride on American security protection and keep its constitution, while using its freed-up resources to pursue economic development.[8]

The 1951 U.S.-Japan Security Treaty

Yoshida proved remarkably adept at leveraging Japan's structural weakness into concessions on independence and sovereignty, but the resulting basing treaty was a model of imbalance. Indeed, of all the basing agreements studied in this book, the 1951 U.S.-Japan Security Treaty is the most hierarchical on several fronts.[9] The first article of the treaty granted the United States the right to base "land, air and sea forces in and about Japan" with unrestricted use-rights and no explicit guarantee that these forces would protect Japan. The article also allowed the United States to use these facilities to maintain "peace and security in the Far East" and to assist the Japanese government to put down "large scale internal riots and disturbances in Japan." The latter clause that sanctioned American direct involvement in domestic Japanese affairs was especially conten-

---

5. Dower 1999, 548, Pyle 1992, 24.

6. "Residual sovereignty" was more than a label justifying American control. Over the next two decades, it became the legal basis for the government of Japan's efforts to secure full reversion. On Yoshida's role and bargaining over the Okinawa issue, see Eldridge 2001, 314–28; Pyle 1992 21–30.

7. Samuels 2003, 223.

8. On the domestic institutionalization of the doctrine, see Chai 1997; Pyle 1992, 32–41.

9. "Security Treaty between the United States of America and Japan," signed September 8, 1951, *TIAS* 2491, 3329–3340.

tious. Article II of the treaty prevented Japan from granting base rights to any other powers without American consent, and Article IV allowed the treaty to expire only upon the mutual consent of both governments. No official status of forces agreement was signed at the time, with the issue designated for a separate administrative agreement.

The accompanying bilateral administrative agreement was negotiated in 1952 by Dean Rusk, then assistant secretary for Far Eastern affairs, with Foreign Minister Okazaki Katsuo, and it mirrored the Security Treaty in its imbalance.[10] U.S. personnel were granted near extraterritoriality, as U.S. authorities were given exclusive jurisdiction over crimes committed by U.S. personnel and dependents anywhere in Japan, although Japanese negotiators managed to modify the jurisdiction clause to allow Japanese courts to try "special cases." U.S. authorities were also granted the power to arrest Japanese citizens outside of designated base areas. Japanese negotiators vehemently objected to a U.S. proposal to establish a "combined command" in times of war that would have subordinated Japanese forces under an American commander. Like the Security Treaty itself, the hierarchical nature of the administrative agreement reminded the Japanese public of the unequal treaties that Western powers had forced on Japan in the late nineteenth century.[11] Some commentators have even speculated that Yoshida tactically accepted the inclusion of some of these blatantly unfair clauses in the treaty in order to more easily make the case later that the humiliating treaty should be renegotiated.[12] Not surprisingly, the Japanese public almost immediately questioned the agreement's legitimacy as a voluntary contract.

The Base Network on the Main Islands
The end of the occupation in 1952 brought about a significant reduction in military facilities on the home islands, from 3,800 in 1952 to 125 in 1970.[13] For political purposes, the U.S. Army had withdrawn nearly all of its ground forces by 1957, although it retained a headquarters complex in Zama and a supply and repair depot in Sagamihara (see fig. 6.1).[14] Important naval installations were established at Yokosuka and Sasebo,

10. For these details of the bilateral administrative agreement, see Takemae 2003, 505–6.
11. Takemae 2003, 506.
12. I thank Paul Midford for his thoughts on this point. See Welfield 1988, 50–51.
13. Greene 1975, 47.
14. The army also ceded certain installations to the Self-Defense Forces of Japan and to other U.S. services; for example, the northern area of Camp Fuji was ceded to the marines.

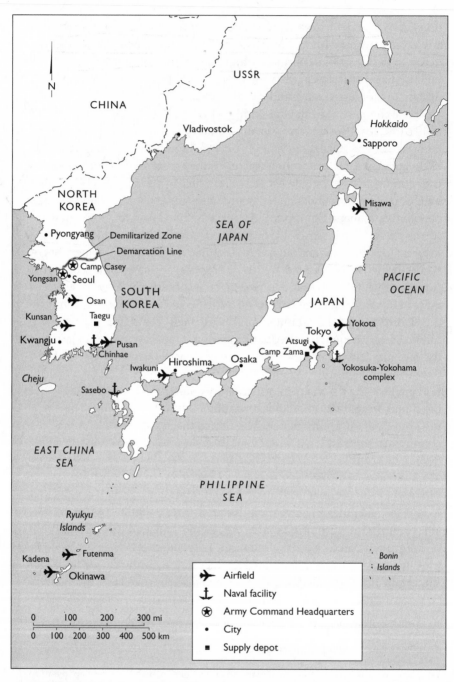

Figure 6.1. Major U.S. military facilities, South Korea and Japan, 1979.
Source: National Defense University

which serviced the Seventh Fleet, and an airbase in Atsugi.[15] Yokosuka in particular has been a critical naval service facility; for several decades it has serviced the largest of aircraft carriers in several dry docks and has served as their home port. The air force established major bases in Yokota, still the site of United States Forces Japan Command, and in Misawa. The marines, mostly based in Okinawa, controlled an air facility in Iwakuni in western Japan. Okinawan reversion in 1972 initiated a reorganization and consolidation of U.S. forces on the main islands, as several facilities were moved to the island prefecture (it would host 75 percent of all USFJ forces and installations after 1972). On the main islands after 1972, 70 percent of base area and 77 percent of U.S. military personnel were located within sixty miles of Tokyo, with five major installations in the area under exclusive U.S. control or shared use with Japan's Self-Defense Force.

Public Reaction and Opposition to the Treaties
The terms of the Security Treaty had immediate effects on the Japanese political system. The peace treaty split the Japanese Socialist Party into a left-wing faction (Left-wing Socialist Party) that opposed both treaties and a center and right-wing faction (Right-wing Socialist Party) that was mostly willing to accept the peace treaty but was opposed to the Security Treaty.[16] The Japanese public too was overwhelmingly opposed to the security provisions and the continued stationing of U.S. troops in Japan, which, along with the U.S. military's administration of Okinawa, was now viewed as a new form of American occupation.[17] Just three days after the formal return of sovereignty on April 28, 1952, more than a million demonstrators took to the streets to participate in a total of 330 May Day rallies across the country; many of the demonstrators carried banners and signs opposing U.S. military bases and U.S. rule over Okinawa.[18]

Democratization, Factionalism, and the Contested 1960 Treaty Ratification

High levels of dissatisfaction with the Security Treaty among Japan's public and politicians in the 1950s coincided with a volatile and fragmented political system. In 1955 the merger of right- and left-wing parties yielded

15. This list of major facilities on the main islands is from Greene 1975, 47–49. Also see Giarra 1999, 119–24.
16. Curtis 1988, 12; Stockwin 1962, 36.
17. For survey data on Japanese attitudes, see Mendel 1959.
18. Dower 1999, 554.

the so-called 1955 system, under which the LDP ruled Japanese politics for nearly four decades.[19] At the time of the LDP's formation, the conservative party was more fragmented than the unified opposition Socialist Party (JSP) that appeared to be in political ascendancy.

The 1958 elections seemed to confirm that the 1955 system would become a consolidated two-party system as the LDP won 57.8 percent of the popular vote and 287 out of 467 Diet seats, whereas the JSP won just 32.8 percent of the vote and 166 Diet seats. The deep ideological polarization of the parties at the time and antisystem orientation of the JSP were exacerbated by their contrasting views on constitutional reform and foreign relations.[20] Intense party competition also bred nationalism, which was further fueled by Japan's rapid economic recovery; the country's newly found prestige was viewed as incompatible with the highly imbalanced Security Treaty that had been imposed on it.

Finally, a steady wave of Japanese media stories about base-related crimes, accidents, and scandals further fueled antibase sentiment and fostered the perception that the United States was behaving like an unchecked colonial power. Between 1953 and 1956, U.S. servicemen were charged with 12,581 criminal offenses, with Japan waiving jurisdiction for all but 386 of them, an unparalleled 97 percent of all cases.[21] The most infamous of these was the Girard case of 1957 in which a U.S. Army Specialist on a U.S.-leased range fired an empty cartridge from a grenade launcher and killed an elderly Japanese woman who was scavenging for scrap metal.[22] The case inflamed Japanese public opinion against the bases and was only resolved after months of a deadlock over Girard's duty status. Reports of widespread base-related black marketeering, prostitution, and pollution further inflamed these negative perceptions.

One consequence of these negative stories about U.S. personnel was the steady erosion of the Japanese public's support for U.S. bases, which was already at a low level. Table 6.1 shows that in September 1950, before the

---

19. On 1955 and the subsequent evolution of the party system, see Curtis 1988.

20. Curtis 1988, 16–18.

21. *New York Times*, June 16, 1957, as cited in Packard 1966, 36–37. Also see Stambuk 1963a, 113, for data on Japanese waiver rates from 1954 to 1958.

22. Girard's commander initially refused to hand him over to Japanese authorities, claiming that he was on duty at the time of the accident. In what is now considered a landmark opinion for SOFA issues, the U.S. Supreme Court in July 1957 ruled that Girard, subject to a previous bilateral administrative agreement, could be tried in Japanese court. In November 1957 Girard was tried and convicted in Japanese court, received a three-year suspended sentence, and was immediately repatriated to the United States. See Stambuk 1963a, 88–92; Moore 1959, 285–96.

TABLE 6.1
Japanese public opinion about U.S. bases, 1950–58

	September 1950	June 1953	October 1957	February 1958
Approve	30	27	18	8
Oppose	38	48	60	58
Don't know	32	25	22	34
N	2641	2515	859	2422

Source: Compiled from Mendel 1961, 102.
Note: The question posed in the survey was, "Do you approve or oppose the presence of U.S. bases in Japan?"

1951 treaty was signed, 30 percent of respondents approved of U.S. bases in Japan, whereas this number dropped to a paltry 8 percent in February 1958. Conversely, 38 percent of respondents in 1950 opposed U.S. bases, whereas in 1958 the number had grown to 58 percent.

By 1958, then, antibase sentiment and nationalism were at their peak, and all of Japan's political parties publicly favored revising the Security Treaty in order to reclaim Japan's "national interest," although they differed as to the substance and extent of these changes.[23]

Kishi Renegotiates the Security Treaty

Against this polarized backdrop, Prime Minister Kishi Nobosuke immediately set about to revise the 1951 treaty following his 1958 election victory. Kishi was already a controversial figure in Japanese politics, having been imprisoned (but not tried) for war crimes before joining the pre-LDP-merger Democratic Party. He forcefully advocated negotiating a new treaty rather than amending the old one, but he faced considerable dissent among members of his own party, including Yoshida, who viewed the 1951 arrangements as having little wrong with them.[24] Kishi prevailed internally and, over the course of two years of hard bargaining, convinced initially reluctant U.S. officials, including Ambassador Douglas MacArthur and Secretary of State Dulles, that if he could not secure a fundamental revision, the Socialists might come to power and public opinion would push Japan "progressively into neutralism."[25] U.S. intelligence and defense analysts concurred and supported the revision. The revised

23. Packard 1966, 35.
24. Junnosuke 1995, 25.
25. A good account of the bargaining is given in Schaller 1997, 127–42. Also see Destler et al. 1976, 12–23; Packard 1966, 54–81.

treaty, together with a new administrative agreement for SOFA issues, was signed in Washington in January 1960. In a preview of the political struggle to come, Kishi's plane was delayed by the more than one thousand student demonstrators who had barricaded themselves in Tokyo's Haneda airport in an effort to prevent the prime minister's plane from leaving for the ceremony.[26]

In purely legal terms, the 1960 Treaty of Mutual Cooperation and Security (or Mutual Security Treaty) between the United States and Japan was significantly less hierarchical than the founding 1951 Security Treaty.[27] The treaty officially replaced the 1951 agreement (Article IX) and dropped any reference to the right of the United States to intervene in Japan's internal affairs. Article V explicitly provided for a U.S. security commitment to Japan, as part of a mutual security commitment, but mandated that Japan only defend those territories that fell under its administration and not U.S. territory, thereby preserving Article IX of the Japanese Constitution. Article IV allowed the bases to be used for preserving "international peace and security in the Far East," which Americans took to include Korea, Taiwan, and later, Vietnam. The parties agreed to adopt the treaty for ten years, after which it would be automatically extended with one year's notice unless either party called for its revision. Again, for Japan this was a fundamental improvement on the 1951 accord's requirement that both countries were required to approve a revision. In an exchange of notes that accompanied the treaty, the United States agreed to engage in prior consultation before undertaking a major deployment, using the bases for combat operations in third countries, or introducing new types of combat equipment.[28] The exchange of notes also created a Joint Committee on Security to institutionalize cooperation on security and basing matters and introduced a new SOFA that replaced the 1952 administrative agreement with NATO-style concurrent criminal jurisdiction procedures.[29]

---

26. Schaller 1997, 142.
27. "Treaty of Mutual Cooperation and Security between the United States and Japan," signed January 19, 1960, *TIAS* 4509, 1632–1651. For a nuanced assessment of each clause, see Welfield 1988, 141–46.
28. Greene 1975, 32.
29. "Agreement under Article VI of the Treaty of Mutual Cooperation and Security: Facilities and Areas and the Status of United States Armed Forces in Japan, U.S.-Japan," signed January 19, 1960, *TIAS* 1652. Although unlike the NATO SOFA, the 1960 U.S.-Japan SOFA was not reciprocal, its provisions did not apply to any Japanese forces stationed in the United States.

Democratizing Pressures and the Contentious Ratification

Despite the new treaty's considerably more balanced provisions, the Japanese opposition parties and the media mounted a strong challenge to it, and its ratification gave rise to the most turbulent political events of postwar Japan. The LDP had already recently clashed with the JSP on a security-related matter when Kishi suddenly introduced a bill that expanded police powers, the controversial Police Duties Law.[30] With party and ideological polarization at an all-time high in the Diet, the treaty's ratification was going to be difficult, but few predicted the deep political crisis it would precipitate.

The treaty required the approval of both Houses, which immediately posed a showdown between the LDP and the opposition. Because the agreement had been signed as an international treaty, its substance as a bill could not be recrafted or compromised, unlike other legislation, meaning that the outcome would be zero sum for the government and opposition parties. When the bill was introduced into the Diet in February 1960, questions and objections were immediately unleashed about the precise meaning of the new clauses on mutual defense and prior consultations, the requirement that Japan increase its self-defense forces, and the treaty's ten-year duration. The JSP, in the middle of a party struggle, tacked left during the debate in order to strengthen its credentials with its union base and differentiate its position from that of the more rightist Democratic Socialist Party (DSP), which had recently broken away.[31] The JSP resolved to deliberately obstruct and delay the actual vote on procedural grounds, while it publicly opposed the controversial clauses of the treaty itself.[32] Intra-LDP difficulties also emerged during the debate, as Kishi positioned himself for a third term as party leader and LDP members conflated support for the treaty with backing Kishi. As a result, several LDP members remained critical of Kishi and certain treaty provisions throughout the ratification session, wanting to see the treaty barely scrape through so as to inflict maximum political damage on the LDP president.[33]

30. Junnosuke 1995, 26–28.
31. According to Packard (1966, 222), the Socialists "faced new competition from Zenro and the DSP and the loss of some workers who were attracted by Zenro's current emphasis on economic over political struggles. Sohyo actually feared that the DSP and Zenro might try to cause splits within its unions. For this reason, the anti-treaty movement after May 19, with its appeal to nationalist sentiment, came at an opportune time for Sohyo. It seemed to justify Sohyo's politically oriented struggle as opposed to the more moderate economic offensive of the DSP and Zenro."
32. Packard 1966, 192.
33. Schaller 1997, 147; Junnosuke 1995, 35–36.

The Japanese media and the public focused more intensely on the Diet debate than they had on any other foreign policy matter since independence. During April and May, while the bill languished in committee, the JCP and JSP organized a number of massive demonstrations and a national petition drive against ratification. Then, on May 1, the press and opposition seized on breaking news that an American U-2 spy plane had been downed in Russia as evidence of the security risks that the U.S. bases had brought to Japan. Because some U-2s were based in Japan, and one had even made an emergency landing near Fujiwasa in September 1959, the Socialists accused the United States of turning the country into a Soviet military target by flying spy missions from Japanese territory.[34]

Kishi now faced a number of significant deadlines, the most important of which was U.S. president Eisenhower's impending visit to Japan on June 19, 1960. Under Japanese Diet rules, the Mutual Security Treaty would be automatically ratified after Lower House approval if the Upper House took no action within thirty days, which meant the treaty had to be approved by the Lower House by May 19 for it to come into effect before Eisenhower's arrival. With the DSP reversing its position on a closure vote and threatening to join the JSP in opposition, Kishi was left politically isolated and facing the collapse of his government if he backed off ratification. Instead, on May 19, in a day regarded as pivotal in Japanese politics, Kishi called for an extension of the Diet session and, while the Socialist delegates were staging a sit-in outside the speaker's office, called for an unannounced vote on the treaty. During an upsurge of confusion and physical tussling among Diet members, the Speaker called on the police to forcibly remove each Socialist from the blockade of the House floor, as packs of photographers recorded the dramatic confrontations. The morning papers stated that Kishi had "unilaterally" approved the treaty; the JSP declared that the passage was "null and void" and that they would begin a boycott of all Diet proceedings.[35]

Violent Protests and the Role of the Media

The following day marked the beginning of a month of demonstrations against Kishi. Students and workers took to the streets in hundreds of separate marches, as Socialist members continued to protest outside of the Diet. The JSP called for a national strike on June 4, and then again for June 15

---

34. Packard 1966, 232.
35. Packard 1966, 241–42.

and 22, while demonstrators targeted Kishi's residence, the Diet, and the U.S. embassy. All the opposition parties called on the government to cancel Eisenhower's visit, and on June 10, U.S. press secretary James Hagerty was mobbed in his car near Haneda airport shortly after arriving to make arrangements for the summit. On June 15, the day of the second general strike, some 70,000 demonstrators, mostly students, stormed the main gate of the Diet and clashed with Japanese police. One girl was killed, several hundred were injured and arrested, and eighteen police trucks were destroyed.[36] On June 16, in an atmosphere of widespread shock at the previous day's events, Kishi announced the cancellation of Eisenhower's visit. Then, on June 20, the prime minister stealthily collected the necessary signatures of LDP cabinet ministers to bring domestic laws into conformity with the treaty that had automatically just gone into effect. On June 23 Kishi resigned, effectively ending what had become a full-blown constitutional and democratic crisis.

The Japanese press played a critical role during the crisis and displayed all the hallmarks of a democratizing media.[37] During the 1950s a number of new national newspapers had been established, and by 1960 they could count on 37 million readers daily. Also, television ownership had rocketed: in 1953, only from 0.1 percent of the Japanese public owned television sets, whereas by 1960 that figure had increased to 33.2 percent.[38] The newspapers were highly critical of the 1960 treaty, but they played a more important role in covering and fueling the extraparliamentary demonstrations during the May crisis. Throughout the ratification crisis, in an intense competition for readership, news outlets focused on sensationalist stories, especially the violence and police actions at the Diet. The various strikes and labor actions were covered sympathetically, partly because of the high union membership (67 percent) among newspaper and news agency staff, with the media accepting uncritically the Socialists' arguments and failing to print the views of political moderates or protreaty advocates.[39] At the same time, the press almost uniformly condemned Kishi and conflated discussions of the problems of treaty with Kishi's own personal shortcomings.[40] Although newspaper editorials did not advocate violence, they warned that more violence was inevitable unless Kishi resigned.[41] In a

36. Packard 1966, 297.
37. See Packard 1966, 278–84; Whittemore 1961.
38. Junnosuke 1995, 49.
39. Packard 1966, 280–81.
40. Whittemore 1961, 40.
41. Packard 1966, 280.

remarkable move, and in the aftermath of some of the worst clashes, on June 15 the country's seven leading newspapers issued a joint editorial, "Wipe Out Violence, Preserve Parliamentary Democracy," which called for Kishi to "respond to the sound judgment of the people" (meaning resign) and for the political opposition to return to the Diet.[42] The statement seemed to have a moderating effect, even as Eisenhower's visit was officially cancelled. But the media's newly found self-reflection was challenged two weeks later by a devastating article in *Time* magazine about the Japanese press's role in inciting demonstrations, a charge Japanese journalists vigorously dismissed.[43]

As it turned out, the 1960 ratification crisis marked the peak of the political fracas over U.S. bases on the Japanese main islands. The popular sentiment that the 1951 Security Treaty had been unfairly imposed on Japan, coupled with genuine concerns about the revised accord, created fertile ground for mobilization against ratification of the 1960 treaty by opposition parties. The 1960 ratification, when combined with intraparty factionalism, intense media scrutiny, and Kishi's heavy-handed parliamentary tactics, was an explosive convergence of democratization dynamics and an illegitimate security contract that produced Japan's most intense postwar political crisis. However, as the political party system stabilized and the new treaty took effect, the basing issue started to recede from the political agenda.

Okinawa's Reversion and the LDP's Consolidation

After Kishi's resignation, Hayato Ikeda assumed the LDP presidency and turned the government's attention to domestic matters and away from the divisive treaty. Under the slogan of reconciliation and development, he introduced the high-profile ten-year income-doubling plan, which targeted more remote regions for economic development. But after his resignation in 1964 due to failing health, issues of bases and sovereignty once again become intertwined with the domestic political fortunes of an LDP politician. The outcome, however, would be much more favorable to the new prime minister and the LDP than Kishi's controversial ratification campaign had been.

---

42. For the text, see Packard 1966, 380.
43. See *Time* 1960; for a response by a Japanese journalist, see Tatsumi 1960.

Sato and Okinawan Reversion

Sato Eisaku's political tenure was instrumentally tied to the Okinawa issue, which in the 1960s remained the major sore spot in U.S.-Japanese relations. Upon declaring his candidacy for LDP president in 1964, Sato promised to demand the reversion of Okinawa to Japan from the United States, although he did not press the issue hard the following year in his summit with President Lyndon Johnson.[44] In October 1968, the election of the fiery revisionist Yara Chobyo as governor of Okinawa (see chap. 5) thrust reversion back onto the political agenda, and just a couple of weeks later Sato was challenged for the LDP presidency by former foreign minister Miki Takeo. Sato forcefully criticized his opponent's position on Okinawa as not resolute enough and openly staked his political career on achieving a reversion deal that would place all remaining U.S. bases in Okinawa under the terms of the 1960 Mutual Security Treaty.[45] He was reelected to a third term as LDP leader on November 27, 1968 and during the next spring began preparations for the reversion talks.

The substance of the negotiations leading up to the November 1969 summit with Nixon was handled mainly through the back channel of Wakaizumi Kei, who directly negotiated with Henry Kissinger on behalf of Sato.[46] As with Kishi in his base negotiations, Sato effectively invoked his audience costs as a bargaining tactic and warned of his government's possible collapse if an agreement on reversion could not be achieved. The final Nixon-Sato communiqué in November 1969 announced that the reversion of Okinawa to Japan would be completed by 1972 and that the United States would be allowed to keep military bases on the island subject to terms of the 1960 Mutual Security Treaty, including the denuclearization of the military installations and the "prior consultation" clause.

The most difficult issue for the United States to accept was Sato's insistence on the denuclearization of Okinawa, in line with the "nonnuclear" principles that Sato had introduced to govern the mainland.[47] The U.S. joint chiefs strongly objected to any change in Okinawa's nuclear status,

---

44. Junnosuke 1995, 100.
45. Junnosuke 1995, 101; Wakaizumi 2002, 37–38.
46. Wakaizumi's personal account of the reversion talks created an uproar upon its publication in Japan because it confirmed a number of tacit deals surrounding the reversion agreement that had previously only been rumored in the press. I rely on the English translation, Wakaizumi 2002.
47. The three "nuclear principles" were prohibitions on the manufacture, possession, and introduction of nuclear weapons into Japanese territory. As in other cases, the transit issue was more ambiguous.

but Sato argued that neither he nor his party could politically survive an agreement that publicly accepted nuclear weapons on sovereign Japanese territory.[48] In the end, Sato signed a top-secret minute (which he signed in a back room during the White House ceremony) that agreed to favorably consider the reintroduction of nuclear weapons in Okinawa in the event of an emergency, a deal he publicly denied making in his first press conference in Japan after the signing.[49] On his part, Nixon demanded that Sato agree to enact voluntary textile export quotas, a move the U.S. president considered critical for his reelection prospects in the textile-producing South. Even on this demand, however, Sato stalled, and when he reluctantly accepted in principle, he insisted that the matter be brought up at the next meeting of the GATT so as to avoid any appearance of a quid pro quo that would hurt him with his domestic business base.

The reversion agreement was favorably received on the Japanese mainland as the "nuclear-free, homeland-level" reversion that Sato had promised to deliver. Just weeks later, Sato was elected to a fourth term as LDP leader, and the LDP made sweeping gains in the December 27 elections at the expense of the JSP, mostly riding public satisfaction with the deal. In February 1970, a public opinion poll on the reversion agreement indicated that 65 percent approved of the deal as opposed to just 5 percent who disapproved (with 30 percent undecided).[50] Through Sato's skillful, if not entirely transparent, reversion deal, the LDP had simultaneously consolidated its domestic dominance and put to rest the final outstanding bases-related issue for the main islands.

Depoliticization and the 1970 Extension of the Security Treaty

One noteworthy "nonevent" that supports my interpretation of base politics was the lack of political contestation in 1970 surrounding the extension of the 1960 Mutual Security Treaty, which was about to expire. Although a number of commentators and observers of Japanese politics predicted a

48. In fact, Sato did his best to turn the nuclear issue to his domestic political advantage. For example, he suggested that Nixon publicly remove the Mace B missiles in time for the general election in January 1970. See Wakaizumi 2002, 207–8.

49. Wakaizumi 2002, 314–15. In his plea to Kissinger for absolute secrecy regarding the minute, Wakaizumi (2002, 211) said, "Only you and the president know about the minute. And of course nobody knows on the Japanese side. . . . If the contents become known, not only would Prime Minister Sato's cabinet split, but the LDP, an ally of America, would face a major challenge at the next general election. And that's not all. The friendship and alliance between Japan and the United States will end up being destroyed, and the significance of Okinawa's return would be fundamentally altered."

50. Mendel 1971–72, 533.

volatile 1960-type showdown over the treaty's extension, it did not materialize.[51] Sato's public victory on Okinawan reversion took the sting out of the bases and sovereignty issue, and the LDP adopted a political platform in October 1969 that allowed the treaty to automatically extend without a Diet vote, thereby avoiding a potential institutional veto point. The JSP, suffering from severe electoral losses, did not coordinate protests on the "automatic" ratification, nor did it mobilize demonstrations that remotely approached those of ten years before.[52]

More important, the procedural legitimacy of the 1960 treaty as a democratically ratified contract was not publicly contested the way the 1951 Security Treaty had been. Polling in 1970 indicates that the Japanese public differentiated between their still negative views of the U.S. bases and Japan's commitment to the security contract in which the bases were embedded. In a February 1970 survey, 39 percent of respondents agreed that the Mutual Security Treaty "should be automatically extended beyond 1970," whereas 19 percent opposed it (42 percent answered "don't know"). The 20-point plurality in favor of extension contrasts sharply with results from the same survey that found 17 percent viewed U.S. bases as "good" for Japan, whereas 57 percent considered them to be "bad" (with 26 percent "don't know").[53] With the 1960 treaty now accepted as a legitimate contract, the LDP firmly in control of the consolidated party system, and the issue of Okinawan reversion resolved, the 1970 "security crisis" got no political traction.

In the space of ten years, the U.S. basing presence, while still opposed by the majority of the Japanese public, had ceased to be the country's most pressing foreign policy and domestic political issue. Certainly, Japan's rapid economic development and the LDP's focus on domestic economic priorities were important factors in explaining the decline of the base issue's salience, but so too was the changing structure of Japanese democracy and the party system. The JSP had been critically undermined in the 1960s by the rise of centrist parties, including the DSP and Komeito, and a particularly sharp decline in JSP support in urban areas.[54] After 1970, political mobilization against the U.S. basing presence was confined mostly to Okinawa, especially as the issue became embedded in the triangular politics of the Okinawa-Tokyo-Washington relationship (see chap. 5).

51. See, e.g., Kobayashi 1968.
52. Junnosuke 1995, 108–9.
53. Mendel 1971–72, 527, 530.
54. Curtis 1988, 19–21.

Today, the 1960 Mutual Security Agreement is still in force and governs the operation of U.S. bases in Japan.

1970s and 1980s: Bureaucratization and the Rise of Cost-Sharing Politics

Institutionalizing LDP Hegemony

By the 1970s, the Japanese system effectively had morphed from a two-party to a multiparty system in which the LDP remained dominant and the opposition parties became fragmented.[55] During the late 1970s and the 1980s, after the party briefly lost its absolute Diet majority in 1976, the LDP became resurgent and once again achieved a commanding parliamentary majority and hegemony. This success owed much to the LDP's incrementalism and policy flexibility that, starting with its slim overall majority in the mid-1970s, allowed the LDP to make compromises with opposition parties and fold their input into the legislative process.

In matters of defense and security, including base policy, opposition parties were included in the process, with the result that political opposition shifted from opposing the legality of issues relating to security and the U.S. bases, and toward focusing on restraining the increase of defense-related expenditures.[56] For example, the adoption of the 1 percent ceiling on defense spending in the mid-1970s was a concession to opposition parties to support various other defense-related policies.[57]

One result of this new consultative politics was that the party political system that once thrived on ideological contestation now forced opposition parties to moderate their views on foreign policy, including the bases issue and the governing Mutual Security Treaty. For example, the Komeito (Clean Government Party) dropped its anti-U.S. base position in the mid-1970s as part of a broader shift to the center on defense issues.[58] Even the JSP, which had remained committed to abrogating the Mutual Security Treaty and had suffered a protracted electoral decline from 1960 to 1980 because of its intransigence on security matters, modified its position in the early 1980s to seek a "phased dismantling" of the treaty in consultation with the United States.[59]

---

55. Curtis 1988, 35–38.
56. Keddell 1993, 89–90.
57. Katzenstein 1996, 124–25; Keddell 1993, 49–55.
58. Keddell 1993, 97.
59. Keddell 1993, 95. On the JSP's ideological intransigence and resulting electoral decline, see Curtis 1988, 117–56. Instructively, Curtis (1988, 137–38) contrasts the JSP's reluctance to change its security views with the Italian Socialists' politically successful opening toward the West and support of NATO during the 1960s.

Further, the greater institutionalization of bureaucratic and interest-group politics within the Japanese political system subsumed and routinized the governance of base-related issues and related societal demands. As the LDP expanded its patronage machine, the institutionalization of *zoku*—specialized policy tribes linking politicians, the bureaucracy, and interest groups—extended into defense.[60] At the same time, the management of base-related issues was delegated to the Defense Facilities Administration Agency (DFAA), a cabinet-level agency charged with overseeing the planning and coordination of base-related maintenance, employment, and local community complaints.[61] Ever since its establishment, the DFAA has mediated and responded to local economic and political demands relating to the bases, and provided compensation payments and "public welfare" to local base-hosting communities.[62] Its jurisdiction over base issues has occasionally been questioned by community activists and local mayors, but it has remained the main conduit through which the central state has resolved and proactively managed base-related disputes.[63] In sum, during the 1970s the LDP's strategy of incremental change and political compromise had transformed the base issue from something that was contested at the highest level of party politics to an issue that was primarily managed by technocrats within a special agency. Other security issues—such as the joint production of military technologies and more active cooperation between the U.S. military and the Japanese Self-Defense Forces—would replace the bases as the main topic of bilateral debate and contention.[64]

The Politics of Burden Sharing and Host-Nation Support

The underlying domestic politics and evolution of the burden-sharing issue—the major topic of base-related negotiations between the United States and Japan during the 1980s—further illustrate how the Japanese government managed to entrench support for the U.S. basing presence by creating new domestic constituencies and interest groups, and as a

60. On *zoku* and Japan's iron triangles, see Curtis 1999, 53–55. On their role in defense, see Green 2001, 47–50; Keddell 1993, 79–124.
61. On the DFAA's role, see Smith 1999.
62. By the 1990s, the major categories for the DFAA's budget were "costs for presence of U.S. forces" (composed of facilities' improvement, labor costs, and utilities), "acquisition of land and building and compensation" (composed of rental payments for USFJ facilities and fishery compensation), and "countermeasures for the region around bases" (composed of sound insulation for housing and environment improvement). Unpublished DFAA briefing packet, Tokyo, June 2003.
63. See Jain 1991 for a case illustration.
64. For an overview, see Katzenstein 1996, 131–52.

consequence, more internal veto points to any fundamental changes. Starting in the mid-1970s, the yen's appreciation vis-à-vis the dollar led to substantial increases in base-related costs for the United States. Under U.S. pressure to contribute to these costs, the LDP introduced "sympathy payments," which were meant to fund and stabilize declining Japanese employment on the bases. The number of Japanese base workers had declined from 34,000 in 1974 to 23,000 in 1977, and American defense officials were threatening even more cuts in the absence of Japanese contributions.[65] The JSP was supported by the All-Japan Security Forces Labor Union, so it could not oppose the cost-sharing measure. In 1977 the Japanese government made its first offset payment of $580 million; in 1979 the payment was increased to $1 billion, and it represented 30 percent of all base-related expenses (not including U.S. military salaries).[66]

Over time, the United States and Japan signed four Special Measures Agreements that increased the amount and kind of Japan's host-nation support for the U.S. basing presence, as new categories of direct costs were incrementally added to the cost-sharing formula.[67] U.S. pressure certainly was a constant in encouraging Japan to increase its support, as were external crises and international events such as the Gulf War, but the categories of outlays and support were driven by Japanese domestic political considerations. Consistent with other elements of the LDP patronage and public works machine, internal lobbying and LDP brokering extended Japan's support payments into areas that included covering all Japanese workers' wages and national insurance contributions (1980), supporting U.S.-proposed base construction (1981), footing the bill for utilities payments (1991), and paying for base relocation costs for the SACO process in Okinawa (1996).[68] In turn, the important beneficiaries of these outlays, including construction companies and electric power companies, were political clients of the LDP factions that brokered the deals.[69]

Again, although the JSP periodically criticized aspects of the host-support payments, mostly arguing that the United States should bear the full financial burden for its presence, it could not oppose the govern-

---

65. Keddell 1993, 68.
66. Sandars 2000, 172.
67. For overviews of the origins and evolution of HNS levels, see Calder 2006; Yoda 2005, 60–102; 2006, 940.
68. On the domestic dimension, see Calder 2003, 53–54; 2006, 159–65; and Yoda 2006, 939–42.
69. Calder 2006, 162–64.

ment's increased contributions to labor costs.[70] In fact, since the onset of Japan's financial support, the absolute number of Japanese employees at U.S. bases increased from 20,000 in 1979 to nearly 25,000, as did the number of Japanese employees per U.S. military personnel.[71] In 1995 host-country support climbed to $3.95 billion or 74.0 percent, and by 2002, Japanese contributions had reached $4.4 billion or 74.5 percent of basing costs, by far the highest amount and proportion of any country hosting U.S. bases.[72] From fundamentally contesting the legality of the U.S. bases in the 1950s, the Japanese government in the 2000s was paying their operating costs and had created an elaborate network of domestic political clients with interests in the bases' continued operation.

Italy: Christian Democracy, the West, and the Nonissue of the Bases

From Vanquished Belligerent to NATO Ally

Although in Italy, unlike Japan, the Allied occupation did not attempt to fundamentally transform the country's domestic institutions, still the postwar settlement could hardly be termed favorable to the Mediterranean country. In 1943 Italy joined the Allies as a cobelligerent against Germany, and the U.S.-led Allied military government supported the formation of a tenuous new multiparty coalition, hoping that the new Italian authority would purge the Italian bureaucracy of its fascist elements and effectively reorganize the country's security forces.[73] In September 1947 the Italian government signed a formal peace treaty that stripped it of its African colonies and Greek islands. The treaty also made the northern city of Trieste a UN-governed territory and imposed ceilings on the size of Italian armed forces. The treaty stipulated that the Allied occupation troops would be withdrawn within ninety days, but Prime Minister Alcide De Gasperi requested that the withdrawal be delayed for internal reasons.[74] At the end of 1947, U.S. troop movements in Italy primarily serviced the contingents in Austria and Trieste. Soon after, two important events set

---

70. Keddell 1993, 144.
71. Yoda 2006, 951–52.
72. U.S. Department of Defense 2004, B-21.
73. On the difficulties of reconstruction, see Miller 1986, 131–210.
74. Nuti 1993, 255; Smith 1991, 30–31.

the stage for the reestablishment of the U.S. military presence on Italian territory.

The Critical 1948 Election and the Turn to NATO

The first event was the landmark 1948 national elections. In early 1947, Italian politics had grown increasingly volatile as a result of the tripartite coalition of political parties headed by the pro-Western Christian Democrats (DC), but included ministerial positions for the Socialists (PSI) and Communists (PCI). De Gasperi dissolved the tripartite coalition in May 1947 in favor of an exclusively DC cabinet with a Western orientation, in part to secure Western support for his party eleven months before the national April 1948 parliamentary elections.[75] The United States followed through, providing De Gasperi, for the first time, with large amounts of economic aid under the Marshall Plan. To further bolster De Gasperi's domestic standing just a few weeks before the April elections, the United States issued a joint declaration with Great Britain and France demanding the return of Trieste to Italy and calling for the immediate consideration of Italy's membership in the United Nations. With substantial American economic assistance and covert support, the DC scored an unexpected landslide victory in the highly contested and ideological 1948 elections, securing 48 percent of the total vote and a healthy parliamentary majority.

Following the historic 1948 vote, De Gasperi set out to obtain a security arrangement with the United States, although he was cautious that any formal alliance would cause a major domestic political storm. Great Britain initially opposed Italian membership in the proposed Northern Atlantic Treaty (NAT), as did some members within Truman's cabinet. Domestically, De Gasperi and Foreign Minister Carlo Sforza rallied the support of all parties except the PCI and PSI, arguing that NAT membership would provide an American security guarantee and more U.S. aid for the cash-starved Italian state.[76] U.S. supporters of Italian membership, who included Secretary of State Dean Acheson and President Harry Truman, believed not only that Italy's strategic location could provide useful facilities to the alliance but that a rebuff of De Gasperi at this point could push Italy back to neutrality or even decisively tip the country back toward Communism. In addition, both Italian and American advocates of Italy's inclusion saw membership as a potential mechanism, under the

75. On the evolution of U.S. engagement with the Italian regime, see Resnick 2005, 100–184.
76. Smith 1991, 77.

general mandate of indirect aggression, for intervening in Italian affairs in the event of a Communist takeover.[77] De Gasperi himself proceeded cautiously through the summer and fall of 1948, trying to secure more concessions from the Allies on Italian territorial questions and economic assistance in order to satisfy skeptics in his own party's moderate faction.[78]

The Italian left launched a vigorous campaign against any type of Western security treaty and warned of continued Western intervention in Italian politics and "warmongering."[79] Both the Communists and Socialists vehemently opposed the proposed Atlantic Pact, whereas some of the smaller parties that were pro-Western criticized De Gasperi for not having secured an adequate revision of the unbalanced peace treaty as quid pro quo for Italy's membership. By March 1949, De Gasperi had secured support for the NAT from his DC members, but he had also gained the politically important backing of Giuseppe Sarargat, head of the Party of Italian Socialist Workers (PSLI). During the parliamentary debate on ratification in March, PSI leader Pietro Nenni warned that the treaty would undercut Italian sovereignty and Italy would have to accept U.S. military bases on Italian soil. The PCI leader Palmiro Togliatti proposed an amendment that would have prohibited foreign governments from establishing military bases on Italian territory, but the amendment was defeated, and soon after the pact itself passed by a 323–170 vote.[80]

For Italy, membership in NATO launched a formal alliance with the United States within a multilateral framework, giving the DC government legitimacy and a new international forum through which to pursue its prestige in the international arena and enhance its domestic standing. Far from having the Alliance or security clientelism imposed on it, Italian leaders skillfully "invited" engagement with the United States and Western integration for their domestic political purposes.[81] As Richard Samuels observes of De Gasperi's efforts,

> He was not "pushed" into alliance with the West. He aggressively "pulled" Italy into it—over the doubts of the United States and Great Britain, and over the strong opposition of his domestic allies. . . . He also understood

77. Smith 1991, 90.
78. Miller 1986, 268.
79. Brogi 2002b, 95–96.
80. Smith 1991, 96.
81. See esp. Brogi 2002b. This is a variant on Geir Lundestad's broader "empire by invitation" thesis. See Lundestad 1986.

that, while the United States strongly preferred a non-Communist Italy, it did not have to be a democratic one. De Gasperi fought creatively and tenaciously to convince these allies that Italy ought not to go that way and played up Italian vulnerability to communism to win their support.[82]

The Bases Established, 1952–1954

The agreement to host U.S. forces and establish NATO bases was negotiated a few years later. The terms of the bilateral general military facilities agreement, signed in January 1952, were deliberately vague and took the form of an exchange of notes so as to avoid parliamentary debate.[83] The agreement committed the Italian government to a number of general principles, for example, to "join in promoting international understanding and good will, and maintaining world peace" and "fulfill the military obligations which it has assumed under the multilateral or bilateral agreements or treaties to which the United States is a party."[84] In August 1952, the two countries also signed the multilateral NATO Protocol on the Status of Headquarters of the Alliance in Paris.[85] However, many of the specific operational arrangements for the bases were left open for specification and negotiation under a later implementation agreement.

The Italian elections of 1953 delayed the signing of the implementation agreement. In a two-level interaction, the new and emboldened Italian parliament now explicitly demanded a favorable conclusion of the Trieste issue as a quid pro quo for ratifying the facilities implementation agreement, a demand that Eisenhower viewed as tantamount to blackmail.[86] Just as Kishi and Sato leveraged audience costs in Japan, Italian officials postured to U.S. counterparts that failure to resolve the Trieste issue would precipitate the collapse of parliament and hand the country

---

82. Samuels 2003, 222. Italian political scientist Gianfranco Pasquino (1986, 61) similarly observes of the DC's domestic maneuvering in economic reconstruction at the time that "what was not inevitable was an almost complete reliance on the United States on the part of Christian Democrats and, consequently, the referral of many important decisions in the field of economic reconstruction to American preferences. Once more, it is not that the U.S.A. *dictated* policy choices, but that dominant forces in Italian politics and economy opted for a capitalist reconstruction in order to obtain advantages from their allegiance to the United States."
83. "Agreement Effected by the Exchange of Notes," signed in Rome, January 7, 1952, *TIAS* 2611. Nuti 1993, 259.
84. Duke 1989, 197.
85. Nuti 1993, 259.
86. Nuti 1993, 260–61; Brogi 2002a, 15.

to the left.[87] Prime Minister Mario Scelba, who had replaced De Gasperi, and the DC also had internal political reasons for attaching Trieste to the facilities implementation agreement. Forcing a vote on the Trieste issue put the left-wing parties in the politically awkward position of having to defend, or at least explain, a vote against securing Italian territorial integrity. After a few more months of political posturing and threats by both sides to break off the negotiations, an agreement on Trieste was reached in October 1954, which was followed three weeks later by the Italian government's signature of the Bilateral Infrastructure Agreement (BIA) as an executive agreement.[88] The exact terms and technical annexes for the use of each facility were kept secret and even now remain classified.[89] In November 1955, after a lively parliamentary debate and considerable left-wing opposition, both chambers ratified the accompanying London Status of Forces Agreement.[90]

The Range and Location of Facilities
The range of military installations and facilities established in the 1950s and 1960s was broad and served a number of functional and coordinating needs for all the U.S. services (see fig. 6.2).[91] The headquarters of Allied Forces Southern Europe (AFSOUTH), located in Naples, was responsible for coordinating military planning for the entire region. In addition, Naples was the headquarters of Allied Naval Forces Southern Europe (NAVSOUTH) and, together with the nearby port of Gaeta, was established as the home port for the Sixth Fleet. Antisubmarine warfare functions were carried out by the naval air facility at Sigonella (Sicily), established in 1959 initially to support aircraft performing antisubmarine reconnaissance. The installation in La Maddalena (Sardinia) was established in 1972 to service nuclear attack submarines. Major U.S. Army facilities were established in the northeast of the country, at Camp Darby and Camp Ederle, with

---

87. Brogi 2002a, 16.
88. Agreement between the Parties Regarding Bilateral Infrastructure in Implementation of the North Atlantic Treaty (BIA), October 20, 1954 (classified). One former official of the Italian Ministry of Defense observed that the enduring secrecy of the BIA may be a function of some of these provisions' unconstitutionality. Author's interview with former Italian Ministry of Defense official, Rome, May 2006.
89. The BIA remains in force, despite the negotiation in 1995 of the "Memorandum of Understanding Concerning the Use of Installations/Infrastructure by United States Forces in Italy," signed in Rome, February 2, 1995, *TIAS* 12317.
90. Nuti 1993, 261–62.
91. For a list and description, see Duke 1989, 199–203, 207–14.

Figure 6.2. Major U.S. military facilities, Italy, 1984.
Source: Congressional Research Service

Vicenza serving as Southern European Task Force (SETAF) headquarters.[92] An extensive network of air force facilities included Aviano near the Yugoslav border and a range of joint-use bases in the southern region. Finally, a number of nuclear installations were established in Italy during the cold war, including the stationing of Jupiter missiles around Gioia del Colle and later, ground-launched cruise missiles (GLCMs) at Comiso in Sicily.

In general, relations between locals and U.S. troops proved friendly in just about all areas of deployment. The Nash report in 1957 singled out the warm reception that U.S. troops had received in Italy and explained:

> Italy is one of the most enthusiastic supporters of NATO and is a strong advocate of collective security. Even stronger is the desire for cooperation with the United States, and Italy looks to the United States as the most powerful member of NATO for leadership as well as material support. The majority of Italians, chastened by their experiences of the last 30 years, believe that their own survival depends upon a close association with other and stronger nations; the United States is therefore an ideal ally if Italy is to be protected and assisted. Psychologically, ties with the United States are strong; there is a long tradition of friendship with America and Americans and a sense of gratitude exists for the US part in the liberation of Italy in World War II.[93]

In a matter of just a few years, Italy had undergone a remarkable transformation in its relations with the United States. From its status as vanquished World War II power, Italy soon emerged as host to a number of critical military installations, and a vital member of NATO and Western security efforts.

Italy's DC Rule and Atlantic Security Policy

Like Japan's LDP, the DC became the pro-Western party that was supported by Washington, and it would be the most vigorous political backer of the U.S. security presence, albeit within a NATO framework. These domestic political lines were clearly drawn during the seminal 1948 election that propelled De Gasperi to his parliamentary majority and initiated

---

92. According to Nuti (1993, 265), the choice of Vicenza as SETAF headquarters reflected its favorable political orientation as a DC stronghold.
93. Nash 1957, 76.

over forty-six years of DC-led Italian governments, most of them in coalition. Remarkably, the 1952 bilateral exchange of notes, along with the 1954 BIA, remained in force for the duration of the DC's political tenure and was only revised in 1995.[94] The durability of the agreement, despite its considerably unbalanced and secret provisions, testifies to its institutionalization within Italy's party political system and the DC's reluctance to, in any way, revise or modify its provisions.

Starting in the mid-1950s, the DC adopted a vigorous neo-Atlanticist agenda, actively promoting cooperation within NATO and enhancing its own international prestige by participating in as many multilateral venues as possible.[95] As in Japan, Italy's one-party political system gradually forced Italian left-wing parties to adopt more moderate foreign and security policies that openly accepted Italy's NATO membership and the presence of U.S. troops, although both the Italian Socialists and Communists did so considerably sooner than their Japanese counterparts. In turn, these parties' shifts toward the center prompted countermobilizations and two-level reactions by Italy's ruling elites.[96] An example of this dynamic occurred when DC officials vehemently objected to U.S. plans to remove troops or nuclear weapons, including proposed SETAF reductions in 1958 and 1963.[97]

94. In 1995 the two sides replaced the 1952 agreement and all previous bilateral and local agreements (except the BIA) with the "Memorandum of Understanding [MOU] Concerning the Use of Installations/Infrastructure by United States Forces in Italy," signed in Rome, February 2, 1995, *TIAS* 12317. For the MOU text, see http://rome.usembassy.gov/ussso/files/shell.pdf (accessed May 2007). Also known as the Shell Agreement, the MOU did not replace the 1954 BIA, which remains the main implementing base agreement and whose provisions still remain confidential. The 1995 MOU provides for the negotiation of individual technical arrangements (TAs) for each installation. As of 2007, one of the TAs, governing Sigonella, had been concluded. I thank Olimpio Guidi, former host-nation liaison for the Office of Defense Cooperation in the U.S. embassy in Rome, for clarifying these legal nuances.
95. See Brogi 2002a, 2002b.
96. As Leopoldo Nuti (2002, 49–50) instructively observes, "Far from passively submitting to the diktat of the international system, Italian politicians played an active role in trying to channel and even shape developments on the international scene to suit their goals. In many cases they urged Washington to pursue actions at the international level that would be conducive to their own domestic purpose. During the Eisenhower administration, for example, Italian politicians repeatedly warned U.S. leaders not to rush toward a dialogue with the Soviet Union lest too hasty a détente yield unpredictable consequences for the Italian political system. Italian leaders sometimes even fabricated an American request in order to influence domestic politics."
97. Nuti 1993, 267–69. The Nash (1957, 77) report also observed, "Compared with the attitude in most countries toward the presence of US forces, the reaction in Italy is paradoxical. Instead of desiring a reduction, Italian officials have gone on the record as wanting

The first of the opposition parties to moderate its positions on NATO and the U.S. military presence was the Socialists led by Pietro Nenni, one of the first critics of Italy's integration into the Western security system. Until the mid-1950s, the PSI had aligned itself firmly with the PCI and had advocated a foreign policy of neutrality.[98] Eisenhower openly distrusted the PSI, as did his outspoken and controversial ambassador to Italy, Clare Boothe Luce, and both resisted calls for an "opening to the left" and negotiations. From 1953 to 1963, prompted in part by events in Hungary in 1956, Nenni moderated the party's foreign policy positions and marginalized its pro-Soviet factions. The transformation was sealed in 1963 when the Kennedy administration openly accepted the PSI and offered it some covert assistance, much to the chagrin of DC political leaders.[99] In 1963 the revamped PSI was included in Italy's first center-left government, led by Aldo Moro. As Maurizio Cremasco observes of the structural dynamics of the shift, "the development of the Socialist Party implied that for any party to be considered a government party, it would have to accept, without reserve, Italy's fundamental foreign and defense policies. The centre-left coalition . . . allowed the Socialist Party to use its support of Italian military and foreign policy to gain external legitimacy and, indirectly, greater bargaining power within the Italian political system."[100]

Over the next decade, the PCI evolved in a similar fashion.[101] From 1973 the PCI aimed at a historic compromise under which it could finally enter a government with the DC and PSI. The PCI abandoned its long-time opposition to NATO in an effort to diffuse its vulnerability on foreign policy—a weakness the DC exploited whenever possible—and focus voters' attention on domestic issues. At a military affairs conference in 1975, PCI policy planners accepted Italy's membership in NATO's integrated defense system and affirmed that they would not unilaterally reduce NATO bases on Italian territory.[102] In a now famous 1976 interview with the leading

---

additional units. Officially, the reason given was the increased instability in the Middle East, the dangers this holds for NATO, and Italy's favorable strategic position from which to deploy forces as necessary. Equally important factors behind this decision were, however, the knowledge of the very important economic contribution by the U.S. forces, and the feeling that the greater the number of US personnel stationed in Italy, the greater the call Italy would have on US protection and assistance."

98. See Nuti 2002.
99. Nuti 1999; 2002, 45–47.
100. Cremasco 1988, 203–4.
101. The actual sincerity of the PCI's changes on foreign policy issues remains a matter of historical and scholarly debate, however dramatic its evolution in its public positions.
102. Putnam 1978, 307.

newspaper *Corriere della Sera,* PCI leader Enrico Berlinguer declared that he would "feel more secure" under the NATO umbrella than within the Communist bloc.[103] This adjustment in the party's foreign policy position seemingly reaped its political reward in June 1976 when the PCI gained 34.4 percent of the vote, putting it just a few points within the DC.[104] Under the historic compromise of 1978, the PCI was invited to join the parliamentary majority but remained excluded from cabinet positions and wielded little influence, prompting it to withdraw in 1979. In the national election of that same year, and in the wake of the kidnapping and killing of Aldo Moro by the extremist group Red Brigade, the PCI's share of the vote declined for the first time in its postwar history, prompting the beginning of its political decline.

The Debate over the Euromissiles

The Euromissile debate of the late 1970s illustrates the structural effects of the Italian one-party political system on defense issues and shows how Italy's governing elites wielded base-related questions to further domestic political advantage. In 1976, the Soviet Union began to deploy more than a hundred new SS-20 missiles, which allowed it to strike targets in western Europe from deep inside its own territory. In response, U.S. and NATO planners accelerated plans to deploy their own Theater Nuclear Forces (TNF) in Europe, and a formal decision toward that end was tentatively approved by Britain, France, and Germany at the Guadalupe summit in January 1979. German chancellor Helmut Schmidt, facing severe political opposition from his own Social Democratic Party members, stated that he would deploy the new intermediate-range Pershing 2 missiles (Euromissiles) only if another NATO country also accepted deployment. American officials agreed to seek approval from Italy but doubted that the country's volatile political environment and the PCI's strong parliamentary presence would ultimately allow Italian leaders to accept the missiles.[105]

As it turned out, the structure of the Italian political system worked in favor of the deployment. The critical political figure was Bettino Craxi, the PSI leader, who offered strong support for the DC promissile position. Craxi saw a political opportunity to use the issue to effectively distance his party from the surging PCI. Having just spent much of the decade reassuring

---

103. *Corriere della Sera,* June 15, 1976, as quoted in Putnam 1978, 308.
104. On Washington's policy toward the PCI, see Gardner 2005; Njølstad 2002.
105. See Gardner 2005, 228–30.

the Italian public that the PCI was now committed to the Western security system, the Socialists' strong support for the Euromissiles threw the PCI on the defensive on a critical foreign policy issue. In the end it was not the opportunity to strategically counter the Soviet move but, according to Craxi's main adviser on the Euromissile decision, the domestic political benefit, as well as the opportunity to forge links with the German SDP, that ultimately convinced Craxi to back the proposal.[106] The ploy worked as planned: the PCI was forced to adopt a convoluted position that called for a six-month moratorium on the TNF deployment to allow for arms control negotiations between the superpowers.[107]

During the heated December 1979 debate in parliament, Berlinguer pleaded that his party's rejection of TNF was not indicative of a broader rejection of NATO and complained that the governing parties were "eager to use this vote instrumentally as a weapon of agitation and pressure for their own domestic political plans."[108] The effort was successful as the parliament approved the resolution 313 to 262, with the support of the DC, Social Democrats, Liberals, Republicans, and Craxi's Socialists. According to one Italian observer of the episode, "the Socialists' support of the government's Atlantic policy isolated the PCI, reduced the Communists' room for maneuver and the prospects of another grand coalition. It also underlined the PCI's incapacity to take decisions truly independent of Moscow and opened up new avenues of collaboration between the PSI and DC."[109] As it turned out, Craxi's calculated gambit to support the Euromissiles paid off for him personally as well, when he became the first Socialist prime minister of Italy in coalition with the DC in 1983.

Sovereign Tensions: The Sigonella Affair and the Libyan Bombing
It was under Craxi's leadership of the Italian government in the mid-1980s that two of the most controversial and politically sensitive base-related episodes in Italy occurred. The first, known as the Sigonella affair, was a blatant breach of the base host's domestic sovereignty and served as a dramatic illustration of some of the legal ambiguities that have characterized the status of U.S. forces in Italy.

106. Author's interview with Stefano Silvestri, former defense adviser to Benedetto Craxi, Rome, May 2006. The U.S. ambassador Richard Gardner (2005, 236), in his memoirs, maintains that Craxi's decision was based on the strategic merits of the question.
107. For an overview of the domestic politics informing Craxi's decision and the ensuing 1984 implementation of the agreement, see Nuti 2004.
108. As quoted in Gardner 2005, 245.
109. Cremasco 1988, 207.

The episode had its origins in the October 1985 hijacking of the Italian cruise liner *Achille Lauro* by four members of the Palestinian Liberation Front (PLF).[110] The ship had been sailing in Egypt when four hijackers took control of it and its 420 crew and passengers and demanded the release of fifty Palestinians from Israeli prisons. After Syria refused the ship permission to dock at the port of Tartus, the hijackers killed a wheelchair-bound Jewish American hostage, Leon Klinghoffer, and then set sail again for Egypt. In their second round of negotiations with Egyptian authorities, the hijackers demanded and secured safe passage to Tunisia (PLO headquarters at the time) via an Egyptian commercial airplane. On October 10, on the direct order of President Ronald Reagan, U.S. naval fighters intercepted the airliner carrying the hijackers and forced it to land at the NATO naval airbase in Sigonella, Sicily. Both Italian defense officials and high-ranking military officers who were involved in the episode insist that the United States had mistakenly assumed Sigonella was an American facility when in fact it was a sovereign Italian installation used by NATO.[111] Accordingly, the U.S. fighters had already breached Italian sovereignty by forcing the landing.[112]

The events that followed were remarkable: as the airliner landed and stopped on the tarmac, it was surrounded by a group of Italian military conscripts stationed at the base. Moments later, another plane carrying a U.S. Delta Force team—which had been instructed to capture the hijackers and bring them back to the United States for trial—also landed and proceeded to encircle the Italian troops. As Italian and American authorities discussed the matter during the tense standoff on the tarmac, the Italian base commander put out an urgent dispatch to all surrounding towns and villages for additional national police (carabinieri). After their arrival, the carabinieri formed a third concentric circle that surrounded the Delta Force. Craxi was unflinching on the question of Italian jurisdiction over the plane, and American officials eventually relented, allowing the plane to take off for Rome and the hijackers to be tried in Italy. As negotiations between Italian and American officials dragged into the middle of the

110. On the legal aspects of the *Achille Lauro* episode, see Cassese 1989. Also see Sandars 2000, 234–35.
111. Author's interview with retired Italian general who was sent to Egypt during the hijacking, Rome, May 2006.
112. According to Michael Bohn (2004, 31), National Security staff member during the episode, the U.S. side decided to request permission for landing only after the airliner had been intercepted in order to present the Italian side with a fait accompli that might have "ensure[d] better Italian cooperation."

night, the Sigonella base commander attempted to diffuse the tension among the Italian and U.S. forces by instructing his assistants to serve coffee on the tarmac to the various concentrically arranged parties.[113]

Ultimately, the Italian side was successful in asserting its various claims of sovereignty over the Sigonella base and the hijackers, but the episode signaled a low in U.S.-Italian relations and for Italian public opinion regarding U.S. base rights in Italy. Whether the American decision to force the Egyptian airliner to land in Sicily was taken more out of ignorance of the base's legal status or in intentional disregard of Italian jurisdiction is still unclear, but the resulting sovereign violation prompted Craxi to publicly state in November 1985 that "NATO bases in Italy can be used only for specific NATO ends and in conformity with NATO accords."[114]

A few months after the Sigonella episode, the issue of American base rights in Italy was once again in the political forefront. During the Gulf of Sidra confrontation between Libya and the United States in March 1986, Craxi emphasized that U.S. actions against the North African country had occurred "outside of the framework of NATO" and that NATO bases in Italy "cannot constitute a starting point of war operations outside of the NATO framework."[115] The following month Craxi refused American requests to use Italian facilities and airspace for U.S. air strikes on Libya. After the U.S. bombing, the Libyan government launched a retaliatory SCUD missile that missed the Italian island of Lampedusa, host to a U.S. Coast Guard station, by several hundred meters.

Accepting the Torrejón Wing: The Partnership Reestablished
Perhaps the most remarkable aspect of the Sigonella affair, from an analytical standpoint, was just how exceptional it was in the cold-war base history of U.S. forces in Italy. Despite intense political opposition to the United States during the episode, Craxi did not contest the governing terms of the U.S. military presence in Italy, nor did the Sigonella or Libya episodes precipitate a further deterioration in security cooperation or base issues.

Rather, just two years later, Italy once again volunteered to provide the United States with much needed base-related access, although it did so out of both international and, again, domestic political motives. At issue in early 1988 was finding an alternative site to host the seventy-two F-16s that

113. Author's interviews with Italian retired generals, Rome, May 2006.
114. Grimmett 1986, 23.
115. Grimmett 1986, 27.

had been based in Torrejón, Spain, but which Spanish negotiators wanted removed as a prerequisite to any new basing agreement (see chap. 3). The new Italian government, now led by DC prime minister Ciriaco De Mita, volunteered to take the fighter wing, with NATO providing the $520 million to fund the transfer.[116] Typically, De Mita's offer not only reflected the DC's traditionally strong pro-NATO orientation but also was intended to split the political left and slow a resurgent Socialist Party, which had almost attained the level of PCI support in local elections in 1988. Mikhail Gorbachev had called for the fighter wing to be included in comprehensive European disarmament talks, something that DC members and U.S. officials vigorously resisted. The transfer was approved by the Italian parliament in June 1988 and completed in 1992, although the original site of Crotone in Calabria was abandoned as a result of escalating costs and replaced with the existing U.S. Air Force–operated base at Aviano in the northeast.

De Mita's decision to accept the fighter wing is an apt example of how the cold war–era Italian party political system entwined domestic political calculations with base-related issues. DC officials and their coalition supporters always presented basing commitments and nuclear deployment as essential to Italy's multilateral commitment to NATO and its pro-Western orientation. By contrast, excluded left-wing parties had to negotiate the fine line between maintaining their ideological base of support while steadily moderating their positions on foreign policy and security issues to appear credible and responsible to median voters. Yet, at each point, governing politicians pushed the limits of these new opposition positions, as with the Euromissile debate, and used base issues to cast doubts on the opposition's security commitments. Like the LDP in Japan, the DC during the cold war was a political client of the United States, but this position also afforded it significant political resources to use for its domestic purposes.

The Post–Cold War Political System and Basing Issues

The Collapse of One-Party Political Rule

The domestic dominance of both the LDP in Japan and the DC in Italy collapsed almost immediately after the end of the cold war. Although the endurance of these one-party systems cannot be reduced exclusively to

116. Jenkins 1988.

the parties' ties to the United States, their anticommunist foreign policy platforms were an important element in unifying party factions as well as their voting publics. As Richard Samuels observes, "the new international balance of power removed many of the external pressures that had shaped postwar Italy and Japan. Suddenly it was less important to be anticommunist and—at least in Italy—suddenly it was less important to *be* Communist. No longer did any group or party *have* to be included or excluded from power."[117] New possibilities for political coalitions and unpredictable alignments emerged, as did demands to reform these countries' electoral systems.

In both countries, however, the coming to power of left-led coalitions in the 1990s had no practical impact on the countries' permissive attitudes toward U.S. basing and indeed helped to further institutionalize the U.S. military presence by bestowing on it the left's official acquiescence. As prime minister of the short-lived LDP-JSP coalition, Socialist Murayama Tomiichi distanced himself from nearly all of the JSP's traditional core positions on security when he declared Japan's Self-Defense Forces constitutional and accepted the U.S.-Japan Security Treaty as "indispensable."[118] Murayama also accepted the recommendations of the famous report authored by Assistant Secretary of Defense for International Security Affairs Joseph Nye (Nye report) in 1995, which called for the reversal of U.S. troop drawdown in Japan and their continued forward deployment in order to preserve East Asian security;[119] the Socialist prime minister also had to manage the mainland's response to the 1995 rape incident on Okinawa and directly confront Governor Ota over his refusal to extend the base land leases (see chap. 5).

In Italy, Romano Prodi's Olive Branch coalition of 1994–96, and the 1996–2000 eclectic left-wing coalition led by former Communist Massimo D'Alema, not only agreed to support Italy's participation in NATO and its security framework but actively managed Italy's military involvement in NATO-related missions in Bosnia and Kosovo. During these Balkan missions, "Italy became NATO's aircraft carrier," despite severe misgivings among these parties' rank and file that their government was allowing the use of the bases for an "American war."[120] And in January 2007 a left-wing government once again found itself defending the sanctity of basing

117. Samuels 2003, 272–73.
118. Curtis 1999, 198.
119. On reaction to the Nye report, see Funabashi 1999, chap. 12.
120. Cremasco 2001, 170–71.

agreements when Prime Minister Romano Prodi, having succeeded the vigorously pro–United States regime of Silvio Berlusconi, bucked his own left-wing coalition members over plans to expand the base at Vicenza. Under the agreement, the base is expected to expand from 2,750 to 4,500 troops to house the full 173rd Airborne Brigade from Germany. Although in January 17, 2007, Prodi shepherded through the Italian Senate the approval of the base expansion measure, he did so under severe criticism from his Communist and Green coalition members, and in the following month, tens of thousands of protestors demonstrated in Vicenza over the plan.[121] Shortly after, Prodi's government briefly fell and was reconstituted, but the Italian prime minister remained resolute in maintaining his backing for the expansion agreement.[122]

New Base-Related Crises and Host-Government Responses

Both the governments of Japan and Italy have had to manage the political fallout of highly publicized base-related accidents and crimes involving U.S. personnel, and their reactions reveal much about the relatively depoliticized status of U.S. bases in these countries.

The aftermath of the 1995 rape in Okinawa typifies Tokyo's style of managing base-related issues. Okinawa governor Ota and his supporters questioned the legality of the U.S. presence on the island and challenged Tokyo's legitimacy to act on behalf of the island prefecture. In response, the main island government, in coordination with Washington, used compensatory politics and created new institutions such as the Special Action Committee on Okinawa to respond to the local crisis, without structurally changing the overall terms of the actual U.S. basing presence.[123] Public opinion in Japan was again tested in 2001 by the sinking of a Japanese fishing vessel by a U.S. Navy submarine off the coast of Hawaii, an accident that cost the lives of nine of the thirty-five educators and children aboard. And in January 2006, a U.S. sailor based on the USS *Kittyhawk* confessed to murdering a Japanese woman in Yokosuka.[124] The sailor was handed

---

121. See Brown 2007; *International Herald Tribune* 2007.
122. Fisher 2007. Prodi's continued commitment to the base expansion occurred even as U.S.-Italian bilateral relations deteriorated over maintaining Italian peacekeepers in Afghanistan and an Italian court's indictment of twenty-six CIA officers for violating Italian law during the kidnapping and rendition of a terror suspect in Milan in 2003.
123. In 2001, the government of Japan agreed to support a request to modify the SOFA to allow Japanese pretrial custody for suspects accused of major crimes such as arson, rape, and armed robbery.
124. BBC News 2006.

over to Japanese authorities and tried and convicted. The most instructive aspect of this latest criminal jurisdiction case is how relatively little uproar it caused in Japan. Contrary to some claims that the murder might unleash a new wave of anti-U.S. base sentiment and negatively affect ongoing realignment negotiations, the orderly resolution of the matter seemed to draw significant contrasts, not comparisons, between the politics of U.S. base-related crimes in mainland Japan and in the more volatile settings of Okinawa or Korea.[125]

In Italy, too, a high-profile dramatic accident that initially threatened to set off a backlash against the U.S. presence had few lasting negative effects. In February 1998 a Marine EA-6B prowler stationed in Aviano severed the cable of a ski-lift gondola near the resort town of Cavalese, in the process killing all twenty passengers on board. The pilot had been flying at a low altitude of 370 feet, well below the recommended 2,000-foot level, leading observers to question whether he had been deliberately negligent or was "flat-hatting" in the Alpine mountain pass. An attempt by a local prosecutor to try the pilot in an Italian court was dismissed by an Italian judge on the grounds that jurisdiction clearly resided with U.S. military officials, in accordance with the NATO SOFA.[126] Media observers and the Italian public were further stunned when the U.S. Congress blocked a plan to provide compensation to the victims' families.[127]

On March 4, 1999, a U.S. military court in North Carolina acquitted the pilot of all twenty counts of involuntary manslaughter. The verdict coincided with a U.S. visit by Prime Minister Massimo D'Alema, who was first informed of the verdict at a press conference in Boston. But despite the Italian prime minister's shock at the verdict and promise to "explore all legal ways" to ensure that "justice is done," the Italian government took no additional action on either the specific case or any base-related issues in retaliation.[128] In fact, one year later the two countries formed a bilateral commission to draw up new rules and procedures for low-level American flights, and the U.S. administration overruled Congress and paid compensation to the Cavalese victims' families.[129] Rather than inciting political

---

125. See, e.g., the warnings about the incident's adverse impact given by Sheila Smith (2006).
126. For a legal analysis, see Ciampi 1999.
127. See Reisman and Sloane 2000.
128. Thompson 1999.
129. U.S. ambassador Tom Foglietta and U.S. president Bill Clinton both issued public apologies to the Italian public and families of the victims.

mobilization around antibasing issues, the accident's aftermath, Carla Monteleone observes, "actually resulted in enhanced cooperation regarding military flights, more clarity regarding the chain of command between Americans and Italians, and the elevation in importance of the Aviano base in overall U.S. strategy."[130]

The tragic nature of these accidents and crimes in Japan and Italy is not at issue, but their severity has indeterminate political consequences. The range of reactions to these high-profile base-related incidents reflects the variations in the politicization of the U.S. basing presence within the different host countries. On the main islands of Japan and in Italy, serious incidents relating to the U.S. military presence did not ignite a host-country challenge to the basing relationship, as they had on Okinawa and in South Korea.

The Global Defense Posture Review and the Politics of U.S. Troop Realignments

The relatively favorable political climate in Italy toward U.S. bases is a key consideration in the Pentagon's current base realignment (see chap. 7). As of 2007, U.S. officials plan on the continued use of nearly all current Italian bases and facilities, making Italy one of the few overseas base hosts likely to see an increase in current U.S. troop levels.[131] U.S. defense officials acknowledge that Italy's strategic positioning on the Mediterranean and near North Africa, the Italian military's antiterrorism doctrine, as well as the country's favorable political disposition toward U.S. forces are important factors in the Pentagon's decision to retain more than 14,000 troops there.[132]

One instructive exception to this general pattern was a brief "island politics" dynamic on the island of Sardinia. In 2004 Renato Soru, as a candidate for the island's governorship, campaigned on a platform that emphasized Sardinian nationalism and opposed Prime Minister Silvio Berlusconi and the American military presence on the island, especially the nuclear submarine repair station at La Maddalena. As in the other cases involving island politics, Soru drew support from local activists and separatists by claiming that the Italian central government did not adequately

130. Monteleone 2007, 78.
131. Author's interviews with U.S. officials, U.S. embassy, Rome, May 2006. Also see Monteleone 2007, 73–77.
132. Author's interviews with U.S. officials, U.S. embassy, Rome, May 2006.

represent the regional government's concerns and positions in base-related negotiations. A year earlier in 2003, a grounding accident involving the nuclear submarine USS *Hartford* near the Sardinian naval station had alarmed local residents and activists.[133] In tests after the accident, U.S. and Italian inspectors found no unusual damage or radiation, but the incident bolstered Soru's campaign promise to close down the naval installation in order to develop the island's tourism industry.[134] Soru also demanded that the Italian government financially compensate the island for a loss of tourism resulting from the *Hartford* accident. American officials claim that the campaign had minimal political impact on their planning as the station had been targeted for closure before Soru's election.[135] Indeed, according to one insider's account of the meeting between Soru, after his successful election, and U.S. officials, the Sardinian governor offered to backtrack on his calls for an immediate closure and instead proposed a phased dismantling over the next five to six years.[136] Shortly after, however, in November 2005, Italian minister of defense Antonio Martino and U.S. secretary of state Donald Rumsfeld announced that the two countries had agreed to close the facility by 2008.

In Japan, too, it appears as if the Global Defense Posture Review–related realignment may differentially impact U.S. bases on the main islands and Okinawa. In May 2006, U.S. and Japanese officials announced that 8,000 marines and about 9,000 dependents stationed in Okinawa would be moved to a new complex on the Pacific island of Guam by 2014 in an effort to ease the island's "special burden." Consistent with its previous burden-sharing efforts, the government of Japan agreed to pay $6.1 billion of the total $10 billion estimated costs for the move.[137] The plan also calls for the construction of a Futenma replacement facility near the city of Nago and moving the F-15 combat training that currently takes place in Kadena to a number of Japanese Self-Defense Forces locations on the main islands. In addition, Yokosuka near Tokyo will, for the first time, become the home port for a nuclear-powered aircraft carrier. These moves will be politically facilitated by a new set of programs and grants that Tokyo will target to base-hosting locales.

133. See *Washington Post* 2003.
134. Wilkinson 2005.
135. Author's interviews with U.S. officials, U.S. embassy, Rome, May 2006.
136. Author's personal communication with an official who attended these negotiations.
137. For preliminary details, see Marquand 2006.

Conclusions: Base Politics in Client Democracies

Despite expectations that their heavy dependence on the United States for security needs might make Japan and Italy exceptional cases in the overall universe of base hosts, the evolution of their postwar base politics broadly conforms to the expectations of the base politics theory and exhibits instructive differences (see fig. 6.1). Both countries accepted the U.S. military presence in the early 1950s and, despite their relatively weak positions, both demanded important sovereign concessions—the return of Trieste to Italy and the granting of independence and a peace treaty to Japan—as quid pro quo for these original basing contracts. Not surprisingly, the legal terms of these security contracts were considerably one-sided, reflecting the new client status of these defeated World War II powers and their dependence on the United States for political support and security.

Nevertheless, the different internal political characteristics and institutional developments of these countries also account for important variations in the evolution and contestation of the basing presence (see fig. 6.3). By the late 1950s in Japan, the 1951 Security Treaty was widely perceived as an illegitimate and unjust contract that had been imposed by an occu-

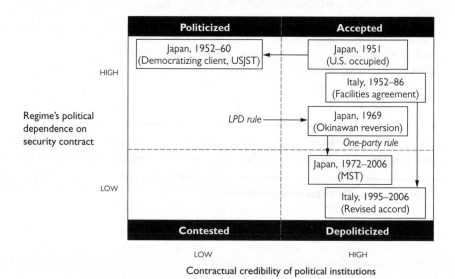

Figure 6.3. Evolution of base politics, Japan (main islands) and Italy

pying power. Accordingly, Japanese leaders successfully made the case to U.S. policymakers that the treaty should be revised in the interest of maintaining internal stability. Yet despite the 1960 treaty's considerable concessions to Japan, its ratification produced an unprecedented crisis in Japanese politics. The critical factors during this period of dramatic political turmoil were Japan's volatile party system, extensive factionalism, and a fiercely competitive media that seemed out of control during the treaty's ratification. By contrast, the contours of the Italian postwar party system were defined by the 1948 election, when the DC triumphed on an openly pro-American and pro-Western platform. Subsequently, Italy joined NATO and signed an extensive base facilities agreement. Although Italy's left-leaning parties vigorously opposed these security treaties and objected to their secrecy and lack of parliamentary ratification, democratic governments voluntarily signed them, lending them a more general legitimacy that the 1951 peace treaty in Japan lacked.

One-party democratic rule in both countries further institutionalized the acceptance of the U.S. basing presence and its governing agreements. As the LDP and the DC established themselves as advocates for the U.S. security umbrella, political statements against the bases necessarily carried connotations of supporting left-wing opposition parties. And elites in both the LDP and the DC used base-related issues to question the foreign policy credentials and competence of left-wing opposition parties. In Italy, one-party rule drove the PSI in the 1960s, and then the PCI in the 1970s, to adopt more pro-Western and pro-NATO positions and accept the legitimacy of the basing presence in order to appeal to the median voter and to appear responsible and competent on foreign policy issues. In Japan, following its contested ratification, the 1960 Mutual Security Treaty was accepted by most of the Japanese public as a legitimate security contract, even though opinion polling on the bases indicated that most Japanese still held strong reservations about the American military presence.

After Okinawa's reversion, the basing presence became almost a nonissue in the high politics of the main islands, as an intransigent JDP declined in electoral support and most U.S. military facilities after 1970 were moved to the island prefecture and became a regional issue enmeshed in Okinawan politics. By the 1980s, a special agency in Japan effectively managed the economic and political demands of base-hosting communities, and the Japanese government made significant payments to directly support the costs of U.S. bases in Japan, while it simultaneously supported a number of domestic interest groups and political clients. And although periodic incidents involving the bases continue to draw attention to their presence, and even generate some public protests, the democratic institutions of both base hosts ensure a continued commitment to the U.S. presence, even as these governments change and the basing presence itself undergoes a major reorganization and realignment.

want some
recognition of their
tribulations, and after that,
more amenable

CHAPTER 7

Central Asia and the Global Defense Posture Review

New Bases, Old Politics

The theory of base politics advanced in this book explains the political evolution of the issue in many of the southern European and East Asian base hosts. Beginning in about 2005, however, the United States has been undergoing a fundamental restructuring of its overseas basing network. As part of the Global Defense Posture Review (GDPR), U.S. defense planners are downsizing large cold war–era facilities and replacing them with a chain of so-called lily-pad bases, a global network of smaller facilities of a nonpermanent nature that can be quickly expanded when needed.[1] These bases will host fewer permanent troops, rely more on contractors for their maintenance, and because of their small size, leave a much lighter social "footprint" in their host country than the large bases of the cold war era. U.S. planners have sought guarantees of "strategic flexibility" or nearly unrestricted use-rights from these new hosts, as these bases are designed to cope with contemporary security threats that are small in scale, unpredictable, and localized. Many of these new bases are located in regions where the United States traditionally has not maintained a presence, including Africa, Central Asia, and the Black Sea.

---

1. See Campbell and Ward 2003 and the report by the Overseas Basing Commission (OBC) 2005.

The strategic reasoning behind this global base restructuring may be compelling, but the assumption of U.S. planners that these new-style bases will be less politically controversial within host countries is unwarranted. The theory of base politics that I've presented in this book argues that the politics of the basing issue tends to be driven by political and institutional changes within the host country itself, not by the actual size of the base or the external security situation. Accordingly, even in these smaller lily-pad installations, base politics should be subject to political developments within base hosts, especially survivorship politics as played by authoritarian hosts or during periods of democratic transition.

The recent evolution of the new U.S. bases in post-Soviet Central Asia offers such a warning. During fall 2001, the United States established bases in Uzbekistan and Kyrgyzstan, both independent states of the former Soviet Union, to support military operations in Afghanistan. The bases themselves—at Karshi-Khanabad (K2) airfield in southern Uzbekistan and Manas (Ganci) airport near the Kyrgyz capital of Bishkek—were relatively small, not intended to be permanent, and typified the new lily-pad facilities of the GDPR.[2]

The U.S. basing presence initially was welcomed by the Central Asian states, but by summer 2005 host attitudes had changed dramatically. In July 2005 the Uzbek government evicted the United States from K2, dealing a major operational and diplomatic blow to U.S. planners. At the same time, the Kyrgyz government demanded a renegotiation of its basing contract and then the criminal jurisdiction procedures underpinning the SOFA. The Central Asian cases demonstrate how authoritarian rulers and democratizing elites manipulated the base issue in a manner strikingly similar to that of their cold war counterparts. In Kyrgyzstan, a democratic-style revolution in March 2005 ousted President Akayev, and new elites soon after challenged the procedural legitimacy of the Akayev-era governing contracts. In Uzbekistan an authoritarian regime calculated that its strict domestic political control and repressive tactics were threatened by the continued U.S. presence and best guaranteed by aligning itself instead with Russia and China. Far from stabilizing the domestic political situation through its lily-pad presence, the United States became embroiled in the internal politics and regime survival strategies of these Central Asian

---

2. U.S. officials sometimes refer to the Manas site as Ganci, a reference and tribute to Peter Ganci, a New York firefighter who died on 9/11. In regard to Manas and the lily-pad base strategy, see, e.g., Tyson 2004. Also see Cornell 2004.

hosts. Importantly, the cases also caution that establishing a global network of multiple new bases in other authoritarian and democratizing host countries may increase, not moderate, internal political volatility.

In the following section I recount the establishment and political evolution of the U.S. military presence in post-Soviet Central Asia and then examine how their base politics quickly changed from nonpolitical to contested in Kyrgyzstan and from nonpolitical to nonexistent as a result of outright eviction in Uzbekistan. In the final section I look at the logic and scope of the GDPR by comparing and contrasting the dramatic base-related events in Central Asia with the likely political trajectories of new bases being established, as of 2007, in Africa and the Black Sea region. Although the GDPR is still relatively recent, the available evidence suggests that a lighter, more global U.S. military presence will not alter the fundamental two-level interactions and base politics played by political elites within base hosts. These lessons are important for U.S. planners, who simultaneously promote democratization and negotiate basing agreements within these same transitioning polities. Ironically, these processes may well work at cross-purposes in that democratization may unleash political momentum to curb, renegotiate, or even expel the U.S. military presence.

New Allies and Base Hosts in Central Asia

America and Central Asia: Background to the Basing Presence

Shortly after the events of September 11, 2001, U.S. officials began preparing to topple the Taliban in Afghanistan and eliminate al-Qaeda fighters and training camps. The planning for Operation Enduring Freedom (OEF) was complicated by the fact that the United States lacked forward-deployed installations near Afghanistan and that it had not developed strong security ties with the post-Soviet Central Asian states. In fact, in initial operational discussions, U.S. planners envisaged that basing would be almost exclusively in Pakistan (see fig. 7.1).[3]

Uzbekistan was the first post-Soviet Central Asian state to offer its support for the Afghanistan campaign and signed an initial agreement on October 7, 2001, that offered basing rights to U.S. forces. The Karshi-Khanabad facility—site of Camp Stronghold Freedom—hosted several thousand light infantry troops and Special Forces and, in December 2001,

---

3. Klepp 2004, 3–4.

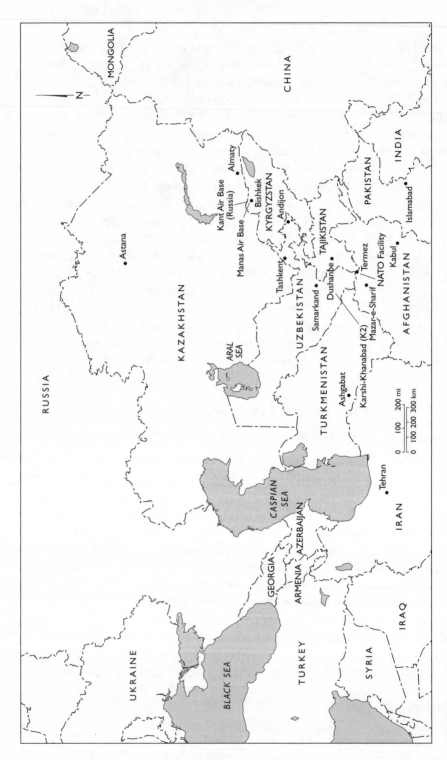

Figure 7.1. Central Asia and major foreign military installations, 2004.
Source: University of Texas, 2003

started trucking shipments of supplies to Mazar-e-Sharif in Afghanistan.[4] Much to CENTCOM's irritation, however, Uzbek officials refused to openly allow the deployment of combat aircraft and insisted that the base be used primarily for "humanitarian purposes." This event drove the State Department to explore additional possible basing sites among the former Soviet states. Kyrgyzstan was found to be the most suitable in that a Japanese-led consortium had just repaved the runway of Manas airport, near the capital of Bishkek.[5] In December 2001, U.S. negotiators reached an agreement with Kyrgyzstan to establish a coalition airbase at Manas, which was later named Ganci. The United States and its coalition partners supplemented these main bases with separate refueling and air corridor agreements with the governments of Tajikistan, Turkmenistan, and Kazakhstan, although these agreements were less publicized for political reasons.[6] The Russian government was not happy to accept American military forces on former Soviet territory but agreed not to oppose the arrangements as long as they were temporary and would be withdrawn after major combat operations in Afghanistan.[7] In addition, Russian intelligence officials—who had for a long time been concerned about the destabilization of Afghanistan—shared information and contacts in the Northern Alliance with their U.S. counterparts.[8]

Uzbekistan and Kyrgyzstan after the Soviet Collapse

The domestic political institutions of the two new Central Asian base hosts shared a number of characteristics. Although both states had officially shunned Communism and Soviet rule, they retained a strong executive that governed with relatively few democratic institutional constraints.[9] Their presidents ruled not so much through formal institutions such as a parliament as through informal networks of clan and subregional identities that institutionalized a system of patron-client ties.[10] Civil society

4. For operational details, see globalsecurity.org. By summer 2002, the base had defined its role as a major supply hub for operations in Afghanistan and hosted a presence of about 1,000–1,300 U.S. troops and hundreds more contractors. Security was strict, as Uzbek security forces guarded a five-kilometer perimeter around the base.
5. Klepp 2004, 4–5.
6. See Oliker and Shlapak 2005, 11–19; Wishnick 2002, 13–14. Also see *Radio Free Europe/ Radio Liberty Report (RFE/RL)* 2001a, 2001b.
7. See Cornell 2004, 245–46; Menon 2003, 192–94.
8. Wallander 2003, 96.
9. On elites and how they shaped electoral systems and legislatures in order to consolidate their power, see Jones Luong 2002.
10. See esp. Collins 2006; Schatz 2004.

remained weak throughout the region, and access to state power remained paramount at all levels of government.[11] Neither Uzbekistan nor Kyrgyzstan had an overriding sense of national identity or purpose, as neither had developed broad-based nationalist movements to oppose Moscow's rule in the late Soviet period.[12] Both had to cope with the collapse of the Soviet-era system of economic distribution and allocation, as well as the loss of fiscal subsidies from Moscow.[13] Finally, the collapse of the Soviet system adversely affected the security institutions of each country. National armies in both countries were far less powerful compared to internal security forces, which upon independence became the main guarantors of state security and regime protection.[14]

However, these two Central Asian countries differed significantly in size and regime priorities. With a population of 25 million and a location in the heart of post-Soviet Central Asia, Uzbekistan was considerably more powerful than Kyrgyzstan and regarded itself as the foremost regional power. Kyrgyzstan, with a population of only 5 million, was a small state with significant ethnic fissures, including a majority Uzbek population in the south and a large percentage of ethnic Russian speakers in the northern capital of Bishkek. Of the two, Kyrgyzstan had liberalized to a greater extent both politically and economically in the 1990s, and had allowed the growth of a number of NGOs representing a nascent civil society; the Uzbek government had become one of the most repressive regimes in the region and had not implemented any meaningful political reforms.[15] In terms of economic activity, Kyrgyzstan received large amounts of foreign aid and development assistance projects from the international community and, nominally at least, embraced many of their reforms.[16] By contrast, Uzbekistan was relatively better endowed with hydrocarbon and mineral wealth than its smaller neighbor was, and it pursued a more gradual set of state-sponsored reforms with relatively little involvement by any international financial institutions.[17]

By the late 1990s, the institutional development of Kyrgyzstan, a country long regarded as a liberal outlier and positive role model in the region,

---

11. On civil society and problems of state building, see Jones Luong 2004.
12. See Beissinger 2002.
13. On these economic legacies, see Cooley 2005d; Zhukov 1996; Pomfret 1995.
14. Cooley 2005d, 111–15.
15. On NGOs and democracy promotion in these countries, see Adamson 2002.
16. Cooley 2000.
17. In both states, however, economic and social conditions remained relatively poor, even according to late-Soviet metrics.

had begun to resemble that of its more authoritarian neighbors. President Akayev's regime was not as brutal or repressive as that of Uzbekistan's President Karimov, but Akayev backtracked on his democratic commitments and had steadily tendered power to his extended family and political allies.[18] Kyrgyz economic reforms also had stalled by 2001, and general economic malaise and endemic corruption characterized the small central Asian country. Neither Kyrgyzstan nor Uzbekistan was anywhere close to implementing the types of structural political and economic reforms of their postcommunist counterparts in the Baltic states or east central Europe.[19]

How the U.S. Basing Presence Promoted Regime Survivorship

The varying internal political traits and institutional characteristics across these states dictated the types of benefits and quid pro quo that each regime sought from the United States for granting base access. Certainly, both regimes were eager to be associated with a global antiterrorism campaign. This desire was out of genuine concern for the destabilizing activities of regional militant Islamic groups and, in the Uzbek case, in order to justify a harsh new crackdown on all opposition political movements. The small size of the Kyrgyz economy and its patronage networks made the Kyrgyz regime particularly eager to leverage U.S. base access for its private economic benefit, something it managed with great success. On the U.S. side, few officials in the State Department or Pentagon were unduly concerned about these states' peculiar institutional characteristics, nor did they voice public concern about the states' undemocratic tendencies.[20] For the United States, the overriding and compelling need was to secure base access for the Afghanistan campaign by any reasonable means.

K2 and Uzbekistan: Strengthening Karimov's Dictatorial Grip

Uzbekistan was the most eager of the Central Asian countries to be associated with Western efforts in Afghanistan. For a decade after independence, hardliner president Islam Karimov had ruled with an iron fist, minimizing political and economic reforms and fending off internal political rivals. By

18. For a good overview of this backtracking, see Spector 2004.
19. See Bunce 2003; Cooley 2003; Kopstein and Reilly 2000.
20. See the apt warning in Jones Luong and Weinthal 2002.

the late 1990s the Uzbek regime was most concerned with the growing popularity of Islamic movements, especially in the impoverished Ferghana Valley and eastern part of the country, and particularly with the subversive activities of the militant Islamic Movement of Uzbekistan (IMU). Led by Djuma Namangani, the IMU reportedly had allied itself with elements of the Taliban in Afghanistan and other regional Islamist groups, and the group had claimed responsibility for a bombing attack in Tashkent in February 1999. During the summers of 1999 and 2000, it skirmished with state security forces in Uzbekistan and Kyrgyzstan after it carried out a series of kidnappings and raids.[21] Allying Uzbekistan with the United States afforded Karimov the opportunity to crush the IMU with Western blessings and justify his regime's crackdown against all opposition movements.

The K2 Agreement and Tacit Quid Pro Quo

Under the October 7, 2001, SOFA agreement, the Uzbek government offered the United States the right to station up to 1,500 troops at K2, ninety miles from the Afghan border.[22] Uzbek officials insisted that the United States retain a low profile in a remote part of the country and asked the U.S. negotiators to conclude a new status of forces agreement that would further specify the legal status of U.S. forces.[23] The United States was granted access to the base and Uzbek airspace for OEF operations, with the duration of the agreement left open-ended; each side retained the right to terminate the agreement within 180 days after giving formal notice. Officially, the United States was prohibited from deploying combat aircraft at K2 and was limited to humanitarian and surveillance missions.[24]

The United States provided, as quid pro quo, a number of benefits to the Uzbek regime. First, and perhaps most important, the United States agreed to target members of the IMU who were fighting alongside the Taliban and al-Qaeda in Afghanistan.[25] The agreement bestowed on Karimov important internal legitimacy and granted international credibility to his efforts to eradicate the IMU.[26] By allying Uzbekistan with Western antiterror coalition members, the agreement emphasized the country's

21. For an overview of the IMU and its activities, see Rashid 2002.
22. Nichol 2005, 1–2.
23. The U.S. side was more hesitant to negotiate a new SOFA, preferring to retain the agreement from its Partnership for Peace activities. Oliker and Shlapak 2005, 17.
24. Cornell 2004, 241.
25. Nichol 2005, 1–2.
26. Jones Luong and Weinthal 2002.

autonomy in foreign policy matters and put some distance between Uzbekistan and Moscow. In terms of military assistance, in 2002 the United States provided $120 million in hardware and surveillance equipment to the Uzbek army and $82 million to the security services, as well as $15 million in base-related operating expenses; indeed, many U.S. officials have since observed that this highly advanced equipment was sought by Uzbek security forces for personal and organizational prestige rather than for use in the battlefield.[27] In the same year, not coincidentally, the U.S. Export-Import Bank granted $55 million in credits to the Uzbek government. U.S. officials did not formally admit that these disbursements were linked to the base, but total U.S. government aid to Uzbekistan significantly increased from $85 million in 2001 to nearly $300 million in 2002.[28]

The new security relationship was formalized in March 2002 when Presidents Bush and Karimov signed a U.S.-Uzbekistan Declaration on Strategic Partnership. The exact provisions of the actual accord were kept secret, but the leaked items included a U.S. pledge to preserve the "security and territorial integrity" of Uzbekistan and Tashkent's agreement to support the U.S.-led war on terror and OEF operations. The Uzbek government agreed to undertake an ambitious set of internal political reforms and committed itself to "ensuring respect for human rights and freedoms . . . enhancing the role of democratic and political institutions in the life of society; establishing a genuine multiparty system . . . ensuring the independence of the media . . . [and] improving the judicial and legal system."[29] It is unclear whether U.S. officials viewed these Uzbek commitments as genuine or as political cover to justify the deepening of security ties between the countries.

Karimov's War on Terror and Democratic Retrenchment

Despite signing this commitment to democratic reforms, the Uzbek regime, emboldened by the presence of the United States in K2, began to backslide on its democratic commitments and human rights practices.[30] In January 2002, Karimov arbitrarily extended his presidential term of office

27. Oliker and Shlapak 2005, 18.
28. Akbarzadeh 2005, 75, 78.
29. *Washington Post* 2002.
30. In the annual global survey of political freedoms conducted by Freedom House, Uzbekistan remained at or near the bottom, scoring a 7 for political rights and a 6 for civil liberties (out of 7, with 7 being the worst). These scores remained unchanged in 2002–4 and declined to 7 and 7 in 2005, placing the regime in Uzbekistan among the most repressive in the world.

to 2007, a move about which U.S. authorities were conspicuously silent. Later in 2002, Uzbek security services arrested hundreds of suspects on accusations of fomenting terrorism. In a highly critical report issued after a December 2002 visit, UN envoy Theo van Boven found rampant and systemic torture of terrorist suspects in Uzbek prisons.[31] And as part of the Bush administration's policy of extraordinary rendition, the United States secretly flew dozens of suspects to Uzbekistan and turned them over to authorities there.[32] According to former British ambassador Craig Murray, who was stationed in Uzbekistan in 2003, both Uzbeks and non-Uzbeks were brought to Uzbekistan from Bagram airbase in Afghanistan, and some reportedly were actually interrogated at K2.[33] For his part, Karimov skillfully used his new coalition position to crack down on all political opposition under the mantra of fighting terrorism, whether these groups actually had ties to Islamic militants or not. Karimov violated democratic norms and reneged on his own international political commitments, calculating that the U.S. government, to maintain its base access, would not denounce these actions.

Kyrgyzstan: Akayev's Reprieve and the Depoliticization of the Base Issue

Joining the OEF international coalition offered President Akayev of Kyrgyzstan a political reprieve, especially after his democratic backsliding during the late 1990s. Manas-Ganci airport became a key coalition facility for OIF, and Akayev was keen to be associated with the effort. By May 2002, the base hosted 2,000 coalition troops from nine countries and an array of international cargo aircraft, refuelers, and even some marine fighters.[34] In response to this U.S.-led Western presence, Russia the following year established its own airbase in Kant, just twenty kilometers away from Manas, making Kyrgyzstan the first country to officially host both a Russian and U.S. military facility.[35]

31. See Van Boven 2003.
32. See Grey 2006, 170–89. Also see Van Natta 2005.
33. Murray, an outspoken critic of U.S. and UK policy toward Uzbekistan, was dismissed from his post of British ambassador to Uzbekistan for making outspoken comments against the human rights record of the Karimov regime. In his writings, Murray (2006) has also claimed that Uzbek security services deliberately fed false information from these detentions in order to maintain their cooperative ties with Western intelligence and security agencies.
34. For details of operations and the types of aircraft stationed at Manas, see Hendren 2002.
35. See Blagov 2003; *RFE/RL* 2003.

Like Karimov, Akayev sought to play up the potential regional Islamic threat so as to lock in security cooperation with the United States. In fact, Kyrgyz officials and security services exaggerated and even fabricated terrorist plots to bolster the government's status. The most striking example was in November 2003 when Kyrgyz security services allegedly foiled a plot to bomb the base by three members of Hizb ut-Tahir, a regional Islamic group with no track record of violence in Kyrgyzstan. The would-be perpetrators were supposedly caught with explosives and a map of the base. Although they were subsequently tried and convicted, Western and Kyrgyz observers expressed major doubts about the accuracy of the Kyrgyz government's account of the plot.[36]

Economic Benefits: Patronage and Selective Incentives
For Akayev, the economic dimension of his base deal with the United States was far more important than it was for Karimov. Kyrgyzstan's small population and struggling $1 billion economy meant that even a relatively small basing presence could exert a major economic impact. The base represented the biggest U.S. economic investment in Kyrgyzstan and, from its first year, contributed about $40 million annually to the Kyrgyz economy, while employing about five hundred Kyrgyz nationals in a variety of positions.

The lion's share of base-related funds, however, flowed to national and private Kyrgyz entities with close ties to the ruling regime. Manas International Airport remained an 87 percent government-owned joint stock company and collected $2 million annually in lease payments plus additional landing fees of $7,000 per takeoff, calculated in accordance with civil aviation standards. The airport company also was awarded most of the base-related service contracts and ad hoc fees for extra parking slots that it allocated to coalition aircraft outside of the designated military area.[37] These revenues flowed directly to Manas airport and were neither accounted for nor taxed by the Kyrgyz government.

The most lucrative source of base-related payments, however, was the fuel contracts secured by the airport-run Manas International Services Ltd. and Aalam Services Ltd. Manas International Services, a legally independent entity partly owned by the president's son Aydar Akayev, was spun off from the airport authority to manage the fuel services and storage

---

36. Author's interviews with Western diplomatic officials, Bishkek, January 2005.
37. Author's interview with Ganci/Manas military official, Manas, Kyrgyzstan, January 2005.

tanks at Manas.[38] Aalam Services was a legally independent fuel company owned by Adil Toiganbayev, Akayev's son-in-law. A *New York Times* investigative story revealed that out of a total of $207 million spent by the U.S. Department of Defense on fuel contracts during the Akayev era, Manas International Services received $87 million and Aalam Services $32 million in subcontracts from the main Western contractors, Avcard (2002) and Red Star (2003–5).[39] The amounts and structure of these payments were kept opaque and were not reported in the Kyrgyz media. A subsequent FBI investigation uncovered the Akayev clan's embezzlement of tens of millions of dollars of these base-related revenues through a network of offshore accounts.

U.S. Pentagon and State Department officials contend—and they are legally correct—that none of these payments or contracts violated U.S. laws or Department of Defense tender procedures. But such claims do not change the fact that these payments had significant *political* connotations and consequences. Base-related revenues supported the Akayev regime and its political clients, who viewed these contracts as the private quid pro quo for granting basing rights to the United States and its coalition partners. In fact, commenting specifically on the adoption of the seemingly generous landing rights formula, former U.S. ambassador John O'Keefe suggested that the fees could have been avoided but were viewed by the American side as an important economic inducement that would secure the Kyrgyz government's commitment to U.S. base access.[40] Just as base-related payments had helped feed the patronage machines of other authoritarian figures such as Syngman Rhee in Korea and Ferdinand Marcos in the Philippines, the U.S. military presence in Kyrgyzstan was predicated on providing economic incentives to ruling elites and their cronies in order to maintain their commitment to U.S. base access.

The Depoliticization of the Base Issue

These private or selective incentives also served to keep the basing issue depoliticized in Kyrgyz politics, as political parties, the Kyrgyz parliament,

---

38. I thank Scott Horton for clarifying the legal status of these entities.
39. According to Cloud (2005), Avcard received $31.2 million in 2002 from the Pentagon, but the contract—after drawing attention because of potential irregularities—was subsequently retendered and awarded to Red Star Enterprises, a London-based company. However, Red Star still relied on Aalam and Manas as its exclusive fuel providers. From 2003 to 2005, Red Star received $175 million from the Pentagon and paid $87 million to Manas and $32 million to Aalam for jet fuel and delivery services.
40. See Klepp 2004, 8–9.

and the media neither publicized nor overtly criticized the terms of the Manas agreement.[41] This situation lasted until the collapse of Akayev's regime in March 2005. Much as they had with the influx of foreign assistance and development aid during the 1990s, Akayev and his backers skillfully used external funds to both enrich themselves and pay off key political supporters in the Kyrgyz system.[42] With the exception of Russian-owned newspapers, the Kyrgyz media did not run negative news stories about the base, nor did it publicize the contractual ties between the U.S. military and the Akayev family. In one of the few public opinion surveys taken about the base, a September 2002 poll by the Informational Support Fund found that 18 percent of respondents supported the government's decision to host the base, whereas 34 percent opposed it. A 45 percent plurality had "no opinion" on the matter.[43] The public's high level of indifference to the basing issue was consistent with its overall lack of interest in foreign policy matters.

More important, domestic opposition movements and NGOs showed little interest in addressing the issue. Some domestic NGOs were aware of the need to investigate base-related activities, such as the adverse environmental impact of fuel dumping by transport planes, but they lacked either the funds or sufficient government cooperation to investigate these issues.[44] Other opposition figures and pro-democracy NGOs were more concerned with planning for a Ukrainian-style democratic revolution to remove Akayev from power rather than worrying about the base. The opposition also considered it tactically important to support the base and the coalition effort in Afghanistan in order to secure the backing of the United States and the international community for a future regime change.[45] As it turned out, the nonpolitical status of Manas did not last much longer. After Akayev's ouster in March 2005, the basing issue and the legitimacy of basing contracts with the previous regime were confronted head on by the new democratizing regime in Bishkek.

41. See Cooley 2005c.
42. Cooley 2005c, 4.
43. Author's interview with U.S. public affairs official, Bishkek, Kyrgyzstan, January 2005.
44. Author's interview with Kyrgyz environmental NGO, Bishkek, Kyrgyzstan, January 2005.
45. Author's interviews with Kyrgyz opposition figures and political NGOs, Bishkek, Kyrgyzstan, January 2005.

Changing Domestic Politics and Base Politics: Eviction and Contestation

The year 2005 marked a major turning point in U.S. relations with both Uzbekistan and Kyrgyzstan over the base issue. Domestic political changes in both countries led to the rapid politicization and then struggles over the U.S. basing presence. During the course of a few months, U.S.-Uzbek relations deteriorated to the point that on July 30, 2005, the Uzbek government officially evicted the U.S. military from K2. In Kyrgyzstan the collapse of the Akayev regime in March 2005 prompted new president Kurmanbek Bakiyev to question the procedural legitimacy of the Manas agreement and demand a new deal on terms more favorable to the Kyrgyz republic.

Uzbekistan: Eviction from K2

The Andijon Uprising and Crackdown
On May 11, 2005, the Uzbek government ruthlessly cracked down on thousands of demonstrators who had gathered in the town square of the eastern city of Andijon. Uzbek government officials claim that the crackdown was necessary because earlier that day armed militants with Islamic ties had staged a prison break and used automatic weapons to capture a local police station and military barracks. International human rights organizations and journalists' accounts maintain that the vast majority of the demonstrators were peacefully protesting the government's jailing of twenty-three local businessmen accused of militant ties and were voicing their opposition to Tashkent's increasingly heavy-handed involvement in local political and economic matters. Local eyewitnesses claim that Uzbek security services in armored vehicles surrounded the demonstrators and then started to fire indiscriminately into the crowd, mowing down hundreds of civilians as they tried to flee the square. Government officials maintain that the death toll that day was limited to 180 mostly armed insurgents, whereas international NGOs such as the Crisis Group and Human Rights Watch conservatively estimate the toll at between 700 and 800.[46]

Events in Andijon sent shockwaves across the region and the West. In Washington, officials reacted tentatively at first.[47] White House press

46. On the events in Andijon, see the page "Uzbekistan: Aftermath of Andijon," *RFE/RL* Special, http://www.rferl.org/specials/uzbek_unrest/(accessed May 2007). Also see International Crisis Group 2005c, 2006; Human Rights Watch 2005a.
47. This section draws on Cooley 2005a, 86–88.

secretary Scott McClellan refused to condemn the Uzbek government's actions, while the Pentagon and CENTCOM were silent about the matter. At NATO headquarters in Brussels, U.S. officials refused to issue a joint communiqué calling for an international investigation into events at Andijon on the grounds that Uzbek authorities might retaliate and restrict military operations based in K2.[48] Just a few weeks later, however, Secretary of State Condoleezza Rice publicly backed the formation of an international inquiry, and a group of U.S. senators called for an investigation into whether Uzbek security forces had used U.S. military hardware in the crackdown.[49] In June, in response to growing criticism by these U.S. bodies, Uzbek officials restricted nighttime flights and heavy airlift out of the base.[50]

The U.S. position in July 2005 on the Andijon refugee issue was the final straw for the Uzbek government. After the violent clashes, 430 refugees had fled Andijon and crossed the border into southern Kyrgyzstan. The Uzbek government demanded that Kyrgyz officials forcibly return the refugees, whom they accused of being militants and instigators, to Uzbek security services for interrogation. Instead the refugees were allowed to remain in southern Kyrgyzstan in makeshift camps run by the United Nations. On July 28, 2005, the United States backed a United Nations decision to move the refugees to Romania and then on to various European nations that had agreed to grant them political asylum. Just a day later, the Uzbek government formally notified the U.S. embassy in Tashkent that it was activating the 180-day termination clause in the SOFA.[51] The last U.S. troops left K2 in November 2005, just four years after their historic deployment in the Central Asian state. Even after the U.S. departure, some base-related tensions lingered as the Uzbek government claimed the United States still owed it $23 million for back rent and base-related expenses.[52]

Karimov's Changing Political Calculations and Eviction
Some have pointed to the growing regional influence of Russia and China in Uzbekistan as an alternate external cause of Karimov's decision to evict the United States and geopolitically realign.[53] Certainly, both Russia and

---

48. Personal communication with NATO political affairs officials, Brussels, June 2005.
49. See Chivers and Shanker 2005.
50. *RIA Novosti* 2005.
51. Weisman and Shanker 2005.
52. On debates between the U.S. Congress and the Department of Defense regarding the payment of the debt, see Nichol 2005, 6.
53. For a nuanced overview of the post-K2 geopolitical environment, see Gleason 2006; Rumer 2006; Baev 2005.

China had developed important economic ties to Uzbekistan, especially in the hydrocarbon and electricity sectors.[54] Immediately after Andijon, Russian president Vladimir Putin and Chinese premier Hu Jintao strongly endorsed the Uzbek president's actions and supported the official Uzbek account of events. This strong political backing ultimately convinced Karimov that his domestic survival and political tenure would be best guaranteed by turning to Moscow and Beijing, and away from the United States, which recently had supported three "democratic revolutions" in quick succession in the post-Soviet space (those of Georgia, Ukraine, and Kyrgyzstan).[55] Thus, Russian and Chinese actions were important less for furthering Uzbekistan's external defense interests and more for maintaining the regime's internal cohesion and tight grip on power. After the K2 eviction, the Uzbek president signed a formal security alliance with Russia in November 2005 and then proceeded to expel a number of Western NGOs and media outlets from Uzbekistan.[56] The Uzbek president clearly believed that all U.S. and Western-backed political activities in the country might undermine his exercise of power.

Kyrgyzstan: Democratization and the Politicization of the Basing Presence

The political collapse of the Akayev regime was as sudden as it was unexpected. Antigovernment activists and groups had planned a democratic revolution, a Tulip Revolution, that would be similar to the popular uprisings in Georgia in 2003 and Ukraine in 2004. However, few political observers of Central Asia or even diplomats in Kyrgyzstan took these claims seriously.[57] Fraudulent parliamentary elections held in late February 2005 sparked uprisings in the southern provinces, and these steadily gathered momentum as various opposition factions and civic NGOs united on an anti-Akayev platform.[58] On March 20, riots erupted in the southern cities of Jalalabad and Osh, and on March 23 demonstrations took place in Bishkek. The security services failed to decisively put down these crowds,

54. See, e.g., Blank 2006.
55. On the colored revolutions in the former Soviet states, see Beissinger 2007; Bunce and Wolchik 2006.
56. See Blagov 2005; *RFE/RL* 2006.
57. None of the foreign officials interviewed in Kyrgyzstan in January 2005, just two months before the regime change, considered a regime change or a democratic revolution likely.
58. On the events leading up to the ouster of Akayev, see International Crisis Group 2005b.

and Akayev's regime crumbled the next day when protestors stormed the presidential White House in the capital. Akayev fled to Russia, and on April 4, 2005, he formally resigned the presidency.

Bakiyev's New Tough Stance

Kurmanbek Bakiyev, a former prime minister turned critic of the regime, became Kyrgyzstan's new acting president. In a political pact for national unity, Bakiyev agreed to grant the post of prime minister to his main rival, Felix Kulov, who had been imprisoned by Akayev.

The first signs of the impending politicization of the base issue occurred when the Shanghai Cooperation Organization, a regional security body comprising Russia, China, Kazakhstan, Kyrgyzstan, Tajikistan, and Uzbekistan, declared during the run-up to the July 10, 2005, Kyrgyz presidential election that the U.S. bases in Central Asia had served their original purpose and that a timetable for their withdrawal should be adopted by member states. Then, in his first press conference after his landslide election victory on July 11, 2005, Bakiyev announced that the purpose of the Manas base would be reexamined and that Kyrgyzstan would pursue a more "independent foreign policy."[59] A quick visit by U.S. secretary of defense Donald Rumsfeld on July 26 seemed to quell the issue as the Kyrgyz president reiterated his commitment to hosting the base, but the matter once again was revived in the aftermath of the United States' expulsion from Uzbekistan.

Sensing increased bargaining leverage now that Manas was the only remaining U.S. base in Central Asia, and under pressure internally for failing to deliver on his post-Akayev reform agenda, Bakiyev once again raised the base issue during the fall 2005. In a series of interviews and speeches Bakiyev questioned the legitimacy of the basing contract, pointed to Akayev's embezzlement of base-related revenues, and claimed that its terms were not favorable to Kyrgyzstan. During an October 2005 visit by Secretary of State Rice, Bakiyev demanded increased payments for base rights as well as a formal accounting of all base-related payments made during the Akayev era. Then, in December 2005, the Kyrgyz president called for a "hundredfold" increase in compensation from the United States, quoting a figure of $200 million for rent and services, and accused

59. At that conference on July 11, 2005, Bakiyev stated, "today it's possible to move toward reviewing the question concerning the expediency of the American military deployment," and then, "time will show when this [U.S. withdrawal] will happen and what specific process [it will follow]." See *Eurasia Insight Report* 2005.

the United States of having previously paid only "symbolic" amounts. In January 2006 the Kyrgyz Foreign Ministry issued a formal request to the U.S. embassy demanding a significant increase in payments, including a $50 million payment for leasing and parking fees alone, as well as separate compensation for base-related environmental damage and the Akayev-era fuel contracts.[60] In April 2006, before a visit to Moscow to meet with Russian president Putin, the Kyrgyz president issued an ultimatum to the United States to conclude a new deal by June 1. In response, U.S. negotiators steadfastly refused to offer such a substantial and explicit quid pro quo and told Kyrgyz officials that they could secure alternate regional-basing arrangements for well below the new $200 million price tag.[61] U.S. officials explored possible alternate basing sites in the region, including in Tajikistan and Mongolia, but the two sides eventually reached an agreement in July 2006.

The July 2006 Accord, the Hatfield Shooting, and Contestation of the SOFA
After months of prolonged negotiations and political brinkmanship, Kyrgyz and U.S. negotiators finally announced a deal on extending the United States' use of the base. The publicly released joint statement is a creative and carefully crafted document that satisfies the main needs of both sides.[62] The U.S. side "expects to provide over $150 million in total assistance and compensation over the next year," thereby allowing Bakiyev to claim that he extracted much of the $200 million he had demanded from the Americans. However, U.S. officials can claim that the actual lease payment for Manas only rose from $2 million annually to $20 million and that the compensation package includes an array of bilateral assistance programs (many of them already in place) as well as more general base-related economic contributions. To emphasize the point, the statement explicitly states that the base deal is part of a "larger, robust bilateral relationship" between the United States and the Kyrgyz Republic; it also points out that the United States has provided more than $850 million in aid to the Central Asian state since independence. Thus the same document that seemingly acknowledges a total of $150 million quid pro quo for

60. See Socor 2006.
61. Personal communication with official from the Kyrgyz Ministry of Foreign Affairs, March and May 2006. According to this Kyrgyz representative involved in the negotiations, U.S. officials claimed that they could get access to two bases for the $200 million annual price tag.
62. For the text, see "U.S. Embassy" on Kyrgyzstan's Web site: http://kyrgyz.usembassy. gov/july_14_joint_statement_on_coalition_airbase.html (accessed May 2007).

U.S. base rights also reaffirms the broader framework and bilateral relationship. The statement does not set a formal duration for the lease, but in a public statement made a few weeks later at Manas to commemorate the fifth anniversary of 9/11, Bakiyev affirmed his commitment to allow the base to operate until major operations in Afghanistan are concluded.

Although the two sides seemingly resolved the tricky issue of compensation, several high-profile accidents late in the year opened up the issue of criminal jurisdiction and the SOFA. The most serious of these occurred on December 6, 2006, when U.S. serviceman Zachary Hatfield shot and killed a Kyrgyz fuel-truck driver, Alexander Ivanov, just outside the base's checkpoint.[63] Hatfield claimed that the driver had threatened him with a knife (only a nail file was found on Ivanov), but the incident soon spiraled into a media and public relations crisis as several Kyrgyz politicians openly denounced the one-sided SOFA and Manas agreements. A few days after the incident, the Kyrgyz parliament passed a resolution calling for review of the 2001 SOFA and the Kyrgyz Foreign Ministry demanded that the serviceman's immunity be lifted and that he be extradited. In February 2007 on a visit to Washington, D.C., Kyrgyz parliament speaker Marat Sultanov demanded a renegotiation of the criminal jurisdiction procedures that govern U.S. troops and the formalization of yet another base deal, whereas in March 2007 the prosecutor general's office in Bishkek announced that the case would have warranted a murder charge in the absence of immunity.[64] Public relations further soured after U.S. authorities offered Ivanov's widow the small sum of $1,100 as compensation, and Hatfield was soon after removed from the country, on March 22.[65] As with similar incidents in democratizing climates, the Kyrgyz media, civic groups, and politicians used the SOFA issue to question the legitimacy and inequality of the overall basing accord.

Domestic Politics and Base Politics in a Democratizing State

The new Bakiyev regime in Kyrgyzstan contested the validity of the basing contract because it had been signed with a previous nondemocratic regime. In the Kyrgyz case, the fuel contracts and embezzlement scandals involving Akayev and his family allowed Bakiyev to publicly question the

---

63. For overviews, see Pannier 2007; Daly 2007.
64. See Kucera 2007; *RFE/RL* 2007.
65. The Ivanov family received $50,000 from the airport company that Ivanov had worked for. U.S. officials insisted, following Hatfield's removal, that they would keep him under investigation in the United States. See Daly 2007.

validity of the original basing deal. With Bakiyev's declining popularity in Kyrgyzstan, his turning to the base issue and questions of sovereignty also offered the new president a political respite from domestic criticism and provided a political issue with which to ingratiate himself among ethnic Russian citizens.[66] But even after the compensation issue was renegotiated, the basing issue once again exploded politically in the aftermath of the Hatfield shooting as a number of Kyrgyz politicians demanded the renegotiation of the SOFA's criminal jurisdiction procedures.

The loss of K2 and Russia's perceived new political offensive into Central Asia strengthened Bakiyev's bargaining position, but it did so in terms of increasing the price that Kyrgyz perceived as reasonable for the facility; it did not precipitate the initial demand for a renegotiation. And although the true democratic credentials of the Bakiyev regime remain in doubt, Bakiyev's actions demonstrate how sudden democratization in base hosts, even in a country in which the basing issue had long been dormant, can precipitate nationalism and the sudden contestation of base contracts. Any successor to Akayev would have politicized and contested the procedural legitimacy of the Manas agreement in the same manner, regardless of external developments. Using the base politics theory that I expound in this book, I expect that the U.S.-Kyrgyz base agreement and legal arrangements will continue to be a major political issue within Kyrgyz domestic politics during this tumultuous democratization period.

New Bases and New Locations: The Global Defense Posture Review

The Central Asian cases suggest that base politics, even with these new-style bases, are likely to follow trajectories similar to those of the historical cases. This finding is all the more important given the Pentagon's current restructuring of the U.S. global basing network under the Global Defense Posture Review (GDPR). The GDPR will replace many of the large forward-deployed facilities of the cold war era with an extensive global network of smaller installations scattered across regions in which the United States has previously not maintained a military presence.[67] Yet the small size and temporary nature of the bases may not stop U.S. officials from becoming embroiled in a number of domestic political disputes in these new host countries. However, the attitudes taken toward the bases by

66. See Gorst 2006.
67. See OBC 2005; Campbell and Ward 2003.

politicians and citizens of these new host countries will once again be a result of the contractual credibility of their countries' regime and its level of dependence on the U.S. basing presence.

Dimensions of the GDPR: A New Type of Lighter Base?

The GDPR creates three different categories of overseas bases: (1) main operating bases, (2) forward operating sites (FOSs), and (3) cooperative security locations (CSLs).[68]

Main operating bases, such as the large facilities in Germany, Japan, and South Korea, will continue to function as regional hubs with permanent support structures and facilities to host permanent forces and personnel families. These main bases will serve as connecting nodes to the other types of facilities. In contrast to main operating bases, FOSs are designed as smaller facilities and bases that will host a limited number of military personnel—no more than one or two thousand—and may store some prepositioned equipment. Such bases, like the U.S. bases in Central Asia, will have the capacity to expand and host troop deployments and logistical lift in times of crisis. CSLs are designed as facilities to be run primarily by host countries and/or military contractors, with few or no U.S. troops or equipment, but they could be activated in times of crisis.[69] FOSs and CSLs will lack the extensive hub of housing complexes, and social and recreational facilities, that have traditionally characterized U.S. bases and their spatial planning, and instead will feature more barebones facilities.[70] Because of their relatively small size and lack of large troop deployments, FOSs and CSLs have been referred to as "light switch" bases or lily pads. The widespread use of contractors to organize, maintain, and run these facilities also reflects the U.S. military's broader tendency to outsource military-related functions and services to the private sector.[71]

New Locations and Installations
In addition to creating new types of bases, the GDPR will radically alter U.S. basing posture by establishing FOSs and CSLs in new locations. In

68. For more background, see OBC 2005; Cooley 2005a; Klaus 2004. On future U.S. basing needs, also see Harkavy 2005.
69. For a full description of these different installations, see http://www.globalsecurity.org/military/facility/intro.htm (accessed May 2007).
70. On the political and social effects of these larger facilities and their spatial needs, see Gillem 2004.
71. See Avant 2005; Singer 2003.

eastern Europe, long-standing cold war–era facilities in Germany are being downsized, while new FOSs have been established on the Black Sea coasts of Romania and Bulgaria.[72] In addition, CSLs are planned for the Balkans, Poland, and, if possible, Azerbaijan and Georgia. In Central Asia, the Pentagon will attempt to preserve its FOS in Kyrgyzstan and gain CSLs in neighboring countries, especially Kazakhstan and Mongolia. In Southeast Asia, PACOM (U.S. Pacific Command) has established an FOS in Singapore and is negotiating a series of CSLs in India, Thailand, Philippines, and Australia. The U.S. unincorporated territory of Guam will host the Third Marine Expeditionary Force, which will be relocated from Okinawa by 2014. In the Americas, U.S. forces will continue to maintain their FOSs in Columbia, Ecuador, and Honduras and will maintain or add CSLs in El Salvador, Paraguay, Peru, Curaçao, and Aruba. Finally, Africa will host a number of new facilities under EUCOM (U.S. European Command) and CENTCOM (U.S. Central Command). São Tomé and Príncipe is eager to host a new naval FOS, and the FOS established in Djibouti in 2002 will be maintained. Possible new CSLs have been negotiated with Algeria, Mali, Mauritania, Gabon, Ghana, Kenya, Senegal, and Uganda.

The establishment of FOSs and CSLs across the Black Sea, Central Asia, and Africa is particularly significant and reveals that under the GDPR the United States is abdicating its traditional role of offshore balancing in favor of an onshore presence in remote and even isolated regions.[73] New bases and installations are being established to expand U.S. reconnaissance and intelligence-gathering capabilities; combat terrorist networks, criminal gangs, and pirates; and protect large infrastructural hubs and projects, especially energy pipelines and distribution networks, that are deemed important to U.S. security and economic interests.[74] The "lily-pad" nature of the bases is designed to provide the U.S. military with a set of installations to cover almost every global hotspot. In his 2004 statement to Congress about the basing realignment, Undersecretary of Defense for Policy Douglas Feith stated that "we're dealing with challenges that are global in nature—so global strategies and actions are necessary to complement our regional planning. We need to improve our ability to project power from one region to another and to manage forces on a global basis."[75]

---

72. See the appendices of OBC 2005. For an overview and analysis of the European transfers, see Fields 2004.
73. On the United States as an offshore balancer, see Layne 2006; Mearsheimer 2001.
74. On the energy security-basing link, see Johnson 2004.
75. Feith 2004.

Debating the Merits of the GDPR

Scholars and policymakers have debated the merits of the GDPR, but mostly in terms of its strategic logic and operational feasibility. Proponents have argued that base restructure is long overdue and better reflects the strategic requirements of a post–cold war security environment and the global war on terror.[76] Some security specialists also view the establishment of new facilities in new regions, such as Africa and Central Asia, as the best way for the United States to stabilize and secure remote areas of the world in which new-style threats, such as terrorist groups and criminal gangs, might proliferate. For example, Thomas Barnett advocates establishing an extensive U.S. military presence in "the Gap," that is, regions whose governance structures are weak and disconnected from globalizing processes, in order to "export security" and ultimately connect the regions to the stable and well-functioning global "core."[77] Policymakers also have argued that the FOSs and CSLs, because of their reduced size and role, will likely minimize the U.S. military's footprint in host countries and avoid some of the social problems and accidents that surround larger bases in Okinawa or Japan.[78] Thus, at first glance the strategic and political logic of the GDPR appears clear and compelling: the new base posture of the United States needs to reflect new global realities and security threats.

New Regions, Old Base Politics: Political Dynamics in Africa and the Black Sea

Regardless of the strategic logic of the GDPR, the Central Asian cases suggest that the internal institutional dynamics of base hosts may complicate or even undermine the anticipated stabilizing political effects of these new bases. In Uzbekistan and Kyrgyzstan the characteristics of these new bases—smaller deployments, increased reliance on contractors, and a more barebones physical structure—did not fundamentally alter the domestic political calculations of base-hosting elites. But what of future base politics in Africa and the Black Sea, the other two new regions that will host U.S. military facilities?

76. See Feith 2004; Klaus 2004, 3. The GDPR is also consistent with the 2001 Quadrennial Defense Review and the National Security Strategy of 2002.
77. See Barnett 2004, 2005.
78. According to Under Secretary of Defense for Policy Douglas Feith (2004, 3), "We seek to tailor the physical U.S. 'footprint' to suit local conditions. Our goal is to reduce friction with host nations, the kind that results from accidents and other problems relating to local sensitivities."

The arguments I've made in this book suggest that the political dynamics and problems may vary across these regions, as base politics in Africa are likely to be significantly more contentious than those of the Black Sea hosts. In Africa, the region's volatile internal politics and lack of democratic consolidation threaten to involve the U.S. military in a number of internal disputes and democratizing transitions in which it may favor and even actively support the actions of unaccountable or unpopular regimes. Over the medium term, U.S. security contracts in Africa run the risk of being contested, declared procedurally invalid, or renegotiated by new political actors, especially if the hosts democratize. By contrast, the new Black Sea hosts of Bulgaria and Romania have fairly consolidated democratic institutions that ratified the agreements to host U.S. forces. Under the political logic developed in this book, these two countries are more likely to remain reliable hosts and accept these initial base contracts as a legitimate and enduring political commitment, despite future scandals or use of the bases for internationally controversial purposes.

The Growing U.S. Military Presence in Africa

Traditionally, Africa has not been considered a region of pressing importance to the United States, a fact illustrated by the longtime absence of a distinct regional command and the allocation of Africa-based operations between EUCOM (responsible for activities in North Africa and western Africa) and CENTCOM (east Africa and southern Africa).[79] But in February 2007, reflecting a renewed interest in establishing an onshore presence in the region, the Defense Department announced that it would create a new U.S. Africa Command headquarters (AFRICOM). The new command, which will be operating by September 2008, will coordinate U.S. military activities and the deployment of permanent military forces on bases in the African continent, bar Egypt, which will continue to operate under EUCOM.[80]

Purpose and Scope of the Future U.S. Presence
The Pentagon's new interest in Africa is driven by two main objectives. The first is an interest in securing oil supplies and American energy investments in the region, especially along the western coast in Angola,

79. See Smith 2004.
80. Crawley 2007.

Gabon, Cameroon, Equatorial Guinea, Nigeria, and São Tomé and Príncipe.[81] In 2006, oil production on the African west coast already accounted for 16–18 percent of all U.S. oil imports.[82] Second, the Pentagon, in cooperation with African state governments, plans to combat Islamic militants and prevent state collapse that might create the anarchical conditions for incubation of future terrorist groups.[83] An example of this type of engagement is the Pan-Sahel Initiative (PSI), which was begun in late 2002 by EUCOM.[84] Over the next two years, U.S. forces trained soldiers and elite units in Mali, Mauritania, Niger, and Chad to build a regional capacity for counterterrorism activities, including conducting a joint mission against the Algerian-based Islamist organization Groupe Salafiste pour la Prédication et le Combat (GSPC). A follow-on project, known as the Trans-Sahara Counter Terror Initiative (TSCTI), has expanded to include military cooperation and assistance to the governments of Algeria, Morocco, Tunisia, Senegal, Ghana, and Nigeria.[85]

With these objectives, the Pentagon is negotiating a number of base access and CSL agreements on the African continent. In 2002, the United States established an FOS in Djibouti, the ex-French colony strategically located on the Red Sea in the Horn of Africa.[86] A follow-on three-year accord was signed in 2003, and the base has hosted about 1,500 to 1,800 U.S. troops. The base, known as Camp Lemonier, initially was used for training missions, large-scale joint exercises, and as a staging post for operations in nearby Yemen.[87] The base has hosted the Horn of Africa Combined Joint Task Force for Operation Enduring Freedom, whose job it is to build local military capacity and complete humanitarian and infrastructure projects in the region.[88] The base was also used to train and support Ethiopian forces for their intervention against Islamic militants in Somalia in December 2006, and in January 2007 to launch AC-130 air strikes against al-Qaeda

81. See Klare and Volman 2004, 2006; Johnson 2004; Smith 2004.
82. Mason 2005.
83. E.g., see Stuart Powell's (2004) analysis that identified the Sahara and the Horn of Africa as potential new "breeding grounds" for terrorists.
84. For an overview, see "Pan-Sahel Initiative," http://www.globalsecurity.org/military/ops/pan-sahel.htm (accessed May 2007). For a critical overview of these cooperative activities, see Keenan 2004.
85. For an overview, see "Trans-Sahara Counter Terrorism Initiative," http://www.globalsecurity.org/military/ops/tscti.htm (accessed May 2007).
86. England 2002.
87. For some casual observations about the Djibouti base and its functions, see Barnett 2007; Kaplan 2005, 273–305.
88. For details, http://www.globalsecurity.org/military/agency/dod/cjtf-hoa.htm.

suspects who had retreated to southern Somalia. Although not officially linked to these base rights, an aid package of $90 million was offered to Djibouti for 2003 and 2004 by U.S. officials, a substantial increase from the $7 million aid package the country received in 2002.[89] Djibouti is rapidly developing into a critical, "new-style" onshore facility for U.S. defense planners right on the Horn of Africa.[90]

In addition to establishing the FOS in Djibouti, U.S. officials have signed a number of CSL agreements, most to secure access to airfields, with Senegal, Ghana, Gabon, Uganda, Cameroon, Zambia, Namibia, Equatorial Guinea, and Kenya. The latter includes access to Mombassa port, the largest in East Africa, to the Manda Bay naval facility and to Mombassa International Airport.[91] Negotiations over similar types of arrangements were conducted in 2005 with Nigeria, Benin, and Ivory Coast. New facilities are also rumored to be under consideration in several locations, including Algeria (where the United States is building a surveillance station in the south), Morocco, Mali, and Senegal. Some reports suggest that the United States may construct a naval FOS on the oil-producing islands of São Tomé and Príncipe, thereby guaranteeing access to the Gulf of Guinea.[92]

Looming Political Problems with New Bases in Africa

New bases in Africa, even relatively small ones, are likely to generate similar political problems for U.S. planners as those experienced in Central Asia: political elites in these hosts will manipulate the U.S. military presence for their own purposes, while their volatile domestic political institutions may not guarantee the long-term credibility of initial basing arrangements. Most of these current and future base hosts are characterized by poor governance, shaky democratic credentials, and governments that crave the legitimacy associated with cooperating with U.S. security, as well as the military training, hardware, and technical assistance. Unexpected political changes, democratic transitions, or authoritarian coups may precipitate the sudden contestation of basing contracts and politicize the U.S. presence and its governing agreements. Therefore, any new basing agreements concluded with these states, no matter how minor the facility, are likely to signal U.S. approval or support for the prevailing regime. In turn, these host governments may involve the United States in a number of

89. *EIU Viewswire* 2004.
90. See Weiss 2006.
91. Barnett 2007; OBC 2005, F13.
92. See Columbant 2004; BBC News 2002.

local political struggles or even exaggerate a local security threat in order to receive attention and assistance from the United States.

In fact, the Pan-Sahel example offers some warning about how African rulers may use the U.S. military presence as a vehicle to advance their own domestic political interests. Critics of the U.S. security cooperation program have accused local African leaders of exaggerating the threat to the Sahara region posed by regional Islamic insurgents in order to secure U.S. assistance, training, and military hardware.[93] Algeria and Chad are particularly good examples of unpopular authoritarian regimes in Africa with which the United States has cooperated.[94] Moreover, the ambiguous legal nature of some of these CSLs and assistance agreements may offer political opportunities to oppositional elites and groups to greatly exaggerate or otherwise mischaracterize the U.S. presence and its actual missions.[95]

Finally, establishing new military facilities or CSLs in these African hosts runs the risk of undermining the credibility of future U.S. efforts to impose economic or political conditionality for domestic reforms. Thad Dunning has noted how foreign assistance in Africa became more effective during the post–cold war era because the end of superpower competition made the imposition of conditions by the West seem more credible in aid bargaining.[96] Under this logic, establishing a network of permanent or semipermanent military installations on the African continent, especially in host countries with authoritarian regimes, runs the risk of hindering parallel U.S. efforts and programs designed to promote good governance and institutional reform within these hosts. And like the U.S. experience with its bases in Uzbekistan and Kyrgyzstan, establishing new military installations and cooperation initiatives in these African hosts carries the risk of triggering a backlash during future democratization or demands for contractual renegotiation should these regimes be toppled or swept away.

More Credible Base Hosts: The Consolidated Democracies of the Black Sea

The theory of base politics suggests that the new U.S. bases recently established in Romania and Bulgaria, in contrast to those in Central Asia and

---

93. E.g., see Hallinan 2006; Keenan 2004.
94. On Algeria, see Keenan 2004; Barth 2003. On Chad, see Khatchadourian 2006.
95. I am grateful to Barry Posen for his thoughts on this point.
96. See Dunning 2004.

Africa with their current and future volatile politics, are much less likely to become politicized or contested in a manner that might force a contractual renegotiation.

Both Black Sea countries now host new FOSs and a number of supporting facilities scattered throughout their territory. In Romania, a bilateral ten-year agreement concluded in December 2005 granted the United States access to the large Mihail Kogalniceanu base and airfield near the Black Sea city of Constanta as well as the Babadag training facility and ranges at Cincu and Smardan. The U.S. force in Romania is anticipated to reach about 1,500 and will be rotational.[97] Similarly, a ten-year agreement signed with Bulgaria in April 2006 permits the U.S. military to use the Bezmer airbase, Novo Selo range, and Graf Ignatievo airfield and storage facilities at Burgas on the Black Sea. U.S. forces will total a brigade size, about 2,000–3000, with the number possibly increasing to 5,000 at peak times.[98] In both cases, the bases will remain the sovereign territory of the host countries and under the symbolic command of a host national officer, although both hosts agreed to waive their primary right of criminal jurisdiction under the NATO SOFA except for cases involving serious crimes.[99]

Beyond offering attractive facilities, these countries have in place internal institutional features likely to ensure that, politically, they will remain favorable base hosts, or at least that they will maintain their commitments to these initial contracts. First, these bilateral agreements were concluded with postcommunist democratic governments and ratified by their parliaments, rendering the agreements procedurally legitimate.[100] The Romanian accord was approved by the Romanian parliament in May 2007 by a vote of 257–1 with 29 abstentions, whereas the Bulgarian legislature ratified its agreement in May 2006 by a vote of 150–20 with 2 abstentions.[101] Accordingly, future governments should regard these basing agreements as procedurally valid international agreements.

Second, the party systems in both countries have consolidated and witnessed orderly turnover.[102] None of the major political parties in Romania

97. See Sullivan 2006.

98. See Associated Press 2006.

99. For further U.S. official positions and budgetary details on the Bulgarian bases, see http://sofia.usembassy.gov/shared_facilities_faq.html (accessed May 2007).

100. For U.S. official positions on the Romanian bases agreement, see http://bucharest.usembassy.gov/US_Policy/FAQ_US_Forces_Presence_in_Romania.html (accessed May 2007).

101. Associated Press 2007; *USA Today* 2006.

102. On party system consolidation in Romania and eastern Europe, see Bochsler 2005.

opposed the basing accord, and even the extreme Motherland nationalist party generally supported the deal.[103] Allegations by human rights groups in fall 2005 that the CIA had operated a secret prison on one of the Romanian bases prompted some Romanian parliamentarians to call for an investigation into the matter, but the allegations did not change party positions regarding the actual basing deal.[104] In Bulgaria, the Socialist Party that signed the May 2006 agreement actually had campaigned a year earlier on a platform of demanding more concessions from the United States. But despite some popular protests against the agreement, the nationalist Attack Party was the only political party to actually oppose the deal.

Third, with their admission to NATO in 2004 and the EU in 2007, both countries enacted a number of domestic institutional reforms as part of the accession and conditionality process.[105] These reforms have streamlined and clarified internal jurisdiction over defense-related issues. The two countries reformed civil-military relations, downsized the military, increased transparency of the defense sector, and consolidated elected civilian control over the armed forces. Although governance problems and corruption issues still trouble both countries, Romania and Bulgaria are much improved and transparent in their management of defense matters, ensuring that civilian bureaucracies and agencies will monitor and deal with base-related issues.

Finally, governments in both countries view these basing agreements as a key component of their new pro-Western orientation in foreign policy matters.[106] Perhaps ironically, both countries' ability to reach a bilateral security cooperation agreement with the United States emphasizes their independence from Moscow. And although Romanian and Bulgarian officials do not want to choose among demonstrating loyalty to the EU, NATO, or the United States, concluding a separate defense agreement with the United States is viewed as an important symbol of their irreversible integration into the West and an important complement to their newly acquired EU membership of January 2007.[107]

103. Author's interview with Romanian Ministry of Foreign Affairs and Defense officials, Bucharest, July 2005.

104. On the covert prison allegation, see Human Rights Watch 2005b.

105. For a discussion of the transformative impact of conditionality, see Epstein 2005; Vachudova 2005.

106. On managing relations with the EU and the United States after the Iraq crisis, see Linden 2004.

107. Author's interviews with Romanian officials in NATO and the Ministry of Foreign Affairs, Brussels and Bucharest, July 2005.

The one set of actors that may politicize or draw attention to various aspects of the basing agreements in both countries is their democratizing media. In Romania and Bulgaria, the media are relatively young and remain fiercely aggressive, with dozens of newspapers and television channels competing for public attention and new stories. As a result, negative stories involving U.S. personnel or the use of the bases may be heavily publicized and scrutinized, especially if they involve criminal jurisdiction procedures.[108] In addition, under the terms of both agreements host countries must be consulted before the bases are used in strikes against a third party, making the consultation process during a military campaign the likely object of intense media scrutiny.

In sum, the domestic political features of the new Black Sea base hosts will likely make them reliable security partners for U.S. basing needs, especially when compared with their Central Asian counterparts. The establishment of the bases after the two countries' democratization, the ratification of these deals by their parliaments, their consolidated party systems, and their pro-Western security orientation will likely yield a more supportive base politics in Bulgaria and Romania than in other new base-hosting regions. The same holds true of other east European countries that are considering hosting other types of U.S. defense installations, such as Poland and the Czech Republic, which in the future may host U.S. national missile defense and radar installations.[109]

Conclusions: Integrating the Gap or Creating a Dozen Uzbekistans?

The GDPR represents the most important change in the U.S. overseas basing posture since World War II. A network of smaller, more flexible installations scattered throughout remote areas of the world will replace the older large, hublike bases of the cold war. By keeping the U.S. military footprint relatively small, U.S. planners hope to deal more flexibly and effectively with new security threats and ensure that the U.S. basing presence neither draws public attention nor generates anti-American backlash in these new locations.

---

108. See Cooley 2005a.
109. On the importance of the political dimension of missile defense, see Larrabee and Karkoszka 2007.

Regardless of the strategic merits of the base restructuring, the cases of Uzbekistan and Kyrgyzstan cast doubts on many of the GDPR's political assumptions. U.S. military facilities in these Central Asian countries were relatively small, yet they rapidly became major political issues, following previous patterns of base politics. In Uzbekistan, authoritarian president Islam Karimov evicted the United States, thereby proving he was neither a reliable strongman nor a dependable security partner, when he perceived that continued U.S. presence might undermine his domestic rule. In Kyrgyzstan a democratizing backlash after the ouster of corrupt president Askar Akayev catapulted the Manas base agreement and compensation formula onto the national political agenda after their years of low-key, nonpolitical status. Much like the cases in Spain, Philippines, Turkey, Korea, and Greece, in Kyrgyzstan the new president Bakiyev challenged the legality and legitimacy of the basing contract by arguing that the original deal had served the narrow interests of an authoritarian ruler and not those of the country as a whole.

These episodes offer a number of lessons and cautions to defense planners who champion the GDPR. For example, in his compelling analysis of the security challenges posed by globalization, author and Pentagon adviser Thomas Barnett asserts, in a statement he made in 2002, that U.S. bases in Central Asia would become "a permanent feature of the landscape" of the Central Asian region.[110] Barnett's point was that the facilities should endure, like the U.S. bases in Germany, even after the Afghanistan campaign because of their strategic location and potential importance to U.S. planners. Barnett's analysis was not wrong in terms of American interest in maintaining a permanent basing presence in Central Asia, but it did not account for the changing political calculations and two-level politics of elites within these base hosts. Internal political changes, not U.S. strategy, mostly determined the political fate of U.S. bases in Central Asia.

Whatever the strategic merits of the GDPR, expanding the network of U.S. military installations is likely to create significant and unforeseen downstream political problems and obstacles for U.S. planners. Whether they intend to or not, U.S. forces are likely to find themselves enmeshed in the domestic politics of an array of new base hosts. Host governments, as they always have, will use the U.S. military presence for their own purposes, and political opposition figures will associate the United States with the undemocratic practices of new host countries, regardless of whether

110. Barnett 2004, 179.

U.S. officials actually supported the host government's specific domestic policies or not. The political crises that the U.S. presence generated in Central Asia may be repeated in other basing regions that are characterized by political volatility and the lack consolidated democratic institutions.

This final point bears additional consideration, as it also suggests that basing politics and interactions with host regimes may not always support the broader U.S. goal of promoting democratization abroad. During the cold war, U.S. planners often overlooked violations of democratic norms and human rights in base hosts such as the Philippines, South Korea, Portugal, and Spain in order to maintain access and basing rights. During this time, planners were willing to tolerate authoritarian practices in order to achieve the greater strategic objective of defeating the Communist threat. However, in the global war against terrorism, when the strategic objective is the defeat of Islamic extremism and the nurturing of democratic states and institutions, the justification for supporting authoritarian or semiauthoritarian base hosts seems less compelling. The Central Asian cases suggest that not only can an overseas military presence, even a small one, pressure U.S. officials to support the excessive political practices of host country regimes, but that the basing presence itself may become embroiled in and held hostage by the volatile politics of these countries. Rather than promote stability and democracy, haphazard deployments in countries with illegitimate governments may actually sow the seeds for future democratic challenges against the U.S. military presence and increase local political volatility. Over the long run, the conduct of base politics and the promotion of democratization may not mix, at least not within the same target country.

CHAPTER 8

Conclusion

America's Past and Future Base Politics

Over six decades across different continents, rulers and politicians in countries hosting U.S. military bases have played two-level base politics; they have used the benefits provided by basing contracts to further their domestic political goals and have invoked domestic institutions to improve the terms of their security contracts with the United States. The phases during which these basing contracts were contested and politicized by various domestic groups or were ignored and subsequently depoliticized have varied according to the host regime's dependence on the base and the contractual credibility of its political institutions. Cases drawn from southern Europe, East Asia, and the postcommunist states have shown that heads of state in authoritarian regimes, democratizers, and consolidated democracies have faced distinct political imperatives and institutional pressures as they negotiated and managed the U.S. basing presence.

Findings

Authoritarian Rule and Base Politics

Authoritarian leaders such as Franco, Salazar, Park, Rhee, Marcos, Akayev, and Karimov all showed remarkable skill at using the American security presence to further their domestic political survival. Certain rulers—Rhee in the 1950s, Marcos in the 1960s and 1970s, and Akayev in the 2000s— used the U.S. basing presence to secure economic assistance from the United States, which they in turn used to distribute private benefits to political clients such as military supporters, bureaucrats, and companies controlled by their ruling families. Even though these leaders were highly dependent on these aid flows and were supposedly weak "clients" of the United States, autocrats such as Rhee and Marcos showed no hesitation in bargaining hard to secure concessions. The U.S. basing presence may have diminished these host countries' overall national sovereignty, but it also afforded their rulers significant private political benefits.

Other authoritarian leaders used the U.S. military presence to acquire prestige and international legitimacy (Franco and Karimov), while still others used it to justify their harsh repression of internal political opponents (Park, Marcos, and Chun). Chun's calculated invocation of American acquiescence to the crackdown at Kwangju is perhaps the most brutal example of this dynamic and demonstrates not only how supposedly subordinate leaders in these client or semisovereign relationships still retained considerable agency to pursue their domestic political interests, but also how they could signal U.S. approval for their heavy-handed actions. U.S. diplomats and defense officials did not condone many of the repressive excesses carried out by these regimes, but their passivity in regard to these internal political matters was certainly noted by regime opponents. And in certain cases, such as Salazar's demand in the 1960s that the United States stop supporting African decolonization in Portuguese territories or Marcos's dismal human rights records in the late 1970s, U.S. presidents who were otherwise committed to promoting liberalization and human rights abroad had to back down over concerns that these authoritarian hosts would revoke U.S. base rights for strategically important locations. These concessions to authoritarian rulers exacted a great price, both politically and operationally, in later years.

Base Politics in Democratizers

The cases I've examined show how countries in the process of democratization have consistently lacked contractual credibility on the basing issue and have been the most politically volatile of base hosts. The cases also show how all three causal mechanisms as outlined in the first chapter— the contesting of procedural legitimacy, competition among institutions for jurisdiction, and fragmenting of the party system—contribute to the recurring periods of politicization and contestation of basing contracts. In every case in which a base deal was signed with a previously nondemocratic regime, the procedural legitimacy of the security contract was questioned in the subsequent democratizing era in one of two ways. In the cases of Spain, post-Marcos Philippines, Korea, Turkey, and Kyrgyzstan—as well as other cases such as Greece, Thailand, and Panama—democratizing elites explicitly questioned the validity of basing contracts, arguing that these deals were initially signed with authoritarian rulers and never ratified by democratic institutions. In the cases of postindependence Philippines, Japan (main islands), and Okinawa, heads of state argued that the United States had unfairly imposed basing accords during a period of military occupation. These powerful narratives undermined the procedural legitimacy of these security contracts and forced renegotiation of both their overall terms and, in the non-NATO cases, the provisions of their SOFAs.

Internal jurisdictional competition further exacerbated these periods of contractual uncertainty. Tensions between the executive and parliament inflamed the base issue in Japan in 1960, Turkey in the 1960s through 1970s, and the Philippines in 1991, whereas base-related clashes between regional governments and central authorities have dominated post-reversion politics in Okinawa and, during the mid-1970s, in the Azores. The activation of civil society, NGOs, and the new media in Korea and Okinawa has challenged elite-led politics and allowed new social actors to directly pressure government actors to renegotiate elements of these basing deals, especially the environmental and criminal jurisdiction elements of the SOFAs.

New and fragmented party systems further encouraged ideological appeals and electoral campaigns with antibase platforms. Not coincidentally, new socialist parties in Spain and Greece in the early 1980s skillfully used an antibase and anti-NATO platform to attain national power for the first time. The fragmented party system and party factionalism also contributed to the difficult ratification of the 1960 Mutual Security Treaty in the Japanese Diet, the highly charged base controversies in Turkish politics in the 1960s, and the successful national presidential campaigns of Korean progressives in 1997 and 2002.

Of the cases of outright evictions (Spain in 1988, Philippines in 1991, and Uzbekistan in 2005) or unilateral abrogation (Turkey in 1974), three out of the four occurred in democratizing environments. The exact pathways for each of these evictions differed. In the Spanish case, negotiators used a crafty national referendum as negotiating leverage and justification to expel U.S.

forces from Torrejón, whereas in the Turkish case nationalist pressures and competitive party politics forced a new coalition led by Süleyman Demirel to curtail U.S. base activities in response to the United States' post-Cyprus embargo. In the Philippines, the expulsion of the U.S. military was the result of domestic institutional competition as the failed ratification in the Philippine Senate effectively vetoed the executive's agreement to extend the lease of Subic. In all of these cases, the combination of domestic democratization and the fact that these new host-country regimes no longer relied on the bases for political survival afforded hosts the political motive and opportunity with which to challenge and expel U.S. forces.

The Credibility of Consolidated Democracies

Equally striking is how the basing issue in overseas hosts has receded as democracies and party systems have consolidated. In countries such as Spain, Greece, and mainland Japan, the basing issue no longer carries anywhere near the political resonance it once did, despite occasional crimes and accidents involving U.S. troops, or even the United States' use of these bases for unpopular military missions such as the 2003 Iraq campaign. Democratic consolidation has contributed to the depoliticization of the base issue in three ways.

First, as new elites and political actors in the democratization era renegotiated and amended basing contracts, these new deals have been ratified by domestic legislatures and granted the procedural legitimacy that was lacking in authoritarian-era agreements. Thus, the PSOE in Spain in 1988 negotiated a new post-Franco deal that was ratified, and the LDP in Japan in 1960, despite intense opposition, ratified the Mutual Security Treaty that would correct some of the imbalances imposed on Japan during its postwar occupation. Subsequently, the Japanese public came to view the treaty as a democratic commitment to the United States, even if it did not particularly care for the enduring U.S. basing presence on Japanese territory. After these treaties were ratified, political actors and negotiators in these host countries could no longer claim that the basing agreements lacked democratic accountability or host-country consent.

Second, as host countries have consolidated their political institutions after democratization, the internal jurisdiction over base issues has become routinized and institutionalized. Base issues now are managed by bureaucracies or specialized agencies and are rarely engaged by political elites. They have become matters for technocrats to implement and manage, not an issue for politicians to question or debate. Indeed, the Japanese case shows how the government of Japan, through its host-nation support and establishment of the DFAA, bureaucratized and created whole domestic interest groups within Japanese society to benefit from the continued U.S. basing presence. As the base issue has been disassociated from "high politics" and delegated to bureaucracies and specialized agencies, the opportunity for fundamentally altering these deals has also faded. Consistent with the literature on political delegation, the bureaucratization of the basing issue, especially in Japan and Okinawa, has created multiple veto points that promote the stability of basing contracts.[1]

Third, the consolidation of party politics in democratic base hosts has further depoliticized the base issue and, in some cases, has created the utter indifference displayed by current leaders of major parties on the matter. Chapter 6 discussed how the party political system in Japan and Italy steadily forced left-wing parties to abandon their opposition to the bases in order to appeal to the median voter, and when these parties finally attained political power in the early 1990s, they took no policy positions to undermine prevailing basing contracts and security agreements. In the Spanish case, mirrored by the Greek case, the PSOE's party platform now makes no mention of the U.S. bases as a political matter, and only marginal parties in European countries now bring up the issue (a position that seemingly reinforces their marginality). As evidenced by the Iraq War in 2003, major national parties no longer debate the bases, even as they criticize American foreign policy and the very missions supported by bases on their territory. I predict that the same will hold true of Korea in the near future. Antibase NGOs will certainly continue to campaign against the U.S. presence, but these single-issue appeals are less likely to sway the median voter over time. My argument leads to the conclusion that party politics will encourage Korea's progressive and conservative parties to converge on matters of foreign policy and security, just as parties have done in Japan, Italy, Spain, and Greece.

Example: The Evolution of Use Rights in Southern Europe

This political shift is borne out when we examine the evolution of use rights and access agreements among southern European base hosts for major "out-of-area" military missions led by U.S. forces. The sample size is

---

1. Tsebelis 2002.

TABLE 8.1
Permission by southern European countries to use bases for major U.S. military campaigns

Military campaign	Greece	Italy	Portugal	Spain	Turkey
Yom Kippur War, 1973	No	No	Yes	No	No
Libya air strikes, 1986	No	No	No	No	No
Gulf War, 1990	Yes	Yes	Yes	Yes	Yes
Bosnia, 1995	Yes	Yes	Yes	Yes	Yes
Kosovo, 1999	Yes	Yes	Yes	Yes	Yes
Afghanistan, 2001	Yes	Yes	Yes	Yes	Yes
Iraq, 2003	Yes	Yes	Yes	Yes	No

small, but the trend is unmistakable (see table 8.1). The United States was unable to secure base rights from any southern European country except Portugal to resupply Israel in 1973 (although two years later Portugal stated it would no longer grant access for Middle Eastern missions), and all of these hosts refused to grant base access for the 1986 bombing of Libya. However, beginning with the Gulf War, the United States has secured base access from these same southern European allies (and northern ones as well) for operations in Bosnia, Kosovo, Afghanistan, and Iraq (with the exception of Turkey). The cases of Kosovo and Iraq are particularly noteworthy in that, like the Libyan case, the United States did not obtain a UN Security Council vote, although in the Kosovo case the action was NATO approved. Nevertheless, the campaign was still deeply unpopular among the rank-and-file party members of the prevailing left-wing governments in Italy and Greece. The only recent exception to this pattern was the Turkish parliamentary vote in 2003. But as we saw, the episode itself bore many hallmarks of democratizing politics. The combination of a new political party trying to whip its first major vote and the Turkish military's effort to embarrass Erdogan ultimately contributed to the electoral defeat. Despite the Turkish leader's attempt to spin the vote as a victory for Turkish democracy, it was his party's own inexperience in maintaining internal discipline that ultimately denied the approval's passage.

The argument I advance in this book also suggests that the United States would likely secure base rights from these same countries for a future unilateral or unsanctioned military action, such as air strikes against Iran. Like the 2003 Iraq War, a bombing campaign to destroy various sites tied to an Iranian nuclear program would arouse widespread opposition among European publics, but it is doubtful that European governments themselves would deny base access to U.S. forces. The same permissive stance would be found in Japan and, most likely, in Korea as well. By contrast, the prospect of securing base rights for an Iran campaign from the politically volatile Central Asian states would be considerably dimmer.

Alternative Explanations Considered

The theory of base politics developed in this book and its implications compare favorably with the alternative theories' predictions about the evolution of political attitudes toward U.S. bases in host countries.

Systemic Theories: Realism and Institutionalism

The most prominent alternate theory would draw on realist assumptions about international relations and explain the politicization of security contracts in any given U.S. ally or security partner as a function of the levels of external threat faced by the base host. Certainly the mutuality of security interests explains the close cooperation and the depoliticized nature of the bases in Korea and Turkey during the 1950s. However, the subsequent volatility of the basing issue in Turkey during the 1960s and 1970s cannot be easily explained by realist accounts, as the Soviet threat remained constant throughout this period. Nor can a systemic account explain the timing of the antibase movements and campaigns in Korea in the 1990s and early 2000s, a period when North Korea arguably behaved even more assertively on security-related matters as it escalated its nuclear activity and even tested ballistic missiles. External threat alone did not determine these patterns of political contestation, even in these two cases in which security concerns were so important initially.

Moreover, structural realist accounts that emphasize the primacy of external threat would have still more significant problems in explaining the sudden politicization and contestation of the basing issue across time in almost all of the other cases. Thus, the intense political challenges to the U.S. basing presence brought by anticommunist allies such as the Philippines

(1950s and late 1980s), Spain (1980s), Portugal (mid-1980s), Turkey (1960s and 1970s), Greece (1980s), and early postwar Japan (1950s) make little sense from a realist perspective. Internal, not external, political calculations drove the changing politics of the base issue. Even in Italy, arguably the strongest European case for a realist account, we repeatedly saw how Italian political elites strongly backed the United States on base-related issues such as the Euromissile deployment, less out of genuine concern about Italian national security but rather to further their domestic political agendas and discredit political rivals, especially the Italian Communist Party.

Conversely, realist accounts would give a straightforward explanation for the relative indifference to the basing issue among contemporary U.S. allies, including Spain, Portugal, Italy, and mainland Japan, as well as other cases like Germany, Greece, Britain, and Australia. Realist scholars would argue that policymakers in these hosts consider the U.S. bases just one small part of a much broader set of cooperative security relations and defense partnerships. This observation is certainly correct, but it confuses cause and effect. The bases are no longer a significant issue in some of these countries precisely because their democratic evolution and consolidation have removed them from the realm of national political agenda-setting and rendered them routine or technical defense matters. Yet these very same agreements in Spain, Greece, and Japan were contested when previous basing agreements lacked procedural legitimacy and democratic accountability. The depoliticization and relative indifference to the base issue today are not natural but a function of this domestic political evolution within these base hosts. One need only chart the evolution of the socialist party platforms in Spain and Italy to underscore just how far these parties have changed their original positions on the question of the U.S. military presence and its underlying security commitments.

Similarly, security institutionalists might argue that the basing issue in the European cases has been subsumed under the broad mandate of NATO cooperation and, because of this multilateral framework, has lost its political significance. Again, although membership in a security community is certainly the way political elites and defense officials now justify the presence of U.S. or NATO bases on their territory, the fact that the bases are used for non-NATO-sanctioned missions such as OIF cannot be readily explained by the same reasoning. Such views also cannot account for why out-of-area operations in the Middle East were not authorized by these hosts in 1973 and 1986, but were authorized in 2003, even though all of these Middle Eastern campaigns fell outside of NATO auspices and lacked the sanctioning of the United Nations. Nor can the security community perspective, in reference to NATO, explain Salazar's brazenly self-serving behavior in 1960 when he threatened to expel U.S. forces from the Azores in order to secure American acquiescence to Portugal's continued African colonial campaigns. In fact, parts of this study suggest that NATO's true political significance may lie at the micropolitical or domestic level among member states, not in its role as a security community or multilateral source of security norms. Domestic elites invoked NATO obligations as political cover for unpopular policies or to discredit political opponents.

Base Size and Troop Levels

A second alternative explanation for varying patterns of base politics would focus on the size of U.S. troop deployments as the critical factor in politicizing the bases. Such an argument could explain the peak of domestic political opposition to the bases in Japan in the late 1950s and in Turkey in the early 1960s, times when U.S. troop levels in these countries were also at or near their peak. However, even in these instances the cases showed that internal democratization dynamics such as elite campaigns, party system fragmentation, and institutional competition helped to channel and even mobilize public concerns about the heavy U.S. footprint. Turkey's closure of U.S. bases took place after U.S. officials reduced troops significantly from a peak of about 10,600 in 1967 to 6,599 in 1974 (see figs. 8.1 and 8.2).

More important, the base size explanation does not correlate with any of the other instances of base politicization and contestation. The most significant political challenges to bases in Spain (1981–88), Okinawa (1972–78, 1995–98), Korea (1996–2002), and the Philippines (1986–91) all took place when the number of U.S. forces had declined, often significantly, from their earlier peak. Moreover, the recent cases of Uzbekistan and Kyrgyzstan, both new-style lily-pad bases that hosted small deployments, aptly demonstrate how even a basing presence of 1,000–2,000 troops can become rapidly contested or, in the Uzbek case, lead to outright eviction. These cases should give pause to analysts and policymakers who assume that smaller-sized bases, such as those advocated in the GDPR, will necessarily reduce political frictions with base hosts.

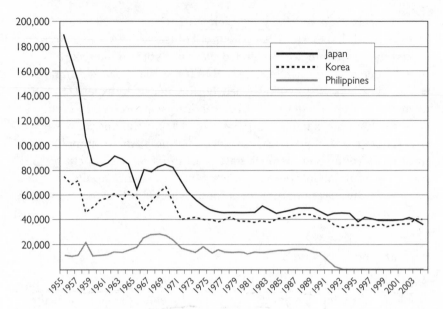

Figure 8.1. U.S. troop levels, East Asian hosts.
Source: U.S. Department of Defense

Base Use and Incidents

A third alternative explanation would describe the politicization of bases as a reaction against their use for unpopular missions or as a result of high-profile base-related accidents or crimes. The Turkish case provides the most support for this view, from the string of base-related incidents in the early 1960s that inflamed public opinion against the bases, to the unpopular Operation Provide Comfort in the 1990s, to the vote in 2003 to authorize Turkish territory for U.S. military forces to launch a northern front against Iraq. However, this account does not explain why so many other European and Asian countries regularly acquiesce to the use of the bases for unpopular or internationally unsanctioned missions. Nor can it explain why there was minimal political fallout directed toward the U.S. military presence in the wake of serious incidents such as the Palomares accident in Spain in 1966 or the clear violation of Italian sovereignty and jurisdiction at Sigonella in Italy in 1986. More recently, such an explanation cannot account for why, after the revelations of CIA prisoner transports and rendition flights through these overseas bases, individual European governments have not repoliticized the

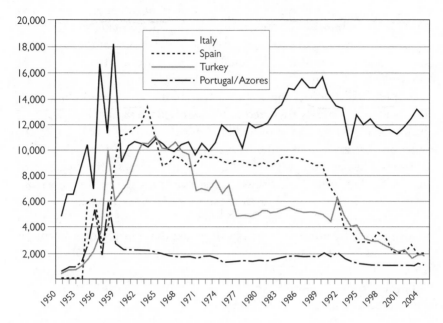

Figure 8.2. U.S. troop levels, southern European hosts.
Source: U.S. Department of Defense

issue and taken operational steps to curtail U.S. basing rights or access arrangements.[2]

At the same time, base politics have been affected, but not driven, by negative incidents involving U.S. personnel. Base-related crimes and accidents are especially damaging when they occur in an already politically volatile, democratizing climate. The Girard case in Japan in 1957, the Highway 56 accident in Korea in 2002, and the shooting of a Kyrgyz base worker in 2006 all exploded as news stories precisely because they seemed to symbolize and reinforce a prevailing perception within the host country that its basing relationship with the United States was unequal. Moreover, in the aftermath of these incidents, the media in these hosts played a critical role in pushing these stories and calling attention to the criminal jurisdiction procedures of the SOFA. But it is just as important to acknowledge, as chapter 6 showed, that when the political climate is stable, base-related

2. In fact, the European Parliament, not national governments, has been the driving political institution investigating the CIA's rendition flights. See European Parliament 2007.

incidents and accidents rarely have long-term political repercussions. The 1998 cable-car tragedy at Cavalese is a case in point, where, despite the tragic loss of twenty lives, the apparent irresponsibility of the U.S. pilot, and the pilot's controversial acquittal by a U.S. court martial, the incident quickly faded from the Italian political agenda.

The one exception to this pattern remains the 1995 rape in Okinawa. The incident effectively triggered a broader backlash against the bases and prompted Governor Ota to mount an antibase campaign, hold a referendum, and refuse to renew the base-related land leases. In its sheer brutality, symbolism, and social impact, it remains perhaps the single most politically damaging base-related crime ever perpetrated by American servicemen. But it is also fair to mention, as we saw in chapter 5, that the Okinawan media significantly fueled the story and emboldened Ota to take a more confrontational stance against the central government on the base issue. From this perspective, it is even more remarkable that Ota actually lost his reelection bid in 1998, after just three years of base-related political confrontation, to a candidate who promised more economic benefits and reconciliation with Tokyo.

Social Attitudes: Anti-Americanism and Political Culture

A fourth, and final, competing explanation to those advanced in this book would focus on the importance of social attitudes toward the bases in a host country. This alternative explanation is perhaps the most easily dismissed simply because it correlates poorly with political shifts on the base issue. For example, levels of anti-Americanism in most European and Asian base hosts have risen significantly over this decade, yet host governments continue to allow U.S. forces relatively unrestricted base access for military missions, even deeply unpopular ones such as Iraq (see table 8.2).

Similarly, as the polling reported in chapter 6 shows, Japanese sentiment toward U.S. bases remained negative throughout the 1960s and 1970s, even as the issue receded from the national political agenda. Conversely, although the amount of antibase activism and anti-Americanism in Korea remains intense among some segments of the population, only a small minority of respondents actually favor the complete withdrawal of U.S. forces. Recall, for example, *Chungang Ilbo*'s poll conducted in January 2003, just months after Roh's controversial election victory, which found that only 13.5 percent of respondents (out of a total of 1,200) favored a complete withdrawal or large-scale pullout by U.S. troops, whereas 42.8 percent favored

TABLE 8.2
Rates of public opinion (%) favorable to the United States among major U.S. military base hosts

Country	1999/2000	2002	2003	2004	2005	2006
Hosts studied in book						
Spain	50	—	38	—	41	23
Turkey	52	30	15	30	23	12
South Korea	58	53	—	46	—	—
Japan	77	72	—	—	—	63
Other major base hosts						
Germany	78	61	45	38	41	37
Great Britain	83	75	70	58	55	56
Pakistan	23	10	13	21	23	27

Sources: Pew Global Attitudes Project, "Global Opinion 2005: The Spread of Anti-Americanism," January 24, 2005, http://people-press.org/commentary/display.php3?AnalysisID=104 (accessed May 2007); "American Character Gets Mixed Reviews," June 23, 2005, http://pewglobal.org/reports/pdf/247.pdf (accessed May 2007).

a small-scale reduction and 41.5 percent favored maintenance of current levels.[3] And in perhaps the most dramatic of U.S. base evictions, that of troops from the Philippines in 1991, opinion polls taken before the Philippine Senate vote indicate that a solid majority of Filipinos actually favored retaining the U.S. bases.[4] Overall, public opinion and surveys of anti-Americanism are poor indicators of political trends on the basing issue.

Similarly, political culture arguments that explain a host's attitudes toward the U.S. basing presence are usually indeterminate. As the Okinawan case shows, despite the island population's strong antimilitarist norms and sense of Okinawan identity, economic arguments and political campaigns for national unity by LDP have regularly trumped antibase platforms in gubernatorial elections on the prefecture. Strongly held notions of host-country identity, nationalism, and sovereignty seem to be activated (and depoliticized) by certain domestic institutional changes—they are not constant factors. So when it comes to explaining base politics, it is difficult to make a case for the independent power of social attitudes and political culture.

3. Cited in Kim 2004, 273.
4. See Bello 1991, 158.

In sum, although the alternative explanations of security pressures, base size, base use, incidents, and social attitudes all have the potential to explain selected episodes or trends in these cases, none of them can explain the full range, from politicization to depoliticization, of the basing issue across these very different regions and historical eras.

Comparative Applications: Other Bases, Other Contracts

The arguments I make in this book need to be explored and evaluated further, both in relation to other cases of overseas basing and other types of bilateral contracting that exhibit properties similar to base contracts.

Comparative Base Politics: Britain, France, and Russia

The comparative study of military basing powers and their political dynamics is still relatively underdeveloped.[5] Certainly, other great powers have maintained military facilities abroad during their rise to international hegemony, although the sheer global coverage and multiplicity of functions undertaken in U.S. installations appear unprecedented. The most obvious of the other modern cases are those of Great Britain and France. Both of these states negotiated base rights and defense treaties, with former imperial holdings, as a precondition for granting decolonization, but these accords were themselves subjected to renegotiation and in most cases termination.[6] For example, Britain negotiated base rights and maintained a presence in Transjordan (1947–56), Ceylon (1947–56), Malaysia (1957–72), and Singapore (1957–72).[7] In the instructive case of Iraq in 1947 and 1948, democratization pressures actually forced Prime Minister Salih Jabr to withdraw from a renegotiated Anglo-Iraqi treaty that would have extended unlimited basing rights to the British after Iraqi independence.[8]

---

5. See, however, the comparative analysis in Johnson 2007; Harkavy 2005.
6. For a more extensive treatment of these decolonization bargains, see the comparative discussion in Cooley and Spruyt 2006.
7. Woodliffe 1992, 77–78.
8. See Mansfield and Snyder 2005, 215–18. As with the American post-occupation cases, Iraqi opposition politicians and populists regarded the original treaty from 1930 as a colonial relic that had been used by the British to justify their internal intervention in Iraq and unrestricted use rights. The Iraqi Regent rejected the renewal in 1948 after intense domestic opposition to the accord.

Presently Britain maintains sizable bases on Belize, Brunei, Cyprus, Gibraltar, British Ocean Territory, and the Falklands. In the latter three cases, bases are located on actual British dependencies, whereas in the first three, basing rights were constitutionally granted as part of their independence agreement.[9] Of these, the Cypriot case is perhaps the most contentious, although the campaign to renegotiate the terms of the British presence was halted by intercommunal violence and then partition of the island following the 1974 Turkish military intervention. The small size and security needs of Belize and Brunei make them relatively welcoming hosts to British forces.

French bases offer perhaps even better opportunities for a comparative application of the argument given that France negotiated a number of basing accords and defense treaties with its former colonies. Several of these agreements—such as those with Algeria and Tunisia—were soon renegotiated and terminated, although these changes were more the product of autocratic nationalism and populist appeals rather than actual democratization. As with Britain, while many of the French postcolonial basing agreements did not last for long, securing them arguably helped to facilitate the decolonization process in the first place.[10] Today France still maintains overseas bases across a network of dependencies and overseas departments, such as Réunion, Mayotte, New Caledonia, French Polynesia, and Guyana, and in Africa, Djibouti, Chad, Mauritania, and the Ivory Coast. The French overseas presence remains controversial politically, with France's periodic interventions in the politics of its African base hosts and its nuclear testing in the Pacific.[11] The theory's predictions would suggest that any real democratization in these countries would initiate a contestation of the status of these remaining French installations.

Perhaps the most politically intriguing cases are contemporary ones involving Russian overseas military bases. As a result of the Soviet dissolution, Russia found a broad range of its fixed assets and military installations stranded outside its borders in the Near Abroad, the non-Russian countries that were once part of the Soviet Union.[12] The Russian government signed a series of leases and other bilateral contracts detailing

9. See the discussion of the British dependencies in Aldrich and Connell 1998.
10. See Cooley and Spruyt 2006; Cooley 2000–2001.
11. For English-language accounts of the French use of bases in Africa for intervention, see Renou 2002; Luckham 1982; Lellouche and Moisi 1979. On French nuclear testing in the Pacific, see Danielsson 1990.
12. For overviews, see Cooley 2000–2001; Drezner 1999, 131–247.

mixed sovereignty arrangements for most of these major assets, such as the Black Sea fleet in Crimea, Ukraine, and the Baikonur cosmodrome in Kazakhstan.

The Georgian case is of particular significance as Russia operated four sovereign bases on Georgian territory for eight years after independence without offering a guarantee for their return. In November 1999 the two countries agreed to close two of these facilities—Vaziani, near the capital Tbilisi, and Gaduata in the breakaway republic of Abkhazia—and further agreed to hold future meetings to discuss the gradual withdrawal of Russia's remaining facilities in Batumi and Akhalkalaki. With the Rose Revolution of 2003–4 and the coming to power of the pro-Western president Mikheil Saakashvili, the status of the remaining Russian bases acquired a new political urgency and was thrust to the forefront of the new government's foreign policy agenda. The democratizing dynamic of jurisdictional competition further fueled withdrawal negotiations, as the Georgian parliament on March 10, 2005, without consulting the president, voted unanimously that the Russians must agree to a removal by mid-May or face a blockade. On May 30, 2005, the two countries reached an agreement that called for the complete withdrawal all Russian troops from the bases by the end of 2007.[13] Georgia's negotiated expulsion of the Russian bases after the Rose Revolution fits the classic democratization pattern outlined in this book. Other countries hosting Russian installations that may exhibit similar dynamics in the near future may include Moldova, which still hosts the Russian Fourteenth Army in its breakaway territory of Transnistria, and Ukraine, whose port city of Sevastopol hosts Russia's Black Sea Fleet under the terms of a leasing deal reached in 1997.[14]

Other Security Contracts and Economic Contracts

My arguments about democratization and uncertain contracting environments also suggest that we should see contractual reneging in other issue areas as states undergo democratic transitions.

In security-related issues, the closest application would be to the study of territorial politics and conflict, another area in which elite appeals to sovereignty and nationalism might politicize and depoliticize governance arrangements. In fact, scholars have explored the link between domestic

---

13. For details, see Corso 2005.
14. On the Black Sea Fleet arrangement, see Cooley 2000-2001.

party system structure and stability and the political capacity of a regime to relinquish territory or decolonize.[15] Similarly, Ian Lustick's comparative study of the dynamics of territorial disengagement emphasizes certain thresholds of regime consolidation that must be attained before host governments can consider the actual security utility of disengagement as a policy option.[16] One final area of application of the base politics argument might be the study of the political governance of strategically important nonmilitary assets, such as the Suez or Panama Canal and the domestic political motivations behind host counties' contestation of the legitimacy of governing contracts.

The most obvious analogy to the base politics issue in the area of international political economy is host-country expropriation of foreign direct investments.[17] Recent studies suggest that democratic change and the nature of political institutions may indeed have several comparable effects in these areas. Adam Resnick argues that the uncertainty surrounding tax and legal regimes in transitioning states dissuades foreign investors and finds that democratic transitions across the developing world have decreased foreign direct investment flows.[18] Similarly, Resnick and Quan Li find that democratic institutions only increase foreign direct investment when they can offer credible guarantees over property rights, otherwise the relationship is negative.[19] Conversely, these authors find empirical support for the analogous claim that consolidated democracies offer more stable contracting environments for international investors, thereby supporting Mancur Olson's claim that democratic institutions are the best guarantors of property rights.[20] Similarly, from a property rights perspective, Louis Wells and Rafiq Ahmed show how democratization, specifically jurisdictional uncertainty and the emergence of new social and political actors, can pressure governments to renegotiate long-term contracts involving large infrastructural projects with international investors.[21]

My argument regarding regime type and contracting environment is broadly consistent with these works and their findings but could specify some of these renegotiation dynamics to an even greater extent. Extending

15. See Spruyt 2005; Kahler 1984.
16. Lustick 1993.
17. For a theoretical account of the U.S. case, see Krasner 1978.
18. Resnick 2001.
19. Resnick and Li 2003.
20. Olson 1993. Also see Jensen 2006.
21. Wells and Ahmed 2007.

the full "base politics" argument to the study of foreign direct investments would involve assessing the level of regime dependence that host countries might have on a particular contract with an external power, or some other form of "mutual hostage" situation. Thus, regimes dependent on technology transfers or specific technical knowledge to use the asset would be less likely to abrogate or renege on the contract than would nondependent regimes. The analogies between security contracts and foreign direct investment contracts seem promising and warrant further investigation.

Politics of the Future Basing Presence in Afghanistan and Iraq

Finally, there is the no small matter of Afghanistan and Iraq. The U.S. military presence and reconstruction effort in both countries have been heavily scrutinized, so I confine myself to analyzing the possible future dynamics of the "permanent bases" issue.[22] Despite official denials that the United States plans to establish permanent bases in these countries, the current high levels of U.S. spending on base construction in both countries suggest otherwise.[23]

One of the ironies is that the bases under construction in both countries look less like the skeletal facilities or lily pads advocated by the GDPR and far more like the enduring, heavy facilities that the United States established after its postwar occupation of Germany and Japan. In Afghanistan, U.S. and NATO forces have developed a network of airfields and bases across the country. The largest is the Bagram airbase, which hosts over 7,000 U.S. and NATO troops and has recently constructed a separate camp for its 400 civilian contractors. U.S. troops also maintain large deployments at airbases in Shinand (near Herat) and Kandahar.[24] In Iraq, as of May 2005, the United States operated 106 bases, along with a number of logistical facilities and four detention centers.[25] By summer of June 2006, reports suggest that original Pentagon plans to build four-

22. On Iraq, see especially Chandrasekaran 2006; Diamond 2005; Packer 2005; Cooley 2005d.
23. In 2004 and 2005, the United States spent $37.4 billion and $41.9 billion on facility construction and maintenance (excluding personnel costs) in Iraq and $6.9 billion and $6.8 billion in Afghanistan. See Belasco 2006, 22.
24. See http://www.globalsecurity.org/military/world/afghanistan/airfield.htm (accessed May 2007).
25. For analysis and maps, see http://www.globalsecurity.org/military/facility/iraq-intro.htm (accessed May 2007).

teen to twenty locations had been scaled back to maintaining four large "enduring bases" or "contingency operating bases."[26] These would be located in Tallil in the south, Al Asad in the west, Balad in the center, and a facility in the north. Balad airbase hosts between 20,000 to 25,000 U.S. troops and contractors, is encircled by a twenty-kilometer security perimeter, and remains the primary hub for movements in and out of Baghdad.[27] As a facility it does not exude temporary qualities.

A book's conclusion should not be the place to hedge bets, so let me clearly assess what my arguments predict about the political future of the U.S. basing presence in these countries.

The Future of the Basing Presence in Afghanistan

The lack of legal procedures to govern the presence of U.S. forces and their actions has already become a political problem in Afghanistan. The United States has yet to sign a status of forces agreement and is highly unlikely to place its troops under any kind of host-country criminal jurisdiction or legal procedure, especially in a time of continuing military operations. Yet negative base-related stories damage political support for the U.S. military presence and increase demands within Afghanistan to establish some legal mechanisms of accountability. Reports that the CIA and Department of Defense used a secret facility in Bagram to detain and interrogate hundreds of Afghan and foreign fighters were heavily criticized within the country.[28] In May 2006 a heavy cargo truck from a U.S. military convoy rammed into Afghan civilian vehicles at an intersection in Kabul. The accident ignited rioting by Afghans against the convoy, the worst since the fall of the Taliban, and resulted in the deaths of 20 Afghans and injuries to 160 when U.S. troops fired into the crowd.[29] The incident prompted demands by the Afghan parliament to try the U.S. driver in an Afghan court and reignited the debate about the need for a status of forces agreement.[30] These developments are all too familiar to students of U.S. base politics and recall previous cases of U.S. forces operating in post-occupation settings.

---

26. The terms used to describe these facilities changed from "enduring bases" in 2004 to "contingent operating bases" in 2005. For representative stories, see Francis 2004; Spolar 2004.
27. See http://www.globalsecurity.org/military/world/iraq/balad-ab.htm (accessed May 2007).
28. Golden and Schmitt 2006.
29. Watson 2006.
30. *Chicago Tribune* 2006.

Tempering reactions to these events on the ground, however, are Afghanistan's enduring weakness and the Karzai regime's extreme dependence on the international community, especially the United States, for its security and economic survival. Simply put, Afghanistan lacks any kind of internal capacity to fund its own state administration or security operations and is unlikely to develop such capacity for many years. Riddled by corruption and poor administration, the Afghan government in 2005 was able to pay for only 28 percent of its budget outlays.[31] Without foreign aid inflows and the continuing support of coalition and International Security Assistance Force (ISAF) deployments, the Afghanistan government would be unable to maintain even the most basic of state functions. Recognizing these needs, Afghan president Harmid Karzai told a national gathering of a thousand local representatives in May 2005 that "we need the assistance of the United States, NATO troops and international coalition forces until we have our own security forces and reach the point that we no longer need that assistance. We are still far from that point."[32]

So although the Afghan parliament and government will press hard for a status of forces agreement and other legal arrangements to clarify and govern the presence of U.S. forces, Afghanistan's continuing weakness ensures that the Karzai regime, or that of his successor, will require the presence of U.S. forces and military bases. Out of the cases we have examined, the political situation in Afghanistan may well come to resemble that of Japan or the Philippines in the 1950s, where elites in semisovereign host governments heavily politicized the bases issue and pressed for a revision of governing agreements but did not contest the overall necessity of the U.S. deployment.

The Future of the Basing Presence in Iraq

The political situation in Iraq looks far less promising from the perspective of the U.S. military. The Iraqi state's dependence on the presence of U.S. forces for security remains high, but the regime's potential fiscal autonomy, guaranteed by oil production, and political independence from the United States are considerably greater than Afghanistan's. Moreover, Iraq's democratizing dynamics are significantly more intense than Afghanistan's, given its sectarian party system, social mobilization, and

31. Rubin 2006, 26.
32. Gall 2005.

competitive media. The theory of base politics would have us predict that these internal political events will threaten a future permanent U.S. basing presence in Iraq, even one that is significantly reduced or concentrated within a few large military installations.

The Iraqi party system remains politically fragmented and was founded along ethnic and sectarian lines, with many small parties adopting aggressive mobilization strategies to attract voters. The May 2006 unity coalition government was founded on a delicate balance of power among parties that remain loyal to the Shiite, Sunni, and Kurdish groups within Iraqi society. Of these, the northern Kurdish parties are the ones most likely to support a future U.S. military presence, both as a guarantee against future centralizing tendencies of the Iraqi government and as a security check against potential incursions by the Turkish military. Shiite leaders have so far split on the issue but appear to be increasingly concerned about the impact of U.S. troops on both the political process and security situation. For example, Muqtada al-Sadr, the young cleric who heads a militia force of thousands in Baghdad, has called for the immediate withdrawal of U.S. forces. Sunni leaders overwhelmingly oppose the U.S. military presence. Accordingly, the U.S. presence threatens to become an issue in debates about party politics and Iraqi federalism and perhaps even a topic in the future political bargaining among these various ethnic factions. The United States may find itself allying with Kurdish factions and bypassing the central government altogether in order to guarantee its future presence in the north.

Iraqi society is increasingly opposed to a permanent U.S. military presence and now blames the United States for both the country's deteriorating security situation and its thousands of civilian casualties. Opinion polls in 2006 showed that a strong majority (over 70 percent) of Iraqis favored withdrawal of U.S. forces, whereas 80 percent believed that the U.S. government planned to establish permanent bases.[33] Relations between the U.S. military and the Iraqi media have grown increasingly strained as the images of Abu Ghraib seemingly confirm every stereotype spouted by anti-American propagandists about the U.S. military. In 2005, reports that the U.S. military paid Iraqi media outlets to plant positive stories as part of its public relations campaign further incensed the Iraqi press.[34] The escalating violence and increasing civilian casualties in 2006 and 2007 have further fueled a public backlash against U.S. forces. Incidents such as the

33. See Program on International Policy Attitudes 2006, 3-4.
34. See *Los Angeles Times* 2005.

Haditha killings, in which eight U.S. Marines were charged with killing Iraqi civilians in cold-blooded retaliation for an IED attack, are now driving demands among all party factions that Iraqi courts play a role in regulating the actions of U.S. forces.[35]

Yet even if the United States and Iraq agree on a SOFA to govern the U.S. presence and resolve thorny questions of criminal jurisdiction, a SOFA's ratification would probably mark the beginning, not the end, of the politicization of the U.S. presence. In Iraq's democratizing environment, legally codifying the U.S. presence will raise national awareness about its provisions and immediately unleash further scrutiny and opposition from political parties, militia groups, regional administrators, and the media. Given the sheer size of the U.S. presence, controversial new incidents are inevitable and will be magnified by the press and denounced by competing political elites. Indeed, during the course of the next national elections, the legal presence of U.S. forces may well become a defining campaign issue.

When all of these considerations are taken together, the prospect of securing and maintaining Iraq's legal support for a permanent U.S. military basing presence appears dim. After toppling the regime of Saddam Hussein, the U.S. military may well be ousted by the very democratic institutions and competitive processes that it helped to install.

Base Politics in a Post-Iraq, Globalizing World

Will the erosion of the United States' international legitimacy and authority as a result of the Iraq campaign adversely affect its global basing network and access arrangements? What, if any, additional political challenges do globalizing trends present to U.S. planners? Looking to the future of basing politics, U.S. policymakers must effectively manage two major trade-offs that relate to the political foundations of its global basing network—the democracy paradox and the low investment/low commitment problem.

The Democratization and Low-Investment Trade-offs

The first trade-off involves the political paradox presented by the United States' current foreign-policy emphasis on promoting democracy. As we have seen, consolidated democracies provide the most reliable contracting partners for the United States. However, as other international relations

35. See *Wall Street Journal* 2006.

scholars have noted, the actual pathway to attaining consolidated democracy is often bumpy, given that democratic transitions are prone to political instability, factionalism, and nationalism.[36] Smooth and quick democratic transitions remain exceptions, although good examples are the east central European postcommunist states, whose successful institutional transformation was catalyzed by the unique role played by the European Union and NATO, especially by the conditions these two institutions imposed as accession requirements.[37] Achieving democratic consolidation has proven far more difficult in other parts of the world, including the non-EU postcommunist countries, Latin America, Africa, Central Asia, Southeast Asia, and the Middle East. As a result, promoting democracy in these regions may trigger a domestic political backlash that targets the local U.S. military presence, as has been the case in Central Asia.

The second trade-off that confronts U.S. planners is the low level of political commitment by the United States to new base hosts that results from the initial low investments made in new-style bases.[38] The move away from heavy bases to a network of lighter FOSs and CSLs affords U.S. officials far fewer mechanisms (i.e., aid guarantees and promises of economic development in base-hosting locales) to offer base hosts as concessions. As a result, U.S. officials will find it increasingly difficult to provide sufficient quid pro quo to guarantee base access, especially in an era when growing democratic oversight may restrict U.S. negotiators' ability to secure regime compliance by disbursing private goods to host elites. On the other hand, the temporary and flexible nature of these new facilities will make it more difficult for U.S. officials to convince potentially welcoming base hosts that U.S. forces are willing to commit for a long-term stay.

Globalizing processes will further magnify these democratization tensions and low-commitment problems. First, the greater political openness, transparency, and information flows brought by globalization will empower the media, civic groups, and the political opposition within base hosts to scrutinize the terms of basing agreements. U.S. officials will find it increasingly difficult to publicly conceal the terms and purpose of the U.S. military presence, even if these facilities are not officially American bases or are located in geographically remote areas. Second, the technological advances in communications and information technology brought about

36. Mansfield and Snyder 2005; Snyder 2000.
37. See Vachudova 2005.
38. I am thankful to Dan Nexon for our discussions on this issue.

by globalization are likely to accelerate antibase mobilization and agenda setting within and across different base hosts. As the Korean and Okinawan cases have shown, contemporary social movements have proven remarkably adept at using information technology and new media outlets to mount highly effective antibase campaigns. Third, growing worldwide anti-Americanism, both in the political and cultural spheres, will make it more difficult for a country's elite to justify hosting U.S. deployments purely in support of U.S. goals. In turn, this situation will further push local elites to demand additional quid pro quo for base access, which may not be readily available to U.S. negotiators.

Beyond Common Purpose: Engaging the Micropolitics of Security Partners
How, then, should U.S. policymakers cope with these political trade-offs and globalizing pressures? One prominent argument made by policymakers and security scholars is that the United States' current unilateralism and fixation with retaining operational flexibility, as embodied in the GDPR, may erode the sense of common interest that has bonded the United States politically to its traditional allies and base hosts.[39] According to this view, reestablishing a sense of mutual purpose and common identification with its security partners is essential if the United States is to retain its authority as a global leader. Yet, as the cases in this book have consistently shown, even staunch U.S. allies during the Cold War supported the U.S. basing network because they derived other domestic political benefits that were often unrelated to the U.S. national security agenda. Besides, it would be difficult to formulate one overriding common global threat, barring the activities of militant Islamic movements in certain areas, that would unite base hosts scattered across disparate continents and regions.

The overarching priority of U.S. policymakers should not be to articulate another new grand strategy or set of global guiding principles. Rather it is to manage more adeptly the micropolitics and new domestic political challenges that arise *within* its partners and that could adversely affect the bilateral security relationship. This purpose will require that U.S. policymakers better anticipate domestic institutional changes in individual base hosts and regions, especially waves of democratization, and assess and prepare for how these are likely to affect the status of U.S. security contracts. It also suggests three specific recommendations:

39. See Campbell and Ward 2003. See also Overseas Basing Commission 2005, 8–11.

First, U.S. diplomats and military planners should politically hedge or maintain contacts with multiple groups and political actors within base hosts, not just the governing regime. Exclusively aligning with and supporting a ruling regime risk alienating political opposition movements or future democratizing forces that might later come to power and abrogate security deals. Further, U.S. policymakers should remain cautious of host-country elites who try to prevent such hedging strategies by labeling political opponents as internal security threats or opponents of U.S. interests.

★ Syria

Second, when possible, U.S. officials should encourage a host country to democratically ratify the presence of U.S. troops or installations. This proceeding flies in the face of current tendencies to rely on informal agreements and more ambiguous legal arrangements. However, even if ratification initially draws public attention to the U.S. presence and generates a lively or controversial debate about its contractual terms, over the long term it will provide critical procedural legitimacy and guarantee a more stable commitment from the host. A ratified fixed-term commitment is more politically reliable than an unsanctioned ad hoc or informal arrangement.

Third, U.S. officials should discard the long-held doctrine that the United States should not pay for overseas basing facilities. Negotiators from actual and potential base hosts will demand quid pro quo for base rights, regardless of this long-standing, and often counterproductive, official U.S. position, especially as the negotiators obtain information about tacit agreements made with other hosts. Moreover, when dealing with an authoritarian regime it would be preferable for the United States to publicly specify a quid pro quo for its base rights, rather than lose its international credibility by endorsing the internal practices of a repressive regime (as it did with Uzbekistan). Similarly, offering an actual compensation package as a base bargain is preferable to providing private goods to a regime that later could jeopardize the legality and legitimacy of the contract, as was the case with the Kyrgyz fuel deals. U.S. officials should draw up a comprehensive list of nonmilitary aid programs and possible economic carrots, such as trade and investment agreements, that could facilitate negotiations and routinely be offered as part of a base rights package.

To be sure, these are just initial suggestions for better managing base politics in a global era. The task will be made even more difficult by geopolitical competition from other powers, such as Russia with its bases in Central Asia or China in Africa, that have no qualms about strongly backing autocrats in the interests of securing strategic access or energy security.

In the short run, U.S. officials may indeed be more constrained in such bid-
ding wars over autocrats. Over the long term, however, U.S. planners will
benefit far more from anticipating and coping with democratic change
in its base hosts than from preventing such change in order to maintain
short-term base access. Ultimately, integrating new partners into a more
globalized, interconnected, legitimate, and democratic network offers the
most politically appealing and stable solution to the United States' security needs.

References

Abramowitz, Morton I. 1993. "Dateline Ankara: Turkey after Ozal." *Foreign Policy* no. 91 (Summer): 164–81.

Abrams, Jim. 1981. "Okinawa Remains an Unwilling Host to U.S. Military Bases." *New York Times*, June 28, 17.

Adamson, Fiona. 2001. "Democratization and the Domestic Sources of Foreign Policy: Turkey in the 1974 Cyprus Crisis." *Political Science Quarterly* 116, no. 2 (Summer): 277–303.

——. 2002. "International Democracy Assistance in Uzbekistan and Kyrgyzstan: Building Civil Society from the Outside?" In *The Power and Limits of NGOs*, ed. John K. Glenn and Sarah E. Mendelson. New York: Columbia University Press.

Adler, Emanuel, and Michael Barnett, eds. 2002. *Security Communities*. New York: Cambridge University Press.

Ahmad, Feroz. 1977. *The Turkish Experiment in Democracy, 1950–1975*. Boulder: Westview Press.

Akbarzadeh, Shahram. 2005. *Uzbekistan and the United States: Authoritarianism, Islamism and Washington's Security Agenda*. New York: ZED.

Aldous, Christopher. 2003a. "Achieving Reversion: Protest and Authority in Okinawa, 1952–70." *Modern Asian Studies* 37, no. 2: 485–508.

——. 2003b. "'Mob Rule' or Popular Activism? The Koza Riot of 1970 and the Okinawan Search for Citizenship." In *Japan and Okinawa: Structure and Subjectivity*, ed. Glen D. Hook and Richard Siddle, 148–66. New York: RoutledgeCurzon.

Aldrich, Robert, and John Connell. 1998. *The Last Colonies*. New York: Cambridge University Press.

Altinay, Ayse Gul, and Amy Holmes. 2008. "Opposition to the U.S. Military Presence in Turkey in the Context of the Iraq War." In *The Bases of Empire: The Global Struggle against U.S. Military Posts*, ed. Catherine Lutz. London: Pluto Press.

Amaral, Carlos E. Pacheco. 1992. "The Azores and the Azoreans: Perspectives on the Self." *Camões Center Quarterly* 3, nos. 3–4 (Winter): 13–23.

Anderson, Lisa, ed. 1999. *Transitions to Democracy*. New York: Columbia University Press.

Andrews, David M., ed. 2005. *The Atlantic Alliance under Stress: U.S.-European Relations after Iraq*. New York: Cambridge University Press.

Antunes, José Freire. 1999. "Kennedy, Portugal, and the Azores Base, 1961." In *John F. Kennedy and Europe*, ed. Douglas Brinkley and Richard T. Griffiths, 148–65. Baton Rouge: Louisiana State University Press.

Archer, Clive. 2003. "Greenland, U.S. Bases and Missile Defence: New Two-Level Negotiations?" *Cooperation and Conflict* 38, no. 2 (June): 125–47.

Arkin, William M., and Richard W. Fieldhouse. 1985. *Nuclear Battlefields: Global Links in the Arms Race*. Cambridge, MA: Ballinger.

Armacost, Michael H., and Daniel I. Okimoto, eds. 2004. *The Future of America's Alliances in Northeast Asia*. Stanford: Stanford University Asia-Pacific Research Center.

Asmus, Ronald. 2003. "Rebuilding the Transatlantic Alliance." *Foreign Affairs* 82, no. 5 (September–October): 20–31.

Associated Press. 2006. "Bulgaria and U.S. Agree to Base Deal." March 24.

——. 2007. "Romanian Parliament Approves Stationing of U.S. Troops in Romania." May 2.

Avant, Deborah. 2005. *The Market for Force*. New York: Cambridge University Press.

——. 2006. "The Implications of Marketized Security for IR Theory: The Democratic Peace, Late State-Building, and the Nature and Frequency of Conflict." *Perspectives on Politics* 4, no. 3 (September): 507–28.

Bacevich, Andrew J. 2002. *American Empire: The Realities and Consequences of American Diplomacy*. Cambridge: Harvard University Press.

Baev, Pavel. 2005. "Russia's Counterrevolutionary Offensive in Central Asia." Russian and Eurasia Program: Center for Strategic and International Studies, PONARS Policy Memo 339. December, 199–204.

Baker, Anni P. 2004. *American Soldiers Overseas: The Global Military Presence*. Westport, CT: Praeger.

Baldacchino, Godfrey. 2004. "Autonomous but Not Sovereign? A Review of Sub-Island Nationalism." *Canadian Review of Studies in Nationalism* 33, nos. 1–2: 77–89.

Ball, Desmond. 1980. *A Suitable Piece of Real Estate: American Installations in Australia*. Sydney: Hale and Iremonger.

——. 2001. "The U.S.-Australian Alliance." In *U.S. Allies in a Changing World*, ed. Barry Rubin and Thomas Keaney, 248–79. Portland, OR: Frank Cass.

Bamford, James. 1983. *The Puzzle Palace: Inside the National Security Agency America's Most Secret Intelligence Organization*. New York: Penguin.

——. 2002. *Body of Secrets: Anatomy of the Ultra-Secret National Security Agency*. New York: Anchor.

Banlaoi, Rommel C. 2002. "The Role of the Philippine-American Relations in the Global Campaign against Terrorism: Implications for Regional Security." *Contemporary Southeast Asia* 24, no. 2 (August): 294–312.

Barkey, Henri. 2000. "Hemmed in by Circumstances: Turkey and Iraq since the Gulf War." *Middle East Policy* 7, no. 4 (October): 110–26.

Barnett, Thomas P. M. 2004. *The Pentagon's New Map: War and Peace in the 21st Century*. New York: Berkley Books.

——. 2005. *Blueprint for Action: A Future Worth Creating*. New York: Putnam Adult.

——. 2007. "Africa Command: The Americans Have Landed." *Esquire* (July 2007): 113–17, 134–37.

Barth, Mustafa. 2003. "Sand Castles in the Sahara: U.S. Military Basing in Algeria." *Review of African Political Economy* 30, no. 98 (December): 679–85.

Baxter, R. R. 1958. "Criminal Jurisdiction in the NATO Status of Forces Agreement." *International and Comparative Law Quarterly* 7, no. 1: 72–81.

BBC News. 2002. "U.S. Naval Base to Protect Sao Tome Oil." August 22.

——. 2003. "U.S. Troops 'To Fight' in Philippines." February 21.

——. 2005. "Spain Quizzes U.S. over CIA Flights." November 17.

——. 2006. "U.S. Hands Sailor over to Japanese." January 7.

Beissinger, Mark R. 2002. *Nationalist Mobilization and the Collapse of the Soviet State.* New York: Cambridge University Press.

——. 2007. "Structure and Example in Modular Political Phenomena: The Diffusion of Bulldozer/Rose/Orange/Tulip Revolutions." *Perspectives on Politics* 5, no. 2 (June): 259–76.

Belasco, Amy. 2006. "The Cost of Iraq, Afghanistan, and Other Global War on Terror Operations since 9/11." *CRS Report for Congress.* Washington, DC. April 24.

Bello, Walden. 1991. "Moment of Decision: The Philippines, the Pacific, and the U.S. Bases." In *The Sun Never Sets: Confronting the Network of Foreign U.S. Military Bases,* ed. Joseph Gerson and Bruce Birchard, 149–66. Boston: South End Press.

Bengzon, Alfredo. 1997. *A Matter of Honor: The Story of the 1990–91 RP-US Bases Treaty.* Manila: Anvil Books.

Berger, Marilyn. 1975. "Turkey Orders Halt in Activities at U.S. Bases." *Washington Post,* July 26.

Berger, Thomas U. 1998. *Cultures of Antimilitarism: National Security in Germany and Germany.* Baltimore: Johns Hopkins University Press.

Bermeo, Nancy. 1988. "Regime Change and Its Impact on Foreign Policy: The Portuguese Case." *Journal of Modern Greek Studies* 6, no. 1 (May): 7–25.

Berry, William E. 1988. "The Military Bases and Postwar U.S.-Philippine Relations." In *The Philippine Bases: Negotiating for the Future,* ed. Fred Greene. New York: Council on Foreign Relations.

——. 1989. *U.S. Bases in the Philippines: The Evolution of the Special Relationship.* Boulder: Westview Press.

Binder, David. 1975. "U.S., in Message to Lisbon, Says Move Left Is a Danger to NATO." *New York Times,* March 27, 2.

Blagov, Sergei. 2003. "Moscow Marches into Kyrgyzstan." *Asia Times,* September 24. http://www.atimes.com/atimes/Central_Asia/EI24Ag01.html.

——. 2005. "Uzbekistan and Russia Sign Mutual Defense Pact." *Eurasia Insight,* November 15. http://www.eurasianet.org/departments/insight/articles/eav111505.shtml (accessed May 2007).

Blaker, James. 1990. *United States Overseas Basing: The Anatomy of the Dilemma.* Westport, CT: Praeger.

Blank, Stephen. 2006. "China Makes Policy Shift, Aiming to Widen Access to Central Asian Energy." *Eurasianet,* March 13. http://www.eurasianet.org/departments/business/articles/eav031306.shtml (accessed May 2007).

Blyth, Mark, and Richard Katz. 2005. "From Catch-All Politics to Cartelization: The Political Economy of the Cartel Party." *West European Politics* 28, no. 1 (January): 33–60.

Bochsler, Daniel. 2005. "The 'Normalisation' of Party Systems and Voting Behavior in Eastern Europe." *Romanian Journal of Political Science* 5, no. 1 (Spring–Summer): 53–74.

Bohn, Michael K. 2004. *The Achille Lauro Hijacking: Lessons in the Politics and Prejudice of Terrorism.* Washington, DC: Brassey's.

Boix, Carles, and James Alt. 1991. "Partisan Voting in the 1986 Spanish NATO Refer-endum: An Ecological Analysis." *Electoral Studies* 10, no. 1 (March): 18–32.

Bonner, Raymond. 1988. *Waltzing with a Dictator: The Marcoses and the Making Of Amer-ican Policy*. New York: Vintage.

Broad, Robin. 1990. *Unequal Alliance: The World Bank, The International Monetary Fund, and the Philippines*. Berkeley: University of California Press.

Brogi, Alessandro. 2002a. "Ike and Italy: The Eisenhower Administration and Italy's "Neo-Atlanticist Agenda." *Journal of Cold War Studies* 4, no. 3 (Summer): 5–35.

———. 2002b. *A Question of Self-Esteem: The United States and the Cold War Choices in France and Italy, 1944–1958*. Westport, CT: Praeger.

Brown, Stephen. 2007. "U.S. Base Protest Poses Dilemma for Italian Left." *Reuters*, February 14.

Bruce, James. 1996. "Erbakan Renews OPC Mandate." *Jane's Intelligence Review*, October 1.

Bueno de Mesquita, Bruce, Alistair Smith, Randolph M. Siverson, and James D. Morrow. 2003. *The Logic of Political Survival*. Cambridge, MA: MIT Press.

Bunce, Valerie. 2003. "Rethinking Recent Democratization: Lessons from the Post-communist Experience." *World Politics* 55, no. 2 (January): 167–92.

Bunce, Valerie J., and Sharon L. Wolchik. 2006. "International Diffusion and Postcom-munist Electoral Revolutions." *Communist and Post-Communist Studies* 39, no. 3 (Sep-tember): 283–304.

Burns, Tom. 1987. "Spain Rejects U.S. Proposal for Renewal of Base Pact." *Washington Post*, February 5, A25.

Calder, Kent E. 1988. *Crisis and Compensation: Public Policy and Political Stability in Japan, 1949–1986*. Princeton: Princeton University Press.

———. 2003. "The Outlier Alliance: U.S.-Japan Security Ties in Comparative Perspec-tive." *Korean Journal of Defense Analysis* 15, no. 2 (Fall): 31–55.

———. 2006. "Beneath the Eagle's Wings? The Political Economy of Northeast Asian Burden-Sharing in Comparative Perspective." *Asian Security* 2, no. 3 (December): 148–73.

Calvet de Magalhães, José. 1993. "U.S. Forces in Portugal, 1943–1962." In *U.S. Military Forces in Europe: The Early Years, 1945–1970*, ed. Simon Duke and Wolfgang Krieger, 273–81. Boulder: Westview Press.

Calvo-Sotelo, Leopoldo. 1990. *Memoria viva de la transición* [Living memory of the transition]. Barcelona: Planeta.

Campbell, Kurt M., and Celeste Johnson Ward. 2003. "New Battle Stations?" *Foreign Affairs* 82, no. 5 (September–October): 95–103.

Cassese, Antonio. 1989. *Terrorism, Politics and Law: The Achille Lauro Affair*. Princeton: Princeton University Press.

Castro, Pacifico A., ed. 1985. *Agreements on United States Military Facilities in Philippine Military Bases, 1947–1985*. Manila: Foreign Service Institute.

Castro-Guevara, Marita, ed. 1997. *The Bases Talks Reader: Key Documents of the 1990–91 Philippine-American Cooperation Talks*. Manila: Anvil Books.

Cha, Victor D. 1999. *Alignment Despite Antagonism: The U.S.-Korea-Japan Security Tri-angle*. Stanford: Stanford University Press.

———. 2000. "Abandonment, Entrapment, and Neoclassical Realism in Asia: The United States, Japan, and Korea." *International Studies Quarterly* 44, no. 2: 261–91.

———. 2003. "Security and Democracy in South Korean Development." In *Korea's Democ-ratization*, ed. Samuel S. Kim, 201–19. New York: Cambridge University Press.

———. 2004. "Shaping Change and Cultivating Ideas in the U.S.-ROK Alliance." In *The Future of America's Alliances in Northeast Asia*, ed. Michael H. Armacost and Daniel I. Okimoto, 121–46. Stanford: Stanford University Asia-Pacific Research Center.

———. 2005. "Anti-Americanism and the U.S. Role in Inter-Korean Relations." In *Korean Attitudes towards the United States*, ed. David I. Steinberg, 116–38. Armonk, NY: M. E. Sharpe.

Chai, Sun-Ki. 1997. "Entrenching the Yoshida Defense Doctrine: Three Techniques for Institutionalization." *International Organization* 51, no. 3 (Summer): 389–412.

Chandrasekaran, Rajiv. 2006. *Imperial Life in the Emerald City: Inside Iraq's Green Zone.* New York: Knopf.

Chicago Tribune. 2006. "Afghanistan Lawmakers Urge Trial in Hit-Run Case." May 31, 15.

Chivers, C. J., and Thom Shanker. 2005. "Uzbek Ministries in Crackdown Received U.S. Aid." *New York Times,* June 18, A1.

Ciampi, Annalisa. 1999. "Public Prosecutor v. Ashby: Judgment No. 161-98." *American Journal of International Law* 93, no. 1 (January): 219–24.

Civil Network for a Peaceful Korea. 2004. "Appeals for Peace in Korea and Northeast Asia." Pamphlet. Seoul: CNPK.

Clarke, Duncan L., and Daniel O'Connor. 1993. "U.S. Base Rights Payments after the Cold War." *Orbis* 37, no. 3 (Summer): 441–57.

Clifford, Mark L. 1998. *Troubled Tiger: Businessmen, Bureaucrats and Generals in South Korea.* Armonk, NY: M. E. Sharpe.

Cloud, David. 2005. "Pentagon's Fuel Deal Is Lesson in Risks of Graft-Prone Regions." *New York Times,* November 15.

Cohen, Sam. 1969. "6th Fleet Stirs up Turk Resentments." *Washington Post,* February 17, A19.

Collins, Kathleen. 2006. *The Logic of Clan Politics in Central Asia: The Impact on Regime Transformation.* New York: Cambridge University Press.

Colomer, Josep. 1991. "Transitions by Agreement: Modeling the Spanish Way." *American Political Science Review* 85, no. 4 (September): 1283–1302.

Columbant, Nico. 2004. "Sao Tome Sparks American Military Interest." Voice of America News, November 12. http://www.voanews.com/english/archive/2004-11/2004-11-12-voa42.cfm?CFID=16320549&CFTOKEN=46206534 (accessed May 2007).

Conde, Carlos. 2006. "Military Cutoff by U.S. Draws Filipino Anger." *New York Times,* December 23, A12.

Cook, Don. 1975. "Alliance Secrets in Jeopardy: Red Power in Portugal Perils NATO." *Los Angeles Times,* March 18, A1.

Cooley, Alexander. 2000. "International Aid to the Former Soviet States: Agent of Change or Guardian of the Status Quo?" *Problems of Post-Communism* 47, no. 4 (July–August): 34–44.

———. 2000–2001. "Imperial Wreckage: Property Rights, Sovereignty and Security in the Post-Soviet Space." *International Security* 25, no. 1 (Winter): 100–127.

———. 2003. "Western Conditions and Domestic Choices: The Influence of External Actors on the Post-Communist Transition." In *Nations in Transit 2003: Democratization in East Central Europe and Eurasia,* ed. Adrian Karatnycky, Alexander Motyl, and Amanda Schnetzer. Lanham, MD: Rowman and Littlefield.

———. 2005a. "Base Politics." *Foreign Affairs* 84, no. 6 (November–December): 79–92.

———. 2005b. "Democratization and the Contested Politics of U.S. Military Bases in Korea: Towards a Comparative Understanding." *IRI Review* 10, no. 2 (Autumn): 201–29.

———. 2005c. "Depoliticizing Manas: The Domestic Consequences of the U.S. Military Presence in Kyrgyzstan." PONARS Policy Memo 362. February 2005. http://www.csis.org/media/csis/pubs/pm_0362.pdf.

——. 2005d. *Logics of Hierarchy: The Organization of Empires, States, and Military Occupations*. Ithaca: Cornell University Press.

Cooley, Alexander, and Jonathan Hopkin. 2006. "Party Politics and Base Politics: The Rise and Decline of the Military Base Issue in Spain, 1975–2005." Manuscript. Barnard College and the London School of Economics.

Cooley, Alexander, and Kimberly Marten. 2006. "Base Motives: The Political Economy of Okinawa's Antimilitarism." *Armed Forces and Society* 32, no. 4 (July): 566–83.

Cooley, Alexander, and Hendrik Spruyt. 2003. "The Political Economy of U.S. Overseas Basing Arrangements: Incomplete Contracts, Specific Assets and Renegotiation." Paper presented to the 99th meeting of the American Political Science Association, Philadelphia. August 30.

——. 2006. "Between Hierarchy and Anarchy: Incomplete Contracts and Negotiations over Sovereign Rights." Paper presented to the Princeton Institute for International and Regional Studies. February 20.

Cornell, Svante E. 2004. "The United States and Central Asia: In the Steppes to Stay?" *Cambridge Review of International Affairs* 17, no. 2 (July): 239–54.

Corso, Molly. 2005. "Some in Georgia Worry That the Russian Base Withdrawal Comes with a Catch." *Eurasia Insight*, June 1. http://www.eurasianet.org/depart ments/insight/articles/eav060105.shtml (accessed May 2007).

Couloumbis, Theodore A. 1966. *Greek Political Reaction to American and NATO Influence*. New Haven: Yale University Press.

——. 1993. "PASOK's Foreign Policies, 1981–1989: Continuity or Change," in *Greece, 1981–1989: The Populist Decade*, ed. Richard Clogg, 113–39. London: Macmillan.

Crawley, Vince. 2007. "U.S. Creating New Africa Command to Coordinate Military Efforts." USINFO, February 6. http://www.globalsecurity.org/military/library/ news/2007/02/mil-070206-usia02.htm (accessed May 2007).

Cremasco, Maurizio. 1988. "Italy: A New Role in the Mediterranean?" In *NATO's Southern Allies: Internal and External Challenges*, ed. John Chipman, 195–235. New York: Routledge.

——. 2001. "Italy and the Management of International Crises." In *Alliance Politics, Kosovo, and NATO's War: Allied Force or Forced Allies?* ed. Pierre Martin and Mark R. Brawley, 165–80. London: Palgrave.

Criss, Nur Bilge. 1993. "U.S. Forces in Turkey." In *U.S. Military Forces in Europe: The Early Years, 1945–70*, ed. Simon Duke and Wolfgang Krieger, 331–50. Boulder: Westview Press.

——. 1997. "Strategic Nuclear Missiles in Turkey: The Jupiter Affair, 1959–1963," *Journal of Strategic Studies* 20, no. 34 (September): 97–122.

——. 2002. "A Short History of Anti-Americanism and Terrorism: The Turkish Case." *Journal of American History* 89, no. 2 (September): 472–84.

Croci, Osvaldo. 2003. "Italian Security Policy after the Cold War." *Journal of Modern Italian Studies* 8, no. 2 (June): 266–83.

Crollen, Luc. 1973. *Portugal, the U.S. and NATO*. Leuven, Belgium: Leuven University Press.

Cullather, Nick, ed. 1992. *Managing Nationalism: United States National Security Council Documents on the Philippines, 1953–1960*. Quezon City, Philippines: New Day Publishers.

——. 1994. *Illusions of Influence: The Political Economy of United States–Philippine Relations, 1942–1960*. Stanford: Stanford University Press.

Cumings, Bruce. 1992. "Silent but Deadly: Sexual Subordination in the U.S.-Korea Relationship." In *Let the Good Times Role: Prostitution and the U.S. Military in Asia*, ed. Saundra Pollock Sturdevant and Brenda Stoltzfus, 169–75. New York: New Press.

——. 1997. *Korea's Place in the Sun: A Modern History*. New York: W. W. Norton.

——. 2005. "The Structural Basis of 'Anti-Americanism' in the Republic of Korea." In *Korean Attitudes toward the United States: Changing Dynamics*, ed. David I. Steinberg, 96–115. Armonk, NY: M. E. Sharpe.

Curtis, Gerald L. 1988. *The Japanese Way of Politics*. New York: Columbia University Press.

——. 1999. *The Logic of Japanese Politics: Leaders, Institutions and the Limits of Change*. New York: Columbia University Press.

Curtis, Gerald L., and Sung-Joo Han, eds. 1983. *The U.S.–South Korean Alliance*. Lexington, MA: Lexington Books.

Daalder, Ivo. 2003. "The End of Atlanticism." *Survival* 45, no. 2 (Summer): 147–66.

Dabrowski, John L. 1996. "The United States, NATO and the Spanish Bases, 1949–1989." Ph.D. dissertation, Department of History, Kent State University.

Daly, John K. 2007. "U.S. Air Base at Manas at Risk over Shooting Suspect?" *Eurasia Daily Monitor*, May 4. http://jamestown.org/edm/article.php?article_id=2372144 (accessed May 2007).

Danielsson, Bengt. 1990. "Poisoned Pacific: The Legacy of French Nuclear Testing." *Bulletin of the Atomic Scientists* 46, no. 2 (March): 22–31.

Davis, Robin L. 1988. "Waiver and Recall of Primary Jurisdiction in Germany." *Army Lawyer* 30 (May): 30–35.

De Castro, Renato Cruz. 2003. "The Revitalized Philippine-U.S. Security Relations: A Ghost from the Cold War or an Alliance for the 21st Century?" *Asian Survey* 43, no. 6 (November–December): 971–88.

——. 2005. "Philippine Defense Policy in the 21st Century: Autonomous Defense or Back to Alliance?" *Pacific Affairs* 78, no. 63 (Fall): 403–22.

——. 2006. "Twenty-First Century Philippine-American Security Relations: Managing an Alliance in the War of the Third Kind." *Asian Security* 2, no. 2 (August): 102–21.

Delbrück, Jost. 1993. "International Law and Military Forces Abroad: U.S. Military Presence in Europe, 1945–1965." In *U.S. Military Forces in Europe: The Early Years, 1945–1970*, ed. Simon W. Duke and Wolfgang Krieger, 83–115. Boulder: Westview Press.

Del Campo, Salustiano, and Juan Manuel Camacho. 2003. *Spanish Public Opinion and Foreign Policy*. Madrid: Instituto de Cuestiones Internacionales y Politica Exterior (INCIPE).

Desch, Michael C. 1989. "The Keys That Lock up the World: Identifying American Interests in the Periphery." *International Security* 14, no. 1 (Summer): 86–121.

——. 1992. "Bases for the Future: U.S. Post–Cold War Military Requirements in the Third World." *Security Studies* 2, no. 2 (Winter): 201–24.

Destler, I. M., Priscilla Clapp, Hideo Sato, and Haruhiro Fukui. 1976. *Managing an Alliance: The Politics of U.S.-Japanese Relations*. Washington, DC: Brookings Institution.

Diamandouros, P. Nikiforos. 1986. "Regime Change and the Prospects for Democracy in Greece: 1974–1983." In *Transitions from Authoritarian Rule: Southern Europe*, ed. Guillermo O'Donnell, Philippe C. Schmitter, and Laurance Whitehead, 138–64. Baltimore: Johns Hopkins University Press.

Diamond, Larry. 2005. *Squandered Victory: The American Occupation and Bungled Effort to Bring Democracy to Iraq*. New York: Owl Books.

Diamond, Larry, and Richard Gunther, eds. 2001. *Political Parties and Democracy*. Baltimore: Johns Hopkins University Press.

Diamond, Larry, and Doh Chull Shin, eds. 2000. *Institutional Reform and Democratic Consolidation in Korea*. Stanford: Hoover Institution Press.

Dower, John W. 1999. *Embracing Defeat: Japan in the Wake of World War II*. New York: W. W. Norton.

Downs, Anthony. 1957. *An Economic Theory of Democracy*. New York: Harper and Row.

Doyle, Michael. 1986. *Empires*. Ithaca: Cornell University Press.

Dragsdahl, Jørgen. 2005. "Denmark and Greenland: American Defences and Domestic Agendas." *Contemporary Security Policy* 26, no. 3 (December): 486–504.

Drake, Waldo. 1958. "Turkey's Deficiencies as a Western Defense Anchor." *Los Angeles Times*, February 16, B5.

Dratch, Howard D. 1975. "High Stakes in the Azores." *Nation*, November 8, 455.

Drennan, William M. 2005. "The Tipping Point: Kwangju, May 1980." In *Korean Attitudes towards the United States*, ed. David I. Steinberg, 280–306. Armonk, NY: M. E. Sharpe.

Drezner, Daniel. 1999. *The Sanctions Paradox: Economic Statecraft and International Relations*. New York: Cambridge University Press.

Druckman, Daniel. 1986. "Stages, Turning Points, and Crises: Negotiating Military Base Rights, Spain and the United States." *Journal of Conflict Resolution* 30, no. 2 (June): 327–60.

Duke, Simon. 1987. *U.S. Defence Bases in the United Kingdom: A Matter for Joint Decision?* Basingstoke, UK: Macmillan.

———. 1989. *United States Military Forces and Installations in Europe*. New York: Oxford University Press.

Duke, Simon, and Wolfgang Krieger, eds. 1993. *U.S. Military Forces in Europe: The Early Years, 1945–1970*. Boulder: Westview Press.

Dunning, Thad. 2004. "Conditioning the Effects of Aid: Cold War Politics, Donor Credibility and Democracy in Africa." *International Organization* 58, no. 3 (Spring): 79–98.

Economist. 2003. "South Korea's Press: A Question of Distortion." April 17, 58–60.

———. 2007. "Overpaid to Move over Here: American Forces in Japan." February 24, 61.

Egami, Takayoshi. 1994. "Politics in Okinawa since the Reversion of Sovereignty." *Asian Survey* 34, no. 9 (September): 828–40.

Egan, John W. 2006. "The Future of Criminal Jurisdiction over the Deployed American Soldier: Four Major Trends in Bilateral U.S. Status of Forces Agreements." *Emory International Law Review* 20 (Spring): 291–344.

Eichelman, Mark E. 2000. "International Criminal Jurisdiction Issues for the United States Military," *Army Lawyer* no. 10 (August): 23–32.

EIU Viewswire. 2004. "Djibouti Economy: Region Is the Main Recipient of U.S. Aid in Africa." May 4.

Eldridge, Robert D. 1997. "The 1996 Okinawa Referendum on U.S. Base Reductions: One Question, Several Answers." *Asian Survey* 37, no. 10 (October 1997): 879–904.

———. 2000. "Okinawa and the Nago Heliport Problem in the U.S.-Japan Relationship." *Asia-Pacific Review* 7, no. 1 (May): 137–56.

———. 2001. *The Origins of the Bilateral Okinawa Problem: Okinawa in Postwar U.S.-Japan Relations, 1945–1952*. New York: Garland.

———. 2004. "Post-Reversion Okinawa and U.S. Japan Relations: A Preliminary Survey of Local Politics and the Bases." Osaka: School for International and Public Policy, University of Osaka.

England, Andrew. 2002. "U.S. Military Grows in Djibouti." Associated Press, September 30.

Enloe, Cynthia. 2001. *Bananas, Beaches and Bases: Making Feminist Sense of International Politics*. Berkeley: University of California Press.

Epstein, Rachel. 2005. "NATO Enlargement and the Spread of Democracy: Evidence and Expectations." *Security Studies* 14, no. 1 (October): 63–105.

Erickson, Richard J. 1994. "Status of Forces Agreements: A Sharing of Sovereign Prerogative." *Air Force Law Review* 37:137–53.

Eurasia Insight Report. 2005. "Bakiyev Wins Landslide Victory, Courts Controversy with the United States." http://www.eurasianet.org/departments/insight/articles/eav071105.shtml (accessed May 2007).

European Parliament. 2007. *Report on the Alleged Use of European Countries by the CIA for the Transportation and Illegal Detention of Prisoners.* Brussels. January 31. http://www.europarl.europa.eu/comparl/tempcom/tdip/final_report_en.pdf (accessed May 2007).

Evans, Peter, Harold Jacobson, and Robert Putnam, eds. 1993. *Double-Edged Diplomacy: International Bargaining and Domestic Politics.* Berkeley: University of California Press.

Facon, Patrick. 1993. "U.S. Forces in France." In *U.S. Military Forces in Europe: The Early Years, 1945–1970,* ed. Simon W. Duke and Wolfgang Krieger, 233–47. Boulder: Westview Press.

Fearon, James. 1994. "Domestic Political Audiences and the Escalation of International Disputes." *American Political Science Review* 88, no. 3 (September): 577–92.

———. 1997. "Signaling Foreign Policy Interests: Tying Hands versus Sinking Costs." *Journal of Conflict Resolution* 41, no. 1 (February): 68–90.

Feith, Douglas J. 2004. "Prepared Statement before the House Armed Services Committee." Washington, DC. June 23. http://merln.ndu.edu/merln/pfiraq/archive/dod/sp20040623–0522.pdf (accessed May 2007).

Ferguson, Niall. 2002. *Empire: The Rise and Demise of the British World Order and the Lessons for Global Power.* New York: Basic Books.

———. 2004. *Colossus: The Price of America's Empire.* New York: Penguin Press.

Fields, Todd W. 2004. "Eastward Bound: The Strategy and Politics of Repositioning U.S. Military Bases in Europe." *Journal of Public and International Affairs* 15 (Spring): 79–98.

Financial Times. 1988. "Future of U.S. Bases: Strained Links in the Chain of Allies' Security." September 30.

Fisher, Ian. 2007. "A Still-Vulnerable Prodi Gets a Second Chance to Lead Italy." *New York Times,* February 24, 8.

Flynn, James Roberts. 2001. "Preserving the Hub: U.S.-Thai Relations during the Vietnam War, 1961–1976." Ph.D. dissertation, Department of History, University of Kentucky.

Foreign Broadcast and Information Service (FBIS). 2002. "Spanish Parliament Backs Defence Accord with the United States." Madrid ABC. Reprinted in *FBIS,* April 10.

Fowler, James. 1999. "The United States and South Korean Democratization." *Political Science Quarterly* 114, no. 2 (Summer): 265–88.

Francis, Carolyn Bowen. 1999. "Women and Military Violence." In *Okinawa: Cold War Island,* ed. Chalmers Johnson, 189–203. Cardiff, CA: Japan Research Policy Institute.

Francis, David. 2004. "U.S. Bases in Iraq: Sticky Politics, Hard Math." *Christian Science Monitor,* September 30.

Funabashi, Yoichi. 1999. *Alliance Adrift.* New York: Council on Foreign Relations.

Gabe, Masaaki. 2000. "Futenma Air Station: The Okinawa Problem in Japan-U.S. Relations." *Japan Echo* (June): 19–24.

———. 2003. "It Is High Time to Wake-Up: Japanese Foreign Policy in the Twenty-First Century." In *Japan and Okinawa: Structure and Subjectivity,* ed. Glen D. Hook and Richard Siddle, 55–73. New York: RoutledgeCurzon.

Gall, Carlotta. 2005. "Afghan Delegates Agree on the Need for Foreign Troops." *New York Times*, May 9, A3.

Gallagher, Tom. 1979. "Portugal's Atlantic Territories: The Separatist Challenge." *World Today* 35, no. 9 (September): 353–59.

———. 1983. *Portugal: A Twentieth-Century Interpretation*. Manchester, UK: University of Manchester Press.

Gardner, Richard N. 2005. *Mission Italy: On the Front Lines of the Cold War*. Lanham, MD: Rowman and Littlefield.

Giarra, Paul S. 1999. "U.S. Bases in Japan: Historical Background and Innovative Approaches to Maintaining Strategic Presence." In *The U.S.-Japan Alliance: Past, Present and Future*, ed. Michael J. Green and Patrick M. Cronin, 114–38. New York: Council on Foreign Relations.

Gillem, Mark L. 2004. "America Town: Building the Outposts of Empire." Ph.D. dissertation, Department of Architecture, University of California Berkeley.

Gleason, Gregory. 2006. "The Uzbek Expulsion of U.S. Forces and Realignment in Central Asia." *Problems of Post-Communism* 53, no. 2 (March–April): 49–60.

Golden, Tim, and Eric Schmitt. 2006. "A Growing Afghan Prison Rivals Bleak Guantanamo." *New York Times*, February 26, A1.

Gorst, Isabel. 2006. "U.S. Facility Faces Eviction from Kyrgyzstan." *Financial Times*, May 19.

Graham, Lawrence S. 1990. "Center-Periphery Relations." In *Portugal: Ancient Country, Young Democracy*, ed. Kenneth Maxwell and Michael H. Haltzel, 23–36. Washington, DC: Wilson Center Press.

Green, Michael J. 2001. *Japan's Reluctant Realism: Foreign Policy Challenges in an Era of Uncertain Power*. New York: Palgrave.

Greene, Fred. 1975. *Stresses in U.S.-Japanese Security Relations*. Washington, DC: Brookings Institution.

Grey, Stephen. 2006. *Ghost Plane: The True Story of the CIA Torture Program*. New York: St. Martin's Press.

Grimmett, Richard. 1986. *U.S. Military Installations in NATO's Southern Region*. Report prepared for the U.S. Congress. Washington, DC.

Gunter, Michael M. 2005. "The U.S.-Turkish Alliance in Disarray." *World Affairs* 167, no. 3 (January): 113–23.

Gunther, Richard, P. Nikiforos Diamandouros, and Hand-Jürge Pule, eds. 1995. *The Politics of Democratic Consolidation: Southern Europe in Comparative Perspective*. Baltimore: Johns Hopkins University Press.

Gunther, Richard, Giacomo Sani, and Goldie Shabad. 1988. *Spain after Franco: The Making of a Competitive Party System*. Berkeley: University of California Press.

Haggard, Stephen. 1990. *Pathways from the Periphery: The Politics of Growth in the Newly Industrialized Countries*. Ithaca: Cornell University Press.

Hallin, Daniel C., and Paolo Mancini. 2004. *Comparing Media Systems: Three Models of Media and Politics*. New York: Cambridge University Press.

Hallinan, Conn. 2006. "Desert Faux: The Sahara's Mirage of Terrorism." *Foreign Policy in Focus*, March 2. http://www.fpif.org/fpiftxt/3136 (accessed May 2007).

Harkavy, Robert. 1989. *Bases Abroad: The Global Foreign Military Presence*. New York: Oxford University Press.

———. 2005. "Thinking about Basing." *Naval War College Review* 58, no. 3 (Summer): 13–42.

Harris, George S. 1972. *Troubled Alliance: Turkish-American Problems in Historical Perspective, 1945–1971*. Washington, DC: ACE-Hoover Policy Studies.

Harvey, Robert. 1978. *Portugal: Birth of a Democracy*. London: Macmillan.

Hemmer, Christopher, and Peter J. Katzenstein. 2002. "Why Is There No NATO in Asia? Collective Identity, Regionalism and the Origins of Multilateralism." *International Organization* 56, no. 3 (Summer): 575–609.

Hendren, Jim. 2002. "Beddown in Bishkek." *Air Force Magazine,* July, 57–60.

Heper, Metin. 2002. "The Consolidation of Democracy versus Democratization in Turkey." *Turkish Studies* 3, no. 1 (Spring): 138–46.

Herz, Norman. 2004. *Operation Alacrity: The Azores and the War in the Atlantic.* Annapolis, MD: Naval Institute Press.

Higa, Mikio. 1963. "Okinawa: Recent Political Developments." *Asian Survey* 3, no. 9 (September): 415–26.

——. 1967. "The Reversion Theme in Current Okinawan Politics." *Asian Survey* 7, no. 3 (March): 151–64.

Hollstein, Mark Clifford. 2000. "Framing Security: A Tri-Cultural Discourse Analysis of Newspaper Reports about the United States Military in Okinawa." Ph.D. dissertation, Department of Political Science, University of Hawaii.

Holman, Otto. 1996. *Integrating Southern Europe: EC Expansion and the Transnationalization of Spain.* New York: Routledge.

Holmes, Amy K. 2006. "Contentious Allies: How Social Movements in Turkey Impacted the American Military Presence." Paper presented to the PIIRS conference at Princeton University. March 19.

Hook, Glenn D., and Richard Siddle, eds. 2003. *Japan and Okinawa: Structure and Subjectivity.* New York: RoutledgeCurzon.

Hookway, James. 2002. "U.S. Troops May Be Unpleasant, but the Abu Sayyaf Are Worse." *Far Eastern Economic Review,* February 7, 16.

——. 2003. "A New Front." *Far Eastern Economic Review,* March 6, 19.

Hopkin, Jonathan. 2004. "From Consensus to Competition: The Changing Nature of Democracy in the Spanish Transition." In *The Politics of Contemporary Spain,* ed. Sebastian Balfour, 6–26. London: Routledge.

Houston Chronicle. 2003. "U.S. Calls off Philippine Deployment." March 1, 29.

Human Rights Watch. 2005a. "Bullets Were Falling Like Rain: The Andijon Massacre, May 13, 2005." Vol. 17, no. 5(D) (June). http://hrw.org/reports/2005/uzbekistan0605/uzbekistan0605.pdf (accessed May 2007).

——. 2005b. "Human Rights Watch Statement on U.S. Secret Detention Facilities in Europe." http://hrw.org/english/docs/2005/11/07/usint11995.htm (accessed May 2007).

Huntington, Samuel. 1993. *The Third Wave: Democratization in the Late Twentieth Century.* Norman: University of Oklahoma Press.

Ikenberry, G. John. 2001. *After Victory: Institutions, Strategic Restraint, and the Rebuilding of Order after Major Wars.* Princeton: Princeton University Press.

——. 2004. "Liberalism and Empire: Logics of Order in the American Unipolar Age." *Review of International Studies* 30, no. 4 (October): 609–30.

Ingimundarson, Valur. 2004. "Immunizing against the American Other: Racism, Nationalism and Gender in U.S.-Icelandic Military Relations during the Cold War." *Journal of Cold War Studies* 6, no. 4 (Fall): 65–88.

Inoue, Masamichi S. 2004. "We Are Okinawans but of a Different Kind." *Current Anthropology* 45, no. 1 (February): 85–104.

Instituto de Cuestiones Internacionales y Politica Exterior (INCIPE). 2003. *Public Opinion and Spanish Foreign Policy.* Madrid: Real Instiututo Elcano.

International Crisis Group. 2005a. "Islamist Terrorism in the Sahel: Fact or Fiction?" *Africa Report* no. 92, March 31.

——. 2005b. "Kyrgyzstan: After the Revolution." *Asia Report* no. 97, May 4.

——. 2005c. "Uzbekistan: The Andijon Uprising." *Asia Briefing* no. 38, May 25.

——. 2006. "Uzbekistan: In for the Long Haul." *Asia Briefing* no. 45, February 16.

International Herald Tribune. 2007. "Thousands Protest U.S. Base Expansion in Northern Italian City." February 17.

Jackson, Patrick T. 2006. *Civilizing the Enemy: German Reconstruction and the Invention of the West.* Ann Arbor: University of Michigan Press.

Jackson, Robert. 1993. "The Weight of Ideas in Decolonization." In *Ideas and Foreign Policy*, ed. Robert Keohane and Judith Goldstein, 111–38. Ithaca: Cornell University Press.

Jain, Purnendra C. 1991. "Green Politics and Citizen Power in Japan: The Citizen Movement." *Asian Survey* 31, no. 6 (June): 559–75.

Japan Economic Newswire. 2006. "Okinawa to Get Extra Grants for Realignment of U.S. Forces." November 21.

Japan Quarterly. 1968. "The Asahi Shimbun's Public Opinion Survey." 15, no. 1, 42.

Jarque Iñiguez, Arturo. 1988. *Queremos esas bases* [We want those bases]. Universidad de Alcalá.

Jenkins, Loren. 1988. "Italy to Agree to NATO Request to Accept U.S. F16s." *Washington Post*, May 26, A15.

Jensen, Nathan M. 2006. *Nation-States and the Multinational Corporation: A Political Economy of Foreign Direct Investment.* Princeton: Princeton University Press.

Joffe, Josef. 1987. "Peace and Populism: Why the European Anti-Nuclear Movement Failed." *International Security* 11, no. 4 (Spring): 3–40.

Johnson, Chalmers, ed. 1999. *Okinawa: Cold War Island.* Cardiff, CA: Japan Policy Research Institute.

——. 2000. *Blowback: The Costs and Consequences of American Empire.* New York: Metropolitan Books.

——. 2004. *The Sorrows of Empire: Militarism, Secrecy and the End of the Republic.* New York: Metropolitan Books.

——. 2007. *Nemesis: The Last Days of the American Republic.* New York: Metropolitan Books.

Johnson, Eric. 2006a. "Nakaima Wins Okinawa Race: Economic Issues Appear to Win Out over U.S. Base Opposition." *Japan Times*, November 20.

——. 2006b. "Okinawa Economic Woes Trump Base Ills for Voters." *Japan Times*, November 21.

Jones Luong, Pauline. 2002. *Institutional Change and Political Continuity in Post-Soviet Central Asia: Power, Perceptions and Pacts.* New York: Cambridge University Press.

——, ed. 2004. *The Transformation of Central Asia: States and Societies from Soviet Rule to Independence.* Ithaca: Cornell University Press.

Jones Luong, Pauline, and Erika Weinthal. 2002. "New Friends, New Fears in Central Asia." *Foreign Affairs* 81, no. 2 (March–April): 61–70.

Jung, Youngjin, and Jun-Shik Hwang. 2003. "Where Does Inequality Come From? An Analysis of the Korea–United States Status of Forces Agreement." *American University International Law Review* 18, no. 5: 1103–1144.

Junnosuke, Masumi. 1995. *Contemporary Politics in Japan.* Trans. Lonny E. Carlie. Berkeley: University of California Press.

Kahler, Miles. 1984. *Decolonization in Britain and France: The Domestic Consequences of International Relations.* Princeton: Princeton University Press.

Kane, Tim. 2004. "Global U.S. Troop Deployment, 1950–2003." http://www.heritage.org/Research/NationalSecurity/cda04-11.cfm (accessed May 2007).

Kaplan, Robert D. 2005. *Imperial Grunts: The American Military on the Ground.* New York: Random House.

Karaosmanoğlu, Ali. 1988. "Turkey and the Southern Flank: Domestic and International Contexts." In *NATO's Southern Allies: Internal and External Challenges,* ed. John Chipman, 287–353. New York: Routledge.

Katz, Richard, and Peter Mair. 1995. "Changing Models of Party Organization and Party Democracy: The Emergence of the Cartel Party." *Party Politics* 1, no. 1 (January): 5–28.

Katzenstein, Peter. 1996. *Cultural Norms and National Security: Police and Military in Postwar Japan.* Ithaca: Cornell University Press.

———. 2005. *A World of Regions: Asia and Europe in the American Imperium.* Ithaca: Cornell University Press.

Katzenstein, Peter, and Robert Keohane, eds. 2006. *Anti-Americanisms in World Politics.* Ithaca: Cornell University Press.

Keck, Margaret, and Katherine Sikkink. 1998. *Activists beyond Borders.* Ithaca: Cornell University Press.

Keddell, Joseph P. 1993. *The Politics of Defense in Japan: Managing Internal and External Pressures.* Armonk, NY: M. E. Sharpe.

Keenan, Jeremy. 2004. "Terror in the Sahara: The Implications of U.S. Imperialism for North and West Africa." *Review of African Political Economy* 31, no. 101 (September): 457–96.

Kessler, Richard J. 1986. "Marcos and the Americans." *Foreign Policy* no. 63 (Summer): 40–57.

Khatchadourian, Raffi. 2006. "Blowback in Africa." *New York Times,* April 28.

Kim, Hun-Shik. 2003. "Media, the Public, and Freedom of the Press." *Social Indicators Research* 62, nos. 1–3: 345–64.

Kim, Jinwung. 2004. "Ambivalent Allies: Recent South Korean Perceptions of the United States Forces Korea (USFK)." *Asian Affairs* 30, no. 4 (Winter): 268–85.

Kim, Samuel S. 2003. "Korea's Democratization in the Global-Local Nexus." In *Korea's Democratization,* ed. Samuel S. Kim, 3–44. New York: Cambridge University Press.

Kim, Seung-Hwan. 2002–3. "Anti-Americanism in Korea." *Washington Quarterly* 26, no. 1 (Winter): 109–22.

Kirisci, Kemal. 1998. "Turkey and the United States: Ambivalent Allies." *Middle East Review of International Affairs* 2, no. 4 (December): 18–26.

Kissinger, Henry A. 1982. *Years of Upheaval.* Boston: Little, Brown.

Klare, Michael T., and Daniel Volman. 2004. "Africa's Oil and American National Security." *Current History* no. 103 (May): 226–31.

———. 2006. "The African 'Oil Rush' and U.S. National Security." *Third World Quarterly* 27, no. 4 (May): 609–28.

Klaus, Jon D. 2004. "U.S. Military Overseas Basing: Background and Oversight." *CRS Report for Congress.* Washington, DC. November 17.

Klepp, Deborah. 2004. "The U.S. Needs a Base *Where*?? How the U.S. Established an Air Base in the Kyrgyz Republic." Unpublished essay. National Defense University, National War College.

Kobayashi, Teruo. 1968. "A Great Debate in Japan: The Fate of the U.S.-Japan Security Treaty in 1970." *Journal of Politics* 30, no. 3 (August): 749–79.

Kopstein, Jeffrey, and David A. Reilly. 2000. "Geographic Diffusion and the Transformation of the Postcommunist World." *World Politics* 53, no. 1 (October): 1–37.

Krasner, Stephen. 1978. *Defending the National Interest: Raw Materials Investments and U.S. Foreign Policy.* Princeton: Princeton University Press.

———. 1999. *Sovereignty: Organized Hypocrisy*. Princeton: Princeton University Press.

Kristensen, Hans M. 2006. "The Neither Confirm Nor Deny Policy: Nuclear Diplomacy at Work." Federation of American Scientists Working Paper. http://www.nukestrat.com/pubs/NCND.pdf (accessed May 2007).

Kucera, Joshua. 2007. "Kyrgyz Officials: Let's Renegotiate U.S. Air Deal." *Eurasia Insight*, February 2. http://www.eurasianet.org/departments/insight/articles/eav020207a.shtml (accessed May 2007).

Kurth, James R. 1989. "The Pacific Basin versus the Atlantic Alliance: Two Paradigms of International Relations." *Annals of the American Academy of Political and Social Science* no. 505 (September): 34–45.

Laganis, Irene. 2003. "U.S. Forces in Greece in the 1950s." In *U.S. Military Forces in Europe: The Early Years, 1945–1970*, ed. Simon Duke and Wolfgang Krieger, 309–30. Boulder: Westview Press.

Lake, David. 1996. "Anarchy, Hierarchy, and the Variety of Security Relations." *International Organization* 50, no. 1 (Winter): 1–33.

———. 1999. *Entangling Relations: American Foreign Policy in Its Century*. Princeton: Princeton University Press.

———. 2007. "Escape from the State-of-Nature: Authority and Hierarchy in World Politics." *International Security* 32, no. 1 (Summer): 47–79.

Larrabee, F. Stephen. 1981–82. "Dateline Athens: Greece for the Greeks." *Foreign Policy* no. 45 (Winter): 158–74.

Larrabee, F. Stephen, and Andrzej Karkoszka. 2007. "(Mis)Managing Missile Defense." *Project Syndicate*. http://www.project-syndicate.org/commentary/larrabee2/English (accessed May 2007).

Layne, Christopher. 2006. *The Peace of Illusions: American Grand Strategy from 1940 to the Present*. Ithaca: Cornell University Press.

Lazareff, Serge. 1971. *The Status of Military Forces under Current International Law*. Leiden, Netherlands: Sijtoff.

Lee, Su-Hoon. 1993. "Transitional Politics of Korea, 1987–1992: Activation of Civil Society." *Pacific Affairs* 66, no. 3 (Autumn): 351–67.

Leffler, Melvyn P. 1985. "Strategy, Diplomacy, and the Cold War: The United States, Turkey, and NATO, 1945–1952." *Journal of American History* 71, no. 4 (March): 807–25.

Legislative Publications Staff of the Senate of the Philippines. 1991. "The Bases of Their Decisions: How the Senators Voted on the Treaty of Friendship, Cooperation and Security between the Government of the Republic of the Philippines and the United States of America." Manila: Secretariat of the Senate.

Leite, José Guilherme Reis. 1992. "The Azores in the Portuguese Republic." In *The New Portugal: Democracy and Europe*, ed. Richard Herr, 62–70. Berkeley: International and Area Studies Institute, University of California.

Lellouche, Pierre, and Dominique Moisi. 1979. "French Policy in Africa: A Lonely Policy against Destabilization." *International Security* 3, no. 4 (Spring): 108–33.

Levin, Norman D. 2004. "Do the Ties Still Bind? The U.S.-ROK Relationship after 9/11." Santa Monica: RAND Project Air Force.

Levin, Norman D., and Yong-Sup Han. 2002. *Sunshine in Korea: The South Korean Debate over Policies toward North Korea*. Santa Monica: RAND Center for Asia Policy.

Liedke, Boris. 1999. "Spain and the United States, 1945–1975." In *Spain and the Great Powers in the Twentieth Century*, ed. Paul Preston and Sebastian Balfour, 229–44. New York: Routledge.

Linden, Ronald H. 2004. "Twin Peaks: Romania and Bulgaria between the EU and the United States." *Problems of Post-Communism* 51, no. 5 (September–October): 45–55.

Linz, Juan J., and Alfred Stepan. 1996. *Problems of Democratic Transition and Consolidation: Southern Europe, South America, and Post-Communist Europe.* Baltimore: Johns Hopkins University Press.

Lipson, Charles. 2003. *Reliable Partners: How Democracies Have Made a Separate Peace.* Princeton: Princeton University Press.

Los Angeles Times. 1981. "Okinawans Mellowing towards U.S. Forces." May 3, 21.

———. 2005. "U.S. Military Covertly Pays to Run Stories in the Iraqi Press." June 5.

Loulis, John C. 1984–85. "Papandreou's Foreign Policy." *Foreign Affairs* 63 (Winter): 375–91.

Luckham, Robin. 1982. "French Militarism in Africa." *Review of African Political Economy* 9, no. 24 (May): 55–82.

Ludington, Nicholas S., and James W. Spain. 1983. "Dateline Turkey: The Case for Patience." *Foreign Policy* no. 50 (Spring): 150–165.

Lundestad, Geir. 1986. "Empire by Invitation? The United States and Western Europe, 1945–1952." *Journal of Peace Research* 23, no. 3 (September): 263–277.

———. 2003. *The United States and Europe Since 1945: From "Empire" to Transatlantic Drift.* Oxford, UK: Oxford University Press.

Lustick, Ian. 1993. *Unsettled States, Disputed Lands: Britain and Ireland, France and Algeria, Israel and the West Bank-Gaza.* Ithaca: Cornell University Press.

Lutz, Catherine, ed. 2008. *The Bases of Empire: The Global Struggle against U.S. Military Posts.* London: Pluto Press.

MacDonald, Donald Stone. 1992. *U.S.-Korean Relations from Liberation to Self-Reliance: The Twenty-Year Record.* Boulder: Westview Press.

Madison, Julian C. 1996. "The United States and the Philippines, 1961–65: Was There a 'Special Relationship'?" Ph.D. dissertation, Department of History, University of Washington.

Manly, Chesly. 1959a. "Tribune Reporter Takes a Look at U.S. Foreign Aid: What Is It? Who Gets It? Does It help Recipient? Turkey Studied as Example." *Chicago Tribune,* March 15, 1.

———. 1959b. "Tyranny Stifles Press, Judiciary in 'Free' Turkey: National Receiving Billions in U.S. Aid Sends Opposition Editors to Prison." *Chicago Tribune,* March 29, 1.

———. 1959c. "Manly Concludes U.S. Should Stop Grant Aid to Turkey." *Chicago Tribune,* April 5, 12.

Mansfield, Edward D., and Jack Snyder. 2005. *Electing to Fight: Why Emerging Democracies Go to War.* Cambridge: MIT Press.

Manyin, Mark. 2003. "South Korean Politics and Rising 'Anti-Americanism': Implications for U.S. Policy towards North Korea." Congressional Research Service Report, Washington, DC. May.

Marquand, Robert. 2006. "Japanese Eye Big Bill to Relocate U.S. Forces." *Christian Science Monitor,* May 10, 7.

Marten, Kimberly. 2005. "Bases for Reflection: The History and Politics of U.S. Military Bases in South Korea." *IRI Review* 10, no. 2 (Autumn): 155–200.

Martin, Lisa. 2000. *Democratic Commitments.* Princeton: Princeton University Press.

Mason, Michael. 2005. "Great Game in West Africa." *Military Technology* 29, no. 2: 7.

Matray, James. 1995. "Hodge Podge: American Occupation Policy in Korea, 1945–1948." *Korean Studies* 19:17–38.

Maxwell, Kenneth. 1991. "Portuguese Defense and Foreign Policy: An Overview." In *Portuguese Defense and Foreign Policy since Democratization*, ed. Kenneth Maxwell. Special Report No. 3. New York: Camões Center, Research Institute on International Change, Columbia University.

———. 1997. *The Making of Portuguese Democracy*. New York: Cambridge University Press.

Maydew, Randall C. 1997. *America's Lost H-Bomb: Palomares, Spain, 1966*. Manhattan, KS: Sunflower University Press.

McDonald, John W., Jr., and Diane B. Bendahmane, eds. 1990. *U.S. Bases Overseas: Negotiations with Spain, Greece, and the Philippines*. Boulder: Westview Press.

Meadows, Martin. 1965. "Recent Developments in Philippine-American Relations." *Asian Survey* 5, no. 6 (June): 305–18.

Mearsheimer, John. 2001. *The Tragedy of Great Power Politics*. New York: W. W. Norton.

Mendel, Douglas H. 1959. "Japanese Attitudes towards American Military Bases." *Far Eastern Survey* 28, no. 9 (September): 129–34.

———. 1961. *The Japanese People and Foreign Policy: A Study of Public Opinion in Post-Treaty Japan*. Westport, CT: Greenwood Press.

———. 1971–72. "Japanese Views of the American Alliance in the Seventies." *Public Opinion Quarterly* 35, no. 4 (Winter): 521–38.

Mendelson, Sarah E. 2005. "Barracks and Brothels: Peacekeepers and Human Trafficking in the Balkans." Washington, DC: Center for International and Strategic Studies.

Menon, Rajan. 2003. "The New Great Game in Central Asia." *Survival* 45, no. 2 (Summer): 187–204.

Mesa, Roberto. 1992. "La normalización exterior de España." In *Transición política y consolidación democrática: España (1975–86)* [Political transition and democratic consolidation], ed. Ramón Cotarelo, 137–62. Madrid: Centro de Investigaciones Sociológicas.

Millard, Mike. 1999. "Okinawa, Then and Now." In *Okinawa: Cold War Island*, ed. Chalmers Johnson. Cardiff, CA: Japan Policy Research Institute.

Miller, James Edward. 1986. *The United States and Italy, 1940–1950: The Politics of Diplomacy and Stabilization*. Chapel Hill: University of North Carolina Press.

Milton, Andrew K. 2001. "Bound but Not Gagged: Media Reform in Democratic Transitions." *Comparative Political Studies* 34, no. 5 (June): 493–526.

Moniz, Miguel. 2004. "Exiled Home: Criminal Deportee Forced Return Migrants and Transnational Identity—The Azorean Example." Ph.D. dissertation, Department of Anthropology, Brown University.

Monjardino, Miguel. 2000. "A base indispensavel" [A vital base]. *Política Internacional* 3, no. 22: 185–215.

Monje, Scott C. 1992. "The Azores in the Atlantic World: Geostrategic Aspects." *Camões Center Quarterly* 3, nos. 3–4 (Winter): 2–12.

Monteleone, Carla. 2007. "The Evolution of a Pluralistic Security Community: Impact and Perspectives of the Presence of American Bases in Italy." *Journal of Transatlantic Studies* 5, no. 1 (Spring): 43–85.

Moon, Chung-in, and Jongryn Mo, eds. 2004. *Democratization and Globalization in Korea: Assessments and Prospects*. Seoul: Yonsei University Press.

Moon, Katharine H. S. 1997. *Sex among Allies: Military Prostitution in U.S.-Korea Relations*. New York: Columbia University Press.

———. 1999. "South Korean Movements against Militarized Sexual Labor." *Asian Survey* 39, no. 2 (March–April): 310–27.

——. 2003. "Korea Nationalism, Anti-Americanism, and Democratic Consolidation." In *Korea's Democratization*, ed. Samuel L. Kim, 135–57. New York: Cambridge University Press.

Moore, Frederick T. 1959. "Criminal Jurisdiction in Overseas Areas." *Journal of Politics* 21, no. 2 (May): 276–302.

Motyl, Alexander. 2001. *Imperial Ends: The Decay, Collapse and Revival of Empires*. New York: Columbia University Press.

——. 2006. "Is Everything Empire? Is Empire Everything?" *Comparative Politics* 38, no. 2 (January): 229–49.

Mujal-Leon, Eusebio. 1983. "Rei(g)ing in Spain." *Foreign Policy* no. 51 (Summer): 101–17.

Mulgan, Aurelia George. 2000. "Managing the U.S. Base Issue in Okinawa: A Test for Japanese Democracy." *Japanese Studies* 20, no. 2 (September): 159–77.

Murphy, Sean D. 1991. "The Role of Bilateral Defense Agreements in Maintaining the European Security Equilibrium." *Cornell International Law Journal* 24:415–36.

Murray, Craig. 2006. *Murder in Samarkand: A British Ambassador's Controversial Defiance of Tyranny in the War on Terror*. London: Mainstream Publishing.

Nam, Joo-Hong. 1986. *America's Commitment to South Korea: The First Decade of the Nixon Doctrine*. New York: Cambridge University Press.

Nash, Frank. 1957. *United States Overseas Military Bases*. White House Report. Washington, DC. December 1. (Declassified February 7, 1990.)

National Security Council (NSC). 2002. *The National Security Strategy of the United States of America*. Washington, DC. September. http://www.whitehouse.gov/nsc/nss/2002/nss.pdf (accessed May 2007).

Nelson, Daniel J. 1987. *A History of U.S. Military Forces in Germany*. Boulder: Westview Press.

Newsom, David. 1990. "The State Department Perspective on the 1977–79 Negotiations." In *U.S. Bases Overseas: Negotiations with Spain, Greece, and the Philippines*, ed. John W. McDonald Jr. and Diane B. Bendahmane, 88–92. Boulder: Westview Press.

New York Times. 1975. "U.S., Greece Agree to End Home Port for the 6th Fleet." April 30.

——. 1987a. "Base Pains in Spain, and Elsewhere." March 23, A18.

——. 1987b. "Weinberger, in Spain, Raises Bases Issue." March 17, A9.

Nexon, Daniel, and Thomas Wright. 2007. "What's at Stake in the American Empire Debate." *American Political Science Review* 101, no. 2 (May): 253–71.

Nichol, Jim. 2005. "Uzbekistan's Closure of the Airbase at Karshi-Khanabad: Context and Implications." *Congressional Research Service Report for Congress*. Washington, DC. October 7.

Njølstad, Olav. 2002. "The Carter Administration and Italy: Keeping the Communists out of Power without Interfering." *Journal of Cold War Studies* 4, no. 3 (Summer): 56–94.

Nuti, Leopoldo. 1993. "U.S. Forces in Italy, 1945–1963." In *U.S. Military Forces in Europe: The Early Years, 1945–1970*, ed. Simon Duke and Wolfgang Krieger, 249–72. Boulder: Westview Press.

——. 1999. "Missiles or Socialists? The Italian Policy of the Kennedy Administration." In *John F. Kennedy and Europe*, ed. Douglas Brinkley and Richard T. Griffiths, 190–202. Baton Rouge: Louisiana State Press.

——. 2002. "The United States, Italy, and the Opening to the Left, 1953–1963." *Journal of Cold War Studies* 4, no. 3 (Summer): 36–55.

——. 2004. "Italy and the Battle of the Euromissiles: The Deployment of the U.S. BGM-109 G 'Gryphon,' 1979–1983." In *The Last Decade of the Cold War: From Conflict*

Escalation to Conflict Transformation, ed. Olav Njølstad, 332–59. New York: Frank Cass.

Oberdorfer, Don. 2001. *The Two Koreas: A Contemporary History*. New York: Basic Books.

O'Donnell, Guillermo, and Philippe Schmitter. 1986. *Transitions from Authoritarian Rule: Tentative Conclusions about Uncertain Democracies*. Baltimore: Johns Hopkins University Press.

Okamura, Reimei. 1998. "U.S.-Japan Relations and the Media in the Information Age: Coverage of the American Bases Issue in Okinawa." *Japanese Journal of American Studies* no. 9:5–27.

Okinawa Military Base Affairs Office. 2000. "U.S. Military Bases in Okinawa." Fact brochure. Naha, Okinawa: Okinawa Prefectural Government.

Oliker, Olga, and David A. Shlapak. 2005. *U.S. Interests in Central Asia: Policy Priorities and Military Roles*. Santa Monica: RAND Project Air Force.

Olson, Mancur. 1993. "Dictatorship, Democracy and Development." *American Political Science Review* 87, no. 3 (September): 567–76.

Olson, Robert. 2005. "Views from Turkey: Reasons for the United States War against Iraq." *Journal of Third World Studies* 22, no. 2 (Spring): 141–60.

Onis, Juan de. 1975. "Oppositionist Turk Calls for the Removal of the U.S. Military." *New York Times*, August 5.

Ota, Masahide. 1999. "Re-Examining the History of the Battle of Okinawa." In *Okinawa: Cold War Island*, ed. Chalmers Johnson, 13–38. Cardiff, CA: Japan Policy Research Institute.

———. 2003. "Beyond *Hondo*: Devolution and Okinawa." In *Japan and Okinawa: Structure and Subjectivity*, ed. Glen D. Hook and Richard Siddle, 114–30. New York: RoutledgeCurzon.

Overseas Basing Commission (OBC). 2005. *Report of the Commission on Review of the Overseas Military Facility Structure of the United States*. Washington, DC. August.

Özbudun, Ergun. 2001. "The Institutional Decline of Parties in Turkey." In *Political Parties and Democracy*, ed. Larry Diamond and Richard Gunther, 238–65. Baltimore: Johns Hopkins University Press.

Özel, Soli. 2003. "After the Tsunami: Turkey at the Polls." *Journal of Democracy* 14, no. 2 (April): 80–94.

Packard, George R., III. 1966. *Protest in Tokyo: The Security Treaty Crisis of 1960*. Princeton: Princeton University Press.

Packer, George. 2005. *The Assassins' Gate: America in Iraq*. New York: Farrar, Straus and Giroux.

Paez, Patricia Ann. 1985. *The Bases Factor: Realpolitik of RP-U.S. Relations*. Manila: Center for Strategic and International Studies of the Philippines.

El País. 1988a. "Un exito de España" [A success for Spain]. January 16.

———. 1988b. "El fin de un capitulo" [The end of a chapter]. May 8.

———. 1991. "La oposición reprocha al gobierno su política de silencio sobre el Golfo" [Opposition rebukes the government for its political silence on the Gulf]. February 3.

Pannier, Bruce. 2007. "Bishkek Wants U.S. to Hand over Airman." *RFE/RL*, March 21. http://www.rferl.org/featuresarticle/2007/03/43ee1a21-85f7-4de8-45a-dd21462d525f.html (accessed May 2007).

Pape, Robert. 2005a. *Dying to Win: The Strategic Logic of Suicide Terrorism*. New York: Random House.

———. 2005b. "Soft Balancing against the United States." *International Security* 30, no. 1 (Summer): 7–45.

Park, Chang Jin. 1975. "The Influence of Small States upon the Superpowers: United States–South Korean Relations as a Case Study, 1950–53." *World Politics* 28, no. 1 (October): 97–117.

Pasquino, Gianfranco. 1986. "The Demise of the First Fascist Regime and Italy's Transition to Democracy: 1943–1948." In *Transitions from Authoritarian Rule: Southern Europe*, ed. Guillermo O'Donnell, Philippe Schmitter, and Laurence Whitehead, 45–70. Baltimore: Johns Hopkins University Press.

Philippine Information Agency. 2007. "RP Credibility at Stake in U.S. Marine's Transfer." January 3. http://www.pia.gov.ph/?m=11&sec=archive&r=ALL&sp=2& fi=p070103.htm&no=30 (accessed May 2007).

Planty, Donald. 1990. "The 1983 Agreement on Friendship, Defense and Cooperation: Overview of the Negotiations." In *U.S. Bases Overseas: Negotiations with Spain, Greece, and the Philippines*, ed. John W. McDonald Jr. and Diane B. Bendahmane, 40–46. Boulder: Westview Press.

Pomfret, Richard. 1995. *The Economies of Central Asia*. Princeton: Princeton University Press.

Pope, Nicole, and Hugh Pope. 1998. *Turkey Unveiled: A History of Modern Turkey*. Woodstock, NY: Overlook Press.

Porrata-Doria, Rafael, Jr. 1992. "The Philippine Bases and Status of Forces Agreement: Lessons for the Future." *Military Law Review* 67:67–132.

Posen, Barry. 2003. "Command of the Commons: The Military Foundation of U.S. Hegemony." *International Security* 28, no. 1 (Summer): 5–46.

Powell, Charles. 2001. *España en democracia, 1975–2000*. Madrid: Plaza y Janes.

Powell, Stuart. 2004. "Swamp of Terror in the Sahara." *Air Force Magazine* 87, no. 11 (November): 50–54.

Preston, Paul. 1993. *Franco: A Biography*. London: Harper Collins.

Price, Richard. 2003. "Transnational Civil Society and Advocacy in World Politics." *World Politics* 55, no. 4 (July): 579–606.

Priest, Dana. 2005. "CIA Holds Terror Suspects in Secret Prisons." *Washington Post*, November 2, A1.

Program on International Policy Attitudes. 2006. "What the Iraqi Public Wants." January 31. http://www.worldpublicopinion.org/pipa/pdf/jan06/Iraq_Jan06_rpt.pdf (accessed May 2007).

Pugh, Mark. 1989. *The ANZUS Crisis, Nuclear Visiting and Deterrence*. New York: Cambridge University Press.

Putnam, Robert D. 1978. "Interdependence and the Italian Communists." *International Organization* 32, no. 2 (Spring): 301–49.

———. 1988. "Diplomacy and Domestic Politics: The Logic of Two-Level Games." *International Organization* 42, no. 3 (Summer): 427–60.

Pyle, Kenneth B. 1992. *The Japanese Question: Power and Purpose in a New Era*. Washington, DC: American Enterprise Institute Press.

Ra, Jong Yil. 1992. "Political Crisis in Korea 1952: The Administration, Legislature, Military and Foreign Powers." *Journal of Contemporary History* 27, no. 2 (April): 301–18.

Radio Free Europe/Radio Liberty Report (RFE/RL). 2001a. "Central Asian States Offer Bases for European, Canadian Warplanes." November 29.

———. 2001b. "Kyrgyzstan, Turkmenistan Give Air Corridors to the U.S." September 25.

——. 2003. "Kyrgyzstan: Putin to Attend Official Opening of Russian Airbase." October 22.

——. 2006. "Uzbekistan: Freedom House Becomes the Latest Casualty." February 10.

——. 2007. "Kyrgyz Say Shooting by U.S. Soldier Was 'Murder.'" March 16. http://www.rferl.org/featuresarticle/2007/03/23BC67A3-3BFD-47DD-9C50-65DF3521CB63.html (accessed May 2007).

Randolph, R. Sean. 1986. *The United States and Thailand: Alliance Dynamics, 1950–1985.* Berkeley: Institute of East Asian Studies, University of California.

Rashid, Ahmed. 2002. *Jihad: The Rise of Militant Islam in Central Asia.* New Haven, Conn.: Yale University Press.

Reisman, Michael, and Robert D. Sloane. 2000. "The Incident at Cavalese and Strategic Compensation." *The American Journal of International Law* 94, no. 3 (July): 505–515.

Renou, Xavier. 2002. "A New French Policy for Africa?" *Journal of Contemporary African Studies* 20, no. 1 (January): 5–27.

Resnick, Adam L. 2001. "Investors, Turbulence and Transition: Democratic Transition and Foreign Direct Investment in Nineteen Developing Countries." *International Interactions* 27, no. 4: 381–398.

Resnick, Adam L., and Quan Li. 2003. "Reversal of Fortunes: Democratic Institutions and Foreign Direct Investment Inflows to Developing Countries." *International Organization* 57, no. 1 (Winter): 175–211.

Resnick, Evan. 2005. "Ties that Bind or Ties that Blind? Assessing Engagement as an Instrument of U.S. Foreign Policy." Ph.D. dissertation, Department of Political Science, Columbia University.

RIA Novosti. 2005. "Uzbekistan Restricts U.S. Flights over Its Territory in Response to Embargo Threats." June 16. http://en.rian.ru/world/20050616/40535701.html (accessed May 2007).

Richelson, Jeffrey T., and Desmond Ball. 1985. *The Ties That Bind: Intelligence Cooperation between the UKUSA Countries—The United Kingdom, the United States of America, Canada, Australia and New Zealand.* Sydney: Allen and Unwin Australia.

Risse-Kappan, Thomas. 1996. "Collective Identity in a Democratic Community: The Case of NATO." In *The Culture of National Security: Norms and Identity in World Politics,* ed. Peter Katzenstein, 357–99. New York: Columbia University Press.

Robins, Philip. 2003. "Confusion at Home, Confusion Abroad: Turkey between Copenhagen and Iraq." *International Affairs* 79, no. 3 (May): 547–66.

Robinson, Ronald. 1968. *Africa and the Victorians: The Climax of Imperialism.* London: Anchor Books.

Rodrigues, Luís Nuno. 2004. "About Face: The United States and Portuguese Colonialism in 1961." *Electronic Journal of Portuguese History* 2, no. 1 (Summer): 1–10.

Roldán, Concha. 1998. *Los americanos en Zaragoza: La presencia de las fuerzas aereas de los Estados Unidos en la base* [The Americans in Zaragoza: The U.S. air force base]. Zaragoza: Iberjaca.

Ross, Michael. 2001. "Does Oil Hinder Democracy?" *World Politics* 53, no. 3 (Spring): 325–61.

Rouse, Joseph H. 1957. "The Exercise of Criminal Jurisdiction under the NATO Status of Forces Agreement." *American Journal of International Law* 51, no. 1: 46–52.

Rubin, Barnett R. 2006. "Afghanistan's Uncertain Transition from Turmoil to Normalcy." *Council on Foreign Relations Special Report,* no. 12. New York.

Rubin, Michael. 2005. "A Comedy of Errors: U.S.-Turkish Diplomacy and the Iraq War." Washington, DC: American Enterprise Institute for Public Policy Research.

Rumer, Eugene. 2006. "The U.S. Interests and Role in Central Asia after K2." *Washington Quarterly* 29, no. 3 (Summer): 141–54.

Samuels, Richard. 2003. *Machiavelli's Children: Leaders and Their Legacies in Italy and Japan.* Ithaca: Cornell University Press.

Sandars, Christopher T. 2000. *America's Overseas Garrisons: The Leasehold Empire.* New York: Oxford University Press.

Sankei Shimbun. 2007a. "Gist of USFJ Realignment Special Measures Law Passed by Lower House on 13 April." April 16. Accessed through the Foreign Broadcasting and Information Service (FBIS).

———. 2007b. "Law on Special Measures for USFJ Realignment: 'Carrot' Used to Press for Acceptance." April 19. Accessed through the FBIS.

Sarantakes, Nicholas Evan. 2000. *Keystone: The American Occupation of Okinawa and U.S.-Japanese Relations.* College Station: Texas A&M Press.

Sariibrahimoglu, Lale. 2004. "Greater U.S. Access to Turkish Bases Unlikely." *Janes Defence Weekly,* October 20.

———. 2005. "U.S. Renews Bid to Increase Use of Turkish Airbase." *Janes Defence Weekly,* January 26.

Sartori, Giovanni. 1976. *Parties and Party Systems.* Cambridge: Cambridge University Press.

Schaller, Michael. 1997. *Altered States: The United States and Japan since the Occupation.* New York: Oxford University Press.

Schatz, Edward. 2004. *Modern Clan Politics: The Politics of "Blood" in Kazakhstan and Beyond.* Seattle: University of Washington Press.

Schlesinger, Arthur M., Jr. 1965. *A Thousand Days: John F. Kennedy in the White House.* Boston: Riverside Press.

Schmidt, Helmut. 1989. *Men and Powers.* New York: Random House.

Seidel, Carlos Collado. 1993. "U.S. Bases in Spain in the 1950s." In *U.S. Military Forces in Europe: The Early Years, 1945–1970,* ed. Simon Duke and Wolfgang Krieger, 283–308. Boulder: Westview Press.

Sell, Susanne K., and Aseem Prakash. 2004. "Using Ideas Strategically: The Contest between Business and NGO Networks and Intellectual Property Rights." *International Studies Quarterly* 48, no. 1 (March): 143–75.

Shanker, Thom. 2006. "Tensions Flare over Custody in Rape Case in Philippines." *New York Times,* December 22, A8.

Shaw, Harry J. 1983. "U.S. Security Assistance: Debts and Dependency." *Foreign Policy* no. 50 (Spring): 105–23.

Shin, Gi-Wook. 1996. "South Korean Anti-Americanism: A Comparative Perspective." *Asian Survey* 36, no. 8 (August): 787–803.

Siddle, Richard. 1998. "Colonialism and Identity in Okinawa before 1945." *Japanese Studies* 18, no. 2 (September): 117–33.

Simich, Laura. 1991. "The Corruption of a Community's Economic and Political Life: The Cruise Missile Base in Comiso." In *The Sun Never Sets: Confronting the Network of Foreign U.S. Military Bases,* ed. Joseph Gerson and Bruce Birchard, 77–94. Boston: South End Press.

Singer, Peter. 2003. *Corporate Warriors: The Rise of the Privatized Military Industry.* Ithaca: Cornell University Press.

Smith, Adam M. 2004. "At Last unto the Breach: The Logic of a U.S. Military Command in West Africa." *Orbis* 48, no. 2 (Spring): 305–19.

Smith, Sheila A. 1999. "Do Domestic Politics Matter? The Case of U.S. Military Bases in Japan." U.S.-Japan Project Working Paper Series, no. 7. George Washington University. http://www.gwu.edu/~nsarchiv/japan/ssmithtp.htm.

——. 2006. "Arrest of U.S. Sailor Complicates U.S.-Japan Realignment Efforts." *East-West Wire,* January 9. http://www.eastwestcenter.org/events-en-detail (accessed May 2007).

Smith, Timothy E. 1991. *The United States, Italy and NATO, 1947–52.* New York: St. Martin's Press.

Snyder, Jack. 2000. *From Voting to Violence: Democratization and Nationalist Conflict.* New York: W. W. Norton.

Snyder, Jack, and Karen Ballentine. 1996. "Nationalism and the Marketplace of Ideas." *International Security* 21, no. 2 (Fall): 5–40.

Sobel, Lester A., ed. 1976. *Portuguese Revolution 1974–76,* by Christ Hunt. New York: Facts on File.

Socor, Vladimir. 2006. "Kyrgyzstan Asks for Manifold Increase in U.S. Payments for Manas." *Eurasian Daily Monitor,* January 26. http://jamestown.org/edm/article.php?article_id=2370703 (accessed May 2007).

Song, Yonghoi. 2004. "News Realities on Crime of the U.S. Military Personnel in Korea: A Constructionist Approach to the Media Coverage of the Death Cases in 1992 and 2002." Ph.D. dissertation, School of Journalism, University of Missouri-Columbia.

Spain, James W. 1984. *American Diplomacy in Turkey: Memoirs of an Ambassador Extraordinary and Plenipotentiary.* New York: Praeger.

Spector, Regine A. 2004. "The Transformation of Askar Akaev, President of Kyrgyzstan." University of California, Berkeley Program in Soviet and Post-Soviet Studies Working Paper Series. http://violet.berkeley.edu/~bsp/publications/2004_02-spec.pdf (accessed May 2007).

Spencer, Caroline. 2003. "Meeting of the Dugongs and the Cooking Pots: Anti-military Base Citizens' Groups on Okinawa." *Japanese Studies* 23, no. 2 (September): 126–40.

Spolar, Christine. 2004. "14 'Enduring Bases' Set in Iraq: Long-Term Military Presence Planned." *Chicago Tribune,* March 23.

Spruyt, Hendrik. 2005. *Ending Empire: Contested Sovereignty and Territorial Partition.* Ithaca: Cornell University Press.

Stambuk, George. 1963a. *American Military Forces Abroad: Their Impact on the Western State System.* Mershon Center: Ohio State University Press.

——. 1963b. "Foreign Policy and the Stationing of American Forces Abroad." *Journal of Politics* 25, no. 3 (August): 472–88.

Stearns, Montague. 1992. *Entangled Allies: U.S. Policy toward Greece, Turkey, and Cyprus.* New York: Council on Foreign Relations.

Stefanidis, Ioanis. 2002. *Asimetri etairi* [Unequal allies: The United States and Greece in the cold war, 1953–1961]. Athens, Greece: Pataki.

Steinberg, David I., ed. 2005. *Korean Attitudes toward the United States: Changing Dynamics.* Armonk, NY: M. E. Sharpe.

Stiles, David. 2006. "A Fusion Bomb over Andalusia: U.S. Information Policy and the Palomares Incident, 1966." *Journal of Cold War Studies* 8, no. 1 (January): 49–67.

Stockwin, J. A. A. 1962. "'Positive Neutrality'—The Foreign Policy of the Japanese Socialist Party." *Asian Survey* 2, no. 9 (November): 33–41.

Stromseth, Jonathan. 1989. "Unequal Allies: Negotiations over U.S. Bases in the Philippines." *Journal of International Affairs* 43, no. 1 (Summer–Fall): 161–88.

Sullivan, Kevin. 2006. "Romania Prepares to Greet the Yanks." *Washington Post,* February 6, A1.

Sunar, Ilkyar, and Sabri Sayari. 1986. "Democracy in Turkey: Problems and Prospects." In *Transitions from Authoritarian Rule: Southern Europe,* ed. Guillermo O'Donnell, Philippe Schmitter, and Laurence Whitehead, 165–86. Baltimore: Johns Hopkins University Press.

Szulc, Tad. 1967. *The Bombs of Palomares.* New York: Viking Press.

——. 1975. "Lisbon and Washington: Behind the Portuguese Revolution." *Foreign Policy* no. 21 (Winter): 3–62.

Takemae, Eiji. 2003. *The Allied Occupation of Japan.* New York: Continuum.

Tan, Reagan D. 2007. "Senators Not Keen on VFA Renegotiation." *Business World* (Internet version), January 7. Accessed through the Foreign Broadcasting and Information Service (FBIS).

Tatsumi, Shimada. 1960. "What Happened in Japan? A Symposium: Free Press Gone Wrong." *Japan Quarterly* 7, no. 4 (October–December): 417–21.

Taylor, George E. 1964. *The Philippines and the United States: Problems of Partnership.* New York: Praeger.

Thompson, Estes. 1999. "Marine Pilot Acquitted of All Charges in Gondola Case." *Washington Post,* March 4.

Thompson, Mark R. 1996. "Off the Endangered List: Philippine Democratization in Comparative Perspective." *Comparative Politics* 28, no. 2 (January): 179–98.

Time. 1960. "Free Press Gone Wrong." June 27.

——. 1975. "The Azores: Unrest in a Way Station." August 18.

Treverton, Gregory F. 1978. *The Dollar Drain and American Forces in Germany: Managing the Political Economics of Alliance.* Athens: Ohio University Press.

Tsebelis, George. 2002. *Veto Players: How Political Institutions Work.* Princeton: Princeton University Press.

Tyson, Ann Scott. 2004. "New U.S. Strategy: 'Lily Pad' Bases: U.S. Forces Are Repositioning Overseas Forces, Opting for Smaller, Transitory Bases in Places like Kyrgyzstan." *Christian Science Monitor,* August 10, 6.

USA Today. 2006. "Bulgarian Parliament OKs U.S. Deal." May 26.

U.S. Department of Defense (DoD). 2000a. *Allied Contributions to the Common Defense.* Report to the U.S. Congress. Washington, DC.

——. 2000b. *Responsibility Sharing Report.* Washington, DC.

——. 2002. *Report on Allied Contributions to the Common Defense.* Washington, DC.

——. 2004. *Statistical Compendium on Allied Contributions to the Common Defense.* Report to the U.S. Congress. Washington, DC. http://www.dod.mil/pubs/20040910_2004 BaseStructureReport.pdf. (accessed May 2007).

——. 2006. *Base Structure Report, Fiscal Year.* Washington, DC. http://www.acq.osd. mil/ie/irm/irm_library/BSR2006Baseline.pdf (accessed May 2007).

Vachudova, Milada Anna. 2005. *Europe Undivided: Democracy, Leverage and Integration after Communism.* New York: Oxford University Press.

Van Biezen, Ingrid. 2003. *Political Parties in New Democracies: Party Organization in Southern and East-Central Europe.* London: Palgrave Macmillan.

Van Boven, Theo. 2003. "Civil and Political Rights, including the Questions of Torture and Detention." *Report for the United Nations Commission on Human Rights.* No. E/CN.4/2003/68/Add.2 (February 3). Available online via Human Rights Watch at http://hrw.org/pub/2005/Uzbekistan_Special_Rapporteur_Report_Feb03.pdf (accessed May 2007).

Van Natta, Don, Jr. 2005. "U.S. Recruits a Rough Ally to Be a Jailer." *New York Times,* May 1.

Vasconcelos, Álvaro. 1988. "Portuguese Defence Policy: Internal Politics and Defence Commitments." In *NATO's Southern Allies: Internal and External Challenges*, ed. John Chipman, 86–139. New York: Routledge.

Viksnins, George J. 1973. "United States Military Spending and the Economy of Thailand, 1967–1972." *Asian Survey* 13, no. 5 (May): 441–57.

Viñas, Angel. 1981. *Los pactos secretos de Franco con los Estados Unidos* [Franco's secret military pacts with the United States]. Barcelona: Grijalbo.

——. 2003a. *En las garras del aguila: Los pactos con Estados Unidos, de Francisco Franco a Felipe Gonzalez (1945–1995)* [In the eagle's talons: The military agreements with the United States, from Francisco Franco to Felipe Gonzales]. Barcelona: Critica.

——. 2003b. "Negotiating the U.S.-Spanish Agreements, 1953–1988: A Spanish Perspective." Jean Monnet/Robert Schuman Paper Series No. 3. Brussels.

Vintras, R. E. 1974. *The Portuguese Connection: The Secret History of the Azores Base*. London: Bachman and Turner.

Wakaizumi, Kei. 2002. *The Best Course Available: A Personal Account of the Secret U.S.-Japan Okinawa Reversion Negotiations*. Honolulu: University of Hawaii Press.

Wallander, Celeste. 2003. "Silk Road, Great Game or Soft Underbelly? The New U.S.-Russia Relationship and Implications for Eurasia." *Journal of Southeast European and Black Sea Studies* 3, no. 3 (September): 92–104.

Wall Street Journal. 2006. "Marine Probe Poses a Crucial Test for Iraqi Leaders." May 30.

Walt, Stephen M. 1987. *The Origins of Alliances*. Ithaca: Cornell University Press.

——. 2005. *Taming American Power: The Global Response to U.S. Primacy*. New York: W. W. Norton.

Waltz, Kenneth. 1979. *Theory of International Politics*. New York: McGraw-Hill.

Washington Post. 1975. "A Pro-American Liberation Front Emerges in the Azores." August 9, A13.

——. 2002. "Uzbek-U.S. Declaration Kept Secret." July 1, A11.

——. 2003. "Sub Officers Relieved of Commands." November 11, A2.

Watson, Paul. 2006. "U.S. Troops May Have Fired at Kabul Crowd." *Los Angeles Times*, June 1, A22.

Weber, Katja. 2000. *Hierarchy amidst Anarchy: Transaction Costs and Institutional Choice*. Albany: State University of New York Press.

Weisman, Steven R., and Thom Shanker. 2005. "Uzbeks Order U.S. from Base in Refugee Rift." *New York Times*, July 31, A1.

Weiss, Stanley. 2006. "After Iraq, a New Model." *International Herald Tribune*, December 26.

Weitz, Richard. 2006. "Averting a New Great Game in Central Asia." *Washington Quarterly* 29, no. 3 (Summer): 155–67.

Welfield, John. 1988. *An Empire in Eclipse: Japan in the Postwar American Alliance System*. Atlantic Highlands, NJ: Athlone Press.

Wells, Louis, and Rafiq Ahmed. 2007. *Making Investment Safe: Property Rights and National Sovereignty*. New York: Oxford University Press.

Wheeler, Fenton. 1975. "Azores Want Independence." *Wall Street Journal*, July 21, A8.

Whitaker, Arthur P. 1962. *Spain and the Defense of the West: Ally and Liability*. New York: Praeger.

Whittemore, Edward P. 1961. *The Press in Japan Today: A Case Study*. Columbia: University of South Carolina Press.

Wilkinson, Tracy. 2005. "Its Time for the U.S. Navy to Leave Port." *Los Angeles Times*, July 17, A1.

Williams, Jerry R. 2005. *In Pursuit of Their Dreams: A History of Azorean Immigration to the United States*. North Dartmouth, MA: Center for Portuguese Studies, University of Massachusetts Dartmouth.

Wishnick, Elizabeth. 2002. "Growing U.S. Security Interests in Central Asia." Strategic Studies Institute, Army War College. http://www.strategicstudiesinstitute.army. mil/pdffiles/PUB110.pdf.

Wolf, Charlotte. 1969. *Garrison Community: A Study of an Overseas American Military Colony*. Westport, CT: Greenwood Press.

Wollemborg, Leo. 1990. *Stars, Stripes, and Italian Tricolor: The United States and Italy, 1946–1989*. Westport, CT: Praeger.

Woo-Cumings, Meredith. 2005. "Unilateralism and Its Discontents: The Passing of the Cold War Alliance and Changing Public Opinion in the Republic of Korea." In *Korean Attitudes towards the United States*, ed. David I. Steinberg, 56–79. Armonk, NY: M. E. Sharpe.

Woodhouse, C. M. 1985. *The Rise and Fall of the Greek Colonels*. New York: Franklin Watts.

Woodliffe, John. 1992. *The Peacetime Use of Foreign Military Installations under Modern International Law*. Dordrecht, Netherlands: Martinus Nijhoff Publishers.

Yoda, Tatsuro. 2005. "Recalibrating Alliance Contributions: Changing Policy Environment and Military Affairs." Ph.D. dissertation, RAND Graduate School.

———. 2006. "Japan's Host Nation Support Program for the U.S.-Japan Security Alliance." *Asian Survey* 46, no. 6 (November–December): 937–61.

Yoshida, Kensei. 2001. *Democracy Betrayed: Okinawa under U.S. Occupation*. Bellingham: Center for East Asian Studies, Western Washington University.

Zhukov, Stanislav. 1996. "Economic Development of the States of Central Asia." In *Central Asia in Transition: Dilemmas of Independence*, ed. Boris Rumer, 106–35. Armonk, NY: M. E. Sharpe.

Index